Better Homes and Gardens® ASK THE garden DOCTOR

1,200 cures for common garden problems

WILEY

John Wiley & Sons, Inc.

Better Homes and Gardens®
Ask the Garden Doctor

Editor and Contributing Writer: Denny Schrock
Contributing Designers: Ken Carlson, Mindy Samuelson; Waterbury Publications, Inc.
Contributing Project Editor: Renee Freemon Mulvihill
Editorial Assistant: Heather Knowles
Contributing Copy Editor: Amy Kuebelbeck
Contributing Proofreaders: Terri Fredrickson, Jody Speer
Contributing Indexer: Marth Fifield
Contributing Photographers: Marty Baldwin, Dean Schoeppner, Denny Schrock
Contributing Photo Researcher: Susan Ferguson

Meredith® Books
Editorial Director: Gregory H. Kayko
Editor in Chief, Garden: Doug Jimerson
Editorial Manager: David Speer
Art Director: Tim Alexander
Managing Editor: Doug Kouma
Executive Director, Sales: Ken Zagor
Director, Operations: George A. Susral
Business Director: Janice Croat
Imaging Center Operator: Randy J. Manning

John Wiley & Sons, Inc.
Publisher: Natalie Chapman
Associate Publisher: Jessica Goodman
Executive Editor: Anne Ficklen
Assistant Editor: Charleen Barila
Production Director: Diana Cisek
Manufacturing Manager: Tom Hyland

This book is printed on acid-free paper.

Better Homes and Gardens Magazine
Editor in Chief: Gayle Goodson Butler

Meredith National Media Group
President: Tom Harty
Excutive Vice President: Doug Olson

Meredith Corporation
President and Chief Executive Officer: Stephen M. Lacy

In Memoriam: E.T. Meredith III (1933–2003)

For general information on our other products and services or for technical support, please contact our Customer Care Department within the United States at (800) 762-2974, outside the United States at (317) 572-3993 or fax (317) 572-4002.

Wiley also publishes its books in a variety of electronic formats. Some content that appears in print may not be available in electronic books. For more information about Wiley products, visit our web site at www.wiley.com.

Library of Congress Cataloging-in-Publication Data

LOC information available upon request.
ISBN: 978-0470-87842-2
Printed in the United States of America

10 9 8 7 6 5 4 3

Note to Reader: Due to differing conditions, tools, and individual skills, Meredith Corporation assumes no responsibility for any damages, injuries suffered, or losses incurred as a result of following the information published in this book. Before beginning any project, review the instructions carefully, and if any doubts or questions remain, consult local experts or authorities. Because codes and regulations vary greatly, you should always check with authorities to ensure that your project complies with all applicable local codes and regulations. Always read and observe all the safety precautions provided by manufacturers of any tools, equipment, or supplies, and follow all accepted safety procedures.

From the Editor

Beginner and experienced gardeners alike run into problems on the plants in their yards and homes. *Ask the Garden Doctor* is designed to help prevent those problems and find solutions when they arise.

The advice on these pages comes from real-life situations. For many years the readers of *Better Homes and Gardens®* magazine have posed tough questions to editors about what to plant where, how to care for particular plants, and asking for help in deciphering pest problems. The questions on the following pages are drawn from those gardening dilemmas posed by real people like you. The answers have been provided by our team of expert garden editors, who have decades of gardening experience among them. Often, we're able to share information based on the results of trials in the *Better Homes and Gardens* Test Garden—a half-acre urban garden located at Meredith corporate headquarters in Des Moines, IA—or from hands-on trial-and-error growing in our personal backyard plots.

The huge task of sorting through the thousands of inquiries and responses, and selecting the ones to share with you has fallen on my shoulders, partly because I've had experience editing more than 30 garden books during my publishing career, and partly because I've had nearly two decades of experience answering questions from the public as an extension horticulturist. Development of this book took me back to my training at the University of Minnesota's Dial-U Clinic where half a dozen graduate students and upper division undergraduates answered more than 200 gardening-related questions daily during the summer. It was like an 8-hour oral exam every day! But I learned a lot in the process, and it served me well through a couple of decades of professional work as an extension horticulturist and state Master Gardener coordinator, and now, as a garden editor.

Questions in the book are organized by plant type to aid in quickly finding the answers. An extensive index also helps pinpoint the place to look for solutions. If you can't find your specific garden problem on these pages, search online at *bhg.com/gardendoctor*. You'll find thousands more answers there as part of *Better Homes and Gardens* long history of problem solving.

Doctor Denny Schrock

Indoor Plants

Easy-Care Houseplants

Q I'd like to purchase some houseplants for my home office. I don't have a green thumb at all. I'd like a tall plant (3 to 4 feet to go by a sliding glass door) and a small potted plant. The room doesn't get direct sunlight, but there is quite a bit of light in the afternoons, and because the room faces west, it can get quite warm. Would calla lilies survive in this environment?

A Calla lilies are better as short-term indoor plants. They need bright light indoors and quite a bit of moisture. Some good easy-care substitutes would be peace lily (*Spathiphyllum*), Chinese evergreen (*Aglaonema*), grape ivy (*Cissus rhombifolia*), spider plant (*Chlorophytum comosum*), and arrowhead vine (*Syngonium podophyllum*).

Q I want to put some plants in my preschool classroom. They need to be easy to take care of and nontoxic. What plants could I use?

A Unfortunately, a lot of the easy-to-grow indoor plants are somewhat poisonous. But some nontoxic types you could try include spider plant (*Chlorophytum*), jade plant (*Crassula*), and Swedish ivy (*Plectranthus*).

Q My cactus rotted off at the base. How can I save it?

A Rotting stems on cactus likely means that you are overwatering the plant. Reduce the amount and frequency of watering to prevent the problem from happening again. To save your cactus, remove any rotted section, allow the cut surface to dry, and reroot the stem in cactus mix.

Q My son is going away to college, and I thought a few plants might liven up his dreary dorm room. There's only one window at the far end of the room. Do you have any recommendations?

A Some of the easiest houseplants to grow in low-light conditions are 1. Snake plant (*Sansevieria trifasciata*), 2. Golden pothos (*Epipremnum aureum*), 3. Peace lily (*Spathiphyllum*), and 4. Cast-iron plant (*Aspidistra elatior*). All tolerate neglect, which can be important for college students around finals time.

Terrariums

Q I have a small glass terrarium and want to fill it with plants. What will thrive in my terrarium? I already purchased two small African violets.

A You didn't mention whether your terrarium is open on top (to permit air circulation) or if it is closed. If it's closed, African violets won't do well, because they like good air circulation and they dislike having water dripping onto their hairy leaves. Suitable choices for a closed terrarium include aluminum plant (*Pilea cadierei*), artillery plant (*Pilea microphylla*), and creeping fig (*Ficus pumila*). Ferns, such as bird's-nest fern (*Asplenium nidus*) or table fern (*Pteris cretica*), also grow well in a terrarium. Nerve plant (*Fittonia*) adds colorful leaves to your planting blend. Consider using miniature versions, which won't outgrow their contained environs as quickly as their full-size cousins will.

Q How often should I water my terrarium?

A Most terrarium plants die as a result of overwatering. If you keep your container closed, you shouldn't need to add water for months after the initial planting. As long as you see condensation inside the terrarium, it needs no additional water. For an open terrarium, add water only when the soil is dry to the touch ½ inch below the surface.

Q I want to make a water terrarium, a plant grown in a container of water that also doubles as a home for a betta fish. What houseplants will grow in water?

A Many plants will thrive in water, including dwarf peace lily (*Spathiphyllum*), Chinese evergreen (*Aglaonema*), and pothos (*Epipremnum*). All grow roots apart from any contact with soil in typical indoor light conditions. Remember that you need to feed your betta fish brine shrimp, water fleas, bloodworms, or other similar creatures for it to survive. Contrary to urban

legend, betta fish are carnivores and will not feed on plant roots. If you observe your fish nibbling at the plant roots, it's most likely that it is eating bacteria on the roots and not the roots themselves.

Dish Garden

Q I have a flowering maple that is growing more all the time. It's in a shallow dish along with a small African violet. Do I repot the whole thing into a larger pot?

A You'll have better luck in the long run by separating the two plants and growing them individually. African violets (*Saintpaulia*) stay relatively small and compact, while the flowering maple (*Abutilon*) can get quite large and shrubby. Eventually the flowering maple will need a much larger pot than the African violet. As another option, you could grow several African violets around the base of the flowering maple as a sort of groundcover.

Watering

Q **We're going on vacation for a couple weeks. Is there some way to keep my houseplants from drying out completely while we're gone?**

A When you go on vacation for longer than a week, your plants will need a little attention while you are gone. You can hire someone to care for your plants or you can use one of these techniques:

• Group plants to conserve humidity and moisture.
• Set all your houseplants in the bathtub and turn on the shower to drench them. Drape a clear sheet of plastic over the plants, but keep it from directly touching them. They'll be fine like this for up to two weeks.
• Set individual plants in large, clear plastic bags, making a mini greenhouse for each. Cut a few slits in the bags, and tuck the tops of the bags under the pots.
• Ask a neighbor or friend to water your plants, leaving a list explaining which days to water and including any special instructions for specific plants.

Q **All of my indoor plants dry out pretty badly. I water them at least once a week, but they still dry out. What should I do?**

A The problem is likely your soil. Most tropical houseplants arrive in a lightweight soil mix that fails to hold water very long. It works well at the greenhouse but can dry out quickly at home and can be difficult to remoisten. Try repotting your plants in a commercial soil developed for houseplants. Loosen the soil around the roots, refill your existing pots with fresh soil, and see how things progress.

Q **How can I get rid of the fungus or mold that is growing on the soil of my houseplants without killing the plant? The color of the stuff ranges from creamy white to light orange. I believe it is responsible for my indoor allergies.**

A Watering too much or too little is the biggest killer of indoor plants. If the stuff on your container soil is soft, it is mold, and that means you are watering too frequently. Wait until the soil is dry to 1 inch down before watering again. If the stuff is crusty, you could be watering too little, or it could be a buildup of salts from the water itself, especially if the crust is white. In that case, ease the plant gently out of the pot, set it aside, and scrub the pot with nine parts water to one part bleach. Then rinse the container thoroughly with clear water and repot the plant.

Q **Is it good to water Boston ferns with ice cubes?**

A Giving Boston ferns or other houseplants ice cubes is fine, but not necessary. Standard liquid water works just fine.

Poisonous Plants

Q We have twins who are now crawling and exploring. Are there any plants we should keep away from them?

A Some plants that you should keep out of reach of kids and pets: 1. Azalea (*Rhododendron*), 2. Croton (*Codiaeum*), 3. Crown-of-thorns (*Euphorbia*), 4. Dieffenbachia, 5. English ivy (*Hedera*), 6. Golden pothos (*Epipremnum*), 7. Peace lily (*Spathiphyllum*), 8. Hyacinth (*Hyacinthus*), 9. Clivia (*Clivia miniata*), and 10. Flamingo flower (*Anthurium*).

1

2

3

4

5

6

7

8

9

10

Low-Light Houseplants

Q **What are some good houseplants for low-light areas?**

A Here are 10 that grow extremely well even in low light: 1. Arrowhead vine, 2. Chinese evergreen, 3. Corn plant, 4. Variegated spider plant, 5. Snake plant, 6. Heartleaf philodendron, 7. Grapeleaf ivy, 8. Parlor palm, 9. Song of India dracaena, and 10. Buddhist pine.

Aloe

Q **I have an aloe plant that was a baby when it was given to me last year. It is now huge, but it's turning brown and starting to go limp. What can I do to help it?**

A Have you repotted the aloe recently? If it has grown a great deal, it may need a larger container. Usually it's best to move the plant to a container that's only 1 inch or so larger than its current one. Although aloe can tolerate dry conditions well, if it's potbound it may not be getting enough water to keep it firm. It also needs bright light.

Q **I have an aloe. What should I do with the pieces of leaves that fall off the main plant? Can I replant them?**

A Shoots that break off the base of aloe plants provide a means to start new plants. Make certain that each shoot has a growing tip and a main stem; an individual leaf won't root. Make a fresh cut at the base of the stem, allow to air-dry a day or two, and then stick the cut end into a mixture of equal parts sand and commercial potting soil. Keep the soil mix moist, but avoid overwatering or you'll rot the cuttings. Hasten the rooting by dipping the cut ends of the stems into rooting hormone (available in liquid or powder form) before inserting them into the soil mixture.

Q **I think I have killed my *Aloe vera* plant! It was doing fine, then I repotted it into a larger pot. I put a layer of rocks at the bottom because the pot didn't have a drainage hole. Now the plant looks soggy or soft in places. Have I killed it?**

A When an aloe plant is overwatered, the leaves develop soft, soggy water-soaked spots. Eventually the entire plant dies. Your plant may be experiencing a waterlogged condition because the pot you put it in lacks a drainage hole. The layer of pebbles in the bottom of

the pot compounds the problem by creating a perched water table over the pebbles. The plant's roots are dying from lack of oxygen. You might be able to save your plant if you dig it up and let it dry out for a day or two. Remove any dead or rotted portions. Replant it in cactus and succulent potting mix in a pot with a drainage hole.

Asparagus Fern

Q **My asparagus fern has yellow spikes. What should be done to correct the yellowing?**

A Some yellowing of spikes is natural. As the spikes age, they turn from green to yellow, then tan before they die. If just a few spikes are turning, you can trim them off. If you see a great deal of yellowing, it may be an indication of disease or insects or an environmental problem such as overwatering. In these cases, the yellowing is more likely to be generalized throughout the plant. Check the plant closely for additional signs of insects or disease, and control those pests, if present.

Croton

Q I have a brightly colored, waxy-leaf houseplant that I believe is a croton. It sits in a sunny spot in our garden room. I only water it when the leaves start to droop. The problem is that the new leaves drop as soon as they appear. Is an insect causing this problem?

A Croton (*Codiaeum variegatum* var. *pictum*) thrives in sunny locations where temperatures hit the 80s during the day and stay at least in the high 60s at night. Cold drafts of air cause plants to drop leaves. Investigate the air seals in your garden room. Do you have cold air that's blowing onto plants? During the summer, even central air-conditioning could cause the problem. Low humidity can also cause leaves to fall. Boost humidity around the plant with a room humidifier.

Q My croton's leaves used to be a brightly colored mix of red, yellow, orange, and green, but now it's turning almost solid green. What am I doing wrong?

A Croton can survive in medium- to low-light conditions, but in order to keep its brightly colored variegation it needs bright light. Try moving your croton to a spot with brighter light. The old leaves that are green won't change color, but new growth should develop the brighter hues.

Dieffenbachia

Q My neighbor told me my dieffenbachia plant is poisonous. Do I need to worry about my dog eating it? Sometimes he chews on leaves.

A Dieffenbachia (above right) is indeed poisonous. One common name for it is dumb cane, because of the

effect it has on those who accidentally ingest it. The plant sap contains calcium oxalate, a chemical compound that causes swelling of the tongue and throat. Swelling can be so severe that airflow through the throat is blocked, preventing normal speech and breathing. Obviously, this can have serious consequences. Fortunately, few accidental poisonings occur. However, to be safe, keep your dieffenbachia out of the reach of small children and pets.

Q When is a good time to cut back my dieffenbachia plant? It's about 8 feet tall and ready to push through the ceiling.

A If necessary you can cut back your dieffenbachia at any time, but the best time is late winter to early spring. When day length and light levels rise in spring, the new growth that results from the cutback will be sturdier.

Dracaena

Q **I have a 5-foot-tall lucky bamboo plant that is out of control. The leaves are turning yellow. Is it dying? I want to cut some of the top off but don't know what to put on the cut ends. Please help.**

A Lucky bamboo is actually a type of dracaena. Is yours growing in water or in potting soil? They can grow for many years directly in water, but you'll need to give it some fertilizer occasionally to prevent the leaves from turning yellow. Use a diluted all-purpose houseplant fertilizer. You can cut back the tops of the lucky bamboo, and it should resprout from just below the point where you make the cut. You don't need to put anything on the pruning wound. Simply let it air dry.

Q **I have a bundle of lucky bamboo that has always been in the vase of water that it was in when I bought it several years ago. It is getting too top heavy for the vase and I'd like to repot it in soil. I'm not sure what type of soil that bamboo should grow in, or should I just move it to a larger vase?**

A Lucky bamboo is actually a type of dracaena, *Dracaena sanderiana*, also sometimes called ribbon plant. It can be grown quite easily in potting soil. Use a good, reliable all-purpose potting soil. Plant it at the same depth as it was growing in water. Keep the soil quite moist at first while the plant adjusts from growing completely in water to growing in soil.

Q **I have had two corn plant trees for more than 13 years, but they have reached the ceiling of my apartment. How do I top them and bring them back down away from the ceiling without killing them?**

A The corn plant dracaena is a tough plant. It can be cut back to a stump and will resprout. You can even root the pieces that you cut off to give you more corn plants. Simply cut off the plant at whatever height you desire. The lower piece should resprout within a month or two, and the upper part that has been cut off will usually root in several months if potted in moist potting soil and kept moist but not soggy.

Q **I just bought a *Dracaena marginata* plant. It is losing all its leaves. I have it under lights, keep it warm, and give it plenty of water. What am I doing wrong?**

A Several conditions could lead to significant leaf loss of your Madagascar dragon tree (*Dracaena marginata*). Tropical foliage plants are grown in bright greenhouses or outdoors under shade cloth. In either case, the plants are accustomed to much more light than you can provide in your home. As the plant adjusts to reduced light conditions, it sheds some of its lower leaves. Another possibility is that your plant might have gotten chilled. Tropical plants such as dracaena react dramatically if they have experienced cold temperatures or drafts. Too much water could also be causing leaf loss. The soil should be allowed to dry to the touch between waterings. If it stays constantly wet, the roots could begin rotting. Yellowed leaves and leaf drop follow.

English Ivy

Q **Ivy plants are my favorites. I have several and just can't seem to keep them healthy. Our house is dry, and we have a water softener—two things that I know don't help. Should I mix or purchase soil? What kinds of pests will I likely be dealing with?**

A English ivy (*Hedera helix*) can be a finicky houseplant, but once you master the basics, your plant will be stunning and reward you with lots of lush, healthy growth. Pot your plants in a good-quality, light houseplant mix. Avoid watering with softened water; it's high in salts, which can damage delicate plant roots. Catch and use rainwater, or use bottled water for your plants. The deathblow to most ivies is the hot, dry environment of homes. Place them in the coolest room you have; aim for daytime temperatures in the upper 60s and nights about 10 degrees cooler. North or east light proves perfect for healthy growth.

Q **I've seen a lot of artificial topiaries being sold, but I'd prefer a live one. How hard is it to create a living topiary?**

A Topiary is an elegant way to dress up even the most common houseplants, and you can create one in a couple hours. If you choose one of the more easy-care houseplants, your topiary will require minimal maintenance. Follow these easy steps to create your own topiary.

1. Fill the pot two-thirds full with potting soil, and insert the wire prong on the topiary frame into the soil. Remove the ivy from its pot.
2. Cut the root ball by slicing down between the stems using a sharp knife. Reassemble the divided root ball around the base of the frame so the trunk of the frame is centered. If needed, add more potting soil.
3. Twine one of the long ivy stems tightly in a spiral up the trunk of the frame, then wind it through the globe at the top. Clip off all the leaves on the trunk section. Repeat the procedure with the remaining stems until you've covered all the wires of the globe.
4. As the ivy grows, pinch new growth occasionally, and clip off errant stems to keep the globe shape dense and round.

Q **My English ivy is turning yellow, and it looks like it has spider webs on it. What is happening to it?**

A It sounds as though your English ivy has spider mites. These tiny pests love English ivy, and most gardeners don't notice them until they have completely infested the plant. Wash spider mites off the plant with a forceful spray of water, or use insecticidal soap or horticultural oil to kill them.

Q **My English ivies just survive without looking healthy at all. Is there any magic to growing great indoor plants?**

A With indoor plants, success depends on matching conditions with the type of plant you're growing. English ivy, for example, needs a cool, moist, partially shaded location such as a north-facing window.

Ferns

Q **I have a Kimberly fern outside and would like to bring it in the house when the weather gets colder. Will it be OK inside?**

A By Kimberly fern, I assume you're referring to the Kimberly Queen fern (*Nephrolepis obliterata*), a close relative of Boston fern. This plant makes a good houseplant as long as you can provide bright, indirect light and high humidity. Keep it slightly moist, but not soggy, at all times.

Q **I bought an indoor fern about a month ago and it seems to be dying on me. The tag says, "Keep in a cool shady place and keep moist." I spray it daily with water and water it every second day, but it's still brown and brittle! I moved it to where it gets some afternoon sun, but it seems to have made no improvement.**

A Ferns do like high humidity and moist soil. If yours is drying out quickly, perhaps it is rootbound and needs to be repotted so that it has a larger mass of soil that can hold more water.

Q **I would like to repot my fern. How do I do this? Rabbit's foot fern has those little feet over the pot, and I don't want to damage the plant.**

A Rabbit's foot fern (*Davallia* spp.) seldom needs to be repotted. If you try to repot it in the traditional way, many of the "feet" will be broken off. You can restart them by pegging the feet down in moist potting mixture. Those that remain attached to the plant will also establish more quickly if they are pegged into the new soil (a hairpin or opened paper clip works well). Potting soil that drains freely is fine, but add some orchid bark if drainage is not good. If you choose not to repot completely, scrape away some of the old soil from between the rhizomes and add some new soil. The most attractive specimens are sometimes almost completely covered with the furry feet.

Q **I just purchased a large foxtail fern. Currently I have the plant in my four-season room and expect that is where it will need to stay over the winter. What type of care does a foxtail fern prefer? Can I plant it outside next spring?**

A Foxtail fern (*Asparagus densiflorus* 'Myersii') is not actually a fern but is related to asparagus. It prefers bright light or filtered shade indoors. Your four-season room should be fine if it stays at about 68°F or so. Feed with half-strength liquid fertilizer every couple weeks through the winter; more frequently during the growing season. Foxtail fern does not like to dry out. If conditions aren't right, it may drop its yellowed needlelike leaves in protest, although it recovers easily. You can put the pot outdoors during the summer in light shade, perhaps under a tree. If you plant it in the ground, you'll need to repot it to bring it in next winter.

Ficus

Q I have a *Ficus benjamina* plant. It's about 3 feet tall and has lost almost all of its leaves. I really don't know how to care for it or what to do.

A Weeping fig (*Ficus benjamina*) is susceptible to leaf drop with any change in environment. However, it usually recovers from periodic leaf drop. Give it medium to bright indirect light. Keep it out of drafts (from open doors, windows, and heating or air-conditioning ducts) and keep it moderately moist.

Norfolk Island Pine

Q My Norfolk Island pine is losing its lower branches. Is there anything I can do to prevent them from dropping?

A Norfolk pine needs bright, indirect light. If light levels are too low, it's not uncommon for it to lose its lower branches. Because the dieback you see is confined to the lower branches, I suspect that this is the case. Norfolk pine is also susceptible to spider mites, which can cause branch browning and dieback. However, spider mites usually attack branch tips and the damage appears randomly. Check the tree for spider mites by holding a sheet of white paper under one of the brown branches. Lightly tap the branch. If you see little specks moving around on the paper, your tree has spider mites. You can control them with a forceful spray of water, insecticidal soap, or a commercial miticide.

Find out more about palms in our online plant encyclopedia at *bhg.com/plantencyclopedia/palms.*

Palm

Q My palm trees have webs with small white dots on the leaves. The leaves are starting to turn brown. Can you help me save them?

A Those webs you've been seeing are a sure sign that your palms have been infested with spider mites. These almost-invisible pests suck plant juices and can cause a plant to go into decline. Give your palms a shower to wash off the mites. Insecticidal soap, horticultural oil, or chemical miticides may be necessary to control the mites.

Q What causes brown tips on plant leaves? I have a palm tree, and the ends are turning brown. Should I cut away the brown edges of the leaves or should I cut off the whole branch?

A Brown leaf tips on palms may be caused by one or more of the following.

Dryness. If the palm is not getting enough water or if the humidity is too low, the leaf tips will turn brown. Water more frequently and on a regular schedule.

Salts. Salts from watering accumulate in the soil over time. The salts may come from fertilizer dissolved in the water or from minerals in the water itself. Prevent the salt buildup by leaching (flushing) the soil with distilled water periodically.

Chemicals. Some chemicals such as chloride can accumulate in leaf tips and cause browning. If your water source has chloride, use distilled water or rainwater instead to water plants.

Philodendron

Q My philodendron seemed to be doing very well. It is getting to be pretty big and full. Lately the edges of some of the leaves have been turning brown. Please help me find the problem.

A If just the edges of the leaves are turning brown, a couple causes are possible. It may be that the potting soil has accumulated salts. These could come from overfertilization or from chlorine or fluoride in your water source. The level of these chemicals may be quite low, but over time they can build up in the soil. You might try flushing the soil with distilled water to wash out any excess salts.

Another possibility for the cause of brown leaf edges is low humidity or dry soil. You may be watering just as frequently as previously, but as the plant grows larger, it will dry out faster. You can remedy the problem by watering more frequently or repotting the plant into a larger container with more soil.

Find out more about other philodendrons in our online plant encyclopedia at *bhg.com/plantencyclopedia/philodendron.*

Q Why are the leaves on my philodendron turning yellow? The yellowing started after the last time I fertilized it. This is the third time this year I have fed this plant.

A The most common cause of yellowing leaves on philodendron is overwatering. Make sure the pot has drainage holes and pour off any excess water that runs into the saucer below. It's unlikely that the fertilizer caused the problem. Excess fertilizer could cause yellowing and browning edges on the leaves.

Q I have a trailing philodendron that I would like to root. Can I do this from a cutting?

A Rooting a philodendron is easy. All you need is a pair of pruning shears and a small container of potting soil. Cut a piece of philodendron stem about 3 to 6 inches long. Make the cut just above a leaf on the same stem. Remove all leaves on the cutting except the top two or three. Place the cutting in moist vermiculite or potting soil. Place the container with the cuttings in bright, indirect sunlight. In two or three weeks roots will sprout, followed by new leaves. Gently tug on the cutting. If you feel resistance you'll know that roots have formed. Pot rooted cuttings in good-quality potting soil in a pot that's 3 to 4 inches wide. If your mother plant is large enough, take three to five cuttings at one time and plant them together in one pot for a full, lush new plant.

Snake Plant

Q **My snake plant has developed yellow leaves and is flopping over. What am I doing wrong?**

A Snake plant is usually easy to care for and trouble-free. However, if it is overwatered and kept too cold, it can develop root rot. The yellowing leaves on your plant are a sign that the roots of your plant may be rotting. Pull it out of the pot, remove any soft or mushy roots, and repot it using a good container-plant potting mix that drains well. Allow the soil to dry to the touch between waterings.

Q **Can I start new snake plants from cuttings, or is it better to divide a large plant?**

A The simplest way to start a new snake plants is to divide a plant. And it's the only way to maintain the marginal light green stripe of variegated types. Plants started from cuttings lose this variegation.

If your snake plant is not variegated, and you're patient, you can start new plants by taking stem cuttings. Cut the leaves into 3- to 4-inch-long segments. Dip the lower end in rooting hormone, and insert it into lightweight potting mix. Keep the mix moist but not wet. In several months you'll see new shoots developing from the base.

Spider Plant

Q **My spider plant seems to be thinning out and becoming unhealthy. The ends of the leaves are turning brown. Am I watering it too much or too little?**

A If your spider plant (*Chlorophytum comosum*) has been in the same pot for a long time, it's probably best to repot it into something a bit larger with fresh soil. Remove the root ball from the pot to look at the roots. A potbound spider plant will have a cluster of thick white roots at the bottom of the pot, circling around the edges and pushing out through the drainage holes.

Those brown tips could be caused by excessive drying or by mineral buildup in the soil. If the plant was potbound, it may have been drying out too quickly. Repotting should remedy the situation. Spider plants are also sensitive to low humidity. Leaf tips can turn brown and shrivel when the air is too dry. You can raise the humidity with a humidifier. To prevent mineral buildup, water more thoroughly. Water enough so that water drains through the pot every time you water.

Q **My spider plant has a lot of babies dangling from it. Can I start new plants from these?**

A Yes, spider plant is one of the easiest plants to propagate. If you look closely at the babies, or plantlets, you'll see little knobs on the underside of the cluster of leaves. These are root initials. If you place them on potting soil, the roots with start to grow, and you'll have new plants. Keep the soil evenly moist until the roots are fully developed.

African Violet

Q **I find growing African violets a challenge, but I love the flowers. Lately the leaves on my violets are turning brown. I water the plants twice a week, always from the bottom. Could I be watering too much?**

A If your violets' leaves are turning brown and mushy, it's likely that you're overwatering the plant. Typically, watering a violet once a week is plenty. To test, push your index finger just beneath the soil surface. If the soil is dry at that depth, water the plant. As you note, it's important to water from the bottom to avoid splashing cold water on the leaves, which can leave unsightly brown spots on the foliage.

Q **African violets are supposed to be easy to grow, but I don't have much luck with them. What's the trick to growing them?**

A Bright, indirect light suits African violets best. A northern or eastern exposure brings the best results. Because they are tropical in origin, they prefer warm temperatures (*in the 70s*). Fertilize monthly with a liquid fertilizer at half strength. Use room-temperature water when watering to avoid brown splotches on the leaves.

Amaryllis

Q How do I get my amaryllis to rebloom?

A After the flowers fade, cut them off to prevent seeds from forming. Remove the stalk after it turns yellow. Keep the plant in a sunny location, and water as needed. After all danger of frost has passed, move the bulb outdoors for the summer. Keep it actively growing through the summer by watering and fertilizing regularly. In fall, bring the plant back indoors before frost hits. Stop watering the plant, and let the foliage die down naturally. Keep the bulb, pot and all, in a cool, dry, dark location for several months. After this resting period, bring it back to a warm location and start watering to initiate new growth and another bloom cycle.

Christmas Cactus

Q I have a dying Christmas cactus. I noticed that the branches were dropping, and then I noticed that they were squishy at the base. At this time, the soil is very dry. I thought maybe I had overwatered it. Please help!

A I think you're correct in your diagnosis that it has been overwatered. Take the stems that have broken off and use them as cuttings. Cut some healthy growth from above where it is soggy, dip the end in rooting hormone, and insert the end in a dampened mix of bark and potting soil. Place in a clear plastic bag perforated with holes so that it does not remain too wet, and keep it in bright light but out of the sun. In a few weeks

roots will develop, and you can pot it. Be sure there is plenty of bark for fast drainage in the potting soil so it does not become soggy again.

Q I have a large Christmas cactus that's been in the family a long time. I don't have much of a green thumb. How do I get it to bloom?

A Holiday cactus (*Schlumbergera*) needs cool temperatures and short day length to form flower buds. Thanksgiving cactus (*S. truncata*) normally blooms a bit sooner than Christmas cactus (*S. buckleyi*). Care requirements for both plants are essentially the same. To induce bloom, give the plants a rest period in fall. Keep them on the dry side, but water enough to prevent the flat, leafy stems from shriveling. Maintain temperatures in the 50s to set the most flower buds. Place the plant in bright, indirect light. After flower buds have formed (you'll see swollen knobs on the stems), increase watering to prevent the buds from dropping. Flower buds also drop if the temperature is too warm, light levels are too low, or the plant is exposed to drafts.

Gardenia

Q I have two indoor gardenias. They were very healthy and had lots of buds on them when I bought them. The leaves are dying and falling off, and the buds are turning yellow. What am I doing wrong?

A Gardenias can be temperamental. Bud drop (and leaf drop) can be irritating problems. Common causes include low humidity, overwatering, underwatering, insufficient light, temperature fluctuations, cold drafts, or a change in plant locations. In midwinter, the problem is most commonly low humidity. Try placing your plant on top of a watertight tray filled with pebbles and filled with water to help maintain a higher level of humidity for your gardenia.

Hibiscus

Q I have tried to keep a tropical hibiscus over the winter inside by a window, watering it once a week, but the leaves have all fallen off, and no new growth is coming. Any suggestions?

A Tropical hibiscus can be a challenge to keep alive indoors during the winter. These plants require a lot of humidity that's hard to re-create inside the home. They also often attract spider mites, which cause the leaves to yellow and drop. If you want to try again next year, make sure your plants get as much sun as possible and mist them frequently. Giving them a weekly shower in the bathroom is also a good idea.

Q I've had an hibiscus tree for six years now which used to flower beautifully outdoors all summer long. I bring it indoors in the fall. Two years ago it had only three flowers in the summer. Last summer no flowers came out once the plant went outside. What do I do to get it to bloom again in summer?

A Hibiscus needs full sun (6 to 8 hours a day) and regular feeding because it takes a lot of nutrients to maintain those big flowers. Add a slow-release fertilizer to the plant's soil or repot the plant, replacing the existing soil completely if your plant has been growing in the same mix for several years .

Q Ever since I brought my hibiscus indoors it hasn't bloomed. What can I do to get it to bloom again?

A Hibiscus plants need a lot of sunshine; they bloom best in a bright window with a southern exposure. Even with the right exposure, they may not bloom through the dark winter months. During this period of slow growth, cut back on watering and fertilizing. When

days lengthen in spring, trim back the plant if it is getting leggy. Increase the frequency of watering, and use a liquid houseplant fertilizer to keep the plant well fed and promote strong new growth.

Q My hibiscus has tiny white bugs on the undersides of the leaves and flying around it. How can I kill these bugs without harming my family?

A These pests are called whiteflies, and hibiscus is one of their favorite host plants. They are difficult to get rid of, but not impossible.

One of the best ways to control without using chemical sprays is to place yellow or blue sticky cards (available at well-stocked garden centers or by mail order) near the plants. The adult flies become trapped in the sticky goo on the cards. Horticultural oil spray is another safe option to control these pests.

Orchids

Q My orchid has lost all its flowers. Do I cut the stem back or leave it as is? My orchids seem to want to grow sideways.

A After your orchid is done blooming, cut the stem back. If it is a moth orchid (*Phalaenopsis*), cut it just below the spot where the lowest bloom was, and you may get a second bloom. For all other orchids, you can remove the entire stem. Most orchids are sympodial, which means their new growth comes from the base of the previous growth. The plant ends up with several plantlets or sections, called pseudobulbs, connected by a rhizome. If you want to cut the plant back so it will fit into the same pot, the oldest pseudobulbs can be cut off and discarded. Always keep at least four pseudobulbs together so your plant won't skip bloom seasons. When you repot the remaining pseudobulbs, put the oldest pseudobulb against the side of the pot so the rest of the space is open for new growth.

Q How often and what should I use to fertilize and water my orchids?

A The amount and frequency to water orchids depends on the type of orchid. Some come from high rainfall areas and should be kept constantly moist. Others need to dry out considerably between waterings. None like to have soggy roots, and most need watering once per week or less. The type of fertilizer to use depends on what type of growing medium the orchid is in. Those growing in bark need a fertilizer with a 3:1:1 ratio of nitrogen to phosphorus to potassium. Those in other growing media should have a 1:1:1 ratio. Some growers like to use a weak solution of fertilizer with every watering. Others prefer fertilizing once a month or so during active growth of the orchids.

Q I have a beautiful orchid that has not bloomed in a couple years. Its leaves are healthy, but there are also these things that look like roots growing up through the soil. What are these and should I cut them?

A The rootlike growths in the soil are likely either rhizomes or pseudobulbs if they are large and coarse, or possibly aerial rootlets if they are fine-textured. Pseudobulbs are where new shoots (and new flower stalks) develop, so you should leave these growths intact. Aerial roots are the orchid's means of attaching itself to a support structure (which could include soil).

Learn more about growing orchids online at *bhg.com/orchids.*

Flowers

Heat-Loving Annuals

Q What are the best plants for flower pots that can stand hot temperatures?

A Some heat-loving annual flowers to consider: 1. Calibrachoa, 2. Cosmos, 3. Geranium (*Pelargonium*), 4. Moss rose (*Portulaca*), 5. Petunia, 6. Salvia, 7. Vinca (*Catharanthus*), 8. Cockscomb (*Celosia*), and 9. Zinnia.

Hanging Baskets

Q **I just purchased several hanging baskets. They are blooming beautifully but already look full for the season. Will they be all right for the whole season, or do they need to be divided so that the plants have room to grow over the summer?**

A Hanging baskets that are quite full to begin the growing season can be kept looking beautiful all season long. They may take more frequent watering and extra fertilizer because the roots are confined to such a small space. Also, by midseason you may need to do some pruning or pinching back of long, trailing stems to keep the plants attractive.

Q **How often do you water plants in hanging baskets? Mine are in full sun. Should they be turned? If so, how often?**

A Plants in containers should generally be kept evenly moist, so test the soil with your finger. If the first inch is dry, water them. Turn the pot to take advantage of (or protect them from) the light on a regular basis—every two weeks, once a month, whatever makes the plant look evenly full.

Q **I have a large hanging basket to put plants in. I would like to put something in the bottom to prevent filling the entire container with potting soil and make it lighter for hanging. What can I fill it with?**

A Many gardeners use foam peanuts to fill the bottoms of large containers. They are light and they take up space. However, keep in mind that the smaller the volume of soil, the more frequently the container will need to be watered.

Q **I live in an apartment with a patio where I have many hanging baskets. What plants would you suggest for growing in baskets?**

A There are many beautiful annual flowers you can grow in hanging containers. Ivy geranium (*Pelargonium peltatum*), verbena (*Verbena* hybrids), ornamental sweet potato vine (*Ipomoea batatas*), browallia (*Browallia speciosa*), and fan flower (*Scaevola*) are a few of the many colorful, trailing plants you can grow. If your patio is shady, consider tuberous begonia (*Begonia × tuberhybrida*), wax begonia (*Begonia × semperflorens-cultorum*), bellflower (*Campanula*), impatiens (*I. walleriana*), or coleus (*Solenostemon scutellarioides*).

Seeding

Q Every year I sow annual flowers directly in my garden, but they come up so thick that I need to thin out many of them. Is there some way I can avoid having to thin out the extra seedlings?

A Flower seedlings growing too closely together create competition just as weeds do. You may be able to dig up the excess seedlings and transplant them to another area of the garden. That way you won't waste any of them. You could also sow the seeds at a wider spacing using one of several options. Some garden centers and mail order catalogs carry seed tapes with seeds embedded at preset intervals. Roll out the seed tape where you want the flowers to grow, and wait for them to sprout. Precision seeders are tools that pick up one seed at a time and plant it at a spacing of your choice. An inexpensive method is to mix sand with your flower seeds before you sow them. The sand adds bulk to the mix, creating wider spacing of the seeds.

Q My flower seeds never sprouted. I soaked the seeds for a couple days before planting them. Is it still possible for them to sprout later on in the year?

A You don't need to soak seeds so long. Soak them overnight only. By soaking for a couple days, you may have drowned the seeds. Some gardeners have better luck by wrapping the seeds in moist paper towels rather than soaking them in water.

Cold soil temperature could also be the culprit. Start the flowers in seed-starting mix in pots. Put the pots on a heat mat to keep the soil and seeds warm until they germinate. Transplant seedlings to the garden later, once they are established.

Q One piece of literature tells me to transplant when the seedling has two sets of true leaves, and another says three sets of true leaves. Does it actually make a difference?

A It varies from species to species. The key is to transplant the seedlings after they're sturdy enough to handle it, but before their roots become long or tangled with those of other seedlings. It's best to handle the seedlings by holding the leaves rather than the stem.

Q I've tried starting flower seeds indoors in our kitchen window, but it's always been a disaster. The seedlings sprout, but they soon grow spindly and fall over. I've also noticed mold forming on the soil surface. Am I overwatering?

A It sounds as though the problem could be too much water and too little light. Even though seeds need lots of moisture and high humidity to sprout, once the seedlings break the soil's surface, they do better when allowed to dry slightly between waterings. Cover the trays and pots with clear plastic until the seeds sprout, then remove it.

If your seedlings are collapsing at the base, they could be getting a fungal disease called damping off. Excess moisture also can cause mold on the soil's surface. Water from the bottom by adding water to the trays, and only add water when the soil surface feels dry to the touch.

Your spindly seedlings may need more consistent light. Fluorescent shop lights provide an inexpensive source of steady light. Place one a few inches above the plants as they first emerge.

Transplanting

Q Do I need to do anything to the flower seedlings that I started indoors before I plant them outside?

A It's a good idea to harden off tender seedlings before planting them in the garden, whether you've started them yourself or purchased them from a greenhouse. Gradually expose plants to more sunlight, cooler temperatures, and less moisture for a transition period of about 7 to 10 days. Place them in a protected location such as under a deck, in the shade of a tree, or next to the house. Seedlings transplanted directly to the garden may sunburn, wilt severely, suffer moisture stress, or possibly die.

Q When can I safely plant my annual flowers in the garden?

A Find out the frost-free date for your area from your local cooperative extension office, a garden center, or an experienced gardening friend. Depending on the cold tolerance of the flowers you intend to plant, use this date as a guideline. Cool-season annuals such as pansies, snapdragons, and calendulas can be set out several weeks before the last frost date. Tropicals that are extremely sensitive to cold, such as impatiens and Thai basil, should wait until a couple of weeks after the frost-free date. Keep an eye on the weather; some years the weather warms up much earlier than in others.

Q I've heard that vegetables should be planted in different areas of the garden each year. Is the same true for flowers?

A Crop rotation is a good idea for flowers as well as vegetables. When you grow the same type of plant year after year in the same spot, diseases and insect problems often develop. To avoid problems it's wise to grow something different periodically to break the pest cycle. On the other hand, if you're having success with a certain variety of flower, you could continue to grow it until a problem develops, then switch to another type.

Easy Annuals

Q I plan to grow flowers from seed for the first time this year. What are some easy ones for first-time gardeners to start with?

A Large-seeded annuals such as 1. marigold, 2. zinnia, and 3. sunflower are good choices for beginning gardeners, including children. These three types of flowers prefer full sun and warm conditions.

1

2

3

Low-Growing Annuals

Q I just moved into a house with nothing in the landscape. Can you suggest some low-growing annuals to line the walkway?

A Several creeping or low-growing annuals that will provide season-long color include: 1. Ageratum, 2. Verbena, 3. Pansy (*Viola*), and 4. Sweet alyssum (*Lobularia*).

Medium-Size Annuals

Q I need some annual flowers for the middle of the border. What are some good medium-size ones?

A Several annuals in the 18 to 24 inch-tall height range include: 1. African marigold (*Tagetes erecta*), 2. Cockscomb (*Celosia*), 3. Petunia, and 4. Globe amaranth (*Gomphrena*).

Large Annuals

Q I need to fill some large spaces in the landscape with annuals. What would be some good large plants to grow?

A Some of the best annuals for the back of a border or to fill in large spaces quickly include: 1. Cosmos, 2. Castor bean (*Ricinus*), 3. Mexican sunflower (*Tithonia*), and 4. Spider flower (*Cleome*).

Storing Seeds

Q Many generous people have given me seeds from their garden plants. How do I store them until I can plant them next spring?

A To preserve your treasures for next year, store the fully dried seeds in airtight containers in a cool, dry place. A refrigerator works well if space is available. Glass jars, plastic food storage containers, or airtight plastic bags make good storage containers. If the inside of a container sweats during storage, the seeds are too wet and should be dried further before storing. If seeds aren't fully dried, they may rot during storage. Be sure to label the containers, including the name of the plant and the date. Fully dried and refrigerated seeds can be viable up to 10 times longer than seeds stored at room temperature.

Saving Seeds

Q I planted flower seeds for the first time. My marigolds were husky, colorful, and long-lasting. It's my first crop of anything, and I'd like to save the seeds. What should I do?

A Marigolds are among the easiest seeds to save. The most important thing is to make sure the seeds are completely mature and dry before you store them. You can let the flowers dry in the garden, or you can dry them after cutting them off the plants. Start with a bouquet of disease-free flowers past their prime for beauty. If the flowers are cut while in full bloom, the seeds will not be completely mature. Wrap a rubber band around the stems and hang the bouquet upside down in a paper bag in a cool spot. As the seeds dry, they will fall into the bag. Keep in mind that if the marigolds you grew were hybrids, they will not come true to type from the seed that you save.

Self-Seeding Annuals

Q I like the look of cottage gardens. Are there some annual flowers that I can plant that will self-seed and fill in my garden?

A A number of annual flowers will self-seed if they are not deadheaded. Some of the best at self-seeding are cosmos, love-in-a-mist (*Nigella*), moss rose (*Portulaca*), and larkspur (*Consolida*).

 Learn all about annual flowers online at *bhg.com /annuals*.

Annuals for Shade

Q **I have a plot of soil surrounded by beautiful brick in front of my home. The house creates a constant shadow over the area so absolutely no sunlight hits it. I have planted impatiens, but they all died in a matter of a week or two. What could I grow there?**

A How dense is the shade in this area? Impatiens should grow in shade, but perhaps you need to amend the soil with compost or organic matter to loosen the soil and provide a better growing base for the plants.

Q **I am a beginner gardener and would like some help on what to plant in an existing bed. It gets dappled sun throughout the day. The dirt is hard. Do I need to till it first? It's kind of rocky underneath.**

A Avoid tilling up the entire area, especially if there are tree roots in the shady zone. You could damage the trees by tilling. Instead, do pocket plantings, amending the soil and digging it up in small sections in and around the tree roots.

Q **I plan to garden in containers on my deck. What kind of flowers should I put in my containers for morning sun and evening shade?**

A Your flower choices depend on how much sun the deck receives during the spring and summer. Sun-loving annuals require at least 6 hours of direct sunlight a day. These include verbena, geranium, marigold, zinnia, and salvia. If your yard gets fewer than 6 hours of sun per day, choose shade-lovers such as begonia, caladium, fuchsia, and impatiens to provide constant color.

Q **I am new to shade gardening and have the usual hostas, ferns, and bleeding heart, but I am looking for some long-blooming flowers for some color. Any suggestions?**

A Annual flowers that provide good color in shade include 1. Impatiens (regular and New Guinea), 2. Wax begonia, and 3. Wishbone flower (*Torenia*). Also consider plants with colorful foliage that are attractive even when not in bloom, such as 4. Coleus (*Solenostemon*).

1

2

3

4

Deadheading

Q What does "deadheading" mean? When and why should this be done?

A Deadheading means removing a plant's flowers as they fade. On some plants—especially annuals—this practice encourages more blooms. Deadhead right after the flowers fade. Deadheading not only improves the plants' appearance, it removes developing seeds. Because most annual flowers are genetically programmed to bloom, produce seed, and die, deadheading pushes the plants to develop more flowers in an attempt to produce more seeds. In other words, deadheading tricks the plants into steady bloom.

Q For the past three years I have had hanging baskets of petunias that start out beautiful but then die branch by branch. They develop something that looks like a bud, but instead of becoming a flower, it turns hard and green. If left on the plant, it turns brown and spills out hundreds of little black specks. This kills the branch. What is this and what can I do to stop it?

A It sounds as though your petunias are setting seed. As with most annual flowers, once the plant sets and matures a crop of seed, its life cycle is completed and it dies. However, you can keep your petunias blooming profusely all season by trimming off the developing seedpods before they turn brown. Most modern petunia cultivars require little deadheading. If you're growing one of the recent introductions and still have trouble with them dying out from seed set, it may be an indication that the plants are being stressed. Container plantings are more likely to be stressed from lack of moisture and excess heat than plants growing in the ground. You might try watering and fertilizing your containers more frequently to minimize stress to the plants.

Q Where on the stem do I cut off dead flowers? I've heard that removing spent flowers encourages more blooms.

A Removing dead flowers, or deadheading, is a good gardening practice. It may make plants produce extra flowers, it makes for a neater garden, and it prevents self-sown seedlings from popping up everywhere. To deadhead, pinch back to the next flower, bud, or leaf on a stem. On flowers such as petunias and marigolds, pinch back the flower stalk to the first set of leaves below the bloom. If you simply pull off spent petals, you may leave behind the developing seedpod.

Pinching

Q I am in the process of transplanting some annual flower plugs annuals into pots and the instructions call for pinching them. Some also call for a "soft pinch." What's the difference and what is the best way to do it?

A The term "pinching" can refer to either soft pinching or hard pinching. A soft pinch means to remove just the growing point of a plant. A hard pinch means removing several sets of leaves from the stem tip. If your seedlings have several sets of leaves, you can pinch back the top set. But don't remove more than one-fourth of the leaves.

Coleus

Q **I always thought coleus was a shade plant. Recently I've seen a lot of them planted in full sun and growing nicely. Are these sun-loving coleus the same species?**

A Coleus (*Solenostemon scutellarioides*) has not only undergone a botanical name change (it used to be *Coleus hybridus*), but it also has recently received a great deal of attention from plant breeders. Although coleus has long been noted for giving colorful splashes of reds, pinks, purples, whites, and greens to shady areas, recent introductions have incorporated sun tolerance. It's a good bet that the coleus you pick up at the garden center these days will grow in full sun as well as in shade, although some of the older varieties remain popular, so it's wise to check the label for sun or shade tolerance.

Q **I bought three pretty coleus plants this spring. They have been in self-watering large pots under some tall evergreens. Is this a good spot for them?**

A Most coleus thrive in a shaded or partially shaded spot and in moist, well-drained soil. Some newer varieties tolerate full sun but require a steady supply of moisture to thrive there. Coleus often produces small spikes of blue flowers when it's happy. Many gardeners don't like this look, so they cut off these spikes. Depending on the age and size of your evergreens, your coleus may not get enough light. Though it thrives in shade, coleus does need some light. In deep shade, the plants will grow tall and spindly.

Fuchsia

Q **I would like to know how to get a fuchsia to bloom again. It's a healthy plant, but hasn't bloomed since the season it was purchased. I live in the Northeast and brought it indoors in fall.**

A Fuchsias require long days of sunlight before they'll bloom. It takes 25 successive days of at least 12 hours of sunlight before the plants will set buds. You may grow them under lights to promote blooms sooner than nature will produce them. Fuchsia also grows best in cool conditions. In hot weather the plant declines and stops blooming.

Q **I got a fuchsia tree plant for a present and I put it in a shaded spot in the yard but moved it up to the deck where it would get more shade. It has been very warm here ever since and it has been losing a lot of its flowers. Is this normal?**

A Fuchsias do tend to drop their flowers when they're stressed. The heat is likely causing the flowers to drop. Let the plant rest during the hot spell; it should start to bloom well again once the heat wave passes.

Geranium

Q **Last fall I brought in a geranium plant. It has been growing new leaves all winter. Can I cut it back to force it to rebloom this summer?**

A You don't have to cut back a geranium to force it to bloom, but it does need bright light to bloom well. It may not get enough light indoors to bloom well. If the growth is spindly, cut it back a couple weeks before you move it outdoors, give it a little fertilizer, and plant it outdoors in a container or in the ground when all chance of frost is past. It should rebloom within a few weeks.

Q **My geraniums are getting too tall and sprawling. I just moved them all outside on my back porch. Should I cut them back?**

A Late winter to spring is the best time to cut back geraniums. Light levels are good at this time of year, and the plants will have time to regrow before the worst heat of summer hits.

Q **How do you grow geraniums? Do they need acidic soil?**

A Annual geraniums (*Pelargonium*) are one of the easiest annuals to grow. They're considered nearly foolproof if planted in the right spot. Best of all, the plants produce numerous clusters of red, pink, lavender, orange, or white flowers all summer. Situate geraniums in well-drained soil; the plants will tolerate most soil types. Geraniums bloom best in full sun and when watered enough to keep them from wilting. To encourage a consistent parade of blooms, cut off flower heads as they fade. If you grow geraniums in containers, fertilize them with a commercial product according to the manufacturer's instructions, and water frequently.

Q **I have a large geranium with beautiful coral flowers. I'd like to start more of these plants. Can geraniums be rooted in water? Also, what fertilizer would you recommend for geraniums?**

A Yes, geraniums can be rooted in water. Take cuttings about 6 inches long and remove all but the top leaves. Put the cuttings in a jar of water in a bright spot but not in direct sun. With luck, the cuttings will send out roots eventually and can be replanted. You may have greater success by rooting the cuttings in moist vermiculite or perlite. These soilless products promote excellent aeration as well as holding in moisture. Dip the lower end of the stems in rooting hormone to enhance root development. Geraniums do well with a slow-release granular fertilizer designed for annual flowers.

Impatiens

Q **Every year my mother and I plant impatiens, and every year they wilt and die. One day they'll be just fine, and the next day they're wilted, both in beds and pots. We thought we might have a spider mite problem, but soap spray didn't work. I water them every day, and most of my yard is in shade.**

A Impatiens are prone to a number of diseases, many of them carried in the soil or by insects such as thrips. Because you plant in the same places every year, your disease problems may be carried over from season to season in the soil or plant residue. You may also be overwatering, which can create a perfect habitat for fungal or bacterial organisms. Impatiens shouldn't need to be watered every day unless they are in the sun. Thrips are tiny insects that feed on impatiens and can spread viral diseases. If you think the problem could be thrips, prevent an infestation from developing by using soap sprays. Once plants are infected with the virus, it's too late to spray. Finally, make sure that you're buying high-quality bedding plants. If any of them show signs of disease or stress in the store, pass them by.

Q **When starting impatiens seeds indoors under fluorescent lighting, should the container be covered until the seeds sprout? When is the right time to start these seeds?**

A Impatiens require about 12 to 16 weeks from sowing to turn into flowering-size seedlings you can plant outside. Impatiens are extremely susceptible to cold temperatures, so make certain that all danger of frost has passed before setting them out. Impatiens seeds require light to germinate, so place the seeds on the surface of the starting mix and provide them with bright light. Keep the flat slightly moist and under grow-lights. Use a sterile seed-starting mix in clean plastic flats or cell-packs. Keep the container covered with a clear top until the seedlings germinate.

Q **Can I bring my impatiens indoors over the winter and plant them outside again next year?**

A It's easy to start new impatiens plants from cuttings. Rather than digging up your old plants to bring indoors, you'll have better luck by taking cuttings late in the season to bring inside. Take cuttings 4–6 inches long. Remove the lower leaves, and place the cuttings in water or moist vermiculite. New roots should form in several weeks. Pot the rooted cuttings, using a good soilless houseplant potting mix. Grow the plants in bright, indirect light. Expect much less bloom indoors than in the garden. In the spring, wait until warm weather settles in to move the plants outdoors.

Q **I bought a beautiful pink New Guinea impatiens two weeks ago and potted it in a terra-cotta pot the next day. We had two very hot days, and it looked really wilty after the first day. I watered it well and brought it inside. It perked up the next day, and looked fine for two or three days, but now it's wilted again. Is there a trick to growing New Guinea impatiens?**

A Most New Guinea impatiens are rather sensitive to moisture stress. Once wilted, they sometimes never recover completely. You did the right thing by watering immediately and moving it to a shady location. If you're lucky, the plant might recover. Because terra-cotta pots dry out quickly, you may have better luck with your New Guinea impatiens by growing in a nonporous container.

Kale

Q **I'm getting ready to plant flowering kale for the first time. Will it survive frost and grow through the winter?**

A Flowering kale is used in the fall because it can handle frosts and actually gets better color after the cold temperatures hit. A hard freeze in the low 20s may hurt it, but these are tough plants and you can generally enjoy them until it's below freezing night and day. It won't overwinter in extremely cold zones, however, so just enjoy it for the season.

Marigolds

Q **Last summer we had a beautiful garden with marigolds until about midsummer. Then the leaves started turning brown and dying even though the flowerheads were still blooming. Eventually entire plants died. Someone told us that it was aster yellows. Can we plant marigolds there again this year? Will they get the same thing?**

A Aster yellows is caused by a phytoplasma (similar to a virus) that is spread from plant to plant by leafhoppers. Symptoms usually start as yellowing of foliage. Plants may grow numerous thin stems, and flowers become distorted. It sounds unlikely that your marigolds were affected by aster yellows. The symptoms you describe sound more like those of phytophthora root rot. This soil-borne fungus causes lower leaves of marigold to wilt and die. The problem is worse in cool, wet soil. Phytophthora remains in the soil indefinitely, so it would be wise to plant something other than marigolds in this bed this year. Dwarf French marigolds (*Tagetes patula*) are resistant to the disease.

Q **I am new to gardening and have marigolds in my garden. Will they rebloom next year?**

A Marigolds (below) are called annual flowers because their life cycle is just one year or growing season. However, marigolds can self-seed in the garden and sprout new plants next year.

Q **I bought a flat of yellow marigolds and planted them around my house. On two of them the yellow buds fell off and rebloomed a bright green with curled petals. It's beautiful, but unusual. What made it do this? Will its seeds grow green marigolds?**

A It sounds like your green marigolds may have a disease called aster yellows. It's a virus-like disease that is spread by insects. Once the plant is infected, there's no way to treat this disease. It's best to remove and destroy affected plants because the disease can spread to other plants.

Pansy

Q If I plant pansies this fall, will they bloom again next spring?

A Pansies and violas are great for cool-season color in fall. In mild-winter areas, they can bloom all winter. In cold regions they may survive (especially under snow cover) and bloom again in the spring.

Q I've heard pansies called hardy annuals. I thought annuals were killed by frost.

A Most annual flowers won't survive over the winter in cold climates, but many tolerate some frost. Pansies and violas survive heavy freezes, so they can overwinter in many climates. Some other hardy annuals to try include kale, alyssum, lobelia, phlox, cornflower, dianthus, nasturtium, poppy, pot marigold, snapdragon, stock, and sweet pea. These plants perform best in cool weather and will bloom best in spring and fall.

Viola

Q My Sorbet Coconut violas are wilting for an unknown reason. They are in the ground, get full sun, and I water them daily.

A Sorbet Coconut viola is a cool-season plant, and it often starts to falter once temperatures heat up. If temperatures are above 80°F or so, that could be it. How moist is the soil? If it's staying wet, the problem could also be that the roots are drowning. The roots die and the plant wilts. If this happens, letting the soil dry out a little more between waterings should help.

Q I love violas and I have tried planting both the perennial and the annual types, but I don't have very good luck with them. They get sun until about noon, and my soil is rich. Does my soil lack something that they need?

A Violas can be picky about hot and cold weather extremes. Johnny-jump-ups, which are one type of viola, are one of the best types to reliably self-seed and survive.

Q I've heard that pansy flowers are edible. Are violas also edible? If so, what's the best way to use them?

A Violas are essentially miniature pansies, and yes, they are edible, just like their larger-flowered cousins. Avoid applying pesticides to flowers you intend to eat, and thoroughly wash them before using them. The most common way to use pansies and violas in food dishes is to add color and zing to salads.

 Learn more about the differences between pansies and violas online at *bhg.com/viola*.

Petunia

Q Every year when I plant petunias, eventually I will see little black specks on the leaves. When I look closely at the petunia, I see little green worms. They start eating the petunia flower and leaves. What are they, and how do I get rid of them?

A This sounds like the budworm caterpillar. This pest usually appears in June and July and is noticed by the black, specklike manure on the leaves. The budworms themselves can be hard to control, but you can knock them out by using a biological control such as Bt (*Bacillus thuringiensis*), often sold as Dipel at your local garden center. It will naturally prevent caterpillars from doing damage to your plants without harming other creatures.

Q One of my petunia plants in a pot has developed light green leaves but still blooms well. This pot has been fertilized the same as all the other pots. The pot is a tall, thin, unglazed light-colored clay pot. I'm thinking that the petunia doesn't like heat. Can you think of any other reason why this plant has developed anemic leaves?

A Petunia is quite heat tolerant. It might need some fertilizer to get it going. Use a complete fertilizer in which the first number (nitrogen) is no larger than the second number (phosphorus) on the label.

Q What do I do with petunias now that the growing season is over and they are dead? Do I pull them out or prune them back to the ground?

A After petunias are killed by frost, it is a good idea to pull them up or cut them off and compost the dead plant parts. That will help prevent diseases and insects from overwintering on the dead plants.

Q How do I get my hanging basket of petunias to put out more flowers? I deadhead, but they don't seem to get new flowers.

A Try fertilizing with low-nitrogen, high-phosphorus fertilizer such as 5-10-10. Phosphorus promotes flowering; nitrogen promotes more green growth.

Salvia

Q **Will red salvias attract hummingbirds?**

A Hummingbirds like brightly colored flowers with lots of nectar and a tubular shape. Red flowers are especially good to attract them. Salvia (below right) is a good choice. Other flowers that attract hummingbirds are coralbells, red-hot poker, hosta, lilac, cardinal flower, bee balm, and fuchsia.

Q **I planted salvia in containers on my deck, and most are doing well. However, I have a few that have lost their flowers, so only the stems and leaves remain. What did I do wrong? Can I correct this, or do I have to start over?**

A You don't say what kind of salvia you are growing. Are they the common red-flowering annual plant also known as scarlet sage or a blue-flowering annual salvia? These plants don't stay in full bloom constantly. As older flowers die out, the plant often goes green for a while until new flower stalks develop. Also, be sure the plants have plenty of sun. Salvia requires at least 6 to 8 hours of direct sunlight per day. Perennial salvias also go through cycles of bloom. Once flower stalks fade, trim off the dead blooms, and within a few weeks the plants start sending out another flush of flowers.

Q **I've seen a couple different kinds of annual flowers called salvia. How do I know if I'm getting the one I want?**

A The genus *Salvia* is a large one, with numerous species, some of them perennial, and some annual. The two most commonly grown annual types are *Salvia splendens*, also known as scarlet sage, and *S. farinacea*, also known as mealycup sage. Scarlet sage takes its name from the tubular red flowers produced by most varieties, although plant breeders have introduced purple, white, orange, and cream forms too. Mealycup sage produces deep purple, blue, or silvery white blooms on narrow spires. Although usually grown as an annual, it is hardy in Zones 8 and warmer.

Snapdragon

Q **What is the trick to growing great snapdragons? Mine always start out nicely, but once the first flowers fade, they get leggy, fall over, and don't come back into bloom very well.**

A Snapdragon (*Antirrhinum majus*) prefers cool weather. In warm parts of North America, it's best to treat it as a spring or fall annual. In Zones 6–9, it may overwinter, so a fall planting can be carried through the winter, providing nice bloom in fall and again in spring. Remove plants when hot weather hits. In cool regions, snapdragons may grow through the summer, languish in midsummer's heat, and perk up again in fall. It's a good idea to remove faded flower stalks to encourage side shoots to form.

Vinca

Q I just planted quite a few vinca plants. They are in full sun, good soil, and mulched. I fertilized them when they were planted. The leaves are turning yellow on several of the plants. What could be causing this?

A Vinca (*Catharanthus*) is susceptible to several different fungal diseases that can cause yellowing of foliage. Phytophthora aerial blight, alternaria leaf spot, and rhizoctonia stem and root rot are all possibilities. If the weather is warm and dry, the plants often grow right through symptoms. On the other hand, if the weather is cool and wet, yellowing leaves on disease-weakened vincas are almost guaranteed. Water only when the soil is dry at least 1 inch below the mulch, and water early in the day so that the foliage dries out before nightfall.

Zinnia

Q My tall zinnias grew malformed, with short, fat, stems on a long main branch. The leaves were small and curly, and the flower buds had stunted growth.

A It sounds as though your zinnias were infected with aster yellows or a virus of some kind. These are often spread by aphids and other sucking insects. Remove and destroy all the affected plant material to keep the problem from spreading to other plants.

Q Can I get seeds from my existing garden zinnias to use for next year?

A If your zinnias are hybrids, the seeds many not come true. In other words, they may not be exact copies of the parent plants, but you can grow zinnias from seed that you collect. Old-fashioned heirloom types are the best for this because they will come true to type.

Q I grew beautiful zinnias last year until late in the season, when they got powdery mildew. How can I keep mildew from getting on them and ruining them?

A The key to keeping zinnias (above) healthy all season is planting them in the right spot and choosing the right variety. Plant your zinnias where there's full sun and well-drained soil. Zinnias planted close together are more prone to fungal attacks. Avoid getting the foliage wet, especially during the evening and night; wet foliage encourages the growth of harmful fungi. Many of the newer varieties are more disease resistant than the older types. The Profusion Series and Zahara Series of zinnias provide large-flowered, mildew-resistant zinnias in a broad array of colors. Small-flowered zinnia species, such as narrowleaf zinnia (*Zinnia angustifolia*) and Mexican zinnia (*Z. haageana*), seldom are affected by powdery mildew.

Shade Perennials

Q There is a spot in the corner of my garden with extremely poor drainage. Even on a hot summer day, the soil is mucky and soft. This area is in part shade. I would like to plant some perennials. What do you suggest?

A Some great perennials for moist-soil conditions and part shade include astilbe, turtlehead (*Chelone*), ligularia, pitcher plant (*Sarracenia*), and creeping Jenny (*Lysimachia nummularia*).

Q I have a shady small hill with about a 25 percent slope. I'd like to combine hosta, ferns, and maybe some astilbes. Will any of these eventually overpower the others if I mix them up on the slope?

A Your plan sounds like a good one. All of these plants should grow well in shade. Whether or not one of them will overwhelm the others depends on what varieties you have and what the growing conditions are. Some types of ferns, ostrich ferns for example, can be quite aggressive. Some types of hosta will spread quickly as well. But in general, the plants should do well together.

Q I have an area in partial shade near pine trees. Nearly everything I have planted rarely blooms. What could I grow in this site?

A There's quite a list of perennials that will thrive in your shady site with acidic soil pH. The list includes anemone (*A. quinquefolia* and *A. virginiana*), goatsbeard (*Aruncus dioicus*), wild ginger (*Asarum canadense*), wood fern (*Dryopteris*), lilyturf (*Liriope muscari*), false Solomon's seal (*Smilacina racemosa*), and maidenhair fern (*Adiantum pedatum*).

Q What easy-care perennial flowers would you suggest for a shady site?

A You have many options of shade-tolerant perennials from which to choose. Here are several that grow well in most areas: 1. Lungwort (*Pulmonaria*), 2. Bugleweed (*Ajuga*), 3. Astilbe, and 4. Bleeding heart (*Dicentra*).

Q I want perennials that will grow under an oak tree. Nothing seems to grow very well there.

A You have plenty of choices from which to select. This short list should get you started: astilbe, hosta, fern, hellebore, creeping phlox, Virginia bluebell, lilyturf, hardy geranium, and barrenwort. Be sure to keep the bed well watered and apply an organic mulch to slow down water loss. Remember that the oak will be tapping into the same soil moisture as the perennials, so you may need to give them a little extra care, as well as prepare the soil thoroughly prior to planting.

Q We have an entry area that has a pine tree and would love to put flowers around the base. Is there a perennial that would grow in these conditions?

A Nothing will do well directly under a pine. It will be too shady and there will be too much root competition. If this is what you were thinking of doing, it may be better to mulch under the tree and add color with low pots or planters. If you are going to plant close by, consider planting a perennial groundcover that is both shade and drought tolerant, such as barrenwort (*Epimedium*), deadnettle (*Lamium*), or lilyturf (*Liriope*).

Q What types of perennials will grow in almost complete shade? I have planted hostas and astilbe. Would ferns, lily-of-the-valley, bleeding heart, or coralbells do better?

A As a general rule, lily-of-the-valley, bigroot geranium, bleeding heart, wild ginger, and ajuga are good for low-light spots. If the shade is extremely dense, thin some of the branches to let in more light.

Dividing Perennials

Q **When can I divide iris, hostas, and other perennials?**

A You can divide perennials anytime from spring to fall. However, the cooler months in spring and fall are usually best because it's less stressful on the plants. In general, it's best to divide spring-blooming perennials in fall, and late-summer or fall-blooming perennials in spring. An exception is bearded iris. Divide it in summer when it is relatively dormant.

Q **What is the best way to divide perennials?**

A There are several methods you can use to divide perennials. The best method depends on the growth habit of the perennial. For those that spread with fibrous rhizomes or runners, such as threadleaf

coreopsis or sundrops (*Oenothera*), simply dig up a chunk of the clump that includes several shoots and healthy roots. For those that spread by thick or tuberous rhizomes, such as daylily (*Hemerocallis*) or iris, it's often easiest to dig up the entire clump, and use a spading fork to tease the rhizomes apart. For those that spread slowly, gradually forming a larger clump it's also usually easiest to dig up the entire clump. After the clump is out of the ground, you can slice through it with a sharp knife or spade to make several divisions.

Q **When is the best time to divide perennials? Will I have to do it often?**

A Most perennials benefit from division every 3 to 5 years and are best divided in early spring, just as new growth is emerging. A few perennials (early-spring bloomers) do best when divided in fall. A few prefer to be left alone throughout their life. Your plant may need dividing if it becomes less floriferous or the flowers get smaller; if the plant's center dies out—leaving a hole, with all the growth around the edges; if the plant loses vigor; or if the plant outgrows its bounds.

Q **How do I know how far apart to plant my perennials when I divide them?**

A You can consult a good book on perennials before planting. *Better Homes and Gardens Perennial Gardening* provides information about spacing as well as soil, sunlight, and water needs. If you are planting nursery-grown plants, refer to the label. The preferred spacing is usually a range, such as 18 to 24 inches. Planting closer will give you a fuller garden more quickly, but you will probably need to divide the perennials sooner. If you can't find information about a specific plant, a general rule is to space small perennials 6 to 12 inches apart, 2- to 3-foot-tall perennials 12 to 18 inches apart, and taller perennials 18 to 36 inches apart.

Transplanting Perennials

Q When should I transplant my summer-blooming daisies?

A Fall and early spring are good times to divide or transplant most perennials. If you don't want to divide the plant, just dig up the whole root ball and move it to wherever you want to replant it. Keep it watered until it becomes reestablished. If the plant is large, you can split the clump into several pieces and replant them.

Q Are there some perennials that shouldn't be divided or transplanted?

A Some perennials resent having their root systems disturbed. Avoid dividing or moving these perennials: baby's breath (*Gypsophila*), balloon flower (*Platycodon*), bugbane (*Cimicifuga*), butterfly weed (*Asclepias tuberosa*), Carolina lupine (*Thermopsis*), false indigo (*Baptisia*), gas plant (*Dictamnus*), goatsbeard (*Aruncus*), monkshood (*Aconitum*), and peony (*Paeonia*), pictured at right.

Q I would like to start perennials from seed and transplant them into my garden. Which ones can I grow from seed?

A Blanket flower (*Gaillardia*) usually blooms from seed its first year. Many others, such as columbine (*Aquilegia*), foxglove (*Digitalis*), false indigo (*Baptisia*), and purple coneflower (*Echinacea*) will grow fairly readily from seed, but they may not bloom until next year unless you start them early enough to receive several weeks of cold that simulates winter weather. Start seeds indoors in late winter, and transplant the seedlings out into the garden after the weather warms and the plants have at least several sets of leaves.

Q I have several perennials that I have planted in containers. Can I plant them in the ground this fall so they come up again in the spring?

A Transplanting your perennials from containers into the ground for winter is a terrific idea. A good time to do this is about the same time as the first fall frost in your area. Mulch the new plantings to insulate and protect the crowns and help prevent heaving if the ground freezes and thaws repeatedly.

Cut Flowers

Q I'd like to start a cut-flower border, but my yard is quite shady. Are there any shade-loving plants that make good cut flowers?

A Unfortunately, few shade-loving plants produce good cut flowers. The best types include astilbe, masterwort (*Astrantia major*), monkshood (*Aconitum* spp.), coralbells (*Heuchera sanguinea*), and cardinal flower (*Lobelia cardinalis*).

If your garden receives some direct sun, you might be able to grow more traditional cut flowers, such as lily (*Lilium*) or blazing star (*Liatris*). However, when grown in the shade, these plants won't bloom as profusely as they would if grown in the sun.

Drying Flowers

Q What is the best way to dry flowers to maintain their color?

A Although no flower will retain its full, bright garden color after it's dried, some plants hold their color better than others. To get the best color, cut flowers just before they are fully open, then tie them in bundles and hang them upside down in a dry, dark, warm location.

Good choices for colorful dried flowers include lavender (*Lavandula*), statice (*Limonium*), baby's breath (*Gypsophila*), cattail (*Typha*), goldenrod (*Solidago*), and yarrow (*Achillea*). Unfortunately, no chemical product is available to enhance the color of dried flowers. Silica gel is used to preserve quick-drying flowers and flowers with closely packed petals such as roses and peonies.

Q I would like to use some of my perennial flowers as cut flowers indoors. Which ones would be best?

A Many perennial garden flowers can serve double duty as cut flowers. Here are some to get you started 1. Blazing star (*Liatris*), 2. Purple coneflower (*Echinacea*), 3. Shasta daisy (*Leucanthemum*), and 4. Yarrow (*Achillea*). Other perennials that make excellent cut flowers are black-eyed Susan (*Rudbeckia*), chrysanthemum, delphinium, false sunflower (*Heliopsis*), goldenrod (*Solidago*), iris, obedient plant (*Physostegia*), and peony (*Paeonia*).

1

2

3

4

Staking

Q A lot of my perennial flowers look great until they start blooming, but then they flop over and look ugly. What can I do?

A If most of your perennial flowers get tall and leggy, it may be an indication that your garden has too much shade or is receiving too much nitrogen fertilizer. Use fertilizer with lower nitrogen content, or grow more shade-tolerant perennials if your garden is shady. You could also grow dwarf versions of your favorite perennials to eliminate the need for staking.

Q What's the best way to stake my perennials?

A Single stakes are best for long-stemmed plants with large, heavy flowers, such as delphiniums, dahlias, and lilies. Make a loose figure-eight loop around the plant stem and stake as the stem elongates. You can also create a staking framework from bamboo stakes and twine. Place bamboo stakes in a circle along the edges of the perennial clump. Weave twine from one stake to another until you've connected all the stakes in a grid pattern. Bushy perennials such as peonies can be supported with circular metal rings. Garden centers carry peony rings and tomato cages that work well for this purpose.

Q I prune many of my shrubs every spring, so I have a lot of twiggy branches. Can I use these as supports for my perennials?

A Yes, you can use twiggy branches to support perennials. When used in this way, they're called pea staking. (They work great to support pea vines too.) Insert the branches into the ground around the edges of the clump. Large clumps may need a few pea stakes in the center as well. Cut the branches several inches shorter than the mature height of the perennial so the staking will eventually be hidden.

Deadheading

Q **I see terms like deadheading a lot. It seems to be a common phrase. I am a beginner though, and I am not well-versed in the jargon yet. What does this term mean?**

A Deadheading is a term that means cutting the flowers off a plant once they begin to fade and look unattractive. There are several reasons to deadhead, including improving the plant's appearance, preventing the plant from producing seed, and encouraging more flower production.

Q **Where on the stem do I cut off dead flowers? I've heard that removing spent flowers encourages more blooms.**

A Removing dead flowers, or deadheading, is a good gardening practice. It may make plants produce extra flowers, it makes for a neater garden, and it prevents self-sown seedlings from popping up everywhere. To deadhead, pinch back to the next flower, bud, or leaf on a stem. You can remove individual flowers as soon as they finish blooming. Many gardeners do this with daylily blooms, which remain open for only one day. You can also wait until the entire flower stalk has finished blooming, then cut the entire stem back to the first set of leaves below the dead blooms. For perennials that go through bloom cycles, such as catmint and salvia, shear the plant after most of the blooms have faded.

Q **I'd like to deadhead my perennials. How far back should I cut them?**

A To deadhead individual blooms, such as those of blanket flower, pinch back to the next flower, bud, or leaf on a stem. For types of flower with long stalks, such as liatris, wait until all the flowers on a single stalk finish blooming, then cut the entire stem close to the uppermost leaves below the base of the flowering stem.

Q **Which perennials will rebloom if I deadhead them?**

A These perennials will usually rebloom if they are deadheaded: balloon flower (*Platycodon*), blanket flower (*Gaillardia*), coreopsis, delphinium, garden phlox, hollyhock (*Alcea*), lupine (*Lupinus*), monkshood (*Aconitum*), spiderwort (*Tradescantia* × *andersoniana*), and yarrow (*Achillea*).

Cleanup

Q **Is it OK to cut back the foliage of my perennials that don't look good, even if it's only August? I just can't stand looking at brown anymore. I don't want to do any permanent harm, though.**

A Cut away. By late August established perennials have been photosynthesizing for long enough to recover with no ill effects from a cutback. Don't be alarmed if a perennial grows back after being cut. Some plants are almost certain to grow back from a late summer haircut—catmint (*Nepeta*), daylily (*Hemerocallis*), globe thistle (*Echinops*), and perennial geranium are a few that are likely to do so.

Q **When should I clean up my perennial flower garden this fall and how should I do it?**

A As long as your perennials look good, leave them alone. Some die back after the first heavy freeze; others remain attractive all winter. I usually go through the garden several times each fall to cut down the plants that no longer look good. A final trip through the garden in late winter removes those that were left for winter interest.

Q **When should I apply mulch for winter protection to my perennial flowers?**

A After perennials have been cut back for winter is a good time to apply additional mulch. With the stems out of the way, it's easier to maneuver around the plants. And the additional mulch will protect the roots and crowns from winter cold.

Learn more about cutting back perennials in the fall with our Test Garden video tips at *bhg.com/fall-cutback.*

Q **Is it better to leave perennial flower foliage in place over winter for protection, or to cut it off in fall?**

A If some of your perennials were attacked by insects or diseases this past year, it would be a good idea to remove stems of those plants to reduce the likelihood that the problems will carry over in the next season. Rather than composting the damaged plant material, dispose of it in the trash. You may leave healthy foliage in place over winter or remove it. Some perennials such as ornamental grasses remain attractive all winter, so leave them in place to enjoy their subtle winter beauty. Others become untidy with harsh winter weather and are more attractive if the foliage is removed.

Perennials

Deer-Resistant Perennials

Q I have lots of deer in my yard. What perennial flowers won't they eat?

A If deer are hungry enough they'll eat just about any plant, but these generally escape damage: 1. Yarrow, 2. Blue star, 3. False indigo, 4. Catmint, 5. Tickseed, 6. Euphorbia, 7. Artemisia, 8. Bee balm, 9. Russian sage, and 10. Stachys.

Mulching

Q I have a flowerbed at the end of my driveway that I can't seem to get flowers to grow in successfully. I think that the bed dries out too much. What colorful perennials could I mix in with the blue fescue that I have growing there? Would mulching help?

A Several perennials will tolerate a hot, dry site after they are established. You can grow sedum; in addition to the upright 'Autumn Joy', there are dozens and dozens of low-growing groundcover types with blooms in red, orange, and yellow. Also, evening primrose (*Oenothera*), blanket flower (*Gaillardia*), and yarrow (*Achillea*) will tolerate hot, dry sites. If you mix compost into the soil and apply a couple inches of mulch on top, you could grow a broad range of plants.

Q Can I use leaves to protect perennials over winter? When do I apply them?

A Fallen leaves may compress too much and cause the perennials underneath to rot. Shredding the leaves first helps prevent this problem. You might also try straw mulch, which stays lighter and fluffier, preventing rot.

Q I have several flowerbeds covered in last year's leaves. Should I leave them on before I cover with bark mulch? Or will the decaying cause disease?

A Tree leaves should not spread disease problems to your flowering perennials, but if they are thick enough on the beds to pack down, they could smother the perennials or keep them so wet that the perennials could develop rot. If the old perennial plant foliage is part of the mix, there could be disease spores on the old leaves of the perennials. It's safest to clean out the beds and compost the material before reapplying it to the beds.

Q Are there any perennials that don't particularly like mulching?

A It's a matter of degree. Mulch helps conserve moisture and keep out weeds. But if it's too thick, it can smother the roots or hold in too much moisture. For most flowers, a mulch layer 2 to 3 inches deep is good. This means that low, creeping types of perennials, such as thyme, creeping phlox, creeping sedum, and hens and chicks (*Sempervivum*) grow best without mulch. In any case, keep the mulch several inches away from the crown of the perennial to prevent rot from developing.

Q When should I clean out all of the mulch that I used in my beds to help protect my plants over the winter? I never know and I am always afraid of cleaning up too early or too late.

A Pull back the winter mulch on your perennials before new growth begins to prevent damage to emerging shoots. You need not completely remove the mulch. If the mulch is no more than 2 to 4 inches thick, it won't hurt to leave it in place. Most perennials will push up through it anyway.

Groundcovers

Q **I have a hot, sunny area that needs some type of groundcover. What plants would you suggest?**

A You have many choices of spreading plants that might work as groundcovers in a sunny site. Here are some ideas to get you started 1. Creeping phlox (*Phlox subulata*), 2. Snow-in-summer (*Ceratostigma*), 3. Bugleweed (*Ajuga*), 4. Thyme (*Thymus*), 5. Creeping sedum (*Sedum*), 6. Woolly yarrow (*Achillea tomentosa*), 7. Spreading juniper (*Juniperus*), 8. Trailing lantana (*Lantana montevidensis*), and 9. Rock rose (*Helianthemum*).

Groundcovers

Q **I have several areas of groundcover in my yard. They're spreading into the lawn and flowerbeds and taking over. What can I do to keep them inbounds?**

A Some groundcovers are more aggressive than others. If mowing fails to keep the groundcovers in line, try edging around the groundcover bed. You may need to add a physical barrier between the groundcover bed and the lawn or flowerbed you're trying to preserve.

Q **I've heard horror stories about certain groundcovers getting out of hand. Which ones should I avoid?**

A Some groundcovers that run rampant in some areas of the country may be well-behaved in other locations. You may be able to keep aggressive groundcovers inbounds by planting them in contained sites, such as a planting bed surrounded by a concrete barrier. Here are some groundcovers that may require containment: creeping buttercup (*Ranunculus*), crown vetch (*Coronilla varia*), English ivy (*Hedera helix*), goutweed (*Aegopodium podograria*), mint (*Mentha*), periwinkle (*Vinca minor*), and yellow archangel (*Lamiastrum galeobdolon*).

Q **My patio is made of flagstones that have spaces between them. What groundcover could I plant in the cracks between the stones?**

A Thyme is one of the most popular choices for this situation. Lemon thyme (*Thymus* × *citriodorus*) has lemon-scented foliage; woolly thyme (*T. pseudolanuginosus*) has fuzzy gray leaves. Other choices include goldmoss sedum (*Sedum acre*), dragon's blood sedum (*Sedum spurium* 'Dragon's Blood'), ice plant (*Delosperma*), and thrift (*Armeria maritima*).

Groundcovers

Q Can you suggest a type of juniper that would make a good groundcover for a sunny western slope? I want something evergreen there.

A Many types of junipers (*Juniperus*) make excellent groundcovers in sites with full sun and well-drained soil. Creeping juniper (*J. horizontalis*) is one of the lowest growing at only 6 to 8 inches tall. 'Bar Harbor', 'Blue Rug', and 'Blue Chip' are cultivars with blue-green foliage. All are hardy in Zones 3–9. Shore juniper (*J. conferta*) is hardy in Zones 6–10. At 1 to 2 feet tall, it makes a great groundcover, especially in coastal areas or locations subject to salt spray from streets and driveways. Low-growing forms of savin juniper (*J. sabina*) are also excellent groundcovers. 'Arcadia' and 'Broadmoor' have bright green foliage; 'Skandia' has blue-green needles.

Q I have steep slope that needs groundcover. I would like to know the fastest spreading perennial that I could plant. The soil is quite sandy and the area gets partial sun.

A Unfortunately, some of the fastest spreading groundcovers can also be invasive, so you'll have to be careful on that front. Some of the safe choices include periwinkle (*Vinca*), ajuga, and spotted deadnettle (*Lamium*). If the hillside is isolated from the rest of the garden and invasiveness won't be a problem, you could even plant variegated goutweed (*Aegopodium*).

Q We are landscaping our backyard. We need to know which flowering perennials will withstand heat and dry conditions. These plants must be planted on a 45-degree slope in the backyard.

A In sunny areas, you can plant low-growing and colorful sedums like 'Blue Spruce' and 'Dragon's Blood', which will knit together to give you a nice, tight mat. There are many drought- and heat-tolerant ground covers for shade, like ajuga and periwinkle. As for taller flowering perennials, try beard-tongue (*Penstemon*), dancing butterflies (*Gaura lindheimeri*), and hummingbird mint (*Agastache* spp.). Just remember that even drought- and heat-tolerant plants need to be watered in their first season to become well-established.

Q My house sits on a steep, grassy slope. What can I plant so I won't have to mow? I'd like something inexpensive.

A It sounds as though a groundcover would work for your situation. Although you don't have to mow a groundcover, you will need to occasionally weed the area and water during dry periods, especially until the groundcover becomes established. Depending on whether your site is sunny or shady, you could try some of the recommendations on pages 50 and 53.

Groundcovers

Q **The lawn under my shade trees is always thin and patchy. Is there a groundcover that would do better there?**

A Numerous groundcovers thrive in shade. Because turfgrass at best tolerates shade, these shade-loving groundcovers will not only look better than your thin, patchy lawn, but they'll also be easier to take care of. 1. Lily-of-the-valley (*Convallaria*), 2. Bugleweed (*Ajuga*), 3. Lilyturf (*Liriope*), 4. Spotted deadnettle (*Lamium*), 5. Vinca, 6. Hosta, 7. Foam flower (*Tiarella*), 8. Wild ginger (*Asarum*), and 9. Bigroot geranium (*Geranium macrorrhizum*).

Astilbe

Q I thought that I was very careful in spraying weed killer in my large flowerbed, but now my astilbe is drooping and dying. The weeds still look healthy. Is there any remedy?

A Broadleaf weed killers containing 2,4-D don't need to be applied directly to a plant to affect it. The chemical is quite volatile and can move readily through the air to susceptible plants. Perennials may outgrow the effects of the herbicide, but it will take time. There is little you can do once the plants have taken up the herbicide, other than prevent them from receiving other stressors such as too much or too little water.

Q Beyond my fern bed I have an area which receives a little sun, so I have planted a variety of columbines. Because they are not always in bloom, I would like to add more interest to the bed and am not sure what would look good with the columbines. I have hostas in different parts of the yard and would like to plant something a little different.

A I would suggest interplanting with different cultivars of astilbe that bloom at different heights and over a long season. Dwarf Chinese astilbe (*A. chinensis* var. *pumila*) is a groundcover type only 6 inches tall, while superba (*A. chinensis* var. *taquettii* 'Suberba') grows to 4 feet. In between are astilbe 'Sprite', japonica types such as 'Peach Blossom', and arendsii hybrids such as 'Fanal'. Various varieties are available in colors ranging from pure white to pink, red, and purple. You could add one bold hosta to tie in with the rest of your garden because repetition always creates a unified look.

Q How do I make my astilbes grow full and lush? They're growing at the edge of the woods and get plenty of shade and moisture. They bloom one little plume and that's all.

A What first comes to mind is competition from the surrounding trees and shrubs. Astilbe does best in partially shady locations. If your spot is totally dark and there is a lot of root competition from the trees, this could cause your plants to become weak. Keep them mulched to maintain constant soil moisture, and use a slow-release fertilizer to keep them fed all year. If they have been growing in the same spot for several years, they would probably benefit from being divided.

Q I have several astilbe plants growing in my part-shade garden. When should I deadhead them?

A Cut off the flower stalks of astilbe as soon as the flowers fade. They won't bloom again, but the foliage is more attractive when the dead bloom stalks are removed.

Baby's Breath

Q I purchased some roots of baby's breath and am wondering when and where I should plant them.

A Because you indicate that you bought roots of baby's breath, I assume that these are dormant, bare-root starts of the plant. They should be potted up or planted outdoors in the ground immediately, if weather conditions permit, so that they don't dry out too much. The perennial type of baby's breath can take some frost, but not hard freezes. This plant likes well-drained alkaline soil, so you might have to amend the soil with lime and compost.

Balloon Flower

Q Am I able to plant the blue balloon flowers from seed or are they a root plant?

A Balloon flower (*Platycodon*) can be started from seed rather easily. If you start seedlings in fall, they will bloom nicely next spring. Or you can start them indoors over winter, and they will bloom with a limited crop of flowers their first year.

Q My balloon flowers seem to fall over, as though the stems aren't strong enough to hold the blooms. What am I doing wrong?

A If they are not getting enough sunlight, the stems will stretch and become weak. Although balloon flower (*Platycodon*) grows in partial shade or full sun, it won't grow well in deep shade. If light conditions are bright enough to grow balloon flower, you might also consider trying one of the dwarf varieties such as 'Scentimental Blue', which only grows 12 to 15 inches tall, and is less prone to falling over.

Bamboo

Q My neighbor has bamboo growing along our fence line, and now bamboo shoots are coming up in my yard. How can I get rid of the shoots and stop more from coming up?

A Growing hardy bamboo (below) as a living fence may seem like a good idea, but bamboo has no respect for property lines. Many hardy bamboo species spread by sending out shallow rhizomes that pop through to the surface as the growing tips of new canes. Two or three times a year, you can use a sharp spade to slice off the new shoots that appear on your property. Once severed, they'll die back and won't need to be dug up. If you were to use an herbicide to kill the bamboo on your side of the fence line, your neighbor's mother plants could be seriously damaged. Because it's virtually impossible to stop bamboo from spreading, the American Bamboo Society (*bamboo. org*) recommends installing a concrete or fabric barrier that works like an underground fence.

Baptisia

Q Should I cut back my false indigo after it has bloomed and the seeds are dried?

A There are two ways to manage your false indigo (*Baptisia*). Gardeners who are fastidious and tidy remove the seedpods after it blooms. Gardeners who are more casual or laidback leave them uncut and are rewarded with grayish black seedpods that rattle after they dry. The drawback to leaving the seedpods in place to dry is that the plant can self-seed and become a bit weedy.

Q I planted some baptisias last year. They have grown very well but I did not get any flowers on the plant. What have I done wrong?

A Baptisia can be slow to establish. It has a deep, extensive root system, and it often won't bloom until the roots are well-established. If the plant has grown well this year, it likely will bloom well next year.

Q I've had a blue false indigo for seven or eight years. I've grown it in three different places and all the transplants have worked out well. Each year the plant grows beautiful and healthy-looking foliage. However, I have never gotten a flower or bloom in all these years. Each location has had between four to six hours of sun a day.

A False indigo needs full sun, which is at least six hours of direct sunlight each day. More sun would be better. It also is difficult to move because of its taproots, which go deep into the soil. If you keep transplanting it, perhaps it is not being given time to reestablish its root system. This particular baptisia also needs fertile, evenly moist soil that drains well.

Bear's Breeches

Q I love the look of bear's breeches but have trouble getting it to grow. What's the secret to getting it established?

A There are several species of bear's breeches. All grow in full sun to part shade in cool regions, but they prefer shade in hot areas. They need well-drained soil. Common bear's breeches (*Acanthus mollis*) and Balkan bear's breeches (*A. hungaricus*) are hardy in Zones 6–9. If you live in a colder area you could try spiny bear's breeches (*A. spinosus*), which is reliably hardy to Zone 5, and may survive in Zone 4 with mulch.

Baptisia is one of the *Better Homes and Gardens* garden editors' top fuss-free plants. Go online at *bhg.com/fuss-free-plants* to discover others.

Bee Balm

Q **I started bee balm in my garden last year. It came back beautifully until I nipped the tops off. Now they don't look like they will flower. Did I make a mistake in nipping them? I thought this would make them fuller and lower to the ground.**

A Depending on how much you cut them back and how late in spring you did it, you may have prevented your bee balm (*Monarda didyma*) from flowering this year. These plants form their buds as they grow in late spring and early summer. You were on the right track, though: You can pinch back the tips of new growth of late-summer-flowering perennials in early spring. Doing so will encourage the plants to have a fuller, more compact habit and will also make them bloom a little later in the season. If you do this, take care not to prune after early spring, and take off only the tips of the new growth.

Q **I like the hummingbirds that are attracted to my bee balm flowers, but every year the leaves turn gray and ugly. How can I keep the plants looking good?**

A It sounds as though your bee balm suffers from powdery mildew. This fungal disease can be severe on bee balm. Plants under stress are more likely to contract the disease, so keep the soil evenly moist, and provide good air circulation to minimize the problem. However, if you're growing a susceptible cultivar, there may be little you can do to prevent your plants from turning gray by the end of summer. A better solution is to grow one of the resistant cultivars, such as 'Colrain Red', 'Raspberry Wine', 'Violet Queen', 'Petite Delight', or 'Marshall's Delight'.

Black-Eyed Susan

Q **The lower leaves on my black-eyed Susan are turning black and spreading upward. Last summer they barely bloomed. Is there anything I can do to stop this and have healthy plants and flowers?**

A The problem on your black-eyed Susan (*Rudbeckia*) sounds like a fungal disease—a very common problem on black-eyed Susans. Help prevent it by growing your plants in a bright, sunny spot (shade makes them more susceptible to the disease). Also, avoid watering the plants with a sprinkler; wet leaves encourage the disease. If necessary, you can try spraying them with a fungicide or look for a variety next year that's better suited to your conditions so it won't succumb to disease as easily.

Q **I found some black worms eating the leaves of my black-eyed Susans. What should I do to get rid of the worms? If I use an insecticide on them, will they continue to grow again this summer?**

A One of the best and safest treatments you can use whenever you see caterpillars devouring your plants is Bt (*Bacillus thuringiensis*). Bt is a natural product; it's actually a bacteria that is toxic to caterpillars but safe for humans. Use it sparingly, however, because it kills all caterpillars—even those that are destined to become butterflies in your garden. You'll find Bt at your local garden center. If the damage to your black-eyed Susans is extensive, you can prune off the worst of it. These durable perennials will likely spring back and bloom for you this summer.

Bleeding Heart

Q A few years ago I planted five bleeding heart plants in an area that I've realized isn't the best place for them. They're too close to some larger plants. I'd like to transplant them but don't know when is the best time or if I should even try.

A You can move bleeding heart (right) in spring or fall, but the best time is in the very early spring when they are just beginning to show some foliage. Dig as large of a root ball as you can around each one. Keep the transplants well-watered for the first growing season until they become established.

Q I bought a bleeding heart around Mother's Day and I planted it the same day. I watered for three days after planting, but now the leaves are looking yellowish brown. Have I watered it too much?

A Yellowing leaves could simply indicate stress from being transplanted. It could also indicate overwatering. Or it may be that your bleeding heart is going dormant for the summer. Old-fashioned bleeding heart—which used to be classified as *Dicentra spectabilis* but has recently been reclassified as *Lamprocapnos spectabilis*—turns yellow and appears to die by midsummer, especially if your area has experienced warm or dry conditions. However, this is perfectly natural and the bleeding heart comes back bigger and better the following spring.

Q My bleeding heart has stopped blooming. How can I get it to bloom again?

A Old-fashioned bleeding hearts have a limited bloom season in spring; so if it's stopped blooming, it's perfectly natural. Your bleeding heart may start to go dormant (show yellowing foliage) in a month or two,

especially if you have hot, dry conditions. Again, this is natural. It will be back again and bloom beautifully next spring. You might like to try Pacific bleeding heart (*Dicentra formosa*) or fringed bleeding heart (*D. eximia*). These types of bleeding hearts are smaller than the old-fashioned type, at just 1 foot tall, but they rebloom sporadically throughout the summer.

Butterfly Weed

Q Can I grow butterfly weed in clay soil if it is in full sun?

A Butterfly weed (*Asclepias tuberosa*) grows well in clay soil as long as it is adequately drained. In wet sites, you could try swamp milkweed (*A. incarnata*). Like butterfly weed, it attracts monarchs and other butterflies, but it bears pink rather than orange flowers.

Catmint

Q **As August approaches, the hot and dry summer has taken most of the color and spirit out of my perennials. My catmint has flopped open and it isn't blooming well.**

A Catmint (*Nepeta*) is a reliable rebloomer as long as you deadhead it when the first cycle of blooms begins to fade. Shear plants back to one-half to one-third their height to promote stocky plants that won't splay open in late summer and to encourage a second round of bloom. This plant grows well in full sun and tolerates dry heat and wind.

Chrysanthemum

Q **How many years do mum plants last? I've had mine eight years. Nothing green is coming up yet this year.**

A Chrysanthemums will overwinter successfully when the variety is hardy to the zone of the garden and if they have good soil drainage. If conditions in early spring are cold and wet, the root systems of mums may rot, especially if they are mulched. Mums may also be lost if they go into the winter too dry. Water well until late in the fall. Even the hardiest mums will suffer from a hard freeze that arrives after the plants have put out tender new growth in the spring. Late frosts can harm plants that are much hardier when dormant during midwinter.

Q **I planted mums this fall and don't know much about them. I was wondering if I should cut them back because they are brown. Will they bloom again next spring and summer?**

A If your mums (*Chrysanthemum*) survive the winter, you'll see new growth developing around the base of the plant early in spring. The old, dead growth from last year can be clipped away. Although garden mums are often called hardy mums, they may not survive the winter if drainage is poor or if you live in an extremely cold climate. If numerous shoots have overwintered, divide and separate the clump. Three to five vigorous shoots are enough to make a showy clump.

Q **My mum plants are growing now, and I would like to know when and how to trim them in order to obtain a nicely rounded flowering plant for the fall garden.**

A Most mum varieties hold up better in the garden if pinched a time or two. Otherwise they may flop over when in bloom. Pinch back mums when they have grown to about 6 inches tall. Pinch back just the growing tips to promote more compact growth. Repeat pinching in late June if the plant is still leggy. Avoid pinching again after the first of July to avoid removing developing flowerbuds. Alternatively, you could grow cushion or carpet mums, low-growing types that get no taller than 8 to 12 inches. These shorter types form a solid mound without the need for pinching.

Columbine

Q **The leaves on the bottom of my columbine are turning yellow and brown. They did have aphids earlier, but that doesn't seem to be a problem now. I am worried that I might lose the whole plant.**

A If it's just the oldest leaves turning yellow on your columbine (*Aquilegia*), it may simply be old age. The yellowing also could be a sign that the columbine is suffering from soil that's too wet or too dry. Columbines are typically short-lived plants; each plant lives two or three years, and after that it dies back. But if you let your columbines produce seed, you should always have a supply of fresh, strong plants because they reliably self-seed in the garden.

Q **I have several columbines growing in a shady area of my backyard. How can I successfully transplant some of the columbines to a shaded area in my front yard?**

A To successfully transplant columbine, move as much of the root system with the plant as possible by keeping a large ball of soil intact around the roots. The best time to move columbine is when it is semidormant, early in spring. Plant the columbine in its new spot, making sure it's at the same depth it was growing before. Water in the transplant, and keep it watered regularly for the first growing season. Alternatively, you might collect ripe seeds after your columbine blooms, and scatter those seeds over the area where you'd like the columbine to grow. Most columbines start readily from seed, often self-seeding in the garden.

Q **One day my columbine plants were blooming, and the next morning they were bare of leaves. I noticed small green worms on the plant. What are they and how do I prevent them from destroying a beautiful plant?**

A Those green worms on your columbine are actually sawfly larvae. Because they are not true caterpillars, Bt (*Bacillus thuringiensis*) will NOT work on them. However, spinosad should control them. You can also remove them by hand and destroy them. Fortunately, columbines can take occasional defoliation with few permanent effects.

Q **I planted two different types of columbines last year. This year I have some plants that don't look like either of the types I planted. Do columbines cross-pollinate?**

A It is common for columbines to hybridize if more than one type is growing close together. And because the plants self-seed readily if not deadheaded, hybrid plants with characteristics different from the parent plants often pop up in the garden the following year. This can be a happy surprise. But if you'd like to prevent it, simply cut off the developing seedheads before they mature.

Coralbells

Q I recently purchased some coralbells and have left them in pots because we will be moving this fall and I'd like to take them with me. Can I leave them in pots in the winter, perhaps in our new insulated but unheated garage?

A If the soil in those pots freezes solid, the coralbells likely won't survive. The unheated garage may be warm enough to prevent the soil from freezing, but it may not be cold enough to prevent the plants from sprouting early. Then you have the problem of keeping the plants alive in the poor light conditions of the garage. You'd be better off planting them in a protected place this fall, mulching them in, and then transplanting them to their permanent location in the spring.

Q I just bought a beautiful heuchera. I presume that it is a perennial, but there were no instructions with it. Can you tell me where to plant it in my garden?

A Coralbells (*Heuchera*) grow best in full sun or part shade and moist, well-drained soil. It does not tolerate clay or poorly drained soil. Cool summer nights are best. Enrich the bed with well-decomposed organic matter. Deadhead to encourage rebloom, cutting the flower stalk off at the base. In winter, cover plants with loose mulch to prevent frost-heaving. Coralbells make good companions with hosta, bleeding heart, and lady's mantle.

Q How does one deadhead coralbells so that they will continue to bloom after their first flush of flowers?

A To deadhead coralbells, remove individual flower stalks all the way to their base. If you grow one of the heucheras (above right) with colorful purple, chartreuse, or copper foliage, you may even want to remove the flower stalks before they bloom. Some gardeners feel that the bloom stalks detract from the beautiful foliage.

Coreopsis

Q I had several coreopsis plants for about five years. This spring, two completely disappeared. I am disappointed not to see them again and am considering replacing them with new coreopsis plants. Is this a good idea?

A It's common for coreopsis to die out after several years in the garden. It's not a particularly long-lived perennial. Five years is a good run for most coreopsis. Unless you saw evidence of disease, you can plant new ones in the same location with little danger of them dying out immediately. Large-flower types such as 'Early Sunrise' often fade away faster than small-flower threadleaf types (*Coreopsis verticillata*). 'Moonbeam' and 'Zagreb' are long-lasting threadleaf types.

Cushion Spurge

Q **Can I grow cushion spurge in clay soil?**

A Cushion spurge (*Euphorbia polychroma*) can be grown in clay soil if it is well-drained. This spring-blooming plant grows best in full sun, although it tolerates part shade. It also holds up well in heat, wind, and in alkaline soils. The plant can melt out in humid conditions or if its crown remains too wet. Plants tend to flop open in midsummer unless you cut them back after their spring bloom. Doing so also prevents them from self-seeding and spreading throughout the garden.

Daylily

Q **Something is cutting the blooms off my daylilies. I come out in the mornings and find that they have been chewed or cut off during the night and are lying on the ground. Nothing has been eaten. How do I stop this?**

A This sounds like the work of some animal pest. Either squirrels or chipmunks could be chewing on the daylily flowerbud stems to get moisture. (The daylily buds are edible, so perhaps they're eating some of them too, but leave some behind.) You could try applying an animal repellent such as Liquid Fence or Messina Squirrel Stopper.

Q **My daylilies are turning yellow at their bases. One plant is in worse shape than the others. At first I thought I fertilized too close to the plants, but now I think it may be a pest. What bugs bother daylilies? What do I use to spray?**

A In general, daylilies (*Hemerocallis*) have few insect problems, but an aphid attack can cause leaves to curl, yellow, and be distorted. You should see a sticky, shiny substance on the leaves if aphids are present.

The yellow, brown, or green insects are visible to the naked eye and are usually found in clusters in the fold near the leaf base. Control aphids by spraying them with an insecticidal soap. Spray only if you are sure you actually have them; soap sprays kill the good bugs too. Daylily foliage can also turn yellow from leaf spot, or leaf streak. This disease starts out as spots on the leaves that gradually turn the entire leaf yellow. It's most severe in warm, humid weather. It can also be a problem if you are overwatering the plants. To combat leaf spot or leaf streak, spray the plants with a fungicide containing basic copper or copper sulfate. Do this every week during periods of warm, humid weather.

Q **My daylily has yellowish spots on the leaves. What is causing this?**

A Daylily rust is a serious fungal disease that produces yellow-orange pustules on the foliage and can cause rapid plant decline. Rust is difficult to control. If you have a susceptible variety, it may be better to replace it with a rust-resistant one. Look for one of the All-American daylily winners such as 'Red Volunteer', a 7-inch midseason bloomer, or 'Miss Mary Mary', a double yellow repeat bloomer. Both have good to excellent rust resistance.

Q Will daylilies grow under the shade of a black walnut tree?

A Yes, daylilies will grow under a black walnut tree. Many plants are susceptible to juglone (the chemical leached from black walnut tree roots), but daylilies are generally unaffected by it. However, keep in mind that daylilies grow better in full sun than in shade.

Q Do hybrid daylilies multiply by seeds, runners, or both? I saved some seeds. Would planting them be a waste of time?

A Thousands of hybrid daylilies are available; unfortunately, none can be successfully propagated true to type from seed. Usually, the seeds collected from hybrid plants produce weaker or inferior plants (or plants that have traits of both parents, if two different plants were crossed to produce the seed). Because daylilies are so easy to propagate by division of their fibrous roots, I'd recommend using that method.

Q Last fall I planted several daylilies that I bought from a local nursery. I covered them with leaves and spruce boughs at the end of November. When I removed the mulch this spring, I discovered that several of my daylilies had rotted, and I lost the plants. What happened, and what should I do this year to keep this from reoccurring?

A Daylilies are hardy through Zone 3. Unless you live in a colder zone, it's not necessary to cover them with winter mulch to the extent that you did. Heavy winter mulch traps moisture and encourages rot. You could put bark mulch around the plants, but avoid covering the crowns (growing points).

Q I need to transplant a large mass of daylilies. When's the best time to divide daylilies and other perennials?

A Daylilies are tough plants and can be transplanted almost any time in early spring, late summer, or early fall. However, the best time to transplant or divide them is in late summer, right after they finish their main flowering spurt. This gives you a full season of bloom and still gives the plants time to establish a strong new root system before winter.

Q What's the best way to divide a daylily? How often does it need to be done?

A Clues that it's time to divide a daylily include a dead center in the crown area, fewer and smaller blooms, and growth that appears crowded. You can divide daylily in late August or early September when the plants are semidormant and the temperatures are dropping. Use a spade to dig the entire clump, then use a sharp knife or shovel to cut off divisions. If you don't want to divide an entire clump, cut divisions from the edge of a clump using a spade or trowel.

Daylily

Q Last year my 'Stella de Oro' daylily bloomed only once. I thought it was supposed to bloom all summer. Why did it stop blooming?

A 'Stella de Oro' is a reblooming daylily. Rather than bloom constantly, it normally has several bloom cycles each year. The longer the growing season, the more numerous the bloom cycles. Daylilies will grow in partial shade but bloom less. If your Stellas bloomed only once last year, it's likely that your plants are not getting enough sunlight or someone sold you a variety that's not really 'Stella de Oro'. It's such a well-known variety that many imitations have shown up. Your plant may have been mislabeled.

Q Should I deadhead daylilies to get them to rebloom?

A You don't need to deadhead reblooming types of daylilies to get them to rebloom, but deadheading keeps the plants looking more attractive and prevents seedpods from forming. Developing seedpods can use up energy that would otherwise be put into forming more blooms.

Q What's the best way to deadhead daylilies?

A If you spend a lot of time in your garden during daylily bloom time, you can remove spent blossoms daily by snapping off the withered blooms. This keeps the plants tidy, and prevents the shriveled buds from detracting from the flowers that bloom in succeeding days. After all the buds on a flower stalk have finished blooming, but the stem back far enough so that the foliage conceals the cut.

Q I have daylilies in my front garden. Two out of five plants have curled, holey leaves. I can't find any insects. We have had a lot of rain lately, but it's been dry for almost a week now, so I have been watering a little late in the evening.

A It may be slugs attacking your daylily plants. They leave holes in the leaves and can mangle the foliage. You can buy slug and snail baits at your local garden center. The curled foliage could also be due to a physiological disorder called spring sickness. Shortly after growth begins in the spring, daylily foliage may appear distorted, ragged, and stunted. Often only a portion of a plant is affected. The cause of this phenomenon is unknown, but it most likely is due to damage to the crown in late winter. The daylily usually grows out of the problem. Regardless, no treatment is necessary.

Delphinium

Q **I just transplanted delphinium seedlings a few days ago, and the leaves were normal color. They are now yellow. Please advise what to do.**

A The leaf yellowing on your delphinium seedlings may simply be transplant shock. This is a normal reaction when you move a plant, especially with seedlings. In most cases, if you keep the seedlings moist while they become reestablished, they'll get settled and grow just fine. If they appear wilted and continue to struggle, provide them with some temporary shade to help them recover.

Q **In my perennial garden, almost everything has come up, except for my delphiniums. Do they come up later than most perennials?**

A Delphiniums are usually short-lived, especially in areas with hot, humid summers. Yours may have seen their last season. Many people grow them as cool-season annuals, enjoying their blooms during the cooler months of spring, and replacing them with heat-loving flowers when summer temperatures soar.

Q **On a recent trip to England I was amazed at the delphiniums in gardens everywhere. How can I grow them successfully here?**

A Plant delphiniums in moist, well-drained soil that's rich in organic matter. How much sun delphiniums need depends on where you grow them. In areas that experience cool summers—such as the Pacific Northwest—the plants thrive in full sun. In areas that experience warm summers, the plants prefer a spot with sun in the morning but shade during the hottest part of the day. They dislike hot summers and are short-lived in the Deep South, Southern California, and the desert Southwest. Delphiniums require regular watering in most areas. Spreading mulch over the soil will help keep them cool and slow evaporation.

Q **My delphiniums have finished blooming for the summer. Am I supposed to split them after they bloom or do anything else?**

A Generally, you don't need to divide delphiniums. Delphiniums like cool summers. In warm areas, they're short-lived and die out before they need dividing. Many gardeners are unaware that delphiniums can produce a second flush of blooms. Right after the flowers fade, remove the flower stalk down to the top set of leaves. If your plant is situated in a spot where it's happy, it should send up another flower stalk. It probably won't be as large as the first, but you will still get two sets of blooms for the price of one.

Ferns

Q **Last year I purchased three Japanese painted ferns. Only two came back this year; both are small. Why are the ferns smaller than when I bought them?**

A There are many possible reasons why your ferns are failing to thrive. If the plants don't like where they are, they won't come back well. For the best luck, plant Japanese painted fern (*Athyrium niponicum* var. *pictum*) in a spot that has dappled shade and soil that's rich in organic matter. Amend the soil liberally with organic matter before planting. Even though Japanese painted fern is hardy in Zone 4, it may not come back well if you've had an especially cold winter or a cold winter without much snow. A hot, dry summer could also weaken your plants, making them less likely to make it through the winter.

Q **Can you tell me which ferns to grow in an area that is dry and shady next to the house? I would like one that grows 2 to 3 feet tall and has large leaves.**

A Although ferns are well-known for moist shade conditions, there are several that will do well in dry shade once they are established. First, amend the soil next to your home by mixing in a lot of loose, crumbly compost. Then plan to do a little babysitting this first season, watering deeply once a week or so, until the plants are established enough to survive the dry shade without your assistance. Any of the following ferns will tolerate dry shade once they are established: Lady fern (*Athyrium filix-femina*), Christmas fern (*Polystichum acrostichoides*), western sword fern (*P. munitum*), soft shield fern (*P. setiferum*), Japanese tassel fern (*P. polyblepharum*), and any of the wood ferns (*Dryopteris* spp.).

Q **I cut down my cinnamon ferns for the winter. Do I mulch them or not? The bed is on the north side of the house.**

A If you just planted your cinnamon ferns (*Osmunda cinnamomea*) this year, cover them with a few inches of leaves for the winter after the temperatures get into the low 20s. More established ferns shouldn't need the mulch, but it wouldn't hurt to mulch them anyway.

Q **I have three different types of perennial ferns I purchased this year—two cinnamon ferns, four autumn ferns, and two lady ferns. Some of the leaves have spots uniformly positioned on the back of their leaves. Is this a bad thing?**

A The spots on the back of fern fronds are perfectly natural; they're the fern's way of reproducing itself. Just as other plants have seeds, ferns have spores. You don't need to do a thing with them. In fact, it could be a sign that the ferns are happy where they're located and growing well.

Q I live in Zone 8 and wonder whether I need to dig up Kimberly Queen ferns to overwinter before frost. They are doing great and I'd hate to have to dig them up if it's not necessary.

A Kimberly Queen fern (*Nephrolepis obliterata*) is considered hardy only in Zones 9 and 10. Where you live in Zone 8, it likely would not survive outdoors unless it is in a very protected location. It might survive outdoors with heavy mulch as protection, but to be safe, you should dig them up and grow them as houseplants over winter.

Q My Japanese ferns look ugly in spring. They always need their brown fronds cut off. It would be easier to cut them all back to allow the new fronds to grow. Can I do that?

A If the fronds on your Japanese painted fern are all brown, you can cut them back completely, taking care to avoid damage to the central core where new fronds emerge. If some of the fronds are still green, it's best to leave them on the plant because they're still photosynthesizing and making energy for the fern.

Q I bought a plant called flowering fern. Where should I plant it?

A Flowering fern (*Osmunda regalis*) prefers a moist site. You can put it where the roots will be in water (such as alongside a stream or pond) and it will do fine. It grows best in light to full shade.

Foxglove

Q **Should foxgloves die back to nothing after blooming? Will they come back with green leaves next spring?**

A It all depends on the type of foxglove (*Digitalis*) you grow. The most commonly grown foxglove (*D. purpurea*) is a biennial, meaning that it will grow only foliage its first year and bloom the next, then die after blooming. Some types of foxglove are truly perennial, however. The most readily available perennial type is strawberry foxglove (*D. × mertonensis*). It looks much like the biennial type but tends to grow shorter, and the flowers are the color of crushed strawberries. The plant is hardy in Zones 3–8. Yellow foxglove (*D. grandiflora*) is another perennial type. It is also hardy in Zones 3–8.

Q **I grow plants in containers on my patio. The patio gets six hours of shade, and I keep the foxglove in the shadiest area. I purchased a foxglove with three flowering stems and additional smaller nonflowering stems. I've had the plant about two months. All of a sudden it looks like death, and I don't know what to do to bring it back to life.**

A Most foxgloves are biennials, so it may be that your foxglove is following its natural cycle. If you grow foxglove in the ground, it can self-seed and start new plants that will bloom the following year. Because you're growing it in a container, you may need to collect the mature seeds and start new plants in seedling trays to keep the cycle of bloom going.

Geranium

Q **I have a grouping of perennial geraniums that didn't bloom very well last year. They're about nine years old, and I've never divided them. Should I be doing this, and if so how and when?**

A It's possible that your perennial geraniums need dividing or thinning. Some types spread quite quickly, while others remain in a tight clump for many years. If they appear to be growing in a thick mass, you can simply dig out sections to transplant elsewhere (or discard if you have no place to plant them). The remaining plants can then fill in the bare spaces, and with less competition may indeed bloom more profusely. If you haven't fertilized in quite a while, it would be helpful to do so. Make sure that you use a fertilizer for blooming plants. Too much nitrogen forces leafy growth at the expense of blooms.

Goatsbeard

Q **I planted a goatsbeard in the spring, and it hasn't done anything. Is this normal?**

A It's not at all uncommon for perennials to sit and seemingly do little the first year they're planted. If your goatsbeard (*Aruncus dioicus*) looks healthy, I'd be patient and see what it does next year. You should find that it will do more. To help your goatsbeard along, top-dress the soil around the plant with organic matter and mulch. Keep the soil moist but not wet.

Goldenrod

Q My neighbor planted some goldenrod in her perennial garden this spring. Doesn't goldenrod pollen cause hay fever?

A Goldenrod (*Solidago*) is a late-summer bloomer with small bright yellow flowers in large clusters. Because it blooms at the peak of hay fever season, some people assume that it is responsible for seasonal allergies. However, goldenrod has gotten a bad rap. Ragweed (*Ambrosia*), which blooms at the same time and produces abundant pollen, is the real culprit. Goldenrod has become a popular cut flower, and many cultivars are available for the garden. Some of the best are the semidwarf 'Crown of Rays', 'Golden Baby', and 'Golden Fleece', which tolerate some shade.

Hibiscus

Q I planted hibiscus last year, and love the big red flowers. It looked like it died last winter, but it started growing again in spring. Is it OK to cut it back?

A Hardy hibiscus (*Hibiscus moscheutos,* at right) does make wonderfully big flowers for 3 to 4 weeks in late summer. Despite its name, the hardy hibiscus usually dies to the ground each winter and should be cut back to the ground line at the end of winter. If yours has already started to grow, you may be able to selectively cut out the dead stems and allow the new ones to grow.

Q I have quite a few hardy hibiscus. I love their tropical look. Is there some way to make them bloom for a longer time through the summer?

A If you pinch back a few stems on each plant in early July, the plant will keep flowering for 2 to 3 extra weeks. Leave some stems unpinched—they'll bloom

first. Remove the top several inches of about one-third of the stems. These shoots will branch and bloom later, extending the season of bloom. You can even trim back a few more shoots in mid- to late July to extend the flowering for an even longer time.

Q I have a hardy hibiscus growing in sandy soil. How do I get this plant to thrive? Can I grow it where it will get only afternoon sun?

A For hardy hibiscus to thrive and bloom well, it needs full sun. If you plant your hibiscus where it gets only a half-day of sun, it may not bloom, and if it does bloom, it will be delayed. The plant prefers rich soil with lots of moisture. Because your soil is sandy, amend the planting bed with compost to help retain moisture.

Heart-Leaf Bergenia

Q **Although my bergenia has been spreading, there are no blooms in the spring. I don't know why. I use a granular fertilizer in the spring for blooms.**

A Is your heart-leaf bergenia (*Bergenia cordifolia*) growing in a shady spot? Too much shade may keep it from blooming well. How often do you fertilize, and what's the condition of your soil? Too many nutrients can encourage a plant to grow only leaves, at the expense of flowers. If you have good, rich soil *and* you're feeding the plant extra, that could be the problem. Also, bergenias tend to flower lightly after harsh winters.

Heart-Leaf Brunnera

Q **We planted heart-leaf brunnera in a semi-shaded area. It's mid-April and they still haven't come up. Will they come up or are they dead?**

A It's not unusual to observe delayed emergence on first-year perennials. I'd give your heart-leaf brunnera (*Brunnera macrophylla*) more time to emerge. If it doesn't, consider a few things before planting new ones. Brunnera is a plant for shade or partial shade. In ideal conditions it will have leaves all through the growing season, allowing the plant to grow and store energy in the roots and crown for the winter. In locations that are too sunny, too hot, and too dry the leaves will burn and die back early. This weakens the plant and it may not survive the winter. Several years of stress will result in the loss of the plant. Be sure the new plants are shaded and keep them moist.

Hellebore

Q **I planted hellebores under the shade of a pine tree last fall. They haven't bloomed this year, and the leaves are brown around the edges. What went wrong?**

A It's common for hellebores (above) not to bloom the first year after you plant them. The brown leaves that you see could simply be winter damage. Brown on the leaf edges commonly comes from cold temperature dips as the new leaves emerge, unseasonably cold temperatures during the winter, or exposure to lots of cold, drying winds.

Q **What's the difference between Christmas rose and Lenten rose?**

A Both are species of hellebores. Lenten rose (*Helleborus orientalis*) is hardy in Zones 4–9, and bears red, purple, green, white, or yellow flowers in late winter to early spring. Christmas rose (*H. niger*) produces green-centered pinkish white blooms earlier in the season, on plants hardy in Zones 3–8. Both grow well in shade and are deer-tolerant. You'll also find many hybrid hellebores with a delightful array of bloom colors from pale pinks with splotches to almost pure black.

Helenium

Q I like the look of Helen's flower, but I've also heard it called sneezeweed. Does it cause hayfever?

A This is one of those cases of a plant getting an unfortunate common name. Helen's flower (*Helenium autumnale*) is sometimes called sneezeweed. It likely got this name because it blooms with yellow, orange, or red daisylike flowers in late summer as ragweed and hay fever season are in full swing. It's not particularly offensive in causing allergies, so you can plant it with good conscience.

Hollyhock

Q Every year my hollyhocks don't do well. They get a rusty coating on the leaves and never thrive.

A Hollyhock (*Alcea rosea*) is notorious for getting rust during hot, humid summers. Two ways to lessen the disease are to remove all old stalks and fallen leaves in the autumn, and to water plants from below to prevent the leaves from getting too wet. Remove infected leaves as you see them. Don't allow plants to get too crowded. Unfortunately, you may still need to apply a fungicide every 7 to 10 days once the leaves begin to develop. Some gardeners report that the fig-leaf types of hollyhock are less susceptible to rust than the old-fashioned kind.

Q My garden had freezing temperatures that damaged my hollyhocks. They didn't turn dark but are limp at this time. Will they still bloom?

A Your hollyhocks should recover and bloom without trouble. Even if the foliage is badly damaged, they can grow more and still bloom this season. Because hollyhock is a biennial plant, it is adapted to withstanding freezing temperatures.

Q Last year I planted some hollyhocks that I started as seedlings. They did not bloom but had many leaves and were at least 12 to 14 inches tall. Do you think they will bloom this year? How can I start more of them?

A The reason that your hollyhocks developed leaves but not flowers the first year is because hollyhocks are biennials. They have a lifespan of two years. The plants that you have now will bloom this year and die at the end of the growing season. However, they often reseed themselves freely after blooming, so you may have plants in the same area again next year. You can scatter ripe seedpods over the ground in late summer or fall to ensure hollyhocks again next year.

Hostas

Q **What is the secret to growing beautiful hostas? Mine are always smaller than my neighbors'. They look yellowed and moth-eaten. What am I doing wrong?**

A Hostas prefer certain sun and soil growing conditions and protection from pests to be at their best. Hostas love filtered shade. Many hostas tolerate a couple hours of morning sun each day if the soil is consistently moist. Some solid green cultivars do nicely in full sun if given enough water. Be sure that your soil has plenty of organic matter, which retains moisture but still allows lots of air to reach the roots. Work well-rotted manure or compost into the soil for a terrific hosta bed. Slugs, snails, and deer find a bed of hostas as appealing as many people find a buffet table. Control snails and slugs with bait or traps, and apply repellents to keep deer away from your hostas.

Q **I moved all my big, beautiful variegated hostas from my previous home and planted them at my new one. Some are in total shade while others are in partial sun. They looked great at first, but now they are gradually turning yellow and fading away. Help!**

A It could be that the plants were damaged during transplanting. Or they could be turning yellow because they were given too little or too much water after transplanting. They also could be suffering from being planted too deeply—especially in clay soil. Lack of oxygen resulting from deep planting damages the roots. Accidentally giving them too much fertilizer—especially right after transplanting them—could also have caused yellowing and browning of the foliage. Also, hostas often turn yellow by the end of the season. It could be that they'll come back just fine next year.

Q **I have a large, beautiful hosta that is beginning to emerge from the soil. I have been told to divide it. I want to know when is the best time to do this and how I should go about dividing it without damaging the plant.**

A You can divide hostas almost anytime, but there is no need to divide them unless they are too large for their location or you want more plants to share or use in other places in your landscape. If you decide to divide them, early spring is best. Simply dig up the plant, cut it into sections with a sharp spade or knife, and replant the sections. Make certain that each section has healthy roots and buds or shoots. Water the new transplants until they are established. A layer of mulch will help maintain even soil moisture.

Q **Should the flower stems growing out of the hosta plants be cut or pulled out in order to let the leaves become more full?**

A Removing the flower stems won't affect the leaves one way or the other. The reason that some gardeners remove hosta flower stems is because they think the tall stems detract from the overall look of the plant. Other gardeners find the flowers charming and prefer to leave them on. In fact, some hostas are bred primarily for their colorful and/or fragrant flowers. Once the blooms have faded, cut the flower stalks off near the base so the foliage can disguise the cut end of the stalk.

Q I love hostas but have failed to get them to grow—my plants always die within six months. A local gardener told me hostas don't thrive in Zone 9 and that I shouldn't waste my money. Do I have any hope?

A Your gardening friend is right. Hostas, which are native to Japan and other cool areas of Asia, dislike hot weather and fail to thrive in areas warmer than Zone 8. They are temperate plants that prefer cool, mild summers and a period of cold and relative darkness during the winter. If you have a cool, moist microclimate in your yard (such as a shady site north of your house), you might get them to survive a bit longer.

Q Last year I acquired some hostas. The variegated one has grown quite large, but the blue-leaf variety is still small. Should I wait another year to split them? When is the best time?

A While you can divide hostas almost any time, it's best to do it in early spring (when the plants are about 2 inches tall) or in late summer (about six weeks before the first killing frost is expected). It's best to wait until your plants are at least three or four years old before you cut them into sections. However, if you are in a hurry to get more plants, chances are good that they will survive dividing the first year after you plant them. Dig around the entire clump, then lift the plant, soil and all, from the hole. Brush away enough soil so you can see the roots. Wash away the remaining soil. Use a sharp knife to cut the clump into sections. Leave as many roots as possible on each section. Replant divisions right away, and keep them moist.

Q Will some hostas take the sun better than others?

A Although hostas prefer shade, there are some that tolerate more sun. They include 'Sunny Delight', 'Squash Casserole', 'Fragrant Bouquet', and 'Fried Bananas'. As a general rule, the yellow-leaved types can tolerate more sun. Most blue-leaf types can't handle much direct sun at all. Also as a general rule, the more organic matter in the soil, the more sun a hosta can take. Similarly, a constant moisture supply will enable hostas to tolerate a greater amount of sun.

Q Deer have eaten the leaves off my hostas, leaving just the stems. Should I cut the plants back to the ground? Will new growth appear this summer?

A Leave the hostas alone. Don't cut back the damaged foliage because even though it's damaged, it's still feeding the plant. The plants should recover with some new foliage before fall unless the deer come back. To prevent the deer from feeding on your hostas again, consider applying a taste-type repellent that deer find unpalatable.

Hostas

Q How do I separate hostas without leaving holes in the bed? I have a line of them in my front yard at least seven years old, and they were not as full last year so I think that it's time to divide them.

A You should be able to dig up your hostas, divide them, and replant in such a way that you don't have holes in your design. Just make sure that your plants are spaced evenly apart so the spaces between them look natural.

Q I have a hosta that lost its lighter color line that went around the leaf. I have divided it many times and shared it with friends. Any idea what's going on?

A It's not unusual for variegated plants to revert back to their solid color. (The variegation usually arises as a mutation from solid green.) The solid green forms of the plant are more vigorous than variegated ones, so once the reversion takes place, the solid form predominates unless it is "weeded out" and removed, allowing the variegated part of the plant to continue on without the competition.

Lady's Mantle

Q Can I plant lady's mantle around my roses to keep them from looking bare near the ground?

A Many roses naturally lose their bottom leaves as the season progresses. Lady's mantle (*Alchemilla mollis*) acts nicely as a companion groundcover to mask the roses' bare stems.

Lamb's-Ears

Q How close should I plant my lamb's-ears to create a groundcover, and how long will it take for them to create a solid blanket?

A If you have good, rich soil, you can plant your lamb's-ears (*Stachys byzantina*) 12 to 18 inches apart. The better your soil is, the faster they'll grow. At the closer spacing, they'll usually fill in completely in one growing season; at the wider spacing it may take a year longer. If you want to maintain the silver carpet effect, cut your lamb's-ears flower stalks as soon as you see them develop. Don't wait until they rise above the foliage, otherwise you may be left with some hard, stubby stems embedded in the leaves. Also, consider planting 'Helene von Stein' (also sold as 'Big Ears'). This variety produces few flowerstalks with leaves twice as large as the species.

Lavender

Q **How often should lavender be trimmed? How close to the woody part can I cut? I have some five-year-old plants that I've trimmed once, two springs ago.**

A The lavender most often grown in North America is *Lavandula angustifolia*. It is hardy to Zone 5. Trim it twice a year. Cut lavender back hard in spring to perhaps half its height. This pruning promotes bushiness and removes dead tips that are common after winter exposure. Leave some portion of each leafy stem rather than stripping it of all its active growth points at one time. As soon as the plant finishes its main June to July bloom, shear it to remove spent flowers. Shearing may promote a second flush of bloom.

Q **I have a small formal garden in Zone 5. I planted 'Munstead' lavender for the edging of the beds within it. However, much of the lavender did not make it through the winter. I thought that lavender was supposed to be hardy to Zone 5.**

A Lavender in Zone 5 can be picky about where it overwinters. 'Munstead' is a good choice of variety, but it needs well-drained soil to survive the winter. And in severe winters, it may die back to the ground. However, don't give up on it immediately if it looks dead in the spring. It may resprout from dormant buds at the base of the plant. Cut back the dead tops and wait at least several weeks for new growth to begin.

Q **I have several different lavenders and wonder how far to cut them back this spring. I did not cut them in the fall.**

A Wait and see where the new growth will occur and then trim back the dead at that time. You may get some new growth on the old wood, or the plant may have died back and you'll only get new growth from the

base. Once you see the new leaves appearing, it's safe to remove everything else. Keep in mind that English lavender (*Lavandula angustifolia*) varieties 'Munstead' and 'Hidcote' are among the hardiest types for Zone 5. Spanish lavender (*L. stoechas*) is hardy only in Zones 7–10.

Q **I have some lavender plants that are more than 10 years old. They are quite woody, and I am wondering what they need. Do I cut them back or divide them?**

A The best way to get lavender in shape is to cut it back in the spring. You can shear the plants back by at least half. Wait until you see the beginnings of new growth before you prune. Lavender does not require dividing because it grows from one crown. It does not develop additional crowns like daylilies or peonies do. If you like, you can give your lavender a little compost or rotted manure, but don't overdo it because these plants thrive best in poor soil.

Ornamental Grasses

Q When should ornamental grasses be pruned? Is it better to do it before winter or in the spring?

A The timing of the pruning is really up to you. After the foliage dies back in fall, it makes no difference to the plant. Some gardeners like the look of the grasses standing in winter to attract birds and provide structure. They cut their grasses down in early spring. Other gardeners don't like to see anything in their gardens over winter, so they cut their grasses back in fall. Some types, such as miscanthus, stand up well all winter long. Others, such as switchgrass, tend to mat down with heavy snow.

Q I have some flame grass. I desperately need to divide it. The middle looks dead. Is that middle dead, or will dividing it make that part grow again?

A Flame grass (*Miscanthus* 'Purpurascens') typically develops a barren spot in the middle of its clump after several years. That middle section is dead and won't grow again. As soon as you see new growth in the spring, dig up the entire clump and use a sharp spade to divide the clump into smaller bits. You can discard the center portion and replant the live, growing portions.

Q I need some ideas for ornamental grasses at the beach in the Northeast.

A There are several ornamental grasses that are hardy and drought- and salt-tolerant. Try these: blue oatgrass (*Helictotrichon sempervirens*), alkali dropseed (*Sporobolus airoides*), little bluestem (*Schizachyrium scoparium*), and Karl Foerster feather reedgrass (*Calamagrostis acutiflora* 'Karl Foerster').

Q My maidengrass is not coming back strong this year. What can I do to help?

A Maidengrass (*Miscanthus sinensis* 'Gracillimus') needs pruning to about 4 inches from the ground before new growth begins in spring. You may lightly prune after it begins growth in the spring, but only to remove the dead brown leaves that may be shading the growing sections of the plant. Sometimes sections of the plant die out over winter and may take a long time to sprout in the spring.

Q **My ribbongrass is turning yellow from the ground up this year. It has been very hot, but I have been watering it, so I'm not sure if it's too much water or if something else is going on.**

A Has the yellowing of your ribbongrass (*Phalaris*) just started happening, or has the yellowing been going on for a while? It sounds like something may have shocked the plant. If the leaves started going yellow all of a sudden, think back to any changes that occurred to the area right before the yellowing happened. It could be something like an application of too much fertilizer, too deep a layer of mulch, exposure to herbicides, or root damage. If the yellowing has developed gradually, the cause may be harder to pinpoint. Too much water can cause yellowing leaves, as could being rootbound (if the grass is in a confined area).

Q **My zebragrass has been beautiful. Now it's lost its stripes. What happened?**

A Depending on the time of year, the stripes in your zebragrass (*Miscanthus sinensis* 'Zebrinus') may return. Zebragrass is a warm-season ornamental that prefers hot weather. Often the first shoots that emerge in spring are solid green. As temperatures warm, additional new shoots develop the characteristic striped variegation. Sometimes a variegated plant such as zebragrass reverts back to its natural single-color form. Usually the solid green form of the plant is more vigorous than the striped or variegated form, so it will overtake the desirable variegated portion of the plant unless you remove the solid green part of the plant.

Q **Is purple fountaingrass a perennial? I planted some last year, and it didn't come back this year.**

A Purple fountaingrass (*Pennisetum setaceum* 'Rubrum') is perennial in Zones 9 and 10, but usually is treated as an annual in colder areas. If you would like to grow a hardier pennisetum, try the green form of fountaingrass (*P. alopecuroides*), which is hardy to Zone 5 or Oriental fountaingrass (*P. orientale*), which is hardy to Zone 6.

Q **I can't get pampas grass to grow in my Zone 5 garden. What am I doing wrong?**

A True pampas grass (*Cortaderia selloana*) is reliably hardy only in Zones 7–10. Many gardeners love the look of its large white plumes, and are disappointed to find that they can't grow it. Several other ornamental grasses are sometimes called pampas grass too. Ravenna grass (*Saccharum ravennae,* also known as *Erianthus ravennae*), produces large seed plumes with shoots to 12 feet tall. It is hardy to Zone 6. Giant miscanthus (*Miscanthus giganteus*) is also sometimes referred to as pampas grass because its large white plumes resemble those of the true pampas grass. It is hardy to Zone 4.

Oriental Poppy

Q Where do poppy seeds used in baking come from? Could I use seeds from Oriental poppies for this purpose?

A The seeds of breadseed poppy (*Papaver somniferum*) are the type used in cooking. They are a close relative of the opium poppy and develop large, pinkish purple flowers on tall stems. You can buy them from mailorder and online sources. They're not the same thing as Oriental poppy, so I'd not recommend substituting seeds of that species for baked goods.

Q I need to move a poppy to a new location. When is the best time to transplant it?

A The best time to transplant poppies depends on the type of poppy. If it's a perennial poppy, such as Oriental poppy (*Papaver orientale*), then early fall is a good time to move it. Annual poppies, such as the Shirley poppy (*P. rhoeas*), don't transplant well. It's best to sow them directly in place. You could harvest seeds of either type and plant them in the new spot.

Q My poppy plants come up beautifully in the spring, but then some of the buds turn black, the stems curl up, and the flower never blooms. What could be causing this? I have several plants in different locations throughout the yard, but they all do the same thing.

A This sounds like a fungal disease is attacking some of your poppies. If only a few flowers are affected, perhaps you can just cut them out as you see them developing to help prevent the spread of the disease. If the problem is widespread, you may wish to use a preventive fungicide spray next year as the flowerbud shoots begin to elongate.

Q My Oriental poppies bloomed beautifully this spring, but now they're dying back. What can I do to save them?

A Oriental poppy naturally goes dormant during the summer. The dieback that you're seeing is likely part of the plant's normal growth cycle. You should see new shoots emerge from the plant in late summer.

Penstemon

Q **Would beard-tongue be a good plant to grow in shallow soil in a rock garden with part sun/part shade? Creeping phlox grows well there, but it needs some taller summer bloomers.**

A Beard-tongue (*Penstemon* spp.) would be a great choice for this situation. There are many varieties and species to choose from. Pineleaf penstemon (*P. pinifolius*) has thin, threadlike leaves and red tubular flowers on stems 18 inches tall. Mexicali penstemon (*P. × mexicali*) offers a couple beautiful selections in 'Red Rocks' and 'Pikes Peak Purple'. The former has pink flowers; the latter deep purple blooms. Both grow 2 to 3 feet tall. Rocky Mountain penstemon (*P. strictus*) has purplish blue blooms on stems up to 3 feet tall.

Q **I have four penstemons in one bed, and all of them are infected with black spots. What causes this?**

A Penstemons sometimes fall under attack from fungal diseases, and that sounds like what may be happening with yours. Make sure that the foliage on your plants doesn't stay wet, and provide good air flow to help reduce the incidence of disease. If the spots are small and are not spreading, the infection period may already be past. If that is the case, there's no need to spray the plants with a fungicide.

Q **I have a penstemon that is crowding some of my other plants. Can I lift and divide it?**

A Penstemon can be lifted and divided. Some types, such as pineleaf penstemon, are much more fibrous-rooted than others and are quite easily divided. Others are more clump formers, but still can be divided by digging the entire clump and slicing through it with a sharp spade. Reset the divided clumps immediately and water them in. The best time to divide or move your penstemon is early spring, just as growth is beginning.

Peony

Q Is there a variety of peony that I can grow in Florida?

A Peony (*Paeonia*) requires a cold spell with temperatures 40°F or less to break winter dormancy. There are some varieties that will do well in Zone 8, and some gardeners have had luck with them in Zone 9. Look for 'Festiva Maxima', 'Kansas', 'Pink Hawaiian Coral', 'Doreen', 'Raspberry Sundae', and 'Sarah Bernhardt'. Provide the coolest conditions that you can by planting on the north side of your house, but make sure the plants get at least half a day of sun. You may have more success with tree peonies. Their woody stems do not go dormant.

Q I've heard that peonies need ants to bloom. I don't see ants on my peony buds. How can I get my plants to bloom?

A Don't worry; ants aren't needed to produce peony blooms. Ants often congregate on peony buds in spring because they come to harvest the sugary nectar that most peonies produce on the outside of their buds. Your peonies should flower just fine even if no ants show up.

Q My peony had a couple of beautiful blooms and then the rest of the buds turned dark and shriveled. What's wrong?

A What you're describing is a fairly common fungal disease called Botrytis blight. It thrives in wet conditions, and the spores can spread when they are splattered around by rainfall or overhead watering. A fungicide isn't generally necessary. All you need to do is snip off and remove all infected plant parts. Then do a thorough cleanup in fall, removing all aboveground portions of the peony plant to reduce overwintering fungal spores. If necessary, you can apply a protective fungicide in the spring, spraying the plant every 10 days from the time the shoots begin to emerge until they're done blooming.

Q Two years ago I divided several clumps of peonies that were quite old, with blooms that were not as large and plentiful as previously. The new bushes look healthy; however, all but one variety are not blooming. What should I do to promote bloom?

A First of all, be sure your peonies are planted in full sun. These plants need at least 6 to 8 hours of direct sun per day. Also, you may have planted them too deeply. Peony roots should have their "eyes" no more than 1 or 2 inches underground. If planted deeper, they may grow, but not bloom well. Also, it may simply take another year for them to recover from their division. Peony often takes several years to recover from division. A final caution: Don't fertilize them. Too much nitrogen, such as from lawn fertilizer, can cause the plants to grow foliage but not flowers.

Q **When should I cut back peony bushes? Is it better to do it right after they finish blooming or in the fall?**

A Leave your peony's foliage alone until it dies back naturally in the fall. Then you can trim the dead foliage, or you can trim it back in the early spring before new growth begins. You can clip back the dead flowerheads after they finish blooming if you want to tidy them up, but leave the foliage alone.

Q **My wife has 50-year-old peony plants. She wants me to transplant them in our yard. They belonged to her aunt, so a successful move is important. Can you give me directions?**

A Transplant peony plants in fall as they begin to go dormant, not in spring as they prepare to bloom. Dig the plants carefully to minimize root injury, and remove the foliage. If the plants are large and old, they'll probably do better if they're divided. Gently wash the soil off the large roots, then use a sharp, clean knife to divide the plant's crown. Make sure each division has 3 to 5 pink buds or healthy stems. Plant divisions at least 3 feet apart, and set each division in a hole so the soil level is no more than 2 inches above the buds on the root. Peonies resent disturbance and may not bloom for several years after transplanting—especially if the plants are old. Water them well, checking to make sure they are not too deep.

Q **I love cut peonies but don't like dealing with the ants. How can I rid cut flowers of ants before I bring them into the house?**

A Your best bet would be to gently shake or brush off the ants. Or cut the peonies as the buds just begin to open, when they are marshmallow-soft. The ants won't be as likely to be hidden in the flower petals, and the peony will bloom beautifully in a few days. You may have heard that ants play an important part in making the peonies bloom, but that is a myth.

Q **I recently bought a tree peony. Does it require any special care?**

A Tree peony (*Paeonia suffruticosa*) does best when planted in a protected spot that receives full sun (at least 6 to 8 hours of direct sun a day). Be sure to amend the soil with abundant organic matter (such as compost) before planting; tree peony will sulk if you grow it in clay. In cold-winter climates, tree peony typically dies back to the ground each year. Unless it's in a really protected spot, it never grows to the 10-foot height it reaches in warm regions.

Phlox

Q **Can you recommend some garden phlox cultivars that are resistant to powdery mildew? The plants I have look terrible by late summer because they are always covered with white powder.**

A You are wise to get rid of your phlox if it is consistently infected with mildew. Several excellent cultivars are seldom affected by powdery mildew. Some of them are 'David', with white flowers; 'Katherine', with lavender flowers; 'Delta Snow', with white flowers; 'Eva Cullum', with pink flowers; 'Robert Poore', with purple flowers; 'Natascha', with purple flowers; and *Phlox carolina*, with lavender flowers.

Q **I recently planted some creeping phlox for a border in front of my home, and they seem to be dying. How can I revive them?**

A Creeping phlox (*Phlox subulata*) requires quick drainage. Too much water can be a problem for

these plants. Avoid fertilizing them if they are struggling. Wait until they begin to grow well to apply fertilizer.

Q **How do I go about dividing creeping phlox?**

A The best time to divide creeping phlox is in very early spring, just as it's coming out of dormancy. Simply use a sharp spade and dig sections the size you want. Replant immediately. These plants like good drainage and full sun.

Q **Mold has started growing on my phlox. Is there anything I can do to save them?**

A The "mold" growing on your garden phlox (*P. paniculata*) is a fungus called powdery mildew. Some varieties are quite susceptible to it and others are very resistant. If yours is severely affected by the fungus, you may want to consider replacing it with a disease-resistant type. Spraying with horticultural oil can provide some protection from the disease, but this likely will need to be done every year as long as you keep this plant.

Q **What can be done about mildew on perennial phlox?**

A Mildew is a perennial problem on this favorite perennial. Try to improve air circulation around the plants next year. As the new stems grow, edit each clump down to about one-third to one-half the stems that appear. If the bed seems crowded with other plants remove some to get better air movement. Grow the plants in full sun and water as needed to prevent moisture stress. If you see infection starting—small white or grayish spots on the stems and leaves—apply a spray of 1 tablespoon canola oil, 1 tablespoon baking soda, and 3 drops of dish soap in 1 quart of water. Mix well and spray to cover the stems and leaves.

Pinks

Q **When should pinks be transplanted?**

A Generally, it's best to transplant pinks (*Dianthus* spp.) when they are dormant. If that's not possible, at least wait until blooming has finished. Perennial dianthus, such as 'Firewitch', pictured at right, can be divided and transplanted after their major flush of bloom in the spring.

Q **All the bloom is gone from my carnations. Should I deadhead them so they will bloom again through the summer?**

A Carnations are a type of pinks (*Dianthus*) that grow best in moderate climates. Remove spent flowers to encourage reblooming. If you have a long-stem variety, you can cut them back if they get scraggly. Clump-forming carnations need to be divided every few years to keep them looking their best.

Q **I bought perennial dianthus and it blooms fine at first, but as the flowers die the whole stem turns brown and doesn't flower any more. I tried deadheading, but that didn't seem to make a difference.**

A Many perennial pinks have one main flush of bloom in the spring and that's all. Some types will rebloom sporadically if deadheaded right after bloom, but most just have foliage the rest of the summer. If entire shoots of your plants are turning brown, it may be an indication that the soil is poorly drained. Dianthus grows best where drainage is good.

Learn about other varieties of dianthus that you can grow at *bhg.com/dianthus*.

Primrose

Q **How long are primroses supposed to bloom?**

A True primroses (*Primula*) bloom only for several weeks in spring. Their foliage may die back in midsummer as well. Most like moist sites with partial shade. Evening primroses (*Oenothera*), on the other hand, bloom throughout the summer and grow well in dry, sunny sites.

Purple Coneflower

Q I'm not sure how I should cut my purple coneflowers. Do I cut the stalk all the way to the bottom? Is it best to deadhead or not?

A You can cut purple coneflower (*Echinacea purpurea*) back to a set of leaves below the flowering stem. It helps to extend the bloom season if you deadhead them. Doing so will keep them from self-seeding and spreading around your garden. However, deadheading also removes the seeds that birds love to feed on.

Q What is happening to my coneflowers? Three different varieties failed to return this year.

A Do you have clay soil in your yard? If so, that could explain your purple coneflowers' disappearing act. They tend to "melt out" or rot in clay soil. These plants need good drainage. Mix in organic matter to improve drainage or plant them in raised beds.

Q I've been seeing a lot of coneflowers in colors other than purple. Are these the same species?

A Plant breeders have been having fun with coneflower breeding in recent years. Purple coneflower is one of the parent plants of these hybrids, but to get different colors, the breeders have crossed that species with several other closely related species, such as yellow coneflower (*E. paradoxa*), pale purple coneflower (*E. pallida*), and Tennessee coneflower (*E. tennesseensis*). The result is a rainbow of color options from traditional purple, pink, and white to orange, red, gold, and burgundy.

Q I've heard that the new hybrid coneflowers don't set seed. Is that true?

A Many of the coneflower hybrids are indeed sterile. Because they derive from wide species crosses, they're unable to set seed. The upside to this is that they won't self-seed and become weedy. The downside is that they're not as bird-friendly as the old-fashioned kind that serve up tasty seeds for feathered friends. Similarly, highly double forms with lots of petals are less likely to set seed. You could grow some of the common purple coneflower to feed the birds and some of the newer ones simply to enjoy their spectacular colors and long season of bloom.

Queen-of-the-Prairie

Q **When can you plant queen-of-the-prairie?**

A Queen-of-the-prairie (*Filipendula rubra*) is a North American native prairie plant that is best planted in early spring. It likes moist soil and full sun. It will grow in part shade, but it tends to get powdery mildew if it doesn't get enough light.

Russian Sage

Q **My Russian sage is about 4 feet tall. I want to rototill the area where it is growing to clean up the garden and loosen the soil. Can I uproot the Russian sage and then put it back in after the new garden is loosened?**

A The best time to move Russian sage (*Perovskia atriplicifolia*) is in the early spring when it's just breaking dormancy. It's not as likely to survive a transplant when moved in summer at its full size. However, it is an extremely tough, drought-tolerant plant, so you could try it if you have no other options.

Q **I want to transplant my Russian sage plants that I planted last year. Do I cut them back before I transplant, or do I leave them as is and move them?**

A Cut your dormant Russian sage back to 4 to 6 inches above the ground and then transplant it. New buds will break the crown of the plant and woody stems that you leave. By the end of summer you should have just as beautiful and full a plant this year as you did last year.

Q **We bought some 'Little Spire' Russian sage last summer. It was so pretty we left it alone all winter. We noticed that the shop where we bought it has cut back their plants to 5 or 6 inches. Should we cut ours back too, or will it grow OK without cutting back?**

A Russian sage (below) can be cut back in late winter or early spring if you want it to grow back a little bushier. If left unpruned, Russian sage sometimes becomes unkempt. By cutting it back close to the ground line each spring, you'll get a more compact and sturdy plant.

Salvia

Q Am I supposed to deadhead my blue perennial salvia?

A Perennial salvia (*S. nemorosa*) will rebloom quicker and with a larger return bloom if you deadhead it as the flower spikes fade. Cut them off back at the foliage. If the plant has a tendency to flop open, you can also cut the plant back more severely—to within 6 inches of the ground—to keep the plant more compact.

Q I bought a Dark Dancer autumn sage with little red flowers on it. Can I put it in a container? What else would you suggest planting with it?

A Autumn sage (*Salvia greggii*) is also sometimes called Texas red sage or cherry sage. It is a perennial that puts down a taproot deep into the soil. This means deep, infrequent waterings. It also means this plant wouldn't be happy in a pot. Give it full sun, well-drained soil (although it tolerates clay), and little water after it's established. Other drought-tolerant plants to put with it that like the same conditions are hummingbird mint (*Agastache* spp.), dancing butterflies (*Gaura lindheimeri*), feverfew (*Tanacetum parthenium*), valerian (*Centranthus*), and lavender (*Lavandula*).

Q I have a beautiful perennial garden planted along the back of my house, but every year I have to tie up the salvia. While driving around town I see other salvias standing tall. Is it because I have them planted next to the house? How do I get them to stand on their own?

A You don't say how much light your salvias are getting. In most cases, if these plants topple it's because they aren't getting enough light. Salvia needs at least 6 to 8 hours of direct sunlight a day. They should not be overfertilized either because this will also cause them to get very tall and weak. You also don't mention which type of salvia you have. I've found that plumed salvia (*S. nemorosa* 'Plumosa') is more likely to split open because it has heavier flower clusters than perennial salvia (*S. nemorosa*). However, if you cut them back to about 1 foot tall after their first flush of bloom, the secondary growth will be shorter and less likely to flop.

Q I want to divide my *Salvia* 'May Night'. It has been in my garden for three to four years. Can I do this and if so, will it not bloom this year? And at what time should I do it?

A Dividing May Knight salvia is easy, and it shouldn't have any trouble reestablishing itself. You can do it in early spring or wait until fall. Dig up the clumping plant and divide it at the root with a sharp knife or trowel. The divisions may not bloom much the first year as they get established in their new locations, but you should get some bloom this year and a full display of flowers next year.

Sedum

Q Some of my sedum plants developed a mushy black stalk. What causes this?

A A basal stem rot fungus can attack sedums near ground level. The fungus survives in moist soil and can splash up onto the stems. Providing better air movement around the plants along with full sun to dry things out is one means of getting the problem under control. If plants are crowded, they may need dividing. Mulch the soil to prevent soil from splashing on the stems. Fungicide sprays can also help prevent the disease from developing.

Q I have had sedum for about five years. The first four years they looked terrific. Now they have gotten so large that they spread out and the stems fall over. How should I trim them? Should they be divided?

A Upright sedums like 'Autumn Joy' thrive in full sun and well-drained soil. They will flop over if they are in too much shade. Also, the plants can become floppy if the soil is overly rich or fertile. You can reduce your sedums' overall height by cutting them in half each June when they reach 8 inches tall. Sedum rarely needs division; once every 8 to 10 years in spring is ideal.

Q I would like to know when is a good time to transplant sedum? Can it be divided? If so, how should that be done?

A Sedum is easy to divide, and it's best to do this in early spring. As soon as the plants begin to poke through the soil use a sharp spade to dig up the clump. Then break or cut the clump into sections, making certain that each section has some healthy roots and at least two or three healthy shoots. Replant the divisions right away at the same depth the mother plant was growing. Water when the soil becomes dry to the touch.

Q I live in Zone 3 and would like a perennial groundcover for a hill with a steep slope and poor, sandy soil. A little color would be nice, but my primary goal is to find something to cover the sandy soil. Low maintenance would also be good.

A One of the creeping sedums may be a good solution for this site. There are many species and varieties, so you could plant swaths of different kinds to get a variety of textures and colors. All do well in sandy, well-drained soil. Flower colors range from yellow to pink, rose, or white.

Q When is the best time to separate and replant my Rosy Glow sedum? How can I separate the plant without killing it? The plant frames our patio and is overgrown and falling over.

A Rosy Glow sedum is a groundcover-type sedum that will naturally sprawl and spread. You can divide and replant it almost any time. It reestablishes quickly and even will root from broken stems without roots placed in soil. If you prefer an upright growing sedum you may want to choose a different variety, such as 'Autumn Joy', 'Neon', or 'Blade Runner'.

Shasta Daisy

Q **My Shasta daisy plants grew and blossomed well, then the stems starting turning black. I checked the root system, and it was almost gone. Could this be slug or grub damage? We did have a lot of rain earlier in the summer.**

A It's possible that the wet weather provided an ideal habitat for a fungal rot disease to attack your Shasta daisies (*Leucanthemum × superbum*), pictured below. They require well-drained soil, and if the soil was constantly soggy, their roots may have rotted in the ground. If that's what happened, amend the soil with a lot of organic matter such as compost to improve drainage before you replant. You could also install raised beds to improve the drainage in this area. The black stems and skimpy root system you describe don't sound like the kind of damage slugs leave behind, and if it were grubs, you'd not only see them in the ground, but you'd also notice other dying plants in your garden and turf in your yard.

Q **How do I deadhead my Shasta daisies? It looks like they are dying. Are they done for the season?**

A Your Shasta daisies will bloom almost the entire season if you deadhead them. That means snipping off the spent blooms once a week or so. Just snip back to the top set of leaves below the dying flowerbud stem. If you look closely you may already see new buds emerging.

Q **When is the best time to separate and transplant Shasta daisies?**

A Early spring is the best time to divide and separate Shasta daisy, but it is an extremely tough perennial and can be moved or divided almost any time of year. Avoid dividing it during hot, dry periods of midsummer, however. Shasta daisy usually needs to be divided every few years to maintain its vigor. If the central portion of the clump begins to die out, it's a good indication that it's time to divide the plant. Dig up the entire clump, then slice through it with a sharp spade to make new plants. As long as the division has at least one healthy shoot and attached roots, it should grow in its new location.

Speedwell

Q **I am having trouble with my blue spike speedwell. It is in an area that gets partial shade. It is growing well but is drooping. Should I stake it? Also, would it be a good idea to pinch off the top leaves?**

A It sounds as though your plant (*Veronica spicata*) may not be getting enough light. Speedwell survives in part shade but does best in full sun. You can pinch back your speedwell in spring—it may grow more compact. If you pinch back in summer, though, you may remove developing flowerbuds, which would prevent your plant from blooming. Your speedwell might also be getting too much fertilizer. With excess fertilizer the shoots aren't as strong and are more likely to flop.

Thyme

Q **I would like a foolproof groundcover to plant on a rocky hillside in the full sun.**

A Thyme (*Thymus* spp.) is one of the best groundcovers for dry, sunny sites. There are many varieties to choose from. Lemon thyme (*T.* × *citriodorus*) has lemon-scented foliage. 'Aureus' has green foliage with gold edging. Creeping thyme (*T. praecox*) has purplish pink flowers. Woolly thyme (*T. pseudolanuginosis*) produces fuzzy leaves.

Toad Lily

Q **I have a garden bed that only receives a couple hours of afternoon sun. Do you have any recommendations for perennials to plant there that will bloom late in the season? It really needs some late-summer color.**

A Toad lily (*Tricyrtis*), pictured below, is a good choice for late-season bloom in a semi-shady site. Some varieties begin to bloom by midsummer and continue until fall. The flowers resemble small orchids.

Yucca

Q **We have a three-year-old yucca plant. It did not flower last year and seems not to be flowering this year. Please help me.**

A It sounds as though you are growing *Yucca filamentosa*, also called Adam's needle, which has a basal rosette of straplike evergreen leaves. It prefers full sun and well-drained, relatively dry soil. It can take five years for its tall spikes of creamy white flowers to appear, so patience may be all that is required for your yucca to bloom. After blooming and fruiting, the rosette dies, sending up side shoots, known as pups, that make new plants around the former base. When your plant finishes blooming, you can trim off the flower stalk, or you can leave it and enjoy the interesting seedpods.

Q **I just purchased a yucca, and the care instructions say that it likes average to sandy, well-drained soil. What if I don't have a sandy spot for planting yucca in my flower garden?**

A Yucca prefers dry to average well-drained soil in full sun. If the soil doesn't drain well, the plant may suffer from rot problems. If you have clay soil, yucca isn't a good plant for your garden. Instead, try it in a container or a raised bed filled with well-drained potting mix. If you have average soil, your yucca may do all right if you avoid overwatering it. Planting it on a sunny, south-facing slope may help create the dry conditions that it enjoys.

 For more ideas on shade garden design, check out our online story at *bhg.com/shadegarden-design*.

Planting Bulbs

Q I don't have much space, but I would like more bulbs in my garden. Can I plant more than one kind of bulb in the same area?

A Layering bulbs is a space-saving technique that many gardeners take advantage of. To do it, select large bulbs, such as daffodils, and also small bulbs, such as grape hyacinths. Once you've made your choices and are ready to plant, put the large bulbs in the ground as usual. Then add soil and plant the small bulbs. Leave at least 1 inch between the top of the bigger bulb and the bottom of the smaller bulb, for best results. Follow recommended planting depths for each type of bulb.

Q I love all the color that bulbs provide in the spring and summer. Are there any I can plant for fall color?

A Here are some good autumn-blooming choices. Autumn crocus, including *Crocus speciosus* and several other species, are wonderful fall bloomers. Colchicum (*Colchicum*) is sometimes called autumn crocus but isn't a crocus at all, though the two plants do share a strong resemblance. Lily-of-the-field (*Sternbergia lutea*) produces crocuslike yellow flowers in autumn. Hardy cyclamen (*Cyclamen hederifolium*) has wonderful shield-shape leaves that are frequently patterned or mottled with silver or light green. It has pink blooms that are often fragrant.

Q Last fall I planted a bulb garden. Now, however, I have to move away. The bulbs have already started to bloom, but I don't want to leave them here. Is there any way I can take my bulbs with me?

A Trying to move spring-flowering bulbs in bloom risks killing them. It's best to make arrangements with the new owners of your home to allow you to come and dig the bulbs later in the year, after they've gone dormant. If you can't move the bulbs later, think of the garden you planted as a contribution to an area where you used to live, knowing you made it a more beautiful place for everyone who's still there to enjoy.

Q My bulbs didn't come up, so I dug them and found that most of them were mush! What causes that?

A The most likely reason for rotten bulbs is that your soil doesn't drain well. Most bulbs require well-drained soil; otherwise, they will suffocate and rot. If planted too late in the season, bulbs may fail to develop roots before the soil freezes. Lack of snow cover may allow cold to penetrate deeper than usual and lead to frozen bulbs that rot. Another possibility is that you planted bulbs that aren't fully winter-hardy in your area. If they can't withstand the cold temperatures, they will die and turn to mush.

Storing Bulbs

Q **I have about 200 spring bulbs that I wasn't able to plant in fall. Should I plant them inside now, save them until next fall, or throw them away?**

A I'm sorry to say that you have few options. Planting them in spring is a waste of time. Depending on the type of bulbs, you could pot them and put the pots in a cool, dark location for 12 to 15 weeks to force them into bloom over the winter. An extra refrigerator is an ideal spot to give the potted bulbs their artificial winter.

Q **I bought some summer-flowering bulbs this spring. The package said to dig them up before winter. When and how do I do that?**

A Carefully dig the plants after the foliage dries up or is killed by a light frost. Cut back stems to 2 inches. Then shake the bulbs free of soil, leaving any remaining stems and foliage in place. Do not wash the bulbs. Lay the bulbs on paper and allow them to cure (dry) for a few days in a shady, well-ventilated spot at about 60 to 70°F. Store bulbs in dry peat moss, perlite, or vermiculite at about 50 to 55°F. Periodically check the bulbs during storage and remove any damaged or rotting material.

Bulb Foliage

Q **I love spring bulbs, but I don't like the ugly fading foliage. Are there other plants I can grow to cover it up?**

A You can solve this problem in a couple ways. The first is to plant spring-blooming perennials that put on a good show at the same time as the bulbs. Favorites include ajuga (*Ajuga*), pasque flower (*Pulsatilla vulgaris*), and periwinkle (*Vinca minor*). Your other

choice is to plant perennial partners that come into their own after the bulbs, so you have an extended season of interest. Small perennials that bloom later include coralbells (*Heuchera*), bellflower (*Campanula carpatica* or *C. portenschlagiana*), or leadwort (*Ceratostigma plumbaginoides*).

Q **How long must I wait to cut back the dying foliage on my spring-flowering bulbs?**

A Allow the bulb foliage to die down naturally before you cut it back. As long as the leaves are green, they're producing photosynthates that build the bulb for next year's bloom. Removing or braiding foliage too soon will weaken the bulbs and lead to their decline.

Allium

Q Due to utility work, I had to dig up a section of my garden. I have many alliums that were budded and close to bloom. Is there a way to save these until fall to replant?

A If your allium bulbs (below) are close to blooming, they need to be in the ground to grow. Success with transplanting the bulbs while they are ready to bloom will be questionable, but if you will lose the bulbs anyway, you might try growing them in containers with potting soil. Allow them to bloom out. Keep the foliage actively growing until it dies down naturally. Next fall, plant the bulbs in your new garden. Expect the bulbs to take several years to recover from this drastic treatment.

Q Can you grow allium from the seeds they produce from the flowerheads?

A The answer is yes and no. It truly depends on the variety. If it's a hybrid like 'Globemaster', the seedlings that result won't come true to type. They may be similar, but you might end up with something quite different from the parent. But if it's a species such as drumstick allium (*A. sphaerocephalon*), you can easily grow them from seed. In fact, many types of alliums, such as drumstick allium, chives (*A. schoenopraesum*), and garlic chives (*A. tuberosum*) will spread on their own, often to the point of becoming weedy.

Q Do allium bulbs have to be lifted after the growing season?

A Allium bulbs don't need to be lifted. In fact, they'll do best if you leave them undisturbed in the ground.

Amaryllis

Q I have amaryllis in pots on my front porch receiving morning sun. I usually put them in the cellar for the winter and bring them up in March and start watering them. This year and last, they did not bloom. How can I get them to bloom again?

A It sounds as though your amaryllis bulbs aren't storing enough food to rebloom. I also think you are giving them a little too much time in the basement. Here are some tips that should help your plants rebloom. First, make sure the plants get enough sunlight on your porch to recharge—at least 6 hours of direct sun a day. The plants require fertilizing when they are up and growing. Use a liquid houseplant fertilizer once or twice a month at half the recommended strength. Keep plants moderately moist until their leaves begin to yellow in late summer. Then stop watering completely. Bring your bulbs back inside before the first frost and store them in a cool, dark spot. After about 2 months, remove the dead, dried leaves. Repot the bulbs in fresh potting soil, if necessary, and water thoroughly. Once top growth begins, move the pots to a sunny window. Flowers should appear about 6 weeks after replanting.

Q My amaryllis bloomed wonderfully. Can I get it to bloom again now?

A Amaryllis bloom only once a season. However, many amaryllis send up at least two bloom stalks. (The older the bulb, the more blooms it can produce.) Only small bulbs put up just one stalk per season. Although the foliage isn't particularly attractive when the plants aren't in bloom, many gardeners feel that it's worth tolerating for the spectacular show when the plants are in bloom.

Calla Lily

Q **I have never planted bulbs. My husband gave me three calla bulbs but no instructions on what to do with them. How and where do I plant callas?**

A Callas (*Zantedeschia*) are adaptable; they thrive in the ground or in containers. To plant them in a container, fill a large pot with good-quality potting soil and set the rhizomes about 4 inches deep. Water well and place the pot in partial shade. Callas accept sun or shade but do best in a location that gets bright, filtered light. Because they are tender, do not plant them outside until all frost danger has passed. You can also easily grow callas directly in the garden. Select the same growing conditions and plant them at the same depth as though you were growing them in containers unless your garden has heavy soil. In that case, plant them only 2 to 3 inches deep.

Q **Do calla lilies need to be dug up for the winter, or can they be left in the ground? When is the best time to plant them?**

A Calla lilies will overwinter outdoors in Zones 9–11, but in most places they need to overwinter indoors. If you've grown the plants in pots, you can simply move the pots inside to a dark location for the winter without having to dig them up. Just repot them in fresh soil in spring. If you've planted them in the garden, dig up the rhizomes at the end of the growing season. Store them in a cool, dry location until next spring. The plants are sensitive to frost, so wait to plant them until all frost danger has passed.

Q **Can you give me some suggestions on how to grow a calla lily?**

A Calla lilies do best outdoors in a partially shady location. They like to be slightly moist but not constantly wet. They are frost-tender, so if you live where you get frosts you'll need to dig up the rhizomes and store

them indoors over winter. Also, they only bloom for part of the summer so don't be surprised if they stop blooming.

Q **My calla lilies develop seedpods after blooming. Can I plant these pods to get more callas? Last year I didn't do anything with them, and this year I have calla lilies everywhere.**

A Like most bulbs, calla lilies are best propagated vegetatively through their underground structure. If conditions are right, seedlings of calla can sprout in your garden from the previous year's seedpods. However, the seedlings will take several years to reach blooming size. Callas spread easily by their underground stems, and that's the best way to increase these plants. Divide rhizomes in late summer or early fall after digging them up for overwintering or in spring before you set them in the ground.

Canna

Q I am in search of information on the correct way to separate my canna bulbs.

A In the fall, after frost lightly blackens their foliage, dig the clumps, and hose them down to wash away the soil. After they dry, place them in a loose mix of sawdust or perlite and store in a cool, dry, dark place for the winter. (If you live in Zone 7 or warmer, you don't have to do this.) In spring, after frost danger has passed, take a sharp knife and simply cut the root mass into pieces, making sure each piece has at least one or two "eyes" or growth spots. If you want to divide a plant that's already growing, dig it, and cut it the same way. The best time to do this is at the beginning of the season before the plant puts on much growth.

Q I have several large cannas in a container. Do I need to remove the bulbs from the container, or can I just cut them back and move the container into my garage?

A You can store cannas directly in pots over winter as long as the pots remain above freezing. If the garage falls below freezing, the canna rhizomes could be damaged. Their ideal storage temperature is approximately 50°F.

Q I planted some cannas for the first time this year. Do I have to dig the bulbs up at the end of the season or can I leave them in the ground for next season? I have also noticed that they have some seedpods developing on them. What are they for?

A Unless you live in Zone 7 or warmer you should dig cannas for winter; they won't survive in the frozen ground. Wait until frost nips or kills the tops, then dig them. Compost the tops and gently work the soil off of the tubers. Wrap them in newspaper or store them in closed paper grocery bags in a cool, dry place. A cool basement is ideal. The seedpods are just that—seedpods.

Some people deadhead cannas so they won't waste energy producing seed, but that's optional. Cannas are generally propagated by dividing the tubers, not by seed.

Q I saved canna bulbs from last year and have now potted them indoors to start them. How long will it take for them to sprout?

A Start cannas indoors 4 to 8 weeks before you want to plant them outdoors. A firm healthy canna rhizome should show new growth in 2 to 3 weeks.

Crocosmia

Q I have a plant called 'Lucifer', but I don't know a thing about it. The leaves look like gladiolus foliage, but the plant has red flowers. Do you know what the name is? Is it a perennial?

A Your plant is a variety of crocosmia. Its resemblance to a gladiolus is correct—both plants are members of the iris family. 'Lucifer' crocosmia is hardy in Zones 6–9. Plant crocosmia in full sun and well-drained soil. In northern ranges of Zone 6, cover the plant with several inches of mulch in winter, just after the soil freezes, to protect the overwintering corms.

Daffodil

Q My favorite yellow-and-white daffodils haven't bloomed in two years. How can I get them to bloom again?

A If daffodils (*Narcissus*) are not divided regularly, the bulbs become too crowded to bloom well. Dig your daffodils in early autumn and plant the bulbs farther apart so they're no longer crowded. Pull individual daughter bulbs from the mother bulb and replant each one in its own hole. I find it helpful to mark where the bulbs are while they're in bloom, so I don't forget where they are after they go dormant.

Q My double yellow daffodils grow well, but the flowers won't open unless I give them a hand. Otherwise, they dry up and turn brown. What's wrong?

A Most varieties of double daffodils are sensitive to a condition called bud blast. It typically occurs when temperatures warm quickly in spring. Unfortunately, there's nothing you can do to prevent it; if the weather warms up fast, you'll need to help open the buds by hand if you want to see flowers. Bud blast is more likely when daffodils are overcrowded. Divide and replant the bulbs if this is the case.

Q I've noticed that after my daffodils bloom, they develop pods on the stems. Can I collect and sow the seeds to start new plants?

A Those capsules you see at the daffodil stem tips are seedpods. Many experts recommend removing them so the bulbs have more energy to produce flowers the following year. You can collect this seed, but if it's from a hybrid bulb, the plant that grows from the seed may not look like the parent. Once the pod ripens, break the hard, dry seeds from the pod. Sow them immediately in a sheltered spot in the garden or in a cold frame. Though they'll germinate the following spring, you'll have to wait 5 to 6 years from seed to bloom.

Q I'd like to try my hand at forcing bulbs. I've heard it's not hard. What is a good bulb to start with?

A Probably the easiest bulb to force is the paperwhite narcissus. In fact, these bulbs are so willing to get growing that they're likely to begin as they sit on your kitchen counter. Pot them in soil or anchor them in a container of pebbles filled with water to the base of the bulbs.

Dahlia

Q How do I plant dahlias?

A Plant the tubers once all danger of frost has passed. Choose a location with fertile, well-drained soil that gets at least six hours of sun a day. For each tuber, dig a hole about 12 inches wide and 8 to 10 inches deep. Tall plants may need to be staked. To avoid damage to the roots, drive a stake into the ground now, a few inches from where you plan to plant each bulb or tuber. Place a tuber horizontally in the bottom of each hole with the eye pointing upward and the roots down. Cover with 2 inches of soil. Shoots should emerge from the holes in about two weeks. As the tall varieties grow, tie them to their stake with twine.

Q I recently purchased a beautiful dinnerplate dahlia. Unfortunately, it froze during a cold spell. Can it be saved?

A The extent of damage to your dahlia depends on how cold it got and for what length of time. If the plant was nipped by frost, it will probably come back; but if it was completely frozen, it may be too late to save it. If the roots didn't freeze, the dahlia should be able to grow from the roots. At this point, the best option is to wait and see if it resprouts. Be prepared to protect them from frost on chilly nights.

Q When do I plant dahlia tubers? I've heard conflicting advice about the right time to plant in my area.

A Plant dahlia tubers after all danger of frost has passed. When it's safe to plant tomatoes, it's safe to plant dahlias. If you'd like to get an earlier start, you can plant the tubers in a pot and start them indoors. That way you'll have a sizable plant to set out when the weather warms. In Zone 8 or warmer, you may leave dahlias in the ground over winter.

Grape Hyacinth

Q My grape hyacinths are starting to come up now. Will they bloom this autumn instead of spring?

A In many areas, grape hyacinth (*Muscari* spp.) naturally sends up foliage in autumn and then again in spring. It's normal and doesn't mean they'll bloom out of season. Look at them as good "marker" plants. If you plant them among your spring-flowering bulbs, their fall foliage reminds you where to dig.

Hyacinth

Q My hyacinth blooms have turned brown. Should I pick them off or just let them be?

A Removing the brown flowers on hyacinth has a couple advantages. Not only do the plants look better afterwards, it also prevents the plant from wasting any energy making seeds.

Q I have some hyacinth bulbs that I bought last fall and didn't plant. Is it too late to plant them now?

A If the ground is already frozen, it's too late to get those bulbs planted outdoors. If they are still firm and healthy, you could try to force them into bloom by potting them in a container and keeping them refrigerated for a couple months to simulate winter cold.

Q My potted hyacinth stems are very heavy so they have drooped to the counter. What causes them to do this?

A Hyacinths that have been forced to bloom indoors often get top-heavy and fall over. You could place a stake by each stalk to hold it upright. Also, the cooler the room, the less likely they'll get too tall and topple.

Iris

Q After blooming, do you cut iris greenery down to 2 or 3 inches or do you leave it as is?

A Cut off the bloomed-out flower stalks, but leave all the foliage intact. The plants needs the leaves to build up reserves for blooming the following year.

Q During the summer months, the leaves on my bearded irises turn brown and shriveled. I don't want to cut them back since they are in a prominent area in the front yard. What can I do to remedy this problem?

A To a certain extent, browning leaves on bearded iris during the summer months is just a fact of life. The older leaves will always turn brown and dry up regardless of what type of care they receive. You can pull or trim off these browning leaves as they develop to keep the plants looking tidier. If the browning problem is severe, you may have a fungal leafspot problem on your irises. Do they first develop yellow or brown splotches before turning completely brown? If so, spraying a fungicide may help prevent the excessive browning.

Q I bought reblooming irises, but they don't flower. Does it take a couple years before they start blooming?

A If you planted the irises late last fall, they may not bloom until late summer at the time of their second cycle of bloom for the year. Also, be sure they are in a sunny spot and that you didn't plant them too deeply. Iris rhizomes do best when they are just barely under the surface of the soil.

Q How often should you divide irises? When is the best time to divide them?

A You can divide iris from mid- until late summer. Either will give them plenty of time to establish new roots before winter. You can cut the leaves to just 6 inches above the rhizomes, and they will grow back lush before the frost kills them back. Space plants 12 to 18 inches apart and position them so that a part of the rhizome is visible at the soil surface.

Q Which irises grow in the shade?

A No irises grow well in shade. Siberian iris (*I. sibirica*) can take a little shade, but won't reliably bloom unless it gets at least six to eight hours of sun a day.

Lily

Q I received several pots of lilies for Easter, including Oriental lilies and white Easter lilies. Can these be replanted so they will bloom next spring?

A Carefully plant your lilies—Oriental and Easter—outdoors at the depth they normally grow (it varies depending on the lily type), and they should bloom when they usually would next season, which is in summer. (Most lilies are forced into spring bloom by greenhouses.) Often, Easter lilies will bloom again in the garden the same summer you plant them.

Q My lilies never have a chance because red beetles eat holes in the leaves. How can I get rid of the beetles?

A It sounds as though your lilies are victims of the lily leaf beetle. Handpick the larvae and adults, or spray plants with a neem-based insecticide once a week from mid-April to September. The sluglike larvae are the main leaf eaters. Look for adults and larvae starting the third week of April. Also look for cylindrical yellow-orange eggs on the undersides. Crush the eggs or pinch off the leaves with eggs on them.

Q I was told that Asiatic lilies bloom most of the summer. Mine don't seem to bloom very long. What is their normal bloom time?

A Lilies (*Lilium*) are a garden staple, but they're not long-blooming. Each plant blooms once a year, and the flowers last a couple weeks. However, with careful selection you can grow a range of lilies that have varying bloom times to provide flowers through most of the summer.

Q I would like to purchase some lilies that are good for cutting and bringing indoors in a vase. I cannot tell the difference between Asiatic, hybrid, and Oriental types.

A Asiatic hybrid lilies bloom the earliest, beginning in late May or early June. They range from 2 to 5 feet tall and bloom in red, orange, yellow, white, and every shade of pink. Oriental lilies (*Lilium orientalis*) follow right along, blooming June through August. They range from 3 to 6 feet tall and bloom in pink, white, yellow, and combinations of those colors. Trumpet lilies range from 4 to 8 feet tall and may need to be staked in the garden. They bloom in July and August. Finally, Orienpets are new crosses between Oriental and trumpet lilies. Bred for durability and a broad range of colors, they bloom in July and August. For the bulbs to survive in your garden and return next year, leave at least half of the stem when you cut the flowers.

Tulip

Q This spring many of my tulips did not bloom. Any ideas why?

A They may be growing in too much shade, or you may have removed the leaves before they turned completely brown and were done manufacturing food to build up the bulb for the following year's bloom. The truth is, however, that most tulips wear out quickly. Some hybrid tulips have more of a propensity for repeat performance. Try 'Charles', 'Christmas Marvel', and 'Couleur Cardinal'. Triumph tulips, such as 'Don Quichotte', and lily-flowered 'Aladdin' and 'Ballade' should bloom reliably for more than one season. Others offering potential for a second season of color include tall Darwin hybrids such as 'Golden Parade', 'Oxford', and 'Holland's Glory'.

Q How and when do I cut my tulips to put them in a vase?

A For the longest-lasting flowers, cut tulips in an advanced bud stage, when the blooms are still closed but the color of the flower is evident. Floral preservative is not necessary for tulips, but replace the water every day, making a fresh cut at the base of the stem. Tulips prefer cool room temperatures. Avoid combining tulips with paperwhite narcissus or daffodils, which exude a gummy sap that can shorten tulips' vase life. If you like to bring tulips indoors as cut flowers, consider growing 'Angélique', 'Don Quichotte', 'Attila', 'Queen of Bartigons', 'Pax', 'Yokohama', 'Ile de France', 'Negrita', 'Leen van der Mark', 'Prinses Irene', or 'Rosario'.

Q When I dug my tulips to separate them, I found many baby bulbs. How do I take care of them so I can have tulip flowers again?

A Saving those baby tulips may not be worth the effort. The daughter bulbs will not likely develop into plants as beautiful as the parent. In most regions, tulips decline in vigor over time rather than increase in

size. However, if you live where tulips grow exceptionally well and you are a bit adventurous, you could replant the daughter bulbs and see what you get. Space the bulbs as you would full-size ones. It will likely take several years for them to reach blooming size.

Q I have a large garden box outside my apartment where I planted tulips last fall. The blossoms are just opening. I'm moving in a few weeks—the box is too large to move and it doesn't have a bottom. How can I transplant the tulips without damaging them?

A You're best off leaving the tulips for the next owner to enjoy and planting new ones for yourself this autumn. The best time to transplant them is in late summer or fall. If your bulbs did recover from being transplanted, they probably wouldn't bloom well anyway, because hybrid tulips bloom well for only a couple years.

Q My tulips don't last. After the first spring, only one sickly leaf comes back. What am I doing wrong?

A Switch to species or botanical tulips, which naturally come back each year and even grow bigger and bigger clumps. *Tulipa turkestanica, T. tarda, T. saxatilis, T. clusiana, T. marjollettii*, and *T. humilis* are good choices for garden use. Botanical tulips are hybrids that remain close to the original species. They include Kaufmanniana, Greigii, and Fosteriana tulips. Species and botanical tulips are generally smaller in bloom size than other tulips, but they can be just as spectacular.

Q I garden in California. I was told that if I want tulips, I have to put the bulbs in the freezer and plant them in December. Is this right?

A The information you received was not entirely correct. In your area you need to order bulbs that are already chilled. Many bulb companies sell prechilled bulbs for gardeners who live in climates such as yours. You can plant those bulbs directly into your garden for springtime blooms.

Q I have a flowerbed with tulips currently growing. I would like to plant summer perennials in the same bed. Do I need to dig up the bulbs and replant them in the fall? How do I care for the bulbs I dig up?

A You may be able to plant perennials in and around your tulips without having to dig them up. How closely are the tulips growing to one another? If there is space enough to stick a trowel between the tulips, you can slip in small perennials from 4-inch pots or smaller. If the tulips are growing close together, you may be able to plant perennials just outside the cluster of tulips. If you decide that the tulips need to be dug to place perennials where you would like them, wait until the bulb foliage dies down naturally. When the leaves are mostly yellow, dig up the bulbs and store them in a cool, dry location until normal planting time this fall.

Q I bought some tulip bulbs last fall and potted them. They're now poking through the soil. Can tulips be grown in pots, or do I have to transfer them to the ground?

A Forced bulbs—potted in the fall, chilled for several weeks and moved to a warm, bright location to bloom—don't do very well when transplanted into the garden. The forcing process zaps their energy reserves so much that they usually just fizzle out in the garden. Most gardeners just toss their forced bulbs into the compost pile after they bloom. If you do want to try to move them to the garden, start by nurturing them right after the blooms fade. Water with a water-soluble fertilizer, and keep the foliage green and healthy for as long as you can. After the foliage has died back on its own, transplant the bulbs into the garden.

Rose Types

Q Can you explain to me the differences in types of roses? I get confused by the terminology.

A Here's a quick guide. 1. Hybrid tea—classic rose form, 2. Hardy shrub rose—cold hardy, disease resistant, 3. Rambler—long canes; bloom just once per year, 4. Climber—more controlled than ramblers; may repeat bloom, 5. Groundcover—low spreading form, 6. Miniature—compact plant with repeat bloom, 7. Tree rose—grafted onto an elongated stem, 8. Grandiflora—cross between hybrid tea and floribunda, 9. Floribunda—many-flowered rose; usually low-growing.

Q What is the difference between a floribunda rosebush and a grandiflora rosebush? I think I have a couple in my yard. When I planted them I thought that they were hybrid teas.

A Floribunda roses are compact, hardy roses with flowers in clusters that mostly bloom throughout the season. They are very suitable for smaller spaces. Examples include 'Betty Prior' and 'Iceberg'. Grandifloras are similar but with clusters of larger flowers, generally borne on long stems, because hybrid teas are in their parentage. The plants tend to be tall with upright growth. They also bloom over a long season. Examples include Cherry Parfait and Glowing Peace.

Hybrid Tea Roses

Q We live just north of Atlanta. I received Black Magic and 'Sweet Freedom' hybrid tea rose plants as a gift. I planted them in full sun, amended the soil, and fertilized them. Now what? I have heard they need pruning and some TLC.

A Hybrid tea roses are really quite easy if you start with disease-resistant plants, grow them in a sunny spot with well-drained soil, and feed them regularly. The best time to prune is in late winter or early spring before new growth begins. Take out the dead wood, thin shoots, or crossed branches. To keep roses healthy, feed with a slow-release fertilizer after the plants break dormancy. Mulch your plants thoroughly to preserve soil moisture and eliminate weeds. Black Magic and 'Sweet Freedom' have good mildew resistance. Even so, spray with fungicide if you have problems with leaf spots in hot, humid weather.

Q I would like to plant hybrid tea roses in my backyard, but I've heard that their roots are strong and may penetrate my basement if the plants are near the house. How far from the house should I plant my roses?

A Fortunately, what you've heard about the rose root system isn't true. How far away from your home to plant roses depends on the size of the full-grown rose plant. If your roses mature at 5 feet wide, for example, plant them no closer than 3 feet from your home (so they don't grow against the side of your house).

Q My husband trimmed our hybrid tea roses to 7-inch stumps. I am afraid he ruined them and they won't grow anymore. What do you think?

A Severe pruning should not kill a healthy rose, though it may affect its overall appearance and bloom production. New canes will grow and replace the old ones that your husband removed. In fact hybrid teas usually wind up with bigger but fewer flowers after such a severe pruning. Just make certain that new shoots arise from above the graft union (the swollen knob near the base of the plant). Shoots from below the graft union will not be the same variety as the top of the plant. If no graft union is present, the roses may be growing on their own roots, in which case any shoots that develop will be identical to the existing shoots.

Shade Roses

Q I just brought a house with a medium-size front yard. I have a tree sitting in the middle of the yard. I love roses and the cottage garden look. Can I plant a garden around the tree?

A Roses, even the new shrub roses, take some work. Roses also do poorly in the shade, so if you're thinking about planting under a tree, roses would not be a good choice. Most varieties will do best with at least six hours of direct sun daily.

Q Can you tell me about the shade tolerance of Flower Carpet and 'Zéphirine Drouhin' roses? How much sunlight do they need?

A Some roses bloom with only four hours of sunlight and withstand the fungal diseases that flourish in shade. Growing roses in partial shade, however, can decrease the number of blooms. 'Zéphirine Drouhin' and Flower Carpet roses offer some degree of shade tolerance, but both bloom better and are more disease-resistant in full sun. *Rosa glauca*, an old-garden rose, also tolerates shade. It's grown more for its purple-tinged grayish leaves and red stems than for its five-petaled pink flowers and handsome red hips.

Q What would be the best rose to grow in a shady spot?

A Most roses need at least six hours of direct sun per day to grow and bloom successfully. However, some tolerate slightly less light. The minimum amount of sun needed is generally four hours of direct sun per day. If your garden gets less than this, consider something other than roses. Roses that are most tolerant of shade are the hybrid teas Blue Moon, 'Christian Dior', 'Fred Edmunds', Garden Party, and 'Swarthmore'. Other shade-tolerant roses include 'Alchymist' shrub rose, 'Etain' rambler, and most hybrid musk roses.

Q I have three rose bushes. They only bloom twice—in spring and summer—and do not have many blooms. What am I doing wrong?

A Do you know what kinds of roses you're growing? Some naturally bloom all season, while others have only a spring and late-summer flush. This is perfectly natural behavior for many shrub roses and old-fashioned roses. In fact, many old-fashioned roses bloom only once a year. Are your roses growing in full sun and rich soil? If not, they won't bloom well.

Rose Pests

Q The stems on my rose bush are turning brown one by one and eventually dying off. I cut one that was starting to do the same thing and discovered a black termite-looking insect eating a hole inside of it. What can I do?

A Several cane borers can attack roses. Because they are protected inside the cane, surface application of an insecticide such as Sevin will not affect them. The best control is to cut out affected canes, cutting back the stem until the pith is white and healthy looking. New growth will resprout from below the cut.

Q How can I get rid of the black spots on my rose bush and keep them from coming back?

A Black spot on roses is a fungal disease that occurs when humidity is high and temperatures are warm. Some varieties of roses are more susceptible to the disease than others. Fungicide sprays are available that can be sprayed on roses to prevent the disease, but as long as environmental conditions are right for the disease, you'll have to continue spraying if you have susceptible roses. If you wish to not have to spray, it might be advisable to replace your roses with varieties that are blackspot resistant.

Q I have a large rose bush that something has stripped most of the leaves. Only the very top of the bush has any leaves or blooms left. What is doing this and how do I stop it?

A If the skeleton of the leaf remains in place, it may be rose slugs devouring the leaves on your rose. These pests are actually a type of sawfly rather than a true slug, but they resemble small, brownish slugs as they feed on the leaves. Most common insecticides will control them. Check to make certain that they are still on the leaves before spraying, however. They often have completed their feeding cycle by the time you observe their damage.

Q My rose bushes develop swollen bumps underground and on the stems as well. Should I dig them and replant resistant varieties? They do bloom, but as soon as they are open they lose the petals.

A These unusual growths are crown galls, tumors caused by a bacterium in the soil. Galls can spread from plant to plant through open wounds. Crown gall often doesn't bother the overall look of the plant, but it can cause less bloom or stunt the plant. If bloom is severely affected, you may want to remove the plant and grow something else there. Do not plant roses in this location because the bacterium is still in the soil. Always sterilize your pruning shears if you cut or prune your infected plants before you use them on another rose to prevent spreading the disease.

Planting Roses

Q I bought bare-root roses and planted them this spring. They were very slow to grow leaves, and when the temperature reached the high 90s they lost their leaves. The stems look dead. Could the rootstock still survive?

A If the canes are brown, your plants are probably dead. If they are still green and pliable, there is some chance that they might recover. If they snap or break easily, the plant will likely not come back next year. If this was a grafted rose and a new shoot arises from below the graft union, it won't be the same variety that you bought. If it is an own-root rose, shoots from below-ground will be true to type.

Q How deep should I plant the new bare-root rosebush that I just purchased?

A The correct depth to plant your bare-root rose depends on your climate and the type of rose. The graft union (a swollen, knobby part of the stem) on roses is easily damaged by cold. In warm-winter climates, place the graft union at or slightly above the soil line. In cold climates (where winter temperatures dip below zero), plant the graft union 1 to 4 inches below the soil line. Plant own-root roses (those without a graft union) with the crown at soil level in warm climates and a few inches below soil level in cold climates.

Q I purchased a bare-root rose this spring. It transplanted well, leafed out, and had a few beautiful blooms. The area of planting receives sun for a minimum of eight hours and is incorporated into a perennial bed with a few other shrub roses. What can I do to encourage blooms for the remainder of this season?

A If your rose's leaves look healthy, it's likely that your plant is putting its energy into getting established in your garden so it can perform well next year. If this is the case, it's actually a good thing it's not blooming a lot because that means it should do better next year than if it flowered profusely this year.

Q I just planted a 'Mister Lincoln' rose that is not looking too good. I got it real cheap at a discount store. It had something on it that looked like wax.

A The problems might be associated with the price you paid. Cheap plants aren't always a bargain. That being said, roses sold as bare root (which is a fine way to start roses) often have a wax coating on them to help keep them from drying out. The wax is fine and should fall off naturally. It takes some time for bare-root roses to sprout, so have patience. The key is how healthy the specific plant is that you purchased. If it's a weak plant, it may never thrive.

Q I am planning to move my well-established 'Cécile Brunner' rose to a better spot in my yard. What is the best way to do this?

A The best time to move an established rose is in the very early spring while the plant is still dormant. Dig as large of a rootball as you can to minimize shock to the plant. Use a sharp spade, and dig a circle around the plant about 18 inches from the crown of the plant. Try to keep the soil ball intact as you move the plant. If the plant is dormant, it won't hurt it if you break some roots during transplanting. And, of course, remember to move it to a sunny spot and plant it at the same depth that it was growing.

Q I bought several potted roses. How should they be planted?

A To plant container-grown roses, start by digging a hole at least twice as wide as the pot. Slide the rose out of its container. If it has circling roots, loosen them with your fingers or slice through them with a knife. Position the rose at the proper depth as for bare-root roses. (See page 106.) Backfill the hole with soil, water well, and apply mulch.

For more details on how to plant container-grown roses, go online at *bhg.com/rose-planting*.

Q Can I plant roses in containers? If so, what sizes and types of containers are best?

A Virtually any rose will grow in a container. The container's size is more important than the type. Small floribunda roses can grow in containers as small as 16 inches in diameter. Large shrub roses will require 24- to 36-inch containers. Roses in containers require more attention. If you live in an area that experiences subzero temperatures, protect your roses during that time. "Plant" the containers somewhere in the yard during winter, or move the potted roses to a protected place, such as an unheated garage, until severe cold has passed.

1

2

3

4

Fragrant Roses

Q **In the past I've bought roses and have been disappointed by their lack of fragrance. Can you tell me which ones would have good fragrance?**

A The roses pictured here are reliably fragrant. Try some of these favorites: 1. 'Fragrant Cloud', 2. Gertrude Jekyll, 3. Honey Perfume, 4. 'Mister Lincoln', 5. 'New Dawn', 6. 'Radiant Perfume', 7. Heritage, 8. 'Fragrant Plum', and 9. 'Sheila's Perfume'.

Rose Companions

Q We have three rosebushes, and I was wondering if there are any types of flowers that will grow well with them.

A Roses look especially nice when you plant shorter companions to help disguise their leggy stems. Dianthus or a clumping variety of catmint such as *Nepeta* 'Walker's Low' would be lovely. You could also plant some spring-blooming bulbs this fall, such as daffodils, to bring some color to the bed early in the season. Later, the dianthus and nepeta foliage will help hide the fading daffodil foliage.

Q How can I keep my roses from looking bare near the ground?

A Many roses naturally lose their bottom leaves as the season progresses. You can plant low-growing plants along with roses. Here are some excellent companion plants for roses: annual geranium (*Pelargonium*), catmint (*Nepeta*), lady's mantle (*Alchemilla mollis*), leadwort (*Ceratostigma plumbaginoides*), perennial geranium (*Geranium*), pincushion flower (*Scabiosa*), pinks (*Dianthus*), and threadleaf coreopsis (*Coreopsis verticillata*).

Rose Hips

Q My roses have developed little red apples. They look pretty, but are they normal? And are they edible?

A What you've observed are fruits of the rose, called rose hips. As you noted, they look similar to small apples, which are close relatives of roses. Rose hips are edible, as long as you haven't used pesticides on your plants. They are a good source of vitamin C. However, most gardeners prefer to enjoy the hips for the color they add to the fall garden.

Q Which roses develop the most colorful rose hips?

A For late-season interest in southern gardens, few roses can top 'Old Blush' (Zones 7–9), a beauty with semidouble lilac-pink blossoms and large orange hips (a climbing form is also available). In the North, 'Frau Dagmar Hartopp' (Zones 2–9) flaunts reddish hips the size of tiny apples, along with foliage that turns reddish purple and golden. Most Rugosa roses also reliably develop colorful hips after they finish blooming.

Disease Resistant Roses

Q I'd like to grow roses, but don't want to have to fuss with them. What are some good low-maintenance types to plant?

A Here are some good disease-resistant varieties of roses to consider: 1. Blushing Knock Out, 2. Carefree Sunshine, 3. Carefree Beauty, 4. Rugosa rose, 5. 'William Baffin', 6. 'Bonica', 7. 'Gourmet Popcorn', 8. 'The Fairy', 9. 'Gemini', and 10. 'New Zealand'.

Shrub Roses

Q **Do you ever have to deadhead self-cleaning roses? Please tell me which roses are self-cleaning.**

A Most of the new landscape/shrub roses don't require deadheading to look good. You can trim off the old flower clusters or shape the stems by pruning if you wish, but it's not necessary. This applies to the Knock Out Series, Easy Elegance Series, and Flower Carpet Series of roses. Two with good fragrance are High Voltage and Sweet Fragrance.

Q **I have winter-hardy roses and this year one of them has shot up a stalk or branch higher than the plant. It is about 2 inches in diameter and extremely thorny. Is this a sucker that should be removed?**

A You don't say what variety of rose this is, but this sounds like a sucker from the rootstock. Most grafted roses are grown on wild rose rootstock, and sometimes they will develop a huge sucker shoot as you have described. It is best to remove this vigorous shoot to prevent it from overwhelming the entire plant.

Q **I have recently purchased the Pink Double Knock Out Roses. It seems they aren't nearly as hardy as the Double Reds. Is it because they are new? I have seen many at stores that look spindly and weak.**

A New shrubs of Pink Double Knock Out rose certainly can be spindly. However, once they become established, they will be fully as vigorous as the Double Red or the original Knock Out rose. Mine that are a couple of years old are quite robust this year. New ones that I just planted this spring are still weak.

Low-Maintenance Roses

Q **I like roses but have heard that they require a lot of care. Are there some you would recommend that are easier to grow than others?**

A Few gardeners have the time to inspect daily for diseases and pests. Top candidates for busy gardeners include the heirloom Gallicas, which flower before Japanese beetles attack. Consider the Rugosas as well. *Rosa rugosa* (Zones 2–9) bears single magenta blossoms throughout the season. Hybridizers have responded to the call for maintenance-free roses with some breakthrough introductions. Flower Carpet (Zones 5–9) boasts large clusters of blossoms from spring through fall on tidy shrubs that are useful as groundcovers. Award-winning Knock Out (Zones 5–9) blooms continuously and asks for nothing in return.

Pruning Roses

Q **Do you cut back roses in late April? If yes, please describe how to do it.**

A For cold parts of the country, spring pruning generally works best. Cut out anything that looks dead. If you're not sure, start at the tip of the rose cane and start snipping a few inches at a time until the centers of the cut stems look white instead of brown. Shorten the living canes to give the plant a compact, balanced appearance. Try to cut back to outward-facing buds to create an open center that will allow sun into the whole plant and provide better air circulation.

Q **How do I prune a rose plant properly to get larger and more flowers?**

A Rose pruning advice depends on what kind of rose you're growing and what climate you're in. Many shrub roses don't require any pruning to bloom well, for example. And in Northern areas, roses die back in winter, so most of the pruning is removal of dead growth. But as a general rule, prune out weak or damaged stems. And deadhead your roses. After the flower fades, cut the stem back to a leaf that's divided into five leaflets. That will encourage the rose to bloom more.

Q **I have two old-fashioned roses and a rose tree that are more than 85 years old. The rose tree base looks almost petrified, but the tree keeps growing like crazy and has hundreds of blooms constantly. But it is only growing thick on one side and thinning on the other. Any suggestions?**

A As roses age, they sometimes start to decline. One way to rejuvenate them is to cut them back severely. In the case of a tree rose, you can cut the top "ball" back to within several inches of the trunk to force new growth from near the graft union above the trunk.

Q **I have quite a few roses that flower most of the time in my Florida garden. When should I trim them?**

A Your roses are probably hybrid teas or floribundas that have been grafted onto the roots of *Rosa × fortuniana*. Highly resistant to nematodes, this rootstock produces vigorous plants that do best when pruned lightly but continuously all year, with a more serious pruning to shape the plants in August. Prune out any old brown canes, then shape the plants as needed, removing up to half of the branches. When black spot or other diseases attack and get out of control, some south Florida gardeners also remove all remaining leaves at this time. However, there is no need to remove healthy leaves. Follow this pruning with a good feeding, which will energize the plants to bloom well all winter.

Climbing Roses

Q Why don't my climbing roses bloom? They are tall but have not set one bloom.

A Climbing roses bloom on what horticulturists call "old wood." That means they bloom on last year's canes rather than this year's. Harsh winters that kill the canes also wipe out a season's worth of blooms. At least you can find comfort in all of this year's tall, healthy canes because you know they'll be the bloomers next year. Protect the canes during the winter by bundling and wrapping them in burlap or burying them shallowly in the ground. Uncover them in early spring and fertilize.

Q I have a climbing rose that has only bloomed one time at the bottom of the plant. It just grows taller but does not bloom. Is there anything I can do to promote blooming?

A Your climbing rose blooms on old wood. When the canes don't survive winter, you won't get any blooms. The reason you had that one season's blooms so low on the plant is because the canes winterkilled back to that point. Provide as much winter protection for the canes as you can. You may need to pull the canes from their support, bundle them together, wrap them in burlap, and mound soil and mulch around the base to protect the crown over winter.

Q I have to move my climbing rose and it's so big I'm not sure the best way to move it or what time of year to move it.

A The best time of year to move your climbing rose is in late winter/early spring just as growth is beginning. To make the move easier, you can cut the canes back to within 1 foot of the ground just before you move it. That will cut off the blooms for one season, but should help the plant survive its transplanting better. Dig up as much of the root system as practical, and move it to its new location.

Q We live in Oklahoma and want to plant some climbing roses on a trellis. Any ideas which ones would be the best?

A Roses have strong regional adaptations. In your area, the only climbers to have gained the EarthKind designation by Texas A&M University are Climbing Pinkie and *Rosa* 'Mutabilis', also known as Butterfly Rose. Other climbers may grow well for you, but these will prove to be the lowest maintenance while still putting on a wonderful flowering show.

For ideas on how to landscape with roses, check out our online story at *bhg.com/rose-landscaping*.

Winter Rose Care

Q I've had a beautiful hybrid tea rose bush for nine years now. We had a rough winter. The canes are black. There is a small amount of green on some of the very bottom of the canes. Can it be saved?

A If your rose still has green on the canes, even if it's just at the base, the plant can come back, but it won't be as large as it was last year. Hybrid teas can be difficult to maintain over time in a northern climate because even with winter protection they can experience dieback. Cut off the black dead portions of the canes and wait for new shoots to develop from the green portion of the stem.

Q What must I do to get my roses to survive the winter in northern Michigan? Do I cut the stems back to the ground?

A The surest way to get roses to survive winter in northern Michigan is to bury them in a trench. Dig a trench right next to the main stem, large enough to accommodate the branches when they are tied up into a bundle. Tip the plant over into the trench, pinning

down with wires if necessary, and bury with soil. Do this after temperatures have gotten down into the low 20s several times. Mulch over the soil with shredded leaves. Alternatively, you can mound up soil around the stems, and mulch heavily. Using this method, the roses will likely die back to the mulch line. Piling snow as additional mulch also helps protect the plant. Avoid pruning the roses severely in fall. That practice decreases their winter hardiness.

Q I had three rosebushes in planters last summer. I brought them into the house for the winter but they dried up. I ended up putting them outside in January and covered them with sheets. Do you think they will survive?

A You roses almost certainly died. It's almost impossible to keep roses over winter inside the house. If you moved them outdoors in January, they would not have been ready for the drastic change in temperature. The best way to treat container roses in the north is to plant them in the fall before the ground freezes. If you like, you can even sink them in the ground, pot and all. Just provide winter protection for them with soil and leaves.

Q How do I go about protecting my roses for winter?

A In areas where winter temperatures dip into the single digits or colder, protect roses after temperatures drop into the low 20s a few times but before the soil freezes. Tie the canes together, then mound soil 8 to 12 inches high around the base of the plants. Cut long canes back to 30 to 36 inches to prevent them from whipping in winter winds. Enclose the mounded plants with a wire cage or fence and cover the soil mound with leaves, straw, or evergreen boughs after the ground freezes. Alternatively you can use mulch instead of soil. Mound up the mulch 15 to 18 inches around the plant's base. You could also use a wire-mesh cylinder or a rose cone filled with mulch.

Heat-Tolerant Roses

Q **It gets really hot here most of the summer. What kinds of roses will grow best in the heat?**

A Roses are rather climate specific in their performance. Some that generally do well in hot areas: 1. 'Oklahoma', 2. 'Harison Yellow', 3. Pink Double Knock Out, 4. 'Royal Highness', 5. Brandy, 6. 'French Lace', 7. St. Patrick, 8. Sunset Celebration, and 9. 'Mister Lincoln'.

Rose Propagation

Q **I kept a commercial cut rose in tap water for over a week, and it is putting out leaves. Is it possible to encourage this to root or graft it to an existing plant?**

A Getting your rose cutting to root is simpler than grafting onto a rootstock. Cuttings should be between 6 and 12 inches long, so it's up to you whether or not to make two cuttings out of your rose stem. Snip off and throw away the bloom immediately. Dip the cut stem(s) in rooting hormone and poke them into a vermiculite-perlite mix to root. Suspend a clear plastic bag over the pot to maintain high humidity for your cutting(s). Put the pot in bright, indirect light and mist the cuttings at least once a day. Roses can be slow to root, so give them a couple months to send out new growth.

Q **How do you root roses?**

A The answer depends on what kind of rose you want to root. Some grafted roses are grown on other rootstocks because they don't thrive on their own roots, so it makes little sense to try to root them. But many older types of rose—especially ramblers and climbers—can be rooted easily by burying a section of cane from the mother plant under the surface of the soil, leaving the tip of the cane above ground. Eventually roots will form on the buried section of the cane and you can separate it from the mother plant.

Cut Flower Roses

Q **I received a dozen roses for my birthday. How can I keep them alive?**

A Recut the stems underwater to prevent air bubbles from reducing the water uptake, and use a floral preservative, which you can find at a florist shop, in the vase water. Floral preservative contains a type of sugar for nutrition, an acidifier to lower the pH of the water, and a compound to inhibit the growth of bacteria. Change the water every day if possible. If you recut the stems underwater every few days, your roses will live even longer.

Miniature Roses

Q **I received a miniature rose bush for Valentine's Day. It bloomed nicely for a few days, but now it appears to be dying. I want to plant it outside in my garden but don't think it will make it until spring. Is there anything I can do to keep it from dying?**

A Keep your rose in a cool location. Warm, dry conditions indoors are hard on miniature roses. Also, keep it slightly moist at all times and in the brightest spot you have—a south-facing window is ideal. Remove the decorative foil wrap to ensure excess water can escape. It can be difficult to keep a miniature rose plant forced into bloom during winter in good condition until spring. (Watch for spider mites. They often attack plants stressed from dry conditions indoors.) Unless the plant dies, however, it will often rebound once planted outdoors when the weather warms. Remember to gradually harden off the rose as you move it outdoors.

Lawn & Landscape

Seeding

Q **May I seed bare spots in my lawn in the summer?**

A Summer is not a good time to reseed a cool-season lawn of bluegrass or fescue. These types of grass seed grow best in the spring and fall when the weather is cool and moist. You can certainly try, especially if the spots are small and you can water them daily, but the best time is in the early fall. Summer-seeded grass also doesn't always develop a very deep root system. If you plan to seed a warm-season grass such as buffalograss or zoysia, early summer is the best time.

Q **We have a new home in need of a lawn. We're trying to decide which method of starting a lawn to go with, seed or sod. We need to keep the price down. What do you suggest?**

A If budget is the primary factor, seed your new lawn. Time of year can also be a consideration. Cool-season lawns, such as bluegrass and fescue, are best seeded and established at the end of summer (late August and September in most of the country). Early spring is another favorable time to seed cool-season lawns. In midsummer to late fall, sodding usually provides better results. Warm-season grasses such as Bermudagrass, buffalograss, and zoysiagrass survive best when established in late spring or early summer.

Q **I am in the process of reseeding my backyard with grass seed. What can I do to neutralize the dog urine problem that I have from two dogs. Is there a product on the market that can do that, or I am left with redoing this process year in and year out?**

A The product that is most effective in neutralizing dog urine is plain water. The burn from urine comes from the uric acid salts. Diluting the salt with water by leaching the affected area is the best solution. You may

also be able to train your dogs to go in a certain area of the yard so that only a small section is affected.

Q **What type of lawn grass will thrive in clay?**

A Turf-type tall fescue is a good choice for clay. This tough grass tolerates slightly wet conditions and will form a dense stand of turf. Thoroughly till the soil before seeding. While you are at it, work in compost, well-decomposed organic matter, or peat moss to improve the soil structure and promote drainage. Any amendments you add now will help the grass thrive later.

Need help calculating how many square feet of lawn you plan to seed? Try our online square footage calculator at *bhg.com/square-feet.*

Q Two areas in my yard have become overgrown with brush, weeds, and prickly bushes. I have been trimming them back every year, but I would like to get rid of all this stuff and make a nice lawn area that I can use. How do I do this?

A Follow these steps for success.
1. Cut, chop, or dig out all the weeds and brush. You may need to spray the area once or twice with a brush killer.
2. Prepare the soil as you would any other lawn.
3. Select the right grass for your new lawn.
4. Spread grass seed or sod over the area.
5. Maintain it regularly. Mow frequently, control weeds, water as needed, and fertilize regularly.

Q How do I start a new bluegrass lawn?

A Spread seeds uniformly over the surface and lightly rake them in so that most of the seeds are just barely covered with soil. To get more uniform seed distribution, calculate how much seed you need for the area, and spread half of that amount in one direction (for example east to west). Then spread the other half at right angles to the first half (north to south).

Q How long will it take for new grass seed to sprout? Does it need to be watered every day?

A Grass seed can take several weeks to sprout depending on temperature and moisture conditions. To ensure good germination, keep the area watered well for the several weeks it takes for your lawn to become established. This may mean watering lightly several times per day if conditions are dry and windy. If you plant seed, it's helpful to apply a thin layer of mulch to hold in moisture.

Seeding

Q **Do you need to do anything special to the soil before seeding grass?**

A If your soil is sandy or claylike, add a layer of organic matter, such as well-rotted manure or peat moss. Till the top 6 inches of soil to incorporate the organic matter. After tilling and amending the soil, smooth it with a rake to create a good seedbed.

Q **The grass seed at the garden center comes in mixtures of various kinds of grasses. Do I need cool-season or warm-season grass? Please give me a good place to start.**

A Cool-season grasses grow best in northern lawns. The grasses grow vigorously in spring and fall but

may go dormant and turn brown in the heat of summer. Cool-season grasses commonly come in blends or mixtures. Warm-season grasses are adapted to growing conditions in the South. They grow well in hot weather but go dormant in cool weather. Before buying grass seed, call your cooperative extension service. Experts there can recommend the best type of grass for your locale and situation.

Q **Someone said that I should use a mixture of grasses for my new lawn. Why do I need a blend of grasses? Why not just buy one kind and be finished with it?**

A Blends and mixtures improve a lawn's appearance. A seed blend contains several varieties of the same kind of grass, such as three types of Kentucky bluegrass. A blend usually gives a lawn a more uniform look. A seed mixture combines several kinds of grasses—for example, Kentucky bluegrass, tall fescue, and perennial ryegrass. Such a combination promotes a green lawn all season.

Q **I want a grass that doesn't need frequent cutting. Can you help me find one?**

A A few grasses need only infrequent cutting. One is buffalograss. It's a drought-tolerant native species, best adapted to the Central and Southern Plains. A slow grower, it may need cutting only a few times a season, depending on how much you water it. (The more you water, the faster it will grow and the more often you'll need to mow it.) Other options are most of the fine-leaf fescues, which are commonly sold for shady lawn areas. These grasses grow only about 6 to 8 inches tall. Some people let them grow all season without mowing. They create a natural look that substitutes well for a traditional lawn. You will need to mow them at least once a season, though, to get rid of the buildup of dead grass.

Q Can I spray weed killer on a recently seeded lawn? I don't want the weeds to take over.

A Lawns seeded in spring tend to get weedy, which is one reason why autumn is the recommended time for planting cool-season grasses (such as Kentucky bluegrass and tall fescue). Before applying an herbicide, wait until new turf grows enough that it requires mowing three times. Young grass plants are sensitive to weed killers and may be damaged if the herbicide is sprayed too soon.

Q Every time I mow, it seems a new rock pops up. My property is on a ledge, which makes planting anything very hard. What can I do to have a nice lawn?

A If you were to start over from scratch, you could hire someone to run a rock picker through the soil before planting. Short of seeding a new lawn, you could gradually add a sand/compost topdressing mix. A little each year will over time build up the turf and root zone. Or you could bring in a bunch of topsoil, raise the grade by several inches, and then replant an entirely new lawn. That's a lot of work but solves the problem in one shot.

Q We're planting a new bluegrass lawn from seed. Can we put down weed killer at the same time that we seed to prevent crabgrass and other weeds from taking over?

A Crabgrass weed preventer is best applied in spring just before the crabgrass seeds germinate. When you plant a new lawn in spring, you cannot use weed preventer because it would also stop your grass from germinating. That's one reason why fall is a better time to start a lawn from seed—most weeds don't germinate and grow at that time of year, so you can get your lawn going without having to fight so many weeds.

Hydraulic Seeding

Q What are the advantages and disadvantages of hydraulic seeding a lawn instead of simply sowing the seed without mulch?

A For very large areas where watering to keep the seedbed moist is difficult, hydraulic seeding is a boon to getting a lawn started. The thin covering of mulch sprayed on with the seed holds in moisture and helps keep the delicate seedlings from drying out too much when they're at the critical stages of germination and establishment. The primary disadvantages are that it is more expensive to hydraulic seed and that seeding a large area may require a professional with hydraulic seeding equipment. (Small patching jobs can be done without special equipment.)

Lawn Repair

Q We recently purchased a home with an extremely poor lawn. I would like some suggestions on repairing the lawn, which includes multiple forms of weeds, tree seedlings, and tree stumps. Or should we just start from scratch and have someone come in and skim off the top 1 to 2 inches of the so-called lawn and start new?

A Skimming off the surface isn't a good idea; along with the weeds, it would remove the most valuable topsoil. Start by wiping out the weeds. You can kill everything with Roundup. Dig out stumps or hire a tree company to grind them out. A week after spraying, you can reseed. Sprinkle bare grass seed over the entire area, and then top it lightly with the expensive seed-and-green mulch mix. It is a good idea to apply a starter fertilizer with your seed, as long as your lawn doesn't slope toward a lake or river.

Q We have large bare spots in our lawn. The grass around them is very green and healthy. What should we do to fix this problem?

A You can overseed the bare spots in your lawn. Lightly work up the soil in the bare spots and seed with a patch repair kit available at nurseries and garden centers. It might take some investigative work to determine what caused the dead patches. It would be good to determine the cause so that you can correct the problem if necessary to prevent it from reoccurring.

Q I used to have the lushest, greenest lawn in the neighborhood; now, I have brown patches. Any advice on whether I should try to repair the spots or start from scratch?

A Repair the patches if:
1. More than 75 percent of the grass is fine-bladed, deep green, and soft to the touch.

2. The grass is slightly thin overall but is generally in good shape.
3. The lawn turns brown uniformly and only during the most severe droughts.
4. Weeds, browning, and insect or disease damage occur in small, isolated patches.

Q My lawn looks bad with lots of weeds and dead patches. Do I need to start over?

A Replace the whole lawn if:
1. The yard is more than 50 percent bare, weed-infested, or diseased, or has additional problems.
2. New bare spots occur because conditions have changed; for example, trees have increased shade.
3. Your lawn is a patchwork of three or more colors or textures of grass.
4. Water puddles on the lawn after a rain.
5. The grass wilts and takes on a grayish cast if not watered regularly.

Overseeding

Q Last year I had new sod put in my front yard. The sod was really beautiful, but now grubs have eaten my entire lawn! The grass just rolled back like a carpet. I've taken care of the grubs, but I don't know what to do now. Should I sod again or should I seed? What do you recommend?

A Wait until the cooler months of late summer or early autumn before you do anything. Then try overseeding your lawn. If the grass seed doesn't fill in the spots by next May, you may have to resort to new sod. To prevent an infestation from happening again, watch your lawn for grubs. (Some products, if used in June or July, do a good job of preventing future grub infestations.) Use chemical or organic grub killers if another infestation occurs.

Q How do I revitalize a lawn filled with crabgrass, clover, thatch, and bare spots? What steps should I take and in what order?

A Assuming you want to preserve whatever grass is still there, the first thing to do is spray broadleaf weed killer on the lawn to get rid of the clover and other broadleaf weeds. Most herbicides require a waiting period of at least several weeks before it is safe to reseed with grass.

Q How do I overseed my lawn to get it to fill in again?

A Here are the general steps to follow. In September rent a vertical mower (or verticutter). Go over your lawn with it a couple of times. Then rake off all the debris (thatch). Use a drop spreader to overseed with whatever kind of grass you have. After you sow the seed, go over your lawn one more time with the verticutter, but this time set the blades to barely nick the soil. This will mix the seeds into the soil, which helps them germinate. The

lawn should become well-established during the fall and winter. Water as needed, and fertilize at least once in fall, no more than a month after you seed.

Q What is the best type of lawn grass that will stay green most of the year along the Gulf Coast?

A Warm-season grasses grow best along the Gulf Coast. All warm-season grasses tend to turn brown in cold weather. However, many homeowners and commercial lawn care firms overseed the warm-season grasses with ryegrass over winter to get a good green color through the cool months. Types of warm-season grasses adapted to your area are Bermudagrass, centipedegrass, and St. Augustine grass.

Sodding

Q We have a new home in need of a lawn. Is it better to seed or sod the lawn?

A If you can afford it, sod where you most need it and seed the other areas. Sod will become established more quickly and permit use of the area faster. Eliminate foot traffic and children's play traffic on the newly sodded areas for two weeks, then allow only light traffic for two more weeks. If you sod and seed, get grass seed of a similar mix and type so your seeded and sodded areas eventually match.

Q When is the best time to lay sod?

A You can lay sod anytime during the growing season, although spring and early autumn are best because cool temperatures combined with occasional rain help sod quickly root. If you lay sod in summer, water at least once a day for several weeks. Lay sod on a cool, overcast day to minimize plant stress. If you lay sod in the heat of summer, moisten the surface of the planting area before putting down the turf. Stagger strips in a bricklike pattern, and be sure that all pieces fit tightly together. Once the sod is in place, run the sod roller over it to eliminate air pockets. Water it immediately, then water daily (depending on rainfall), moistening the soil to a depth of 4 inches, until the sod takes root.

Q What do I need to do to get my soil ready for sodding?

A Remove twigs, stones, and other debris littering the surface. Break up soil clods that are larger than 2 inches in diameter. Fill low areas with good quality topsoil. If the soil is sandy or full of clay, work in organic matter. Take advantage of this opportunity to improve the soil; it's easy to add amendments when the soil is bare. Smooth the soil with a stiff garden rake. Finish preparing the area by compacting it slightly with a sod roller (often available through your local landscape equipment rental outlet).

Q How long will it take for new sod to get established?

A If growing conditions are good, your sod should form new roots in two to three weeks. To find out if sod has rooted, gently tug at it. If you feel resistance, roots are anchored in the underlying soil. Avoid mowing sod until it has firmly rooted.

Q Can I transplant sod?

A Absolutely! Before moving the sod, prepare the area to be sodded by removing twigs and other debris. Fill any low spots with good quality topsoil, and break up clods that are more than 2 inches in diameter. A sod cutter is easy to rent and will make the job of digging out the sod you'd like to transplant a lot easier. You can also use a flat spade to uproot the sod in small areas. After moving the sod, water it regularly until it is well-established.

Q There's a problem area in my yard where the grass has died. I'd like to patch it with sod. How do I do this?

A Prepare the soil the same way you would for a seed patch. Dig out the area 1 inch or so below the soil line so the finished patch will be level with the existing grass. Use a utility knife to cut a piece of sod the same size and shape as the area to be patched. Firm the patch into the soil, making sure the edges fit snugly into the surrounding lawn. Step on the patch to settle it, and water deeply.

Plugs

Q I'm planning a new lawn, and in my research I've read about plugs. Are plugs different from sod? Please tell me more and whether they are a good option for my lawn.

A Plugs are a good way to install Bermudagrass, zoysiagrass, St. Augustine grass, and other creeping grass species. (Plugs don't work as well for noncreepers.) Plugs are little plants with roots, leaves, and a core of soil around the roots. After you plant them and keep them well-watered, they take root and eventually fill in. The main drawback is that weeds can become a problem before the grass has a chance to fill in. Nevertheless, many people plug their lawns and do so quite successfully. Many garden centers sell plugs by the flat. The difference with sod is that it comes in solid "sheets" or rolls, and you lay it down like carpet. It gives you a solid, weed-free turf immediately. Sod is more expensive than plugs, so your budget may determine which you use.

Q I've seen grass sold as sprigs. What are they? How do I plant them in my lawn?

A Sprigs work best with warm-season grasses such as Bermudagrass, zoysiagrass, or St. Augustine grass. Sprigs are 3- to 6-inch pieces of grass stems or runners without soil. Before planting, till or dig organic matter and granular slow-release fertilizer into the soil. Smooth the soil with a rake. To use sprigs, clear the patch. Then till and amend the soil. Sprinkle the sprigs relatively evenly across a moistened bed and cover them with a thin layer of topsoil. Some sprigs won't sprout, but the roots of most will take hold. Keep the area free from weeds. Mow when the sprigs or plugs reach a height of 2 inches.

Moss Control

Q **We have a lot of green moss growing in our yard and cannot seem to get rid of it. One side of the yard is shady, but the sunny side also has moss. Any suggestions?**

A Several conditions favor the growth of moss in the lawn. Shade is one of them. But often poor drainage (possibly from compaction) that allows the soil to stay moist for long periods is another factor. In addition, low pH can sometimes favor the growth of moss over that of turf. You might start by testing your soil to see whether the pH needs to be adjusted with lime. Regardless, it would also be a good idea to core aerate the lawn and topdress with compost.

Core Aeration

Q **Our yard has a lot of clay. What can we do to make grass grow in this clay?**

A The best thing you can do is aerate. You can rent aerators, or have a service do it for you. Typically,

lawns are aerated annually, but it's even better to do it twice a year in spring and fall. That will help loosen the clay and get the grass more deeply rooted. Beyond that, keep the lawn well cared for and it will eventually take root. Clay is tough for plants to get established in, but once plants manage to take root, it's actually good soil. It holds a lot of water and nutrients.

Q **How often should I aerate my lawn?**

A A simple test tells you if you need to aerate. Use a screwdriver to probe the soil a day or so after ¼ inch or more of rain has fallen. If the screwdriver penetrates the soil with little resistance, you probably don't need to core aerate. If you have a hard time getting the screwdriver into the soil, it's time to aerate. Core aerate the lawn at least every year or two to keep it healthy and prevent the soil from becoming compacted.

Q **My lawn was sodded by the house builder and is about a year old. I've followed a lawn maintenance program, but my yard doesn't look much better than the yards that are not fertilized or maintained. Water runs off the top of the soil, and my grass seems to be growing runners on top of the soil instead of underneath. Do you think my soil is compacted?**

A You have already identified the problem: soil compaction. Compaction is troublesome in new landscapes where heavy equipment has been used during construction. Aeration is definitely the cure. All the water and fertilizer in the world are little use if the grass fails to get its roots into the ground. Most grasses are pretty tough, so you can make three or four passes (not just two) with the core aerator, a minimum of once a year (twice is even better).

Thatch

Q **After an unusually cold winter, my grass is brown. It is slowly turning green but seems to be so thick. Is it thatch?**

A A small amount of thatch in grass is beneficial, providing some cushion for foot traffic. However, if thatch becomes more than ³/₄ inch thick it can become detrimental. You can check the depth of the thatch by cutting up a plug of turf and pulling it up. If the thatch is less than ³/₄ inch thick, you don't need to do anything about it. If it is deeper than ³/₄ inch, it may be advisable to dethatch your lawn.

Q **How often should I dethatch my lawn?**

A Dethatching is recommended only if the thatch is ³/₄ inch or more thick, not as a routine practice. If thatch is really thick and has gotten out of hand, aeration won't solve the problem. That's when you bring in a dethatcher (also called a power rake or vertical mower). But if thatch is more or less under control, it should stay that way with regular aeration. Spring and fall are both good times to aerate cool-season grasses.

Q **I have a new house and lawn that was sodded a year ago. This spring we have several large areas in the lawn that are thin and seem to have quite a bit of thatch. Does the lawn need dethatching already?**

A It's unlikely that thatch would build up to a depth of ³/₄ inch or more in that short time. However, some types of grass, such as zoysiagrass, tend to develop thatch more quickly than others. And if you fertilize heavily, you may be promoting thatch development. A good precautionary measure to help prevent thatch buildup is to core aerate every year or two. Pulling some soil up to the surface helps decay the thatch layer from above as well as below.

Mowing

Q We let our bluegrass lawn grow very long, like field grass. It's very thick and lying down on itself. Should I mow it now or let it go dormant in this condition for the summer? I am concerned that it might mat down and smother itself.

A As you now realize, Kentucky bluegrass should not be allowed to become so tall. Mow it right away with your lawn mower at its highest setting, then rake the extra growth off the top of the turf. Lower the setting and mow again a few days later. Try not to remove any more than one-third of the grass height at any one mowing.

Q Would it be better to add my grass clippings to a compost pile or use them as a mulch in the garden?

A Avoid using grass clippings as mulch immediately after pesticide application and mowing. They should be composted first. Most widely used lawn-care insecticides and herbicides break down rapidly during composting or become tied to the organic matter in the compost.

Q Is it a good idea to bag my grass clippings?

A The best option is to leave the grass clippings on the lawn. The clippings will gradually break down, improving soil conditions and reducing the need for fertilizer. Clippings usually do not contribute to thatch buildup, because they decompose readily. If the clippings form clumps on the surface of the lawn, you may need to rake off the excess, or mow again to evenly distribute the clippings.

Q Since I purchased a home a couple years ago, I mow every Saturday morning. Is this regular schedule OK? Or can you mow too much or too little?

A It's a pity to break your weekly routine, but if your grass is growing, you need to be mowing. Each grass type looks best and stays healthiest at a certain height. Letting the grass grow too long can be just as damaging as giving your lawn a too-short crew cut. Avoid cutting more than one-third of the leaf blade. If these guidelines work out to your mowing every Saturday, fine; however, weather and growth spurts may require adjusting your schedule.

Q How short can I cut my grass so that I won't need to mow as often?

A Scalping the lawn (cutting it too short) is a common mistake. In the cooler spring and autumn weather, you can cut grasses shorter. But when temperatures start topping 80°F, let the grass get taller. It won't have the same "perfect" appearance as a lawn cut shorter, but plant health will more than make up for style. Taller blades shade the ground, conserving moisture and preventing weed seeds from germinating. And cutting the grass shorter doesn't slow its growth rate. It will need mowing just as frequently.

Q It's late October and my lawn looks like it needs mowing again. If I don't mow it, will it cause any problems for the grass?

A Leaving long grass blades going into winter can encourage disease development and other problems. The grass mats down under snow, creating an ideal place for fungal diseases such as snow mold to develop and for the protected runways of voles and mice. As long as the grass is actively growing, mow it to its proper height. Growth usually slows down after a few hard freezes, when temperatures consistently remain cold.

Q I need a new lawn mower and would like to be environmentally friendly. What are my choices?

A The old-fashioned manual (reel) lawn mower has been updated for modern times. It's now made of lightweight but sturdy materials; some models feature pneumatic tires, easy-to-use blade-height settings, and adjustable handle length. The reel-mounted horizontal blades give a superior cut by slicing the grass against a lower, rigid bar. Spectacularly quiet and pollution-free, these mowers are especially useful for small lawns. Battery-powered walk-behind lawn mowers are appropriate for lawns of more than 4,000 square feet. Some battery-operated models have the capacity to cut up to two-thirds of an acre on one charge.

Q I have a suburban lot with a beautiful expanse of lawn. I say I need a riding mower to keep it uniform and healthy. My wife says a rider is overkill for the amount of grass we have. Is there such a thing as too much mower?

A For a large expanse of lawn, self-propelled walk-behind models are particularly helpful. Today almost all power lawn mowers are designed as mulching mowers, with a special blade that suspends clippings long enough to be cut several times before they fall back onto the lawn as a mulch. A riding mower may be justified for the convenience it offers: cruise control, joystick steering, zero turning radius, and even a drink holder. Most can pull a cart—useful for mulching and other gardening applications. Larger, more powerful models can handle aeration, tilling, and snow-removal attachments.

Fertilizing

Q **When is the best time to fertilize my St. Augustine grass?**

A St. Augustine grass loves heat, so the hottest times of the year are when it will grow the most and need the most nutrients. Apply a nitrogen-rich turf fertilizer in late spring, then every eight weeks or so until late summer. After that, St. Augustine grass has little need for fertilizer because it goes dormant in fall and winter. The same is true for other warm-season grasses such as Bermudagrass and zoysiagrass.

Q **I have been having trouble making my grass grow in the front yard. I water it as much as I can, but it still has very little patches of green. What can I put on it?**

A Have you had a soil test done to see what the soil may be lacking in the way of fertility? That's the surest way to apply the right mix of fertilizer for the needs of the grass. The soil test should also tell you whether the soil is lacking in organic matter. If the soil is extremely compacted or poor, it will be difficult to grow good grass regardless of how much water and fertilizer you apply. It may be most helpful to add organic matter.

Q **I put down fertilizer with weed killer in the spring and fertilizer with crabgrass killer in July, but I still have lots of crabgrass in my lawn. Why?**

A Most fertilizers with weed killer contain an herbicide that affects only broadleaf weeds such as dandelions. Applying crabgrass killer in July is too late. Although the crabgrass usually isn't easily seen until late summer, it can start germinating as soon as the soil temperature reaches the mid-50s. That means that the crabgrass killer should be in place in early spring (often about the time that the forsythias bloom).

Q **I live in South Texas and have a carpetgrass lawn. I recently fertilized with a brand-name fertilizer and watered it as directed. The grass blades are turning a light yellow-green color. Can you help, please?**

A Are you sure that the product was just fertilizer and that carpetgrass was listed as a type of turf safe to use the product on? Many turf fertilizer products are combinations of fertilizer and weed killer, and the labels look a lot alike. Weed killer often turns turf yellow, especially if it's during a summer hot spell. The good news is, turf usually bounces back pretty quickly. As long as the product is labelled for your type of grass, and you followed all instructions (including temperature and moisture condition cautions), yellowing should not occur.

Interested in organic lawn care? Check out our on-line story on organic lawn care basics at *bhg.com /organic-lawn.*

Fertilizer

Q Is there a commercial fertilizer that I can purchase that is safe for pets? I want to plant grass in my backyard, but I have a dog and want to find a safe fertilizer.

A If you practice good application and cleanup procedures according to the label directions, any fertilizer should be safe for your pet. The label will tell you how long to keep pets off treated areas, which is usually as long as it takes to dry. Many fertilizer companies also offer organic forms of fertilizer, which are slow-acting and much less likely to cause fertilizer burn.

Q My boyfriend first cut the grass low then put down a layer of fertilizer. Now there are stripes of dark green throughout the yard. How can I fix this?

A Striping in the grass is a common result of uneven fertilizer application. It's possible that the spreader wasn't working properly, or that some areas of overlap got a double dose of fertilizer. You have several options. You could apply more fertilizer to the light green areas only, but it's difficult to get an exact match to the stripes. Or you could wait for the color difference to fade; it will even out eventually.

Q When should I fertilize my bluegrass lawn?

A The most important time to fertilize bluegrass and other cool-season grasses, such as fescue and ryegrass, is in late summer and fall. Late-season fertilization encourages root growth to help the grass survive winter. Avoid fertilizing during the heat of summer unless you irrigate regularly to keep the grass actively growing.

Q When should I apply a winterizer fertilizer to my lawn?

A Winterizer fertilizers are usually applied in late October or early November to cool-season lawns. To take full advantage of the effects of winterizer fertilizer, you should also make a fertilizer application to your lawn in early September. The early fall feeding stimulates root growth. If you plan to make only one fertilizer application in fall, the best time is late September or early October.

Watering

Q I keep watering my lawn, but it continues to look sickly and spindly. We're expecting more drought conditions again next summer. What can I do to keep my grass alive?

A Most lawns love water, but you can spoil them by providing too much too often. Overwatering keeps the top layer of soil wet and encourages grass to develop weak, shallow roots, leading to quick injury in hot, dry weather. Infrequent but deep watering stimulates deep root growth and provides the best results. Excess water also leaches nutrients from the root zone and may lead to nitrogen deficiency.

Q Is it OK to water the yard in the middle of the day when it's hot?

A Rapid evaporation makes watering in the middle of the day wasteful. The best time to water grass is in the early morning. Wind and heat are usually minimal at this time, and the majority of the water will reach the lawn. Plus, the grass leaves and stems will dry by midday, lessening the chance of disease. If you must water during the middle of the day, the grass will not be harmed. Many top-notch golf courses spritz their greens on hot days to reduce heat stress on the grass.

Q I have an expanse of lawn mixed with plots of shrubs and flowers. I'll be installing a watering system that will allow me to apply different amounts of water at different intervals. How much water should I program the system to apply?

A The amount of water that plants need depends on many factors, including the growth habit of the plants, soil type, nearby plants, and climate. It's nearly impossible to assign a standard amount of water to apply. If you can, group plants with like water requirements on the same programmable zone.

Q We have a large backyard with a slope. We have underground irrigation, so our yard gets plenty of water. Our lawn does well and looks nice with the exception of the slope. By early summer only weeds grow, and there are bare patches everywhere on the hill.

A Almost always, the problem when lawns fail to grow on hills is lack of water penetration into the soil. The water runs downhill before it can soak in. The cure for this is to increase the frequency of irrigation and decrease the run times. In other words, instead of (for example) watering three times a week for 20 minutes each time, water six times a week for 10 minutes each time.

Q I live in California. I recently purchased a newly built home with a tall fescue lawn. My lawn seems to be yellowing slightly all over. Because the landscape is brand new I think they set the sprinkler to go on every day. Is my lawn getting too much water?

A In your climate, with its high heat and low humidity, even established lawns need water 2 to 3 times a week. A new lawn would need it daily for the first month or so, then cut it back to every other day. Every other day is a pretty typical schedule for watering lawns in your area. The yellowing may very well be due to nitrogen deficiency, which could be worse due to all the watering, which leaches nutrients out of the soil. Try applying fertilizer at half the package rate and see if the lawn responds with better color.

Q How much water should we put on our new sod?

A The amount and frequency to water new sod depends on a lot of factors, including soil type and weather conditions. Essentially you must water frequently enough so that the sod never dries out while

it is rooting in. This may mean watering twice a day if conditions are warm and windy. Apply enough water at each irrigation to wet the soil several inches deep. It will take longer to wet clay soil deeply than sandy soil, but you'll need to water more frequently on sandy soil to keep it moist. You may need to provide daily watering for a couple weeks. Then you can start cutting back on the frequency to every other day, gradually changing to twice a week and even longer time intervals.

Q I don't want to water my lawn all summer, but I do want it to survive during hot, dry periods. Can I water it just part of the time?

A Some lawn grasses are naturally more drought tolerant than others. Kentucky bluegrass and perennial ryegrass go dormant and turn brown when conditions become hot and dry. If you don't care about keeping your lawn lush and green all summer, lightly irrigate with ½ inch of water every 3 to 4 weeks to keep the roots and crowns alive. Avoid the temptation to give the lawn a soaking that could spur new growth, especially if you don't intend to continue watering. It's stressful to the grass to go in and out of dormancy. If you start watering thoroughly, continue to water thoroughly until rainfall returns to sufficient levels.

Shade

Q We live in Zone 4 and have two mature maple trees. Every spring, after the snow melts, we have no grass one-third of the way up our front lawn. We've brought in topsoil and tried many different ways to seed, but still no grass. Help!

A Maples cast dense shade and have shallow roots that compete strongly with grass for moisture. It might help to thin the branches on the maples to allow in more light. But you should also keep in mind that no lawn grass prefers shade. Some tolerate it, but even so, don't grow well in dense shade. You might be better off planting the shaded area to a shade-tolerant groundcover rather than continually fighting trying to grow grass there.

Q Our yard doesn't get much sun, and we have moss growing everywhere in the lawn. We tried treating it with a moss control product, but it comes right back. What can we do to get rid of it?

A Moss loves shade, and lawns love sun. Moss also thrives where the soil is poorly drained or compacted or low in nutrients. If the lawn is struggling, moss will get the upper hand. Prune the trees, or have some of them removed to provide more daylight. Hand rake or power rake the lawn vigorously. Aerate the soil with a core aerator. The core holes should be about 3 inches apart; it may take a couple rounds with the aerator to do a good job. Check the moss control label for application safety when there are pets on the lawn. Fertilize on a regular basis. All lawns need some sun to thrive, but you may help things along by topseeding with one of the shade-tolerant lawn mixes.

Q We have two huge oak trees in our front yard, and there is so much shade that we cannot grow grass. What type of grass seed should I use?

A There are grass-seed mixtures marketed specifically for shady conditions. But I have another idea: Why not replace the sparse lawn under the trees with a groundcover? The trick is to keep from disturbing tree roots too much. Plant pockets of plants and let them spread. To complete the natural landscape, you might include some small boulders and rocks, and intersperse them with some daffodils and crocus for spring splash.

Q I had a large portion of my backyard lawn professionally planted with grass seed in the spring. The lawn came in beautifully and died entirely a couple months later. The area is almost entirely shaded. Should I give up on grass?

A If the area is quite shaded, that is the most likely reason for failure of grass to grow. Although some grasses can tolerate shade, none grow well in dense shade. You could do some pruning to thin out the shade, or you could plant shade-tolerant groundcover that will grow well in the environment that exists.

Q I have a pine tree in my backyard, and it's turning my lawn brown. Help!

A It is tough to grow a lawn under a pine tree. Aside from the shade they cast, it seems as if they never stop producing needles, so it's difficult to keep the area raked. Many gardeners with tall trees underplant them with woodland shrubs and flowers, which generally thrive in the dry, acidic soil under pines.

Q I have a small front yard with two huge oak trees. I tried seeding grass for many years and still am unable to get grass to cover the entire front yard. What do you suggest?

A My recommendation is to try something besides grass. Even shade mixes have their limits, and if you've tried to reseed several times with no success, it would seem that your shade is more than lawn grasses can handle. Shade-loving perennials such as hosta, archangel, ferns, brunnera, and heuchera are good alternate choices that can handle more shade than grasses.

Q I planted a shade-grass mix last spring, and it came back in patches this year. How can I get this grass to spread?

A Some types of grasses, such as perennial ryegrass and St. Augustine grass, are more shade-tolerant than others. But any grass planted in dense shade will come back patchy. Rather than constantly reseeding, try an under-the-tree garden bed filled with shade-loving plants instead.

Q What type of grass mixture can I grow to have a lush lawn? I live in the Northeast, and my yard is a mix of sun and shade.

A The best solution for lawns that encompass a variety of site conditions is to plant a mix of two or three species. In your location, a mix of bluegrass, tall fescue, and fine-leaf fescues (which do better in shade) is a good idea. If the trees that are shading your lawn have low-hanging branches, you might try pruning the lowest ones to allow more light to reach the ground.

Mushrooms

Q We have mushrooms growing in our grass, and I was wondering how we can get rid of them or prevent them from growing.

A When mushrooms appear in your lawn, they are feeding on decaying organic matter near the soil surface. It may be thatch or roots from a tree or shrub that was removed. There isn't much you can do except mow the mushrooms down. Soon enough their food source will be gone, and they'll go away on their own.

Q I have been watering my lawn to keep it green. I mow on a high setting, and all was fine. Now I have mushrooms all over my backyard, even in the sunny locations. How do I get rid of or control these?

A Mushrooms are not a sign that anything is amiss. When conditions are moist for extended periods, they often show up. They do not harm the lawn. You may wish to pick them out by hand or knock them apart with a rake, if you have small children who might eat them.

Q How do I get rid of fairy rings in the lawn?

A Fairy rings are caused by a fungus that often shows up in locations where trees once grew or in lawns with lots of thatch. Typical symptoms are a ring or arc of darker-colored grass with mushrooms growing in the darkened area. Sometimes a dead patch accompanies the ring. They generally appear in spring and go away quickly. They're almost impossible to eliminate, but you can mask their presence. If the circle within the ring is more yellow than the rest of the lawn, fertilize the entire area. That will help even out the coloration and make the fairy ring less noticeable. Extra irrigation also sometimes helps, because the soil-inhabiting fungi create artificial drought conditions by sucking up extra soil moisture.

Q I am having a problem with mushrooms in my lawn. I've put down a fungicide twice and it seems to help a little, but it doesn't solve the problem. I've handpicked them, raked them, and mowed them. I think one of the roots from my tree is rotten, and someone told me that it might be the source of the mushroom problem.

A Mushrooms usually develop in cool, wet conditions. They generally disappear once dry weather returns. Your friend is right; mushrooms derive their energy from decaying organic matter. A rotten tree root could be the source. There's no chemical way to get rid of mushrooms. If you dislike their appearance, keep breaking them off with a rake and hope that dry conditions develop soon. The mushrooms themselves won't cause harm to your lawn, unless they grow densely enough to shade it.

Dog Damage

Q **The grass seed I planted in my backyard sprouted but died. This spring I seeded again and used a high-traffic seed because I have three dogs. I have been told to use lime, but nothing works. What am I doing wrong?**

A People often use lime when they plant, but it's best to hold off using it unless you know that the lawn needs it. If your soil already has a high pH, the lime can be harmful, raising the pH to a level that the grass won't tolerate. The real problem may be the heavy amount of traffic. Dogs are hard on turf. If possible, keep the dogs off the lawn while it is still young. Planting your lawn in sections is one way to accomplish this. Another alternative is sodding. It's more expensive, but it will give you an established lawn that tolerates foot traffic more quickly.

Q **I have a 4-year-old border collie who likes to run. She has created a trench run around a tree, and most of the yard is dirt. What can I do?**

A One drastic solution is to give up on growing grass and mulch the entire yard with wood chips instead. Border collies have active minds as well as active bodies. They need plenty of exercise and plenty of mental stimulation. Give the dog a task. Teach it new tricks. And by all means, tire it out with long walks and runs if you can. You can also put up some barriers. Raised beds, edging, shrubs, and large pots can all be used to change the dog's route. Another idea, although costly, is to put down one of those driveway grids, made of plastic or concrete, where the grass grows through the gaps in the grid. The structure really helps take the wear and tear out of grass.

Q **I have a long narrow yard that has been overrun by my black Lab and weeds. I want to lay sod but don't know how to do so and keep it from being destroyed by the dog.**

A If your dog has free run of your backyard without supervision, you won't be able to have a perfect lawn. Dogs and perfect lawns don't mix. Always exercise your dog away from the yard every day and, when it's in the backyard, be there to supervise. If you must leave the dog in the backyard when you aren't home, install a dog kennel where the dog can stay safe but won't spend the day tramping your turf. Otherwise, it's probably best to install gravel or bark mulch instead of grass.

Q **Our dog burns up our grass with his urine. We tried everything with no results. I heard that the only way to remedy this is to go out and spray water each time he urinates, which is not possible for us. Any suggestions?**

A Sadly, there's not much you can do except keep the dog off the lawn or loosen your standards on how you want your lawn to look. If your dog has free run of your yard, you will never have a perfect lawn. You could try fixing up a corner of the yard and encourage the dog to go only in that spot. With training, over time, this is possible. But, if you just let the dog loose and don't dilute the urine with water, your lawn will continue to develop spots.

Grubs

Q I have moles in my lawn. If I control the grubs in my lawn, will the moles leave?

A It's a common misconception that controlling grubs will get rid of moles. Moles do eat grubs, but the No. 1 food source of moles is earthworms, not white grubs. Moles will eat almost any insect larva they come across while digging through the soil. Rather than assuming that grubs are to blame because you see moles digging in the lawn, check to see how many grubs are present. Unless your lawn has more than 10 grubs per square foot, chemical treatment for grubs is likely unnecessary. Trapping is the most reliable way to eliminate moles. Harpoon or choker traps are effective.

Q I suspect I have a problem with grubs in my back lawn. Could you tell me how I would know if grubs are the problem and suggest a way to combat them?

A Grub-infested lawns are most apparent in late summer when sod starts dying in patches. If you dig in the soil, you'll find white C-shape grubs. There are many effective grub-killing products on the market, under brand-names such as Bayer, Grub Ex, and Grub-B-Gon. If you prefer a more natural approach, there are organic products, as well. For example, some garden centers and mail-order companies sell a type of microscopic worm (nematode) that attacks and kills grubs.

Q I planted grass, and it is starting to die. I have done everything to keep it from getting any worse. Could it be grubs?

A If grubs are a serious problem, you can often peel back the grass rather easily, because they have chewed off the roots. The surest way to sample for grubs, however, is to cut out a piece of sod and count how many grubs you see in the soil. If fewer than ten per square foot are present, you probably need not treat for them.

Q Is there any natural control that gets rid of grubs? Our yard is covered with birds that are eating them.

A Some gardeners have had good success with natural products such as milky spore; others have had less luck. One reason is that milky spore disease targets Japanese beetle grubs; if other grub species infest your lawn, milky spore disease won't affect them. Other natural products that can provide some control, though not as consistently as a chemical control, are diatomaceous earth and beneficial nematodes, which are sold under the name Grub-Away.

Insects

Q **I have bugs in my lawn that are feeding on the roots. How can I get rid of them?**

A The first step is to identify the insects that are feeding on the roots of your grass. Are they wormlike grubs? Or something else? You'll want to make certain that the insects you see are actually causing the damage, and not simply feeding on dead tissue caused by some other problem. A cooperative extension entomologist or lawn care professional may be able to help you identify the insects. From there, you can choose an appropriate insecticide, if necessary.

Q **Insects that look like termites are spreading their tunnels among our grass blades. What can they be and what will kill them?**

A The insects you describe are almost certainly not termites, which do not feed on lawns. One possibility is sod webworms; they make tiny burrows in lawns from which they emerge to feed, mostly at night. Regardless of what your insects are, a general-purpose insecticide—Sevin, for example—will probably eliminate them. However, it's worth a trip to the cooperative extension service to find out for sure what the problem is. Take a sample of the damaged turf and an actual specimen of the bug, if you can find one. Experts will be able to identify it and make a recommendation.

Q **Do you have any suggestions for the lumps that appear in my yard? We have been told that it is night crawlers.**

A The mounds of earthworm castings can be annoying in a lawn, but it's a sign of a healthy lawn. The earthworms aerate the soil and convert decaying organic matter into humus that the plants can use. While you could use an insecticide to kill the earthworms, we don't recommend doing so. Instead try raking out the castings to spread them throughout the lawn. They are a beneficial topdressing for the grass.

Q **I live in Texas and have St. Augustine grass in my yard. The grass has started dying in patches 2 feet wide. What is this? Am I watering too little or is it some insect?**

A One disease that has become a serious problem in Texas on St. Augustine lawns is called take-all patch. It forms large dead patches like you describe. Lawn fungicides seem to work as a control. Grubs and chinch bugs can also cause large dead patches to appear. You should see the actual bugs if this is what the problem is. Grubs can be found just underneath the dead grass, which should pull up easily due to all the eaten roots. Chinch bugs are small, but you should be able to see lots of them if they're causing this much damage. If the problem is insects, garden centers can provide you with insecticides to control them.

Thinking about hiring a lawn care service to take care of your lawn's pest problems? Read our online story about what to look for in a lawn service at *bhg.com/lawn-service*.

Diseases

Q **I have a shady area where the grass blades have a powdery white film on them. What is it, and how do I get rid of it?**

A It sounds as though your lawn has powdery mildew (right). This is a lawn disease that primarily affects Kentucky bluegrass, although some fescues can also get it. Severe outbreaks may occur on bluegrass growing in shaded areas. The mildew usually disappears when environmental conditions change. It seldom causes injury that is severe enough to warrant spraying. If you're patient, the problem will likely take care of itself. If it comes back repeatedly, you may want to consider growing a less susceptible variety of grass in the shady area or plant a shade-tolerant groundcover there.

Q **My lawn has developed a faint orange tint, which someone told me is rust. I have since treated it with fungicide. However, I still see it in many patches in the yard. Where did the rust come from, will the fungicide eliminate it, and how can I prevent this from happening again?**

A Rust is a common disease. It can pop up in any lawn (newly seeded lawns frequently experience worse rust than established lawns), but it doesn't necessarily mean you have a problem that needs solving. Because rust is not terribly harmful and because fungicides are expensive, relatively few homeowners choose this approach. If the right fungicide is used, it can cut down on the rust, but the best way to prevent rust is to keep the lawn healthy, well-watered, and fertilized.

Q **I live in the Chicago area. Now that the snow has melted away, it looks like grubs have eaten my lawn. What can I do?**

A Grubs are dormant in winter. Unless it was already there last fall, whatever you're seeing, isn't grub damage. A fungus called snow mold can attack lawns underneath a snow cover. Did you notice any matting or webbing as the snow melted? If it is snow mold, the turf may recover on its own. The fungus depends on temperatures just above freezing and high humidity for survival. So as the lawn dries out and air temperatures warm up, the problem should go away. If the infestation is not severe, the crown (growing point) of your grass may have survived and will sprout new growth once conditions improve. Help it along by vigorously raking the patch to allow more oxygen to reach the crowns. In severe cases, patches of grass may be killed. In that case, overseed or sod the dead areas.

Q **Why do parts of my grass have red-colored tips on them?**

A This sounds like a fungal disease called red thread, which is generally best controlled with proper maintenance. Keep lawn well-fertilized, don't water in the afternoon or evening (to avoid excessive or prolonged exposure moisture) and dethatch, if your lawn has a thick layer of thatch. By summertime, when weather warms and isn't so damp, the disease will likely disappear. There are also fungicides available to treat for red thread, but unless you're about to lose large swaths of lawn, proper maintenance should work to control the problem.

Q I think the brown circles in my St. Augustine grass lawn are brown patch. I treated them last summer, but the fungus still seems to be active. What do you suggest?

A Although your diagnosis may be correct, remember that many turf diseases look like brown patch. Properly identify the disease by taking a sample to your county extension service. They'll need a patch that contains some healthy turf as well as the dead brown area to make a definite diagnosis. If your lawn does indeed have brown patch, let the disease run its course. Like all fungal diseases, brown patch is condition-dependent—it flares up when the conditions are hot and humid and recedes when the weather turns cooler. Control the severity of brown patch by avoiding heavy nitrogen applications in spring and autumn. Water in the morning so the grass doesn't stay wet overnight. To prevent brown patch from spreading when it is active, remove grass clippings.

Q My lawn has spots that start out circular and yellow, then spread outward in a ring shape, with the center completely dying out to bare ground. I tried fungicide on the rings and it seemed to help, but most keep expanding. Do you have any suggestions?

A Different diseases produce that pattern in a lawn: yellow patch, necrotic ring spot, summer patch, and fusarium blight. All of these diseases are fungus-based. For immediate control, you can apply a systemic fungicide according to label directions (check with a local garden center or county extension service to see what is recommended for your area), but, as you are finding, fungicides are expensive, and you may need to use several applications.

Q Every year my lawn develops brown patches. Do I need to spray something to get rid of them?

A Most healthy lawns are able to outgrow a bout with diseases; you may have to tolerate some discoloration while the lawn recovers. Keep your lawn as healthy as possible. Fertilize regularly to encourage the lawn to fill in. Reseed seriously affected areas, selecting varieties of grass with good disease resistance.

Q I've been told that the brown spots in my lawn are from necrotic ring spot. How do I get rid of the spots?

A To prevent necrotic ring spot, dethatch and aerate your lawn regularly. Irrigate when necessary to avoid drought stress and apply lawn fertilizer at regular intervals. During hot summer months, set your mower a little higher than during cool periods.

Weeds

Q Last spring I applied a fertilizer with a crabgrass preventer. For some reason the crabgrass was actually worse last summer. Is there something else I can do to make sure the chemical works?

A If you wait too late in the season to apply crabgrass preventer, crabgrass (below right) may become established before the herbicide is effective. Be certain to apply the crabgrass preventer before the soil temperature reaches 55°F in spring. On south-facing slopes and near driveways or sidewalks, this may happen early in spring. One cue that many gardeners use for timing crabgrass preventer applications is when forsythia is in full bloom. Soil-temperature measurements are more precise, but the bright golden forsythia blossoms serve as a good reminder.

Q Over the past two years our lawn has been taken over by what looks like purple violets with tiny pumpkin-plant leaves. It started randomly in the yard, then it spread in large patches, killing the grass where it takes over. Are there any organic solutions that really work?

A From your description the weed sounds like creeping Charlie. It's a tough, invasive weed, especially in shady spots. If you spot it early, you can probably manage to eliminate creeping Charlie by hand. Household borax is slightly more toxic to creeping Charlie than to grass, so you can kill the weed but spare the lawn. It does have its limits: It's going to burn the grass if you apply it too heavily, and you can apply it only once a year for two years before you exceed the level that will harm grass. The proper mixture is 10 ounces of borax in 2½ gallons of water for 1,000 square feet of infested lawn.

Q I have clover in my yard. I have tried several weed killers to no avail. I was told that lime would get rid of it, but that didn't seem to work either. The only way I can get rid of it is to dig it up and replant grass in its place. Is there anything else I can try?

A Clover can be killed with repeat applications of a combination selective broadleaf weed killer. Any product will do if it has two or three active ingredients from this list: 2,4-D, dichlorprop, MCPP (mecoprop), dicamba, triclopyr, or clopyralid. Carefully follow the instructions on the label. Add a squirt of dish soap to the solution to help the spray stick to the leaves; otherwise, it may bead up and roll off. Even with a thorough spraying, it's likely that you'll overlook many clover plants and a few will manage to grow back. New ones will continue to germinate, too, so count on some follow-up applications.

Q I have grass burs in my lawn. What can I do to stop them?

A Grass burs (also called sandburs) are common in sandy lawns. Like most lawn weeds, grass burs are opportunists—they thrive when grass is struggling to survive. Proper mowing, fertilization, and irrigation develop a dense turf that will quickly choke out grass burs. In other words, give your lawn plenty

of TLC. Preemergence herbicides are best for getting rid of grass burs. Use a product that contains oryzalin or pendimethalin. Follow the application instructions carefully.

Q My yard has big patches of quackgrass. I've consulted grass experts who have told me that the only thing I can do is tear up my lawn and start over. Please tell me what I can do!

A Quackgrass is one of the worst lawn weeds. Any chemical product that will kill quackgrass will also kill the grass in your lawn. That means you either have to put up with the quackgrass or kill the entire area and start over.

Q I have bentgrass creeping into my Kentucky bluegrass lawn. I've been spraying the spots with Roundup, then reseeding, but there are a lot of spots. Are there any preventive measures I can take to stop bentgrass from overrunning my beautiful lawn?

A Unfortunately, there is nothing that will selectively take out bentgrass while leaving the bluegrass. A nonselective herbicide with the active ingredient glyphosate (Roundup) is the only long-term solution, and it's less than perfect, as you're finding out. Although it won't be cheap, your best option is to spray Roundup over the entire area where bentgrass is showing up, then reestablish bluegrass. To keep out the bentgrass from that point on, never mow it with a lawn mower that has been used elsewhere; some invasive grasses that spread by rhizomes or stolons spread via lawn clippings too.

Q I can't seem to find a solution to the multitude of oniongrass growing in our lawn. The regular weed killers don't affect it. Do you have any ideas?

A Wild oniongrass is hard to kill with chemicals, but it can be done. Use a combination broadleaf herbicide product that contains two or three chemicals; ask for the ester formulation. You'll need to make the application in early spring, when the oniongrass is actively growing. One precaution: Ester formulations are a little more potent than other formulations of the same product. You should apply ester formulations only during cool weather (spring and fall) and never use them close to ornamentals.

Q We have nutgrass everywhere and it spreads like crazy. Do you have any recommendations?

A Several products on the market selectively kill nutgrass, also called nutsedge. If it's in your lawn, use a selective herbicide labeled as nutgrass killer, such as MSMA or Basagran. Often (not always), nutgrass becomes a problem because of poor drainage. Check to see whether the nutgrass is growing in a wet area. If it is, you can probably reduce it by improving drainage and drying out the site.

Landscape Planning

Q **Do I need anyone's permission before starting my landscaping project? One neighbor says the city inspector has to approve and inspect all work; another neighbor builds pergolas and porches without asking anyone.**

A Projects need various levels of approval in different areas. If you're planting a perennial bed in your backyard and aren't altering any existing structures, you generally don't need governmental approval. But that's not the case everywhere. The best thing to do is ask your city or county government what sorts of structures or garden changes need planning approval. Also, you may live in a development with a neighborhood association that has to approve any changes to the exterior of your home. Check local covenants.

Q **We'd like to landscape our yard, but the expense seems overwhelming. Is it possible to landscape on a budget?**

A Yes, you just have to plan and spend wisely. Here are some hints. Hire a landscape designer to develop a plan, then do the work yourself. Another option is to

decide on which parts of the plan you can do, then hire out the more difficult portions. Tackle one part of the plan at a time, and work at your own pace to spread out the cost and the work. You don't have to get the whole project done in a single day, week, or month—or even a season.

Q **After developing our landscape design plan, we find we just don't have enough in the budget to do it all. Do you have some ideas for how we might scale back the cost?**

A Look for inexpensive alternatives. A retaining wall of newly quarried stone is expensive, but concrete blocks from sidewalk-replacement projects work just as well, and some contractors give them away. Plant small trees. Large trees often take a long time to recover from transplanting, while small ones reestablish quickly. Shrubs, which fill in faster than trees, add structure, too, and can be purchased in small sizes to save money. Use annuals for color around new landscaping. These quick bloomers add color until your perennials have time to fill in. A couple flats of bedding plants such as petunias, or a few seed packets of a quick-growing flower such as nasturtiums, are usually enough for full-season color.

Q **I want to get rid of the grass strip along the street and plant it with flowers and a nice shade tree. Are there any special considerations when planting this close to the street?**

A Check with your city or subdivision for ordinances regarding front-yard plantings and structures. For example, some municipalities prohibit plantings on the utility strip between the sidewalk and street. If you live in an area without sidewalks, the strip abutting the street might be public land. Many also impose height limitations on structures in the front yard.

Landscape Professionals

Q **I have a big project in mind for my backyard, and I've decided it is too big for me to tackle on my own. What kind of professional do I look for to help me with the labor?**

A That depends on the scope of the project, how much you want to do yourself, and the amount you want to spend. You may hire a landscape contractor to install design elements, such as a path or retaining wall. Check references and ask questions about the quality and fit of materials used. Sometimes your local garden center or home building center is the best place to start looking for professional advice. They frequently can supply the materials and labor needed for your dream design. You may even get a discount for a package including design, materials, and labor.

Q **What's the difference between a landscape designer and a landscape architect? Which would be better for designing my landscape?**

A Landscape architects are usually licensed and certified. They tackle the biggest projects, such as developing a comprehensive plan for your entire outdoor space. Landscape designers usually are not licensed or regulated by any agency, but they typically have some formal design training and may belong to organizations that offer continuing education or review. Many designers, even if they aren't certified, are gifted in design and have vast plant knowledge. Designers often create planting plans rather than overall landscape designs. The choice of which to use often depends on the scope of the project, but it can also depend on which professional can creatively envision your dream.

Q **We're thinking about selling our home and have heard that landscaping can add value to the home. How much can we expect to increase the value of our home by doing some landscaping?**

A A few flowers and shrubs to spruce up the front yard may not add much value to your home. But if you're thinking of selling, the first impression you create with colorful flowers and tidy shrubs could make the difference between an interested buyer and a drive-by missed sale. Studies suggest that you can increase the value of your home 5–15 percent by upgrading your landscape from poor to good. Strictly going by these numbers, you might figure on spending about 5 to 10 percent or so of the value of your home on a landscape upgrade and expect to get most of it back right away.

Curb Appeal

Q **I'd like a nice-looking yard, but I can't afford a professional landscaper. What can I do myself to get started?**

A There are lots of ways to lift a landscaping project out of the ordinary. Adapt one or more of these ideas to make your yard memorable. Put one tall plant, three medium plants, and five short plants together. Place the tall one slightly off-center; group the medium plants together; then intersperse the small, ground-hugging plants among the others. Add an inviting path and line it with colorful plants. Use containers for architectural interest. Terra-cotta pots, stone urns, and window boxes offer focal points, often in places where nothing can otherwise grow, such as on decks and patios, along walkways, hanging from awnings or latticework, and on top of walls.

Q **I'd like to add more curb appeal to my yard. What can I do to spruce up the front yard?**

A Your budget and personal preferences will guide your final result. Knowing where to start is often a hurdle. One option is to start with a professionally drawn landscape plan. Many landscapers charge a small fee for this if you do the work yourself. You won't pay separately for a plan if you're hiring a landscaper to design and install the hardscaping and plants though.

Q **What can I do to make my front entry more inviting?**

A Look at the walkway from the street to your front door. Just changing a straight walk to a curving one and adding plantings can transform the whole look of a yard. Consider installing retaining walls, landscape lighting, and archways or pergolas. Keep them simple, and use materials that are reliable, require little maintenance, and are compatible with the look of your home. An easy way to add appeal is to put in window boxes or containers near doors or windows. Painting a front door or garden bench also contributes to the look of the landscape without costing much.

Q **I don't know how to get started with landscaping my front yard. Do you have some simple suggestions?**

A Each landscape is unique and often requires an onsite evaluation to determine what landscaping is needed. Step across the street and look at your house for a few minutes. The front entry and access to it should be easy to see and look inviting. The trees, shrubs, and other plants should frame the home, make it look attractive, and not overwhelm it. Even if you're on a limited budget, consider getting professional landscaping help. The more difficult and expensive the project, the more likely you are to need someone trained in this field. A good landscape architect or designer can make suggestions at differing levels of expense. The expert can help you prioritize what needs to be done first and figure out which parts you can do yourself.

Check out our front yard landscaping secrets online at *bhg.com/front-yard*.

Q I love my new home, but the landscape is a mess. Part of it is overgrown with shrubs, small trees, and vines. Other parts of the yard haven't been touched. What's the best way to get started on what seems to be an enormous project?

A Rather than start with things you can add to your landscape, begin by removing the detractors. Then you can move on to adding landscape components that bring enjoyment and value to your home. If tree branches are dying, rubbing against the roof, or threatening to fall in a storm, pruning or removal is in order. For work on tall trees, call in a professional. Does anything pose a safety hazard? For example, look for obstacles on pathways, foliage that blocks sight lines from sidewalks or driveways, crumbling retaining walls, drainage problems, or a blocked view of the front door. Before you dig or plant, have the yard marked for utility lines, property lines, an irrigation system, or a buried pet fence. Avoid damaging the root systems of existing trees by digging too closely to them or compacting soil with heavy equipment.

Q All the magazines I read tell me that I need a focal point for my garden, such as a birdbath, a fancy pot, or a piece of garden art. Why is this important?

A A focal point stops the eye, creating a place to focus—hence, the term focal point. A focal point can transform a garden to make it yours. For example, a classical urn on a fluted pedestal adds an air of formality, whereas a copper fountain that spins and hurls water in an ever-changing pattern injects whimsy. An effective focal point brings with it an element of surprise. It gives visitors something they aren't expecting. A focal point can be practical as well as artistic. Birdhouses, bird feeders, and birdbaths attract wildlife while adding an artistic element.

Q My beds stretch the length of my property, with one side in shade and the other in full sun. Planting the sunny side is easy, but it's hard to balance the look of the garden because I can't grow colorful plants in the shady end.

A It can be a challenge to get bright colors in the shade, but balance in garden design does not have to be symmetrical, with identical plantings on either side of your border. As you noted, bright colors have more visual impact than do dark ones. But you may be able to counterbalance the bright red and yellow flowers of the sunny portion of the border with shade plants having variegated foliage. Creams, whites, and yellows will stand out in the shade. You can also add touches of color in the shade with annuals such as impatiens, begonias, and coleus

Shade

Q My yard is rather shady. What are some plants that I can grow there to add color and interest?

A Here are 10 great perennials and shrubs for a shady landscape: 1. Hosta, 2. Lungwort (*Pulmonaria*), 3. Heuchera, 4. Bleeding heart (*Dicentra*), 5. Toad lily (*Tricyrtis*), 6. Hellebore (*Helleborus*), 7. Serviceberry (*Amelanchier*), 8. Fothergilla, 9. Oakleaf hydrangea (*Hydrangea*), and 10. Summersweet (*Clethra*).

Q **I have a shady spot in front of my home. I planted impatiens, but they all died in a matter of a week or two. What could I grow here?**

A How dense is the shade in this area? Impatiens should grow in shade, but perhaps you need to start with large perennials, or perhaps the soil needs to be amended with compost or organic matter to provide a better growing base for the plants. Many shade-tolerant perennials might work here. Bleeding heart, pulmonaria, ajuga, Japanese painted fern, Jacob's ladder, begonias, and hostas are some to consider.

Q **I have a creek that is slowly eroding away our backyard. The soil is moist, and gets very little sun or no sun at all. I need to find plants that are low maintenance to help with the erosion problem. Do you have any suggestions?**

A Daylilies can tolerate partial shade, but not deep shade. They also prefer well-drained soil. Better bets for your situation would be hosta or sedges (*Carex* spp.). The sedges look like grasses, but aren't true grasses. Most remain under 1 foot tall and prefer shady, moist locations. Hostas come in a wide variety of sizes and shades from green to gold, blue-green, and variegated with white

Q **What would you recommend for a shaded garden on a slope? It gets some morning sun, but is mostly shaded by maples and a willow. It is surrounded by a stone wall of about 10 inches. I am more interested in perennials than annuals.**

A The maples and willow not only create dense shade, but they also have shallow, dense root systems that will compete with your plantings for space, moisture, and nutrients. But the morning sun and good soil you describe make it sound like a habitable garden spot

for lots of plants. Perennials you might plant include hostas, corydalis, lungwort (*Pulmonaria*), brunnera, and sweet woodruff (*Galium*). You might also tuck in a few shade-loving groundcovers such as periwinkle (*Vinca major*), Japanese spurge (*Pachysandra*), lily-of-the-valley (*Convallaria*), or bugleweed (*Ajuga*).

Q **My husband and I have a vacation home where we go many weekends. There are quite a few trees, so there is also a lot of shade. What types of plants grow well without a lot of watering and attention?**

A First, keep plantings to a minimum so there's little maintenance. Dry shade can pose a challenge, but here are some plants that will do well in that situation: yew (*Taxus*), daylily (*Hemerocallis*), cranesbill geranium (*G. sanguineum*), barrenwort (*Epimedium*), bleeding heart (*Dicentra*), dead nettle (*Lamium*), Japanese spurge (*Pachysandra*), and lily-of-the-valley. All of these will fare well on their own once they're established.

Shade

Q I have trouble getting grass to grow under my trees. I've decided that it would look better with groundcover. What are some good ones to grow in the shade?

A You have many choices of shade-tolerant groundcovers. Here are some to consider: 1. Bugleweed (*Ajuga*), 2. English ivy (*Hedera*), 3. Wild ginger (*Asarum*), 4. Deadnettle (*Lamium*), 5. Leadwort (*Ceratostigma*), 6. Mondo grass (*Ophiopogon*), 7. Periwinkle (*Vinca*), 8. Yellow archangel (*Lamiastrum*), and 9. Lilyturf (*Liriope*).

Planting Around Trees

Q I want to plant circular beds around several trees in my yard. Will the soil touching the base of the trees present a problem for the tree trunk?

A Adding soil around the base of a tree can be a problem because it reduces oxygen to the roots. Trees that are susceptible to their roots dying from this practice are sugar maple, beech, flowering dogwood, and many oaks, pines, and spruces. Older trees and trees under stress can succumb to smothering, too. A better idea is to plant shallow-rooted groundcovers under the trees and establish your gardens that way.

Q Last year I made four raised beds, and I want to plant them with various vegetables and flowers. A large portion of the garden is in partial or full shade, and when it rains, the soil retains a lot of water. Can you please suggest the types of plants that can survive these conditions?

A Your question does not specify that the soil in the raised beds holds water. I am assuming they drain fine. If not, an easy fix is to replace or amend that soil. If the beds are holding water because the soil underneath is impermeable to water, that's another problem. Solomon's seal (*Polygonatum*), toad lily (*Tricyrtis*), lungwort (*Pulmonaria*), cardinal flower (*Lobelia*), various ferns, and hostas will grow in wet spots in the shade. Sadly, few vegetables grow well in shade.

Q I would like to establish a garden around our ash tree. One root is coming out into the lawn and extends away from the tree, and directly around the tree are lots of little root shoots. How can I have some flowers around this? Is it best to set containers out around it instead of directly in the dirt?

A Growing plants in containers under the tree is a great solution. If you try to plant directly in the ground, you may damage the tree's roots and could even kill the tree if the root damage is extensive.

Q I am a beginning gardener and would like some help on what to plant in an existing shaded bed. I would love to plant it with perennials. The dirt is hard. Do I need to till it first? It's kind of rocky underneath.

A Avoid tilling up the entire area, especially if there are tree roots in the shady zone. You could damage the trees by tilling. Instead, do pocket plantings, amending the soil and digging it up in small sections in and around the tree roots. You can plant hostas, pulmonarias, heucheras, bleeding hearts, toad lilies, turtleheads, and hellebores, among other shade-tolerant plants.

Drainage

Q My home has a huge, flat rectangular yard that is predominately sunny. If it rains a lot, there are some wet spots. I want to visually break it up and give it interest. Any ideas?

A Berms are a good solution for your flat front yard. By heaping soil amended with organic matter, you can create changes in levels where there were none. And by planting on the berms, you won't have to worry about plant roots drowning due to poor drainage.

Q Our backyard is small and in need of help. We want to landscape the yard, but we need to know how to work around a large red maple and what the best drainage plan would be. The backyard of our neighbor's house drains into our backyard. Could I divert the drainage into the alley behind our home? Could we level the yard or tile it to improve the drainage?

A It's frustrating to deal with runoff from your neighbor's yard. Developers are supposed to design sites so that water is managed on each lot rather than shifted to the neighbor. With a large red maple in a small backyard, you won't be able to level the yard without damaging the tree. Hauling in soil to level things off will smother the roots, and removing soil will physically damage and kill roots. The best thing you can do for your site is to create a rain garden. It's a garden of deep-rooted, moisture-loving perennials planted in a shallow basin-shape bed. The idea is that rainwater runs into the slightly sunken bed where it pools and then percolates down into the soil. See page 154 for some plants adapted to rain gardens.

Q We live on a hill with large sloped front yard, and our septic tank is the only flat surface in the front yard. How do we make it look stunning without causing damage to our septic or drain field.

A Don't let the septic system deter you from installing a lush landscape. With the exception of the tank access area, you can plant perennials and shrubs anywhere around and over the septic tank and drain field. Of course, when you are digging planting holes, be careful not to damage any of the underground apparatus. Drainage tile fingering out into the drain field is likely not tile at all but black plastic tubing perforated with holes. Keep any tree plantings off to the sides of the septic field.

Q We have a drainage ditch that fills with water every time it rains hard, but most of the time it is dry. What could we plant there that will survive flooding, but not die when it dries out?

A You may be able to landscape with plants that tolerate occasional wet feet. Siberian iris (*Iris*), redtwig dogwood (*Cornus alba*), maidengrass (*Miscanthus*), and moneywort (*Lysimachia*) are a few examples of plants that may be suited to periodic wet cycles but which also thrive during drier times.

Q My front yard slopes toward the house. When it rains, water runs down the hill. There is grass there, but it still makes a muddy mess! I'd like to plant a flowerbed. Any suggestions?

A Putting in a flowerbed will only put a bandage on your problems. Your best bet is to contact a landscaper to get some on-site advice about how to drain the water away from your home. Once you get the drainage taken care of, you can work on a flowerbed. You'll then have a variety of options open to you.

Q We have a dry creek bed running through our yard, with mature trees on the banks, and with rock and weeds growing in the creek bed. Can you suggest a groundcover that will grow in sun or shade and withstand the occasional flash flood?

A Few groundcovers thrive in both shade and sun, but here are some options for you to consider. For sun, try daylily (*Hemerocallis*), leadwort (*Ceratostigma*), dwarf speedwells (*Veronica*), and lamb's-ears (*Stachys*). For shade, try periwinkle (*Vinca*), bishop's weed (*Aegopodium*), barrenwort (*Epimedium*), and green-and-gold (*Chrysogonum*).

Q Our yard gets drainage from the road, and with the winter salt, our lawn is bare. Any ideas of what to put there instead of grass?

A Road salt can create a toxic environment for any plant, so you may struggle to get anything to grow along the road. Sprinkle the soil with powdered gypsum. Gypsum is available at garden centers, and it's inexpensive. Then water the area well; it may help flush the salt down through the soil profile. You could try planting a groundcover that is more tolerant of salt than turf is—something like Virginia creeper (*Parthenocissus quinquefolia*), Liriope (*L. spicata*), or cinquefoil (*Potentilla*).

Rain Garden

Q I'd like to start a rain garden. What plants could I grow in it?

A Rain-garden plants must tolerate periodic wet soil but also thrive when conditions are drier. Here are some shrubs and perennials that will work: 1. Cardinal flower (*Lobelia*), 2. Japanese iris (*Iris*), 3. Moneywort (*Lysimachia*), 4. Pink turtlehead (*Chelone*), 5. Spiderwort (*Tradescantia* × *andersoniana*), 6. Red-osier dogwood (*Cornus sericea*), 7. Sedge (*Carex*), 8. Hardy hibiscus (*Hibiscus*), and 9. Black chokeberry (*Aronia*).

Beach Plants

Q We have a place on the beach. The soil is sandy, and we get salt spray from the ocean. What plants could we grow there?

A Here are some good choices: 1. Rose of Sharon (*Hibiscus syriacus*), 2. Tamarisk (*Tamarix*), 3. Russian olive (*Eleagnus*), 4. Peashrub (*Caragana*), 5. Cotoneaster, 6. Little bluestem (*Schizachyrium*), 7. Blue oat grass (*Helictotrichon*), 8. Rosemary (*Rosmarinus*), 9. Salvia, and 10. Jupiter's beard (*Centranthus*).

Slope

Q **We are building a new home and have a basement entrance that has banks that are too steep to mow. Would mulch or groundcovers be a good solution?**

A If the area is too steep to mow, it may need more than just groundcover plantings to prevent erosion. Consider a retaining wall or walls to terrace the slope.

Q **We're trying to find material for a retaining wall about 18 inches high in the front of our home. My husband wants to use treated lumber, but I am interested in something a little better-looking.**

A Landscape blocks are the standard material for this type of situation. I don't think you'll match the low cost of treated landscape timbers. Nevertheless, landscape blocks are affordable and come in a wide range of sizes, colors, and styles. In some areas, fieldstone or boulders may be readily available at nominal cost. They provide a more natural look and will be long-lasting if installed properly.

Q **We'd like to build a retaining wall to break up the slope in our backyard. How difficult is this to do?**

A If the retaining wall is under 3 feet tall, you probably can tackle the task yourselves. Taller walls may need professional engineering. Here are several key points to remember in building your retaining wall. Start with a solid base. For a wall up to 3 feet tall, you'll need to dig 6 to 12 inches deep, lay down a base of compacted sand and gravel, then lay the base course of stone, blocks, or timbers. Tilt each succeeding layer back into the bed. If you make the wall perfectly perpendicular, the pressure of the soil behind the wall will eventually cause the wall to push outward. Overlap gaps in succeeding layers. This will help tie the wall together for greater stability.

Q **Our front yard slopes down to the street. We've decided to put in a retaining wall to create terraces. That means we'll need to have some stairs through the retaining wall. What do we need to know to do this project ourselves?**

A If you've had little experience in landscape construction projects, it may be well worth your time to have a professional contractor design the steps for you. You could also find a good how-to book on landscape construction that will provide detailed instructions. Check local codes and ordinances for regulations on stair dimensions, railing requirements, and other parameters. Choose a durable material that will blend well with the retaining wall and your home. Consider the steepness of the stairs. Treads should be a minimum of 12 inches deep. The shorter the rise (the distance stepped up between each step), the wider the tread should be. Typical combinations include a 6-inch riser with a 14-inch tread, a 5-inch riser with a 16-inch tread, and a 4-inch riser with an 18-inch tread. Break up long, steep slopes by curving the flight of stairs or by shortening the spans with landings.

Slope

Q We have a dry, sunny slope that's difficult to mow. What are some good plants for this location?

A Here are a few to consider: 1. Blanket flower (*Gaillardia*), 2. Daylily (*Hemerocallis*), 3. Barberry (*Berberis*), 4. Creeping juniper (*Juniperus*), 5. Trailing lantana (*Lantana*), 6. Yarrow (*Achillea*), 7. Lavender (*Lavandula*), 8. Creeping sedum, 9. Mugo pine (*Pinus*), and 10. Cinquefoil (*Potentilla*).

Terraces

Q **I have a steep slope with heavy shade. I have tried all kinds of grasses, but they keep dying. When it rains, there is a mudslide into my walkway. I need to walk on that area because it adjoins a stairway with a double gate at the bottom. What can I plant or do?**

A If the area is too shady, no turfgrass will grow well there. Some groundcovers tolerate occasional foot traffic and that grow well in shade, including brass buttons (*Leptinella squalida*), Kenilworth ivy (*Cymbalaria*), and moss. However, if the slope is quite steep, it may be best to terrace the slope with retaining walls and plant the terraces with shade-tolerant perennials.

Q **Our newly purchased home sits on the high side of the street. I'd like to install steps that crisscross the slope. We have the same situation in the backyard, but the incline is not as steep. Any ideas about where I can get pictures of terraced yards?**

A There are a few places to find ideas for terracing. One of the easiest, which you may already have checked, is your neighborhood. Spend some time taking notes on how other people with similar conditions have handled the situation. You'll see what has been successful and what hasn't, what you like and what you don't, and which plants do best in your locale. Second, talk to local landscapers. Dealing with a major hillside usually requires professional help. Even if you don't hire a landscape architect to do the job, it will pay off to have a professional plan in hand. Third, check out the landscaping section at a major bookstore. Most landscaping books include information about slopes and the challenges associated with gardening on them.

Q **Are there any problems associated with using old railroad ties to create retaining walls for a terrace?**

A Creosote oozing from railroad ties can be toxic to plants. But most railroad ties used in landscaping no longer have fresh creosote that oozes into the soil. If in doubt, you can place a plastic liner behind the retaining wall so that nothing can ooze into the soil.

Q **We live in an area with lots of rocks. I would like to create a tiered garden with rocks. Please tell me how.**

A Basically, you dig into the slope to create an even, compact base of gravel, then stack the rocks carefully on the compacted gravel base. The slope of the wall needs to taper back, and rocks should fit snugly. Using mortar will strengthen the wall. Also, it is best to install a drainage system (gravel and perforated plastic drainpipe) behind the wall to keep the weight of water from destroying your retaining wall.

Walkway

Q **We don't have a walkway to the front door. Our funds right now are going toward interior projects, yet I can't help but think there might be some way to create the illusion of a walkway without too much expense and wasted effort until we can build the real thing. Any suggestions?**

A For a quick low-cost walkway, try stepping-stones across the lawn for now. Home improvement centers have all kinds of stone and concrete stepping-stones and pavers. Once you've decided on the style you like, buy enough to lay the walk. Move them around on the lawn until you have the walkway layout that looks just right. Then cut the turf around each stone, set the stone aside, and remove the turf inside the cut area so that the stone will be level with the ground for ease of mowing and to avoid tripping on protruding stones. Set the stone in place, and your walkway is complete.

Q **We have a problem with moss growing on gravel walkways, driveways, and on areas covered with pavers. Lime will not kill the moss. Any suggestions?**

A Moss can be a slippery problem on walkways and paths, especially in damp climates. If you can, improve the drainage surrounding the pavers so that the surface does not remain wet. Also remove overhanging tree limbs if possible to improve air circulation and light conditions. If the infestation is not too severe, sometimes the moss can be removed with a power washer or very strong jet from a garden hose, although it will return. Moss-Aside Herbicidal Soap from Gardens Alive and Safers De-Moss Cryptocidal Soap are relatively safe products that will kill moss. Use these according to the instructions. Biodegradable chlorine bleach is sometimes used also, but it may harm surrounding plants and needs a lot of care to use properly. If the conditions that cause

moss growth in the first place are not corrected, the moss will likely return and need ongoing removal.

Q **Is there some low-growing moss or grass that can be planted between the pavers in my walkway path?**

A You don't say how much sunlight reaches your walkway, and that's really the key ingredient for success. Low-growing sedum, creeping veronica, miniature dianthus, or thyme (*Thymus*) will work fine if you have enough sunlight, but will fail in the shade. Irish moss (*Sagina*), brass buttons (*Leptinella*), or Kenilworth ivy are good choices for a shady site.

Q **I would like to know if you can put down a grass killer early in the spring to stop the grass from starting to grow in the pea stones in my walkway?**

A Preemergent weed controls will control germinating weed seeds, but they won't have any effect on grass rhizomes that creep in from surrounding lawn. To control those spreading grass rhizomes, wait until the grass begins to grow and use glyphosate (Roundup) herbicide on the blades. Take caution to avoid getting any of the herbicide on plants you wish to keep because it will kill other living plants, too, if it comes in contact with them.

Q I have brick path that stretches across the yard. What groundcovers do you recommend that would grow between the bricks? Is there something that when you step on it you could smell the aroma?

A Thyme is a wonderful plant for in-between spaces on a path or patio. It will give off an aroma when crushed, and it does tolerate some foot traffic. There are plenty of thymes to try: lemon thyme, creeping thyme 'Pink Chintz', woolly thyme, and mother of thyme. For a clovelike fragrance, you could try pinks (*Dianthus*), along the outer edges of the path.

Patio

Q I have a patio made of concrete pavers. It is old, but the pavers are in good condition. I'm tired of weeding between the blocks. I tried sand but still get weeds. Would planting creeping thyme stop the weeds and be attractive?

A Creeping thyme will thrive in those between-the-steppers crevices as long as it's a sunny site. It's not only attractive, but it also smells terrific when you brush against it. You'll still have to weed between the blocks while the thyme gets itself established, but after a season or two, it will reduce your weeding chores considerably.

Q I have an aggregate concrete patio that is cracking and discolored. It is surrounded by garden on three sides and my home on the fourth. I want to use the option that will disturb the garden the least. I have thought of pavers or pouring a couple inches of concrete and stamping it with a design. Are there other options?

A Covering the unsightly damaged patio with pavers may be your best option for rescuing the area. Pouring a thin layer of concrete over the existing surface brings the possibility of cracked concrete because it will be thinner than customary depth used for concrete walking surfaces.

Q I need a fast-growing shade tree for my Koi pond, patio, and arbor close to my house. I need something that has a vertical root system. I would prefer a large-leaf deciduous tree.

A I would advise against planting a fast-growing shade tree close to your house. The problem with fast-growing trees is that they're the weakest, so they're the most likely to lose branches or topple entirely in strong winds or an ice storm. And the root system of any type of tree primarily grows in the top foot of soil, spreading outward rather than growing deep into the soil. Typically, the spread of the roots is several times that of the branches. A tree planted next to your patio will definitely develop roots under the patio and create the possibility of heaving of the concrete.

Mulch

Q **I have a round brick patio that is just off my deck. I landscaped with river rock and opened up the landscape fabric that sits under the rock to plant some perennials. The perennials do not seem to grow very well. I am thinking of taking them out and planting something else. Will I need to remove all of the rocks and landscape fabric to do this?**

A Rock mulch isn't ideal for plants because the rock intensifies the heat stress put on plants. If the patio is already hot and in full sun, the rock is compounding the problem and making for a very unfriendly environment for plants. I'd recommend removing the river rock and mulching your new planting with an organic mulch such as shredded cypress or cedar.

Q **We just finished landscaping the front yard of our first home. We dug out holes in the yard to plant our plants but did not dig out all the grass surrounding the plants. We thought that the dirt and mulch we were spreading over the area would kill the grass. A week later there is grass popping up all over. What can I do about this?**

A I have a couple of solutions for you. Choose whichever sounds more manageable for your landscape project. First, you could rake off the mulch you applied, lay four to six sheets of newspaper over all the grass, and spread the mulch over it all. The newspaper layer will smother the grass and eventually break down naturally. The other option is to spot-spray the grass with a herbicide such as glyphosate (Roundup). You'll have to shield your plantings carefully from drift, because the herbicide can kill all plants. You might use a cardboard shield or, if the plants are small enough, overturned buckets to shelter them while you spray.

Q **My husband wants to lay landscape fabric in our new beds that we are creating. Just how necessary is landscape fabric?**

A Landscape fabric is completely optional; some homeowners wouldn't dream of landscaping without it, but some gardeners find it annoying and say it gets in the way. Landscape fabric does help prevent weeds, but is not a completely foolproof weed inhibitor. Determined weeds may spring up in the mulch on top of the landscape fabric and make their way through. If they do, they are especially difficult to remove because you've got to wrestle with the fabric that the roots are threaded through and entangled in. If you use landscape fabric, it has to be cut back as perennials spread and suckering shrubs grow in girth. I mulch my beds and don't use landscape fabric. I think bed maintenance is simpler without the fabric.

Hedge Plants

Q We'd like to install a hedge for privacy in our backyard. What shrubs could we use for this purpose?

A Here are some good choices: 1. Arborvitae (*Thuja*), 2. Upright juniper (*Juniperus*), 3. Arrowwood viburnum (*Viburnum*), 4. Canadian hemlock (*Tsuga*), 5. Meyer lilac (*Syringa*), 6. Oleander (*Nerium*), 7. Privet (*Ligustrum*), 8. Yew (*Taxus*), 9. Ninebark (*Physocarpus*), and 10. Barberry (*Berberis*).

Privacy

Q We recently moved to a new house near our local high school. It can become very noisy on game nights and during band practice. What type of trees do you recommend to enhance our privacy and hopefully reduce some of the noise?

A Because the noise from games and band practice will likely continue into the winter season, I'd suggest some evergreens. You might also consider putting a fountain near your sitting area to mask some of the noise in warm weather. A few evergreen choices are American arborvitae, Atlas cedar or deodar cedar, balsam, noble or white fir, Canadian hemlock, Colorado or Norway spruce, Douglas fir, eastern red cedar, false cypress, holly, incense cedar, and pine.

Q We live on a corner lot, which leaves our entire backyard exposed to view from the side street. What could we do to create more privacy in the backyard?

A You can grow your own living privacy fence. Tall, slender trees and shrubs such as Blue Angel holly, Emerald arborvitae, columnar Norway maple, and Skyrocket juniper are ideal for corner lots such as yours, where space and privacy are at a premium. They also are perfect for exposed front entries.

Q I need some landscaping ideas to block the view of a shopping center from my Zone 8 front yard. Would it be better to block the view from close to the house or out at the front edge of the property?

A A combination of trees and shrubs is always a good idea for privacy and to cut down on noise. Shrubs and trees for Zone 8 include strawberry tree, Mexican orange, New Zealand daisy bush, Japanese pittosporum,

and cherry laurel. Plant a combination of trees and shrubs out toward the sidewalk if you want to use the yard and have some privacy too.

Q I have a deck with a 4-foot-high deck railing. I would like to grow something in containers that would give me more privacy. Would an additional privacy fence look good going around the railing itself?

A Lattice on top of a deck rail is attractive and fairly simple to install. Build a frame of 2×4s the length of your deck rail and the height of the lattice you want. Tack lattice to what will be the outside of the frames. Use deck screws to attach the frame(s) to the railing and the side of the building. If you are installing it around the entire perimeter, you can attach the frames to each other at the corners. An additional 2×4 angled across the top from one panel to the other at the corner will add stability. After the frames are installed, tack a second piece of lattice on the front of the panels. Group pots around the perimeter of the deck.

Fragrance

Q I'd like to surround our patio with some sweet-smelling plants. What would you recommend?

A Here are some to consider: 1. Bearded iris (*Iris*), 2. Cheddar pink (*Dianthus*), 3. Daphne, 4. Holly osmanthus (*Osmanthus*), 5. Hyacinth (*Hyacinthus*), 6. Korean spice viburnum, 7. Lilac (*Syringa*), 8. Lily-of-the-valley (*Convallaria*), 9. Orange jessamine (*Murraya*), and 10. Sweet autumn clematis.

Low-Maintenance Gardening

Q **I am not a seasoned gardener and would like to create a low-maintenance area off my front porch, using a variety of plants that have movement in the wind and are conducive to Zone 8. Also, I am interested in a pine tree that will do well in a 4-foot area without destructive root spread.**

A Several perennial grasses you might consider are bamboo muhly (*Muhlenbergia dumosa*), fountaingrass (*Pennisetum*), and prairie dropseed (*Sporobolus heterolepis*). Perennial flowers for dry sites include yarrow (*Achillea*), purple coneflower (*Echinacea*), catmint (*Nepeta*), and pinks (*Dianthus*). Many dwarf conifers could be used in a 4-foot space. Do you want a true pine, or would some other type of evergreen be suitable? Leyland cypress (×*Cupressocyparis leylandii*) is a tall, narrow upright evergreen that could work in your area. Dwarf Hinoki cypress (*Chamaecyparis obtusa*) should also work. Miniature forms of mugo pine (*Pinus mugo*) could also work.

Q **I need some landscaping suggestions for a large area in front of our home we moved into last summer. There is a sprinkler system in the area, but I need this area to be pretty much low maintenance. Please help me!**

A Did you know you can design your own garden online for free? Go to *bhg.com/gardening* and click on the "Plan Your Garden" tab. Although you're looking for low maintenance, a little work before planting will help you immensely. Be sure to dig out all the roots you can from the previous plants, and if the soil is heavy clay or sandy dry, mix in lots of compost.

Q **I love the look of a cottage garden but live where water shortage is a big problem. Is it possible to have a drought-tolerant, low-maintenance cottage-style garden?**

A The secret to low-maintenance, drought-tolerant landscaping is to plant in zones. Group your plants according to watering needs. Put the thirstiest plants near a rain barrel that collects rain for irrigation. This simplifies watering. Also, be sure to amend the soil thoroughly and mulch your plants to conserve moisture.

Q **Which flowering perennials and low shrubs will withstand heat and dry conditions? These plants must be planted on a 45-degree slope in the backyard.**

A Assuming that your slope has good drainage, you can anchor it with low-growing shrubs such as juniper. In between in sunny areas you can plant low-growing and colorful sedums like 'Blue Spruce' and 'Dragon's Blood', which will knit together to give you a nice, tight mat. There are many drought- and heat-tolerant ground covers for shade, such as bugleweed (*Ajuga*) and periwinkle (*Vinca*). For taller flowering perennials, try beard-tongue (*Penstemon*), whirling butterflies (*Gaura lindheimerii*), and hummingbird mint (*Agastache*). Just remember that even drought- and heat-tolerant plants need to be watered in their first season to become well-established.

Landscape Lighting

Q I'd like to add some landscape lighting next to the walkway in front of my house but wonder how safe it is and how expensive it is to keep it lit all night.

A Most landscape lighting systems use low-voltage lights. The normal household voltage of 110 volts is reduced to 12 volts by a transformer. This low voltage makes the lights extremely safe; you're unlikely to get a shock even if you touch bare wires or hit a buried cable while digging in the garden. Low-voltage systems are economical to operate. Most use less energy than a single 75-watt bulb. To save even more energy, you could put the lights on a timer that automatically shuts them off at a predetermined time each night. Or consider a solar-powered system, which harnesses sunlight during the day to power the lights at night.

Q I've noticed that the leaves on my maple tree near a streetlight hang on through the winter, while those farther away from the light fall off at the normal time. Is the streetlight causing problems?

A Bright streetlights can affect a plant's perception of day length. The plants are tricked into perceiving that days are longer than they really are by the artificial light from the street lamp. Because declining day length is one of the triggers that induces dormancy in a plant, leaf color changes and leaf drop may be delayed by proximity to a bright light. In most cases, plants will continue to grow with no ill effects. But should an extremely early cold snap hit, branch tips that have not hardened off properly may suffer dieback.

Q I put some little white lights among my azaleas and left them up year-round. Will these lights cause any problems with the health and growth of the plants?

A Using lights year-round in your shrubs should have little effect on the plants' health. You might notice that your azaleas don't bloom as well, but this will depend on the brightness of the lights and how long they are burning at night. Azaleas are sensitive to the length of the day—it's what tells them to bloom. If the plants receive too much light during the night hours, it could trick them into behaving as though the days are longer than they really are, thus keeping them from blooming at the right time.

Q We want to add some decorative lights to our landscape. Are LED lights better than incandescent ones?

A Both types of lights have their advantages and disadvantages. LED lights are popular because they have lower energy use than incandescent bulbs and last longer, so they need replacing less frequently. However some people prefer the softer, yellowish glow of incandescent lighting over that of the harsher white light from LED fixtures.

chapter 4

Trees, Shrubs & Vines

Planting Trees

Q We got a good deal on a couple of potted trees at the nursery. How do we plant them?

A Follow these steps: 1. Dig a hole twice as wide but no deeper than the container. 2. Check the root ball and loosen the outer roots. 3. Place the tree in the hole making certain that tree rests 1 or 2 inches above the surrounding grade. 4. Backfill the hole with the soil that you excavated. If the garden soil is heavy clay, it may help to amend it first with organic matter to more closely match the soil mix in the container. 5. Water the root zone to settle the backfill and remove air pockets. 6. Add a 2- to 4-inch-deep layer of mulch to suppress weeds and conserve moisture.

Planting Trees

Q I plan to buy some trees and have found some mail-order ones that are a lot cheaper than those at the local nursery. Are these OK to buy?

A If you plant your trees properly, they will likely be fine, whatever type you choose. Young, small trees are often sold bare root. This is a common method of selling trees by mail order, because it's less expensive to ship the plant without heavy soil. Low cost is the major advantage of bare-root plants. However, they require greater care to prevent roots from drying during transport and planting. Bare-root plants are available only early in spring while the plants are still dormant.

Q What's the best way to plant a bare-root tree? We ordered several from a mail-order nursery and want to be ready when the plants arrive.

A Here's what to do:
1. Before planting a bare-root tree, soak the roots for a few hours in a bucket of water.
2. Dig a hole wide and deep enough to accommodate the roots without cramping them.
3. Prune back any broken or dead roots to healthy tissue.
4. Set the plant in the hole, spreading the roots evenly over a cone of soil.
5. Backfill the hole until it is three-fourths full. Then water thoroughly.
6. Fill the hole with the soil until it is at ground level. If the plant has settled in too deeply during watering, pull it up gently to the correct level.
7. Firm the soil with your foot to eliminate any air pockets that may be left in the planting hole.
8. Shape a ridge of soil around the edge of the planting hole to create a watering saucer, and water again.

Q Our conservation department is selling bare-root evergreens for windbreaks. I thought that only deciduous trees and shrubs could be planted bare root. Will these bare-root evergreens grow well?

A You're correct that most bare-root plantings are done with dormant, deciduous woody plants. However seedling pines, spruces, and citrus are also commonly sold bare root. It's especially important to keep the roots moist on these bare-root plants with needles or leaves because they can dehydrate quickly. It's also important to plant them when weather conditions are cool and moist.

Q What's the best way to pick out trees for our yard?

A Consider what you want the tree to do: look pretty, shade the driveway, block the wind or a neighbor's view, or provide flowers or fruit. Will it be part of a formal planting area, or will it be featured as a specimen? Consider its size at maturity. Will there be enough room for it? Once you have answered those questions, you can move on to selecting the tree that fits your needs. You may even find that a shrub is better suited for a particular location than a tree.

Planting Trees

Q How do I decide whether I need an evergreen or a deciduous tree? Where is the best spot for each kind?

A Because a tree is a permanent part of the landscape, the most important thing about deciding where to put one is envisioning its mature size and shape. Evergreens are the best trees for the northwest side of your house, or between the house and the coldest winds you get on your property. Deciduous trees are the best choice for the southwest and southeast sides of your house. They provide shade in the heat of summer.

Q Can you recommend some shade trees that grow rapidly?

A I typically don't recommend planting fast-growing trees. Fast-growing species generally develop problems because they have soft wood that breaks easily. These trees are much more likely to lose limbs or fall during storms or periods of heavy winds. Many fast-growing species are more likely to catch diseases and die sooner too. About the time they become effective as a shade tree, they may suddenly die or decline. Then you have to start over again. In many cases, trees with a moderate growth rate have gotten a bad rap as slow growers. If provided with the right growing conditions, they can add 1 to 2 feet or more of growth per year.

Q I've noticed that the nurseries are starting to sell plants again for this fall. Is this a good time to be adding to my garden?

A Yes, fall is perfect for buying nursery stock. Avoid plants with wilted foliage, broken branches, or uneven growth. A cheap plant is no bargain if it's going to die or introduce diseases to the healthy plants in your garden. Look for good branching structure with wide-angled branches spaced uniformly around the tree. Avoid trees with competing main shoots of nearly equal size. Buying young trees and shrubs saves you money if you're willing to wait a few extra years for them to mature.

Q When should I remove the stakes from my newly planted trees?

A Some experts recommend that you stake trees only for the first year after planting. Other experts recommend not staking at all. Most trees develop strong trunks faster if allowed to move freely with the wind. In any case, remove the stakes from your trees as soon as they can stand alone. The sooner the supports are removed, the faster the trees will become stronger.

Q I've noticed some trees listed as "B&B." What does this mean? Are they better than other types of trees?

A Trees sold with their roots in soil and wrapped in burlap tend to be larger and more mature. These balled-and-burlapped (B&B) trees grow in the ground and are dug in fall, late winter, or spring, then wrapped and shipped to garden centers. B&B trees are usually more expensive but can be a good value because they are large and can become established quickly.

Q What's the proper way to plant trees? Can I kill them by planting them wrong?

A When planting trees in large beds, prepare the entire area—not just individual holes. If the soil is compacted and poorly drained, create a good root zone by amending the beds with compost or peat moss and working it in well. Place a balled-and-burlapped plant in the hole so the top of the root ball is about 1 inch above the soil's surface. Remove any twine or wire holding the burlap in place, and cut off the burlap as far down as you can. Fill the planting hole about two-thirds of the way with the soil you removed from the hole. Water well to settle the soil and eliminate air pockets. When the water has drained, finish filling the hole with soil. Firm it to make sure there are no air pockets, then soak the soil thoroughly. Finally, add a 2- to 4-inch-deep layer of organic mulch, such as shredded bark. Water young plants as needed to keep the soil evenly moist.

Q When I plant balled-and-burlapped trees, do I need to remove the burlap before planting?

A You need to remove the burlap from the root ball of trees. Suppliers traditionally used standard burlap because it's tough, its natural fibers rot in the hole, it doesn't disturb the soil around the roots, and it makes planting easier. But today's burlap may be made from synthetic fibers, which are difficult to distinguish from traditional burlap and don't decay in the soil. Cut away as much burlap as possible from the sides of the root ball after you've positioned it in the hole. Because most roots grow outward rather than downward, this will allow them to grow without restraint. If the ball is encased in a wire cage, cut away the cage too. Then you can get at the burlap and remove it.

Q I want to have a live Christmas tree that I can plant in the yard after the holidays. What is the best way to do that?

A Success with a live Christmas tree requires some advance planning and cooperative weather. If you live in an extremely cold part of the country, your chances of success are diminished. Dig a planting hole for the tree before the ground freezes. Store the soil in a garage or shed where it won't freeze, or cover it with a thick layer of mulch or leaves to reduce the chance of freezing. You might also want to fill the hole with mulch or leaves to keep the surrounding soil from freezing. Choose a healthy tree from a nursery or garden center. Keep the tree outside until just a few days before the holidays. When you move the tree inside, keep it as cool as possible to prevent it from beginning growth. Leave it indoors for no more than a few days. Be sure the root ball stays moist but not waterlogged. Plant the tree as soon as possible after the holidays. Follow good planting procedures: Water it in thoroughly and mulch heavily.

Small Trees

Q I am looking for a tree that has color all season long and won't grow higher than 20 feet. What do you recommend?

A Few small trees have interest all year, but most look attractive throughout the growing season. Here are several to consider: 1. Amur maple (*Acer ginnala*), 2. Crape myrtle (*Lagerstroemia*), 3. Redbud (*Cercis*), 4. Crabapple (*Malus*), 5. Flowering dogwood (*Cornus florida*), 6. Japanese maple (*Acer palmatum*), 7. Stewartia, 8. Japanese tree lilac (*Syringa*), and 9. Serviceberry (*Amelanchier*).

Planting Trees

Q Do you have any tips about where to put certain tree shapes?

A Columnar trees, such as gray birch and arborvitae, take up little room on the ground but grow tall and stately. They make excellent hedges along property lines to screen views or block wind. Vase-shape and spreading trees, such as red oak, white oak, and sugar maple, produce lots of shade. Weeping trees, such as willow, beech, and Higan cherry, need room to spread because they grow nearly as wide as they do tall. Pyramid shapes include pin oak, littleleaf linden, sweetgum, and larch. Their formal look works well on lawns or along a street. Small flowering trees, such as dogwood, crabapple, flowering cherry, hawthorn, and magnolia make excellent accent trees. They're ideal beneath power lines where they can fill the view yet not interfere with wires.

Q I would like to plant a tree in a spot that's shady. It will be in front of my bedroom window, so I'd like something that's beautiful during all four seasons. I live in Zone 4.

A For your climate, I would recommend native pagoda dogwood (*Cornus alternifolia*). It produces small clusters of white flowers in late spring or early summer. These blooms turn into dark-blue fruits that birds find appealing. Another native tree that tolerates shade is American hornbeam (*Carpinus caroliniana*). It has blue-green leaves that turn yellow or red in autumn. In summer, it produces yellow-green catkins that look like hops. If the shade is not too dense, downy serviceberry (*Amelanchier arborea*) would be a good choice. It has white blooms in spring, blue fruits in early summer, and excellent orange-red color in fall.

Q My homeowners association wants to plant more trees. Could you give us a list of good urban trees to choose from?

A Good trees for urban conditions include the following: 1. Crabapple (*Malus*), 2. Ginkgo (*Ginkgo biloba*), 3. Japanese zelkova (*Zelkova serrata*), 4. Linden (*Tilia*), 5. Norway maple (*Acer platanoides*), 6. Oak (*Quercus*), 7. Sweetgum (*Liquidambar styraciflua*), and 8. Thornless honeylocust (*Gleditsia triacanthos inermis*)

Q Can you suggest some native trees to plant in my landscape?

A Use this regional list of native trees as a starting point.

East: 1. American hornbeam (*Carpinus*), 2. Black gum (*Nyssa sylvatica*), 3. Eastern redbud (*Cercis canadensis*), 4. Honeylocust (*Gleditsia*)

Southeast: 1. Black gum, 2. Carolina silverbell (*Halesia*), 3. Sassafras (*Sassafras*) 4. Sweetgum (*Liquidambar*)

Midwest: 1. Linden (*Tilia*), 2. Bur oak (*Quercus macrocarpa*), 3. Honeylocust 4. Ironwood (*Ostrya*), 5. Kentucky coffee tree (*Gymnocladus*)

Northwest: 1. Bigleaf maple (*Acer macrophyllum*) 2. Douglas fir (*Pseudotsuga*), 3. Pacific dogwood (*Cornus nuttallii*), 4. White fir (*Abies concolor*)

Southwest: Arizona cypress (*Cupressus*), 2. Bigtooth maple (*Acer grandidentatum*), 3. Gambel oak (*Quercus gambelii*), 4. Pinyon pine (*Pinus edulis*)

Small Trees

Q I'd like to plant a couple of trees with good fall foliage color. What would you recommend?

A Fall foliage color is dependent on many factors, including soil type, weather conditions, and species of tree. Here are some deciduous trees that usually produce good fall color: 1. Sugar maple (*Acer*), 2. Red oak (*Quercus*), 3. Ginkgo, 4. Black gum (*Nyssa*), 5. Red maple (*Acer*) 6. Japanese maple (*Acer*), 7. Flowering dogwood (*Cornus*), 8. Aspen (*Populus*), 9. Larch (*Larix*).

Tree Selection

Q I am soon to have a 100-year-old swamp maple tree removed. I would like to replace it with something that will be fast-growing and at the same time sure-rooted for strength. Can you recommend something that will offer good height and broad shade?

A You might not be able to get a tree that meets every requirement on your wish list. The problem is that anything that grows fast is not going to be long-lived or safe in the long term because quick growth means a weaker trunk, roots, and branches. Avoid fast-growing trees such as poplars, willows, or silver maples. Another swamp maple, also called red maple (*Acer rubrum*), might be the answer. A selection called 'Franksred' (Red Sunset) is a good possibility. It grows relatively fast for a maple, is drought-tolerant, and also has a dense habit.

Q Can I plant a red maple in San Diego? If not, can you recommend other suitable trees?

A Although red maple is native to a broad range of climates from Canada to Florida, it does best in Zones 3–9 in more humid climates. Many wonderful trees will do well in your climate, however. One favorite is California live oak (*Quercus agrifolia*). For smaller trees you might consider California buckeye (*Aesculus californica*), Jerusalem thorn (*Parkinsonia aculeata*), or western redbud (*Cercis occidentalis*).

Q I love flowering trees. We live in a new subdivision, and I'd like to bring some color here. What can you recommend?

A Here are some suggestions: 1. Flowering dogwood (*Cornus florida*), 2. Kousa dogwood (*C. kousa*), 3. Saucer magnolia (*Magnolia × soulangiana*), 4. Goldenchain tree (*Laburnum × watereri*), and 5. Flowering cherry (*Prunus*).

Q I just bought a lovely red maple. The tag on the plant says that this tree could grow to be 50 feet tall and 50 feet wide. Right now it is only 2 feet tall and looks like a skinny stick. How long will it take to reach its full size?

A The time it takes for a tree to reach maturity depends on many factors. Some trees are slow growers (20 to 30 years to reach full size) and some are fast (10 to 15 years). Red maple is a moderately fast grower; given good growing conditions, it should put on 1 to 2 feet of growth per year once established. The better the growing conditions you've given it, the happier it will be and the faster it will grow. Choose a planting location with full sun and good drainage. Then help the tree get established with deep and consistent watering for the first three years. As it gets older, annual mulching and supplemental watering in drought times will boost its growth rate as well.

Attracting Birds

Q I enjoy feeding the birds and watching wildlife in my backyard. I have room to plant a couple trees. Which kinds would be best to attract birds?

A Almost any tree will attract some kind of bird because trees are used as nesting sites. Some trees also provide food for birds. Here are some to consider: 1. Serviceberry (*Amelanchier*), 2. Hackberry (*Celtis*), 3. Hawthorn (*Crataegus*), 4. Eastern red cedar (*Juniperus virginiana*), 5. Crabapple (*Malus*), 6. Mulberry (*Morus*), 7. Cherry (*Prunus*), 8. Canadian hemlock (*Tsuga canadensis*), and 9. Plum (*Prunus*).

Messy Fruit

Q We'd like to plant a sweetgum tree but don't want those spiny seed balls, which are a nuisance. Are there any that don't develop the gum balls?

A American sweet gum (*Liquidambar styraciflua*) has male and female flowers on the same tree, so every tree can set fruit. A few cultivars make a claim of bearing "few fruit," but they aren't common. You may have to search for them. 'Cherokee' and columnar 'Shadow' are hardy to Zone 5. 'Rotundiloba' is hardy to Zone 6.

Q I have many seedling mulberry trees that have sprouted in our fence row. We cut them down to the ground several times a year, and they just keep coming back. Is there something I can use to kill the roots and not kill my shrubs and flowers?

A As soon as you make a cut, brush the stump with a brush-killing herbicide. Be sure to cover the entire stump, including the sides. I do this all the time and it works great. You can buy brush killers at your local garden center. This will not hurt the surrounding plants or soil as long as you only brush the tree stumps themselves.

Q I've been told there's a way to stop oak trees from producing acorns. Do you know if this is true? They make mowing underneath the oak trees difficult.

A Acorn production varies from year to year— sometimes you'll get a bumper crop and other times just a few. There isn't a simple way to prevent the acorns from forming. Florel (ethephon) growth regulator can be sprayed on the trees when they bloom to prevent acorn formation. But timing can be tricky for the average homeowner to detect. (Oak flowers aren't showy like those of crabapple or cherry.) And even if you get the timing right, the spray must cover the entire tree, or the portion of the tree missed by the spray will produce some acorns. Home spray equipment typically won't reach to the top of a mature oak tree. That means you'll have to hire a professional tree service to do the job. The spray is effective for only one year, so it would have to be reapplied annually. Over time, that adds up to a significant expense.

Q The fruits on my crabapple tree make a mess when they drop on my patio. Is there anything that I can spray to prevent the fruits from forming?

A There are several possible sprays that you can use. None is perfect, so your tree may still set some fruit. Florel (ethephon) and Fruitone (naphthalene acetic acid) or App-L-Set (also NAA) are growth regulators that can limit fruit set if sprayed at the right time during bloom and if weather conditions are right. Sevin (carbaryl) is also sometimes used as a fruit-thinning agent, but it is highly toxic to bees. These products need to be sprayed every year. A better long-term solution may be to replace the tree with something less messy.

Evergreen Selection

Q I'd like to plant an evergreen tree for year-round color in the landscape. What would you suggest?

A Here are some to consider: 1. Arborvitae (*Thuja*), 2. False cypress (*Chamaecyparis*), 3. Fir (*Abies*), 4. Douglas fir (*Pseudotsuga*), 5. Spruce (*Picea*), 6. Pine (*Pinus*), 7. Holly (*Ilex*), 8. Southern magnolia (*Magnolia*), 9. California live oak (*Quercus*), 10. Atlas cedar (*Cedrus*).

Winter Burn

Q **I planted hollies last year but now, in late March, they look windburned. What can I do to bring them back to health?**

A It's not uncommon for broadleaf evergreens such as hollies to suffer winter burn, especially their first year after planting. After the damage has occurred there is little that can be done except to make certain that they get adequate water and fertilizer this growing season to support strong, healthy new growth. The browned leaves will not recover. They will eventually fall off, usually after new growth emerges in the spring. If the winter dessication was severe, there may be some branch-tip dieback. Wait to see where new growth emerges on the plant, and cut dead stems back to where new healthy growth begins. To prevent winter damage in the future, make certain that the plants are watered well going into the winter. If it is dry and warm over winter, they may even need midwinter watering. Also, if they are sited where they get a lot of direct afternoon winter sun, they may need some shading to prevent them from turning brown over winter.

Q **I live in Michigan, and after the snow melted our dwarf Alberta spruce had a brownish red spot on the front of it. What caused this?**

A This sounds like winter burn. I suspect that it's on the south or southwest side of the tree. During winter when the ground is frozen, the tree can't readily pull moisture out of the ground. Yet, on warm days it is transpiring and losing water. So essentially the plant is under midwinter drought stress. It helps to make certain the soil is saturated going into winter. And if the tree is exposed, you may need to put up a temporary shade barrier of burlap or similar material to keep the browning from recurring.

Winter Protection

Q **With the extreme cold weather this past winter, we lost one of our favorite trees. Some of the other trees and shrubs look as if they were burned. Is there anything we can do to provide winter protection in the future?**

A There are things you can do to protect your trees from killing winter chills. Water your trees and shrubs before winter—until the ground freezes. Shield young tree trunks from low-angled winter sun by wrapping the trunk with tree wrap. Insulate the ground out to the drip line with a 2- to 4-inch-deep layer of shredded bark or wood chips. And when you are shoveling snow, add a little extra around your trees and shrubs; a thick layer of snow also can act as mulch.

Q **What's the correct way to wrap a tree trunk for winter protection? Is the brown paper tree wrap better than plastic trunk guards?**

A The purpose of tree wrap is at least twofold. It protects tender trunks from winter sun damage, and it can prevent gnawing by rodents such as rabbits and voles. I prefer the brown crepe tree wrap because you can get a tight fit with it. Begin at ground level and wrap around the trunk, spiraling upward to the first branch (or even higher if the tree branches are low on the trunk). Use a strip of masking tape to secure the top. Be sure to remove the wrap in spring. Plastic tree guards have their place, but remember that dark-color ones can increase heat buildup on the trunk and potentially add to injury.

Sunscald

Q **I have a nine-year-old Japanese maple which has developed a 6-inch crack about 10 inches from the base. The crack is about 1½ inches deep and was not caused by anything like a plow or car. What can I do to stop the crack from spreading or should I just leave it? The tree is perfect except for this.**

A All maples are susceptible to sunscald (right) and frost crack because they have thin bark until they become older. It may help to wrap the trunk of your Japanese maple with tree wrap over winter, but during spring and summer, the tree wrap should be removed. Allow the crack to be exposed to sunlight and air so that it remains dry and seals itself off from possible rotting fungi. Do not try to cover it up with wound dressing or anything else. It is advisable to keep the tree watered well and fertilized to prevent further stress to it.

Q **I've just planted a new tree in my front yard. Do I need to put tree wrap on it?**

A Depending on the type of tree, you might wrap the tender, young trunk to prevent sunscald and protect it from damage in winter. Thin-barked species such as maples, lindens, and most fruit trees are most susceptible. Generally, after a tree develops a corky bark, it doesn't require tree wrap to protect it from the sun. Also, water your newly planted tree deeply at least once a week through the first growing season. More is better if the summer turns hot and dry.

Lightning Damage

Q **A huge tree in my yard was struck by lightning in a recent storm. Is there anything I can do to help it survive?**

A Tall trees are common targets for lightning strikes. The extent of damage from lightning varies greatly. Bark may be split open the full length of the tree. Branches may explode. A section of the top may be killed. Roots can be killed. You may need to wait and see if the tree needs to be removed or if it will recover; the extent of internal damage can't be determined immediately. Trim back loose bark to where it is solidly attached. Fertilize the tree and keep it watered during dry periods. Continue to monitor the tree's health. Remove dead branches that may appear. If the tree continues to decline, it may need to be removed.

Trunk Damage

Q **I have a hawthorn tree approximately eight years old. The bark of the tree looks as if an animal tried to climb it and scratched up the bark all the way to the branches. What could have caused this? I had wire around the bottom so the rabbits wouldn't bother it, and there is no problem with this area.**

A Do you live in an area where there are lots of deer? It sounds like deer damage, when young bucks scratch their heads on trees as their antlers start to emerge. It's also possible that your hawthorn has frost cracks. These splits can develop in the bark during cold weather with alternating freezing and thawing cycles.

Mulch

Q Is it a good idea to mulch around a newly planted tree?

A A layer of mulch around your new tree saves water, decreases stress, and keeps the grass from competing with the tree for nutrients. The ring of mulch also keeps you and your lawn mower away from the trunk and reduces nicks in the bark, which allow insects and disease to get in. Keep the mulch away from the trunk to prevent rodents from hiding in it and gnawing the tree bark.

Q I have a lot of pine cones and sweetgum balls. Can I use them as mulch?

A Pine cones and sweetgum balls make an attractive mulch, and the practice is far better for the environment than burning them. Chopping them up is not necessary unless you prefer the look of a finer mulch. As a bonus, some research indicates that rabbits don't like to hop across the spiney gum balls. So you may be protecting your trees from hungry bunnies at the same time.

Q How much mulch should I place around my trees? I've seen piles of mulch around trees that look almost 1 foot deep.

A You're right in thinking that deep piles of mulch are bad. When the mulch depth is greater than about 6 inches, it can restrict air to the roots and slow water infiltration into the soil. The result: Roots grow up into the mulch rather than into the soil. When dry conditions arrive, they become more susceptible to drought injury. Another point to remember about mulch application is to keep it away from the trunk. Mulch piled against the trunk can cause rots to develop. On the other hand, spread the mulch far and wide. Tree roots extend several times farther than the branches. By applying mulch over a wide area, you reduce competition for the tree and encourage faster growth.

Q My young red maple has been slow to leaf the last two years. This year the bark started splitting, and the tree turned brown and died. This is the second maple I have planted in the same spot. The same thing happened to the other maple after three years. What could be causing trees to die in this spot? It is in full sun in the center of a lawn.

A Several things might be killing your maples. When maples are young, they have thin bark that is prone to sunscald damage on the trunk. It shows up as a long vertical scar on the south or west side of the trunk. Sunscald does severe damage but usually doesn't kill the tree. There may be planting problems. Could the trees have been planted too deeply? In heavy soils it's best to plant the tree slightly higher than the surrounding soil level so the roots will have better aeration. Mower blight—bruising the trunk with the lawn mower—can kill trees. Try mulching your tree to keep the mower away.

Fertilizing Trees

Q **I added way too much nitrogen to my Japanese maple. Should I add other nutrients to the soil to try to help my tree?**

A Trying to balance an overdose of nitrogen fertilizer with an excess of other fertilizer elements is not a good idea. Fortunately, nitrogen is relatively mobile and comparatively short-lived in the soil. You may be able to help the process along by watering heavily to flush some nitrogen from the soil. The best solution here is to allow time and natural forces break down the nitrogen. By next spring, things should be back in balance for your garden.

Q **I bought two Yoshino cherry trees last fall and recently planted them. Do they require any specific feeding or pruning?**

A The best thing you can do for your new trees is to mulch them. Apply a 3- or 4-inch layer of organic mulch. Keep it a few inches away from the trunk, and extend the mulch ring out to the dripline (the farthest reach of the branch tips.) No fertilizer is necessary right away unless you are concerned about soil fertility. If your soil is poor, a balanced fertilizer (10-10-10 or 12-12-12, for example) is a good idea. Don't prune your trees unless it's just to remove suckers near the trunk. The trees will use every bit of leaf surface they have to support the growth and establishment of their root systems.

Q **I had some chicken manure piled 3 to 4 feet from my new maple tree. The tree had dark green leaves and now has a greenish yellow color to it. My neighbor says I shouldn't have put any manure on the tree.**

A It's unlikely that the manure piled several feet away had a direct effect on the change in leaf coloration of your maple tree. However, chicken manure is high in ammonia content, so if it were quite fresh, the ammonia might have drifted through the air and caused burning. It's true that newly planted trees need little fertilizer. It's best to let them get established the first year before applying many supplemental nutrients. Composted manure would be good. It also adds organic matter.

Q **Is a tablespoon the correct amount of fertilizer to give to one tree or shrub?**

A Fertilizer rates vary based on the product formulation; follow the application rate listed on the package instructions. A tablespoon of 10-10-10 granular fertilizer would hardly make a difference on a tree or shrub outdoors, but would be far too much for a potted plant indoors, for example. Labels may be tedious to read, but are packed with valuable information.

Q **Are fertilizer spikes the best way to fertilize trees?**

A Spikes are a convenient way to apply fertilizer to the root zone of a tree, but they're no better than other forms of fertilizer. Also keep in mind that if you're fertilizing the lawn around the tree, it may be getting plenty of nutrition without supplemental feeding.

Stump Removal

Q What's the easiest and quickest way to get rid of tree stumps?

A The easiest and quickest way to remove unwanted tree stumps is not necessarily the least expensive. You'll want to balance what budget you have for stump removal with the desire for quick removal. Many tree-removal companies have large stump grinders that chip up the stump, including major roots that are just below ground. This can be done within a couple hours but can be expensive. Small stumps (less than 2 inches in diameter) may be pulled out with a tractor or four-wheel-drive utility vehicle. You'll usually need to do some chopping of brace roots to free the stump.

Q Do stump remover products really work?

A Stump rotting compounds are generally ineffective. However, the process usually recommended for their use does increase the rate of decay. Drilling holes into the stump so that moisture and oxygen can get to a larger surface area to begin the decay process will do as much or more to rot the stump than the actual chemical in the stump-rotting product.

Exposed Roots

Q I have a couple pine trees that were planted shallowly and have exposed roots aboveground. Should I cover them?

A Pine trees are sensitive to changes in soil level. You may be able to add a thin layer of soil without causing damage if the trees were recently planted. However, avoid adding more than a shallow layer. If you want to disguise the roots, you can cover them with a mulch of shredded bark or some other material.

Q Several of the large shade trees in my backyard have exposed roots that cause my children to trip when they are playing. Is there a safe and inexpensive way to cover the roots without damaging the trees?

A Covering the roots with soil may harm them. Some trees are more sensitive to added soil than others. Oaks are particularly sensitive to changes in soil level. If the roots die, the rest of the tree will soon follow. You might consider converting the area to a garden filled with shade-loving groundcovers. That way your children will avoid the area altogether. Often, exposed tree roots are an indication of compacted soil. You might try aerating the soil around the tree with a core aerator to encourage deeper rooting.

Ash

Q **The leaves of my green ash tree are falling off. Some of the leaves have brown spots. What should I do?**

A It sounds as though your tree has become infected with a fungal disease called ash anthracnose. This disease attacks white ash and green ash just after bud break in spring. It is more severe in cool, wet weather. Symptoms often don't show up until several weeks later. The fungus causes large, irregular brown patches on young leaflets, usually following the veins. Leaves may be deformed, and leaf drop can be severe, especially in the lower part of the tree where the foliage is slow to dry. By the time you notice leaf drop, the fungus has usually run its course, and no treatment is needed. It is a disease of early spring; as the weather warms and becomes drier, reinfection is unlikely. Even with heavy leaf drop, overall tree health is rarely affected; trees usually send out a second flush of leaves. If a tree has been infected, do what you can to promote growth and avoid stress to the tree. Water the tree during dry periods; fertilize if it's not growing vigorously, and mulch around its base.

Q **I have heard that there is a disease that is sweeping the country that infects ash trees. What is it, and what are the symptoms? I have a large one in my yard that I want to save.**

A There's an insect called emerald ash borer that is spreading from infestation points in the Northeast and Midwest to a broader geographic range. The adult borer is a metallic greenish beetle. Its larvae tunnel under the bark of the tree and can kill it within a year or two. Often you'll see branch dieback first. If you look closely, you may also see D-shape exit holes where the larvae emerge from the bark. For more details, go to *emeraldashborer.info*.

Birch

Q **The leaves on my river birch turned yellow and began dropping in early August. What's wrong with the tree?**

A Early fall leaf color in late summer is probably an environmental problem related to hot, dry weather. River birch lives up to its name; it requires a great deal of water. During drought conditions, it benefits from periodic soaking. Mulching under the canopy of the tree will keep the soil cooler and cut down on evaporation. It is unlikely that your tree will leaf out again this season because the defoliation happened late in summer. The tree should leaf out fine next season.

Q **I planted a paper birch about 15 years ago. I noticed last year that caterpillars infested it in the summer. Before fall arrived, part of the tree started dying.**

A Your birch may be stressed because of environmental conditions, making it more susceptible to insect attack. Birches are short-lived, especially if grown in a sunny, dry location. You can help by watering them regularly and mulching the root zone, but don't expect them to live more than about 20 to 30 years at best. The "worms" that you saw early in summer are likely birch sawfly larvae. These pests can strip leaves off the tree. Because birches continue to put out new growth all season, they usually outgrow the insect attack. The dieback problem is likely due to bronze birch borer. It causes damage to birches similar to that of emerald ash borer on ash trees (see answer at left).

Crabapple

Q **Last year I planted a flowering crabapple tree that had lots of pink flowers on it. The tree came through the winter OK, but it has absolutely no flowers. Is it because it's planted near the road and gets salt spray in the winter?**

A It's not unusual for a crabapple tree to not bloom for the first several years after transplanting. The tree puts most of its energy into developing a new root system first. Then it goes on to flower. If the leaves look healthy and vigorous, it's not likely that road-salt spray is affecting the tree. If that were the case, you would see small leaves with browned edges.

Q **Our flowering crabapple tree is dropping leaves. Many leaves are yellow and have black spots on them. What is causing this?**

A It sounds as though your tree has apple scab, a common fungal disease of crabapples and apples. Apple scab gets off to a great start with humid spring weather. Once it has spread, it's pretty futile to start spraying a fungicide. Rake up and remove all fallen leaves and fruit so that next year there won't be as much spore activity. Then start spraying a fungicide as soon as you see green tips on the buds next spring. You'll have to spray repeatedly, about every 7 to 10 days for two months. You may want to consider replacing this susceptible crabapple with a new variety that has good resistance to the disease. That way you won't have to look at a defoliated tree every year or spray constantly.

Q **We have a crabapple tree that last year had branches with wilted leaves and sappy black branches. Someone told us it was fireblight and that we should probably get rid of it. We trimmed a lot of the branches that were infected and kept it. Do you think we can save the tree, or would it be better to get rid of it?**

A Fireblight can affect other apple trees and close relatives such as pear, mountain ash, and cotoneaster. But if you removed all affected branches last year by pruning them out, it's likely that you have removed the possible source of infection. Fireblight is a bacterial disease that can easily be spread by insects or splashing water from an infected branch to an open wound. Avoid pruning your tree during the growing season to help prevent infection.

Q **Our crabapple looks terrible all year long. It has produced fruit only once in 15 years. It flowers sporadically. In spring, the few flowers it produces fall off, then so do the few leaves. What can we do?**

A There could be several problems happening here. Many older crabapple varieties are more susceptible to diseases than newer hybrids. It's possible that your tree has apple scab, a fungus that defoliates trees by midsummer. Because the tree defoliates every year, it is stressed and may not form many flowerbuds. It may be time to replace your tree with a disease-resistant variety. Tea crabapple (*Malus hupehensis*) has good scab resistance, as do many named cultivars, such as 'Adams', 'Camzam' (Camelot), 'Cardinal', 'Donald Wyman', 'Guinzam' (Guinevere), 'Indian Summer', 'Prairifire', 'Robinson', and 'Sutyzam' (Sugar Tyme).

Crape Myrtle

Q My crape myrtle tree has a powdery whitish substance on the leaves. What is this stuff, and how can I get rid of it?

A The white substance you're seeing is probably powdery mildew, a fungus that appears as a white dusting on leaf surfaces. This is particularly prevalent on crape myrtle (*Lagerstroemia indica*) in hot, humid weather. It won't kill your tree, but it is unsightly, causes early leaf drop and leaf distortion, and won't go away without treatment. Spray a mix of 1 tablespoon of baking soda and a few drops of dish detergent in 1 gallon of water to get the problem under control. Or you could apply a commercial fungicide from a garden center. Clean up and discard fallen leaves promptly. Improve air circulation around infected plants to prevent infection from reoccurring. You could also remove your susceptible plant and replace it with a mildew-resistant one such as 'Catawba', 'Natchez', 'Yuma', 'Zuni', or 'Tonto'.

Q I put in several young crape myrtles this year. The branches look long and leggy. Should I cut them back, and, if so, when?

A Although crape myrtle can be pruned any time after the leaves have dropped in fall through early spring, I'd leave young plants alone for the first growing season and see how they shape up. Then before you prune, decide whether you want to grow them as trees with distinct trunks or as multistem shrubs. If trees are your goal, remove the many suckering inner shoots as they appear. In either case, prune for shape and to remove crossing or damaged branches. Encourage a second flush of flowers in late summer by deadheading (clipping off spent flowerheads) right after the first bloom.

Q My crape myrtles produce lots of blooms, but I've noticed that my neighbor's trees have brighter blooms. What can I do to make my trees bloom brighter?

A Many factors influence a plant's bloom color. The amount of moisture the plant gets while blooming plays a role, as does the temperature during this time. The most likely cause for the bloom color difference, though, is that you're growing a different variety from your neighbor. There are more than 300 crape myrtle varieties in cultivation, and many have slight differences in the color of their blooms. If this is the case, there's nothing you can do to get brighter flowers other than to replace the plants with a brighter blooming selection.

Q Three years ago I planted a crape myrtle that was in bloom. The next two summers it didn't bloom. What should I do?

A Crape myrtle may not bloom for several reasons. Check to see whether it was planted too deeply. (It should have been planted at the same level as it was growing when you bought it.) Another problem could be that it is not getting enough sun. Crape myrtle requires full sun; slightly acidic, well-drained soil; and only minimal fertilizer. Lastly, have you pruned it? The trees should be pruned only from autumn through early spring. Crape myrtle blooms on new wood. If you prune during the early summer months, you may be cutting off that year's flowers.

Dogwood

Q **What kind of care do dogwoods need? Which are the best ones to plant?**

A One of the most popular ornamental trees is flowering dogwood (*Cornus florida*). Myriad pests and diseases threaten its existence in New England and the mid-Atlantic states. Dogwoods like an acidic, well-drained soil that is mulched to maintain coolness and moisture. Most varieties prefer partial shade, but some can handle full sun. Dogwoods that experience poorly drained soil or drought conditions show signs of stress, then decline and die. Kousa dogwood (*C. kousa*) and pagoda dogwood (*C. alternifolia*) are more disease-resistant than flowering dogwood.

Q **Our dogwood trees are not blooming well. It looks like the bark is coming off, and there are several dead limbs. What's wrong with them?**

A Flowering dogwood is hardy in Zones 5–9. If you live in the colder end of the range, your trees may lack flowerbud hardiness. Northern nurseries often sell stock that is southern-grown. With some plants, it makes no difference. In the case of flowering dogwoods, it does. Make certain your dogwoods came from a local source. If that's not the problem, several disease and insect problems may be at work. From borers to anthracnose, stressed dogwoods are susceptible to many foes and woes. Make certain that your trees are planted in the right location and getting proper care.

Q **Last spring, I planted a flowering dogwood in a large pot and placed it where it receives morning sun on my deck. The leaves on the tree keep burning. I want to plant it in my yard but do not know where to put it.**

A Your flowering dogwood might be unhappy in its pot, because these plants don't like drying out. I suspect that moisture is more of a problem than excess sunlight. Dogwoods need protection from hot afternoon sun. If your soil is alkaline, amend it with peat moss or other types of organic matter before planting your tree. Water it well after planting. Be sure the soil has no chance to dry out, especially for the first few years, but avoid overwatering.

Elm

Q **How can I get rid of seedling elm trees? Every year I get lots of them popping up in my yard.**

A It's easiest to kill seedling elm trees when they are tiny. Weed killer applied to seedlings with established root systems will only set the tree back, not kill it. For these larger seedlings, you may need to cut off the top of the seedling and daub the concentrated weed killer directly on the cut surface.

Ginkgo

Q **We want to plant a ginkgo in our yard but have heard that ginkgo fruits smell terrible. Are there some varieties that don't produce fruit?**

A Ginkgo (*Ginkgo biloba*) has separate male and female trees, so purchasing a male cultivar is the best way to avoid the smelly and messy-fruiting female ginkgo. Avoid purchasing a seedling ginkgo; there's no way to know what sex the mature tree will become. Instead, purchase a named male cultivar that has been grafted onto a seedling rootstock or propagated from stem cuttings. Male cultivars to look for include 'Autumn Gold', 'Fairmont', 'Princeton Sentry', 'Saratoga', and 'Shangri-la'.

Q **We live in Minnesota and planted a small ginkgo tree several years ago. Although we were told the tree is supposed to be hardy here, it suffers winter dieback every year. Will it ever get to be a big tree?**

A In Minnesota, you're at the northern end of the hardiness range for ginkgo. But the tree should be hardy in the southern half of that state. One problem may be that you started with a tree that's too small. Immature ginkgo trees are slightly less hardy than mature ones. Those under about 5 feet tall are more likely to suffer winter injury than larger trees. So if you can protect your tree well for its first few years, it may take off for you once it gets a bit older.

Hackberry

Q **The leaves on my hackberry tree have big warty bumps on them. What are these? Will they harm the tree?**

A The problem you're describing is hackberry nipple gall. These protrusions on the leaves are caused by an insect called the hackberry gall psyllid. Although the tree may look bedraggled, they cause no harm to the tree, so there's no need to spray for them.

Hawthorn

Q **I have a Washington hawthorn but don't know anything about it. Will it grow into my power lines?**

A Washington hawthorn (*Crataegus phaenopyrum*) is a small tree that can grow to 30 feet. The tree shouldn't interfere with your power lines unless they are low. Plant Washington hawthorn in full sun and well-drained soil. The tree produces small white flowers in spring and edible red or orange berries in autumn. The foliage has burgundy tones in autumn too. It's an ideal tree for attracting songbirds.

Holly

Q My Burford holly has outgrown its space. The plant is more than 5 feet tall and wide. Can I prune it back?

A Unless you want to prune your holly regularly or it is a dwarf variety, I have bad news: You need to move your plant. Burford holly (*Ilex cornuta* 'Burfordii') typically grows 15 feet tall and wide. Dwarf varieties usually grow about half that. Because the plant naturally grows much larger than the space it is in, if you were to leave it where it is you would need to constantly keep it pruned, which would weaken it. If you decide to prune, avoid cutting the plant back severely. It's best to remove only a small portion of the foliage at a time.

Q My holly tree doesn't produce any berries. What's wrong with it?

A A few species of plants, such as holly, bittersweet, and ginkgo, are dioecious—meaning that their male and female flowers are on different plants. You need to know which is which only if you want to grow one for its fruit. Only a female dioecious plant can produce fruit, and only if a male plant is nearby to pollinate it. You may have a male tree. Or if no other holly trees are nearby you may have a female tree that is not getting pollinated. Many cultivated varieties of holly sold at nurseries indicate on their plant tag whether they are male or female. Make certain that you have one of each to get berries.

Q I have a few different types of hollies. Some seem healthy and full of foliage with nice berries. A couple seem scrawny with little foliage. What is the best time to prune them?

A Late winter to early spring is the best time to prune your hollies. While it's best to make the pruning cuts just above a leaf or bud, hollies are quite tolerant of shearing at almost any point on the stem. Just prune back the long, errant stems to about the same length as shorter ones. They'll usually branch just below the point where you make the cut.

Honeylocust

Q My Sunburst honeylocust tree leaves are small and disfigured. What can I do to save the tree?

A It sounds as though your honeylocust tree has been attacked by the honeylocust plant bug. Both the adult and nymph stage of this insect feed on expanding leaves, causing stippling (yellow spots) and leaf distortion. By the time that you see the damage they may no longer be present. The good news is that well-established trees will not suffer permanent harm from the bugs. If you have a small tree, you can knock the bugs out of the tree canopy with a forceful jet spray of water. Insecticides will also control the bugs but usually are unnecessary.

Magnolia

Q I have a magnolia tree that flowers wonderfully, but the flowers last only two or three days, then turn brown. Is this normal?

A The 2- to 3-day lifespan of your magnolia blossoms is perfectly normal, and there's nothing you can do make the individual blooms last longer. If you fertilize with a high-phosphorous fertilizer (something with a big middle number like 5-10-5 or 10-30-10) you might promote more blooms, but it won't aid in the longevity of the blossoms. You only need to fertilize once per year with a slow-release pelletized fertilizer.

Q I have a nonblooming magnolia tree in my front yard. It does have a live oak shading it. Could this be why it won't bloom?

A Magnolias need full sun to develop flowers, so if the live oak has shaded the magnolia, the magnolia will not reliably develop flowers. Magnolia requires at least six to eight hours of direct sunlight to bloom.

Q I have a saucer magnolia tree, and this is the first year I've seen huge red pods dropping from the tree. Is this normal? If so, can the seeds inside be planted?

A Your saucer magnolia (*Magnolia × soulangeana*) is finally mature. These fruits contain seed. However, most garden magnolias are grown from cuttings or hybrids and won't come true from seed. Plus, they are extremely difficult to germinate and slow to grow. Unless you enjoy a challenge, I'd recommend simply enjoying their burst of color on the tree, and leave propagation of new magnolias to nursery professionals.

Q Last spring we expanded our patio near an established magnolia. This spring it has few flowers and few leaves. What can I do to restore it to its former glory?

A Magnolias have a shallow root system, which may have been damaged when you built the patio. The roots of most trees extend well beyond the branching structure. If you dug within 4 feet of the trunk, you may have removed almost half of the tree's root system. Now that the damage is done, prune out all dead wood. Restrict foot traffic around the tree out to the drip line (the place where the branches end). Spread a layer of compost, and top with mulch to a depth of no more than 4 inches combined, keeping the mulch a few inches away from the trunk. Make sure to water the tree adequately and consistently—but not excessively— throughout the growing season. With time, it may recover.

Maple

Q We planted a maple about 30 years ago. This year we discovered a crack running up the trunk. It is oozing sap and is filled with insects. We tried using tar to cover the crack, but it's still oozing. Is there anything we can do?

A Cracks such as this on maple could be due to sunscald, freezing temperatures, or lightning. In any case, the tar won't help and in fact could be making matters worse for your tree. A layer of tar can seal in moisture and promote further rot. The insects you see are secondary; they're attracted to the sap and may not be harmful at all.

Q I recently pruned my maple tree, and now sap is flowing out of the cut. Will this hurt the tree? Should I put anything on the wound?

A The best time to prune maples and other trees with heavy late-winter sap flow is after they have fully leafed out in early summer. Unless you don't mind stained trunks, avoid pruning your maple tree in late winter when the majority of other trees are pruned. The sap flow doesn't harm the tree, but it can create unattractive wet streaks on the bark. There is no need to seal the cuts with wound dressing. Allow nature to take its course in sealing off the cuts naturally.

Q I have a weeping Japanese maple. It has several shoots coming out of the base. Each shoot is going straight up and does not conform to the look of the tree. Can I cut these shoots at the base and make new trees?

A If these shoots are coming from the base of the plant, they probably aren't the same variety as the weeping top part of your Japanese maple. Most named varieties, and especially weeping ones, are grafted. Grafted plants are two different varieties; one variety

grows on the roots of the other. In the case of a weeping plant, an upright growing cultivar is used for the root system and trunk of the tree, and the weeping stems are grafted on top. Shoots sprouting from the base of the plant develop from the root variety. Your best option is to cut off these shoots at ground level and dispose of them. Although you could try rooting softwood cuttings, chances of success are slim unless you use rooting hormone and have a mist propagation system.

Q I live in the Midwest and have an inset in front of my home that is about 8 feet deep and receives very little sun. I would like to plant a Japanese maple there. Will it like this spot?

A Japanese maple (*Acer palmatum*) often fails to grow well for gardeners in the upper Midwest. The tree prefers warmer winters and cooler summers than your area typically sees. If you have your heart set on a Japanese maple, and you have the right microclimate, you may be able to make it thrive. The tree likes bright but filtered light and a protected spot. The inset in front of your home may be just right for a Japanese maple. It sounds as though it's protected from scorching summer sun, and the inset may also protect the tree from severe winter extremes.

Oak

Q **My pin oak isn't doing very well. Its leaves are pale and sparse. What's wrong, and what can I do?**

A Pin oak (*Quercus palustris*) is an attractive landscape tree, but it can look bad when grown in the wrong spot. Pin oak likes well-drained, slightly acidic soil. If your landscape soil has too high a pH, your tree can't absorb the nutrients (iron in particular) that it needs from the soil, and as a result it develops pale leaves. Typical symptoms of iron chlorosis are yellowed leaves with green veins. A spray of chelated iron, available at garden centers, may green up the foliage. But a long-term fix will require more work. Start with a soil test. If your soil is too alkaline, use elemental sulfur, iron sulfate, or another soil acidifier to lower the pH.

Q **I recently read that gypsy moths are attacking oak trees. What do you recommend as treatment for this?**

A Oak trees are a favorite food of gypsy moth larvae. But they don't necessarily need to be treated or sprayed. Healthy, established oak trees have a lot of energy reserves and can withstand an occasional defoliation. Small trees just getting established may benefit from a protective spray of Bt (*Bacillus thuringiensis*) soon after the larvae hatch out in spring. Gypsy moth populations go in cycles, so they may not need spraying every year. (There are some natural controls that help keep populations down.) Also, severe infestations may require aerial application over a large area, which means that your municipality or county may need to be involved.

Read more about oaks in our online plant encyclopedia at *bhg.com/oaks*.

Q **Can a tree be started from an acorn? If so, how do you do it?**

A Oak trees are easily grown from acorns. Gather acorns when they fall and sow them 1 inch deep in the ground or in pots. Protect your planting from foraging squirrels. Members of the white oak group (bur oak and swamp white oak) will send a root down immediately this fall, followed by a stem and leaves next spring. Members of the red oak group (pin oak, red oak, and black oak) need to go through winter before they'll sprout.

Q **I have a pin oak tree that needs pruning. Should I prune in early spring or wait until it stops shedding leaves and has new ones?**

A Prune pin oak trees only during the winter months (sometime between December and February) to avoid oak wilt disease. Open pruning wounds during the growing season can attract beetles that spread the disease. You can remove the lower branches on your pin oak, but it's best to remove a few each year rather than doing a lot of drastic pruning all at once.

Palm

Q I have a fishtail palm that is about 20 feet tall. My condo complex sent me a notice that it cannot be more than 10 feet tall. How do I trim it to make it survive?

A Most palms have one central growing point near the top of their stems. If this growing point is cut off, the entire palm dies. Only on palms with multiple stems arising from the ground can you cut off the taller stems and the shorter ones will continue to grow. Fishtail palm may be planted with multiple trunks, but you can't cut back the top of the stem without killing that shoot.

Q How do I treat scale on a very large potted palm tree?

A Scale insects are difficult to control because they are protected under their waxy scalelike coating. The most effective means of control is to swab the affected area of the plant with rubbing alcohol. If some fronds are severely infested, it may be simpler to cut them off and destroy them first. It usual takes several treatments with the rubbing alcohol dipped in cotton swabs (or a cloth rag) to bring the scale population down to a reasonable level.

Q I have a palm tree which I think got too cold sitting on my sun porch. Now some of the branches are turning brown. What can I do to save my tree?

A If the problem is cold damage, as you suggest, there's little you can do but wait and see if the palm is able to grow out of it. If the temperatures weren't too cold and the palm wasn't exposed to them for too long, it should start producing healthy new growth from the growing point which is somewhat protected from cold inside the main stem.

Q Can I grow a majesty palm as a yard plant in Zone 8?

A The majesty palm (*Ravenea*) is hardy to about 30°F so it would have to be grown as an annual or container garden plant in Zone 8. Some hardier palms that you might try are fan palm (*Washingtonia*), windmill palm (*Trachycarpus*), saw palmetto (*Serenoa*), palmetto (*Sabal*), and blue-needle palm (*Trithrinax*).

Pine

Q The center of my white pine tree is turning yellow. The tips are still green. Is it something I should worry about?

A Pine-needle drop happens every year. Some years it is more obvious or dramatic than others, but some needle loss occurs every year. Deciduous trees' leaves change color, and all drop pretty much at the same time. Eastern white pine (*Pinus strobus*) drops its third-year needles. The one- and two-year-old needles remain on the tree, making it "evergreen." If the tree put on a great deal of growth three years ago, and produced a lot of needles, the leaf drop will be more noticeable this year. This is a natural occurrence and not something to be alarmed about. Other evergreens also have seasonal needle drop, but it's usually most apparent on white pine.

Q I have a pine tree planted three years ago that is located in a fairly windy area. The limbs are green and supple, but the tips of all the needles are brown. Is the tree dead?

A If the browning occurred over winter this year, it could be that your tree suffered from some winter desiccation, drying out because it didn't have enough protection from winter winds. Recently planted evergreens are susceptible to winter burn, especially if

soil conditions are dry going into winter or if warm weather hits during winter while the ground is frozen. Wait and see whether new growth greens up this spring. If there is ample water available, the tree should put out new healthy green needles.

Q Can anything be grown under my ponderosa pine tree? I can't seem to get anything to grow there.

A It's difficult to grow plants in the ground underneath established pines or other evergreens. Evergreen's massive root systems absorb most of the moisture and nutrients from the soil around the tree. In addition, the evergreens may block out too much light for most plants to grow well. If there's enough light under your pine, you should be able to successfully grow plants in pots or large planters. Try shade-tolerant annuals such as impatiens, begonia, browallia, and torenia. You could also include shade-loving perennials such as sedges, ferns, periwinkle, and lamium.

Q I have a 12-foot-tall pine tree. The long needles have white scale on them. The needles are dropping, and the tree does not seem to be healthy. How do I treat it?

A Control of scale insects is difficult, but with repeated insecticide sprays you can bring the problem under control. The first step is to spray trees with an insecticide in spring when the crawlers are active. Then next year in early spring before new growth begins but after danger of frost has passed, spray the trees with Volck oil spray or lime sulfur (but not both) to kill overwintering eggs.

Q I have sawflies on my mugo pines. The ends are turning brown too. What is a safe and organic way to get rid of them? Is this a problem I will always have with mugos?

A Pine sawfly is a common pest on mugo pine (*Pinus mugo*), but won't necessarily appear every year. Spinosad and neem are natural insecticides that can be used to control the wormlike sawfly larvae.

Plum

Q **I'm having a problem with an ornamental purple-leaf plum tree. The leaves are laced with holes and there is damage to the bark, which is peeling. What should I do?**

A It sounds like your tree has two distinct problems. It's unlikely the leaf and bark problems are related. You clearly had some type of insect feeding on the leaves. If insects are still present you could try a general purpose insecticide, although slight defoliation from insect chewing usually needs no treatment. The bark is more problematic. Plums are rather short-lived, and often they will develop bark problems as they get older. If your tree is 15 years old or older, it could be a natural decline of the tree. If the tree is quite young, it may be winter injury from sunscald.

Poplar/Quaking Aspen

Q **Our neighbors recently cut down five poplars and ground the stumps because little shoots would pop up in their lawn. Now every neighbor has poplar pop-ups. How can we get rid of them?**

A Sadly, poplars (below) are invasive. As they get older, their roots can clog drains and pipes. In general, if everyone diligently mows the shoots, the roots will eventually die. You could call a professional lawn-care service or an arborist for treatment with a brush killer. You can also apply a brush killer especially formulated for persistent woody plants.

Q **I live in Montana and have clay soil. My aspen trees are not doing well, and two have died. They get black around the edges of the leaves and have developed bumps along the trunk. Any suggestions?**

A Quaking aspens (*Populus tremuloides*) are prone to two problems that may be happening here. Aspen leaf spot is a fungus that affects the foliage. Rake up and destroy fallen leaves to help prevent overwintering spores. And avoid wetting the foliage with sprinkler irrigation to cut down on the spread of the disease. If the problem is severe, you can apply a protective fungicide next spring as the trees are leafing out. But the problem is mostly aesthetic and doesn't really require spraying. The bumps on the trunk could be a type of aspen canker, a more serious condition that will often kill trees. I would take a sample to your local extension service or garden center for an upclose evaluation.

Q **I planted three aspen trees by my paved patio in sandy soil. Last summer the leaves got brown spots and holes, and the bark began to turn an orange color and then dark brown. Do the trees need to be removed?**

A Quaking aspens are high-elevation trees that need cool, moist conditions to thrive. Growing them at lower elevations in the Mountain West almost always puts them under stress, which in turn causes disease and insect problems to set in. Anything that you can do to provide conditions closer to those the trees experience at higher elevations would be helpful. That includes mulching the soil around them with 3 to 4 inches of organic mulch and keeping them watered well. Especially in the first couple of years after planting, the trees require extra moisture until their roots become established.

Redbud

Q **Our redbud has seedpods on the limbs that it never had before. The tree looks so sad without its normal profusion of leaves. Is this something we should worry about? Are we watering too much or too little?**

A The seedpods on your redbud (*Cercis canadensis*) are perfectly normal. They'll fall off on their own, and you may even end up with some seedling trees. Heavy seed production often causes a delay in leaf development. (The tree is putting its energy into seed production at the expense of the leaves.) If the leaf canopy isn't as thick as usual, consider applying a slow-release granular fertilizer around the base and out to the dripline of your tree. A balanced fertilizer such as 10-10-10 or 12-12-12 is best. You can give your tree a deep soaking during dry periods.

Q **I have a wooded area at the back of my property and would like to incorporate some blooming trees. I am thinking of planting redbud as well as a few azaleas. Do you think they will work well? There is a lot of shade with some late afternoon dappled sunlight.**

A Redbud should grow well in this situation. It is a native understory tree adapted to moderate shade. You might also consider pagoda dogwood (*Cornus alternifolia*), fringe tree (*Chionanthus virginicus*), and Carolina silverbell (*Halesia carolina*).

Q **I just bought a new house that has a young redbud tree in the front yard. It has very few pink flowers that bloom during the spring and sporadic leaves on its branches. I was considering pulling it out and planting another tree, but I love redbuds. Is it a slow-starting tree? Should I wait longer?**

A Give it more time. Redbud trees do not transplant happily, so it may need a little more time to get established well enough to produce the bloom you want. Another factor is sunlight. Although redbuds grow well in the shade, they bloom best with lots of sun. They prefer moist, but not wet, soil.

Redwood

Q **How can I eliminate the shoots that grow from the base of my redwood trees? Can I spray them with Roundup?**

A Spraying the shoots at the base of the tree with glyphosate (Roundup) could damage the entire tree. Even if you spray only the undesirable shoots, the herbicide will be absorbed by the needles and spread throughout the tree. In addition to dieback of the shoots, you may observe yellowing, browning, and disfiguration of other parts of the tree. A much better option is to prune off the unwanted shoots at ground level.

Spruce

Q My dwarf Alberta spruces have been doing great, but I recently noticed that one has turned brown at the top and lost its needles. Is there any way to save this tree?

A There are several possible causes of browning needles on your dwarf Alberta spruce (*Picea glauca* 'Conica'). One is the spruce spider mite. This tiny mite is active during cool fall and spring weather, feeding on needles of the spruce. If populations are high, you may see webbing. Often needles turn brown later in summer when temperatures rise. You can spray with a miticide or horticultural oil when the mites are present in spring or fall to prevent the problem in the future. Another possibility is winter damage to the spruce. A dry autumn, drying wind, and dry soil can cause browning. The browned needles won't recover from winter damage, though the tree may produce new growth from buds on browned branches.

Q My four dwarf Alberta spruce are getting too wide for my garden. I've been told they cannot be trimmed to make them skinnier. Is that true?

A It sounds as though dwarf Alberta spruce wasn't the best choice for your garden. They can grow 8 feet wide. Trim the new growth that appears on the side branches each year to keep them from getting much wider than they are now. Avoid pruning back into old wood that has no green needles on it.

Q I have several pyramidal blue spruce about 15 to 20 feet high growing throughout my yard. As they get older they are losing their lovely blue tinge. I know some people add certain minerals to the soil to increase the blue color. Have you heard of this?

A Color in spruces tends to fade as the plants mature. Some of the new hybrids remain quite blue through their lifetimes but are not as blue as they were when they were younger. Soil pH does not affect the blue coloration of spruces as it does with hydrangeas. Adding acidifying agents to the soil will have no effect.

Sycamore

Q **We have a sycamore tree in our backyard. This spring, all of a sudden, our tree dropped its leaves. What is this?**

A Rake up those diseased leaves, bag them, and throw them away. Your tree is most probably infected with sycamore anthracnose, a common foliar fungus, which usually appears in spring during wet weather. Normally the tree will leaf out again, and as the weather gets warm and dry, this fungus will subside.

Q **I have a sycamore tree that has webbing on it. There are small black seedlike specks on the leaves, and caterpillars are eating all the leaves! How do I get rid of this problem?**

A Your tree may have a couple insect problems. The webbing sounds like it may be from fall webworm, which attacks sycamore trees. If the webbing is in a location where you can reach it, the easiest control is to physically remove the webbing in the evening when the worms tend to gather back in the nest. If the webbing is on a large tree, the amount of defoliation that the worms do likely will not permanently harm the tree. The black specks on the leaves could be sycamore lace bugs. These pests suck plant sap from the leaves, causing the leaves to develop speckling of lighter yellow. If there is no speckling, it may just be the leftovers from the caterpillar feeding that you see.

Walnut

Q **I've heard that walnuts can kill other plants. Is this true?**

A Yes, walnut (*Juglans* spp.) is toxic to many other plants. Roots and leaves produce a toxin called juglone that adversely affects the growth of some species. Avoid growing the following plants near a walnut tree: American linden, apple, asparagus, blackberry, potentilla, cabbage, lilac, privet, cotoneaster, white pine, birch, peony, pepper, potato, rhododendron, magnolia, and tomato.

Q **What plants can I plant in the yard with a mature black walnut tree? Does the black walnut tree affect the entire yard or just a certain area around it?**

A The black walnut tree (below) can affect plants up to 75 feet away. Lined raised beds or container gardens are a good idea if you're growing vegetables. If you're planting an ornamental garden, try some of these walnut-tolerant plants: Hosta, bleeding heart, daffodil, Solomon's seal, coralbells, yarrow, spiderwort, bearded iris, lily-of-the-valley, astilbe, cranesbill, ajuga, woodland phlox, columbine, and daylily.

Willow

Q **Suddenly a five-year-old corkscrew willow has no leaves. Adjacent trees are fine. Could it be a beetle?**

A If it is a beetle defoliating the tree, you should see evidence of the beetle. There may be some of the veins of the leaves left as skeletons, or there may be insect frass from their feeding. There are leaf beetles that feed on willow and can cause defoliation. Other causes of defoliation would likely leave fallen yellow leaves as evidence.

Q **Will willows grow toward water lines?**

A Willows are notorious for having their roots collect around and in water lines and drainage fields. Actually, all trees will do that to some degree—they need water. If a pipe leaks even slightly, roots will grow in that area. It is wise to not plant trees over drainage fields and on top of water lines.

Q **I have been told not to plant weeping willows because they are hard on water. Is this true? I love weeping trees. Are there any others that are safer to plant?**

A Weeping willows (*Salix babylonica*) aren't necessarily hard on water, but they do prefer a lot of moisture. Their root systems can be invasive in sewer systems. They are weak-wooded and messy, dropping branches during storms. In addition, they are subject to numerous disease and insect problems. Weeping willows have their place along the shorelines of lakes or for stabilizing riverbanks, but they are a poor choice for most home landscapes.

Q **I have a weeping willow in my backyard that is beautiful, albeit messy. I had a sidewalk put in that runs alongside the tree. A large root has lifted the sidewalk to a point where it is now a hazard. Can I cut that root without harming the tree?**

A An established weeping willow can be problematic. As a rule, tree roots larger than 2 inches in diameter should not be cut through. Willows regenerate roots readily, so they may not be as sensitive to root loss as some other types of trees. However, removal of a large root may also compromise the structural safety of the tree. Loss of a large support root could weaken the tree and make it more likely to blow over in a windstorm.

Planting Shrubs

Q How do I plant a shrub?

A 1. Dig a wide, shallow hole. For bare-root shrubs, make the hole wide enough to spread the roots out evenly from the main stem. For container-grown plants, make the hole at least twice as wide as the pot. 2. Place the shrub in the hole so that the soil line on the shrub will be at the same level as it grew previously. 3. Backfill the hole with the excavated soil. 4. Water the newly planted shrub. Keep it watered regularly for at least the first growing season.

Transplanting Shrubs

Q My variegated welgela is overtaking my garden. How and when can I move it with the least stress to the plant?

A You can transplant your weigela in either spring or fall; they're durable and adaptable shrubs that can handle transplanting without difficulty. The cool temperatures during these seasons will help it avoid the stress of hot summer weather while it reestablishes its root system in a new location. Place it in full sun with well-drained soil. Prune off no more than one-third of the stems when you transplant it.

Q I need to move a small lilac. It is not getting enough sun where it was originally planted. Can I do this without ruining the lilac?

A It would be best to move the lilac when it is dormant in winter rather than when it is actively growing. In preparation for moving it next winter you could dig down around the root system now to force the roots to branch out. Whenever you do move it, keep as much soil around the root ball as possible.

Q I want to transplant camellia bushes. All of them have new buds. Can I transplant them without harm to the bushes?

A Camellias handle transplanting pretty well because they have fairly shallow, fibrous root systems. But no plant can easily devote energy to reestablishing its root system and blooming at the same time. It's likely that if you transplant your camellias in full bud, they'll drop the buds and focus on restoring their root systems. If you can, it would be best to wait until they're done blooming for the season before you transplant them.

Q I have a large hydrangea that has gotten too big for its home, and I would like to move it. When is the best time to do this?

A The best time to move most deciduous shrubs, including hydrangea, is early spring, just before it leafs out. Another excellent time is late autumn after the leaves turn color but before the ground freezes. The bigger and older the plant is, the more stressed it will be when you move it. So be warned that your hydrangea may not bloom for a year or two after you move it while it recovers from transplanting shock.

Hedge Plants

Q **What plants could you suggest for a hedge?**

A These shrubs make excellent hedge plants: 1. Summersweet (*Clethra alnifolia*), 2. Oakleaf hydrangea (*Hydrangea quercifolia*), 3. Large fothergilla (*Fothergilla major*), 4. Regent serviceberry (*Amelanchier alnifolia* 'Regent'), 5. Black chokeberry (*Aronia melanocarpa*), 6. Yew (*Taxus × media*), 7. Boxwood (*Buxus sempervirens*), 8. Canadian hemlock (*Tsuga canadensis*), and 9. Privet (*Ligustrum* spp.).

Hedge Pruning

Q I have a yew hedge that needs to be trimmed. What's the best way to do this?

A To shape an evergreen hedge, taper the sides so the lower branches are wider than those at the top. If the sun reaching foliage on the sides of the hedge is insufficient, the foliage will die back. To stimulate growth, trim a hedge with hedge shears or electric clippers below the desired height in spring. When you prune later in the season, remove only a portion of new growth. Stop trimming by midsummer so that any regrowth has a chance to harden off before cold weather sets in.

Q What's the best way to get a uniform height on my boxwood hedge?

A Boxwood is commonly used as a hedge shrub because it tolerates repeated shearing. You can use a tight stringline strung along the hedge to mark a uniform height. Prune frequently enough so that you are cutting only the current season's growth. Consider boxwood for individual plantings too; it contributes attractive, fine-texture evergreen foliage to a mixed border. To prune a boxwood that's not in a hedge, use hand pruners, rather than hedge shears, to clip off individual branches that protrude from the main body of the shrub. Cut the branches at slightly different lengths to avoid creating a sheared shape.

Q How can I keep my hedges looking good? They die out in the middle.

A Hedges often turn brown in the middle without proper care. If you prune your hedge into a formal shape, clip the top of the hedge narrower than the bottom so light can reach the lower branches. Instead of shearing hedges flat, stagger your cuts. Prune some branches deeper inside the plant and others closer to the edges. This allows more light to reach the middle of the plant, keeping it from dying out. In areas with heavy snowfall, prune formal hedges to have rounded tops. This will help protect them from heavy snow accumulation, which can break branches.

Hedge Planting

Q How closely together should shrubs be planted to create a solid hedge?

A The correct spacing to use depends on the mature size of the shrub. If the shrubs grow 3 feet tall and wide, for example, plant them about 2 feet apart so that the branches will intertwine. If they grow 10 feet wide, you could space them 5 to 8 feet apart, depending on how quickly you'd like them to form a solid barrier.

Year-Round Interest

Q What shrubs can I plant for year-round appeal? I'd like a shrub that looks good for more than a couple of weeks in spring.

A Here are some shrubs that can help: 1. Bottlebrush buckeye (*Aesculus parviflora*), 2. Bloomerang lilac (*Syringa* × 'Penda'), 3. Kerria (*Kerria japonica*), 4. Allegheny lantanaphyllum viburnum (*Viburnum* × *rhytidophylloides* 'Allegheny'), 5. Northern Lights azaleas (*Rhododendron* Northern Lights Series), 6. Oakleaf hydrangea (*Hydrangea quercifolia*), 7. Smooth sumac (*Rhus glabra*), 8. Heavenly bamboo (*Nandina domestica*), and 9. Vernal witch hazel (*Hamemelis vernalis*).

Winter Damage

Q I live in Zone 5. How do I protect my hydrangea and boxwoods from the winter?

A There are no guarantees when it comes to keeping tender plants alive during bad winters. Mulch your hydrangea at the base with shredded bark or leaves to help insulate the root system. Boxwoods are more difficult because they are evergreen and can dry out from winter winds. Consider using a burlap screen around but not touching the plant to keep the winds from hitting the foliage. Also consider using an antidessicant such as Freeze-Pruf, which is designed to protect foliage during cold weather.

Q We lost several rhododendrons and many azaleas this winter and can't figure out why. The leaves are curled up and dry but show no blight or spots. Any ideas?

A The plants may have died of dehydration, or in horticultural terms, desiccation. It's common following a dry fall. After the ground freezes the plants' root systems can't take up any moisture. Broadleaf evergreens like rhododendrons are particularly vulnerable because their leaves continue to transpire, and the roots can't keep up with the moisture demands. Leaf curl in winter is a typical response because the leaves are attempting to shelter their own pores (stomates) from drying wind.

Q I purchased a butterfly bush last year and it bloomed until frost. I live in Zone 5. So far this year it has not started greening up. Is it dead?

A Butterfly bush (*Buddleja*) is usually root-hardy in Zone 5, but it often dies back to the ground over winter. Some winters can be severe enough in Zone 5 that butterfly bushes may die completely. It's possible that it will still sprout from the roots, so you might give it a couple more weeks, but I suspect that your butterfly bush is dead.

Q Last year the rose of Sharon in my front yard was beautiful and had plenty of flowers for several months. This year, half of the branches did not produce leaves. Is there anything I can do to save it?

A Many shrubs that are normally perfectly hardy can suffer winter injury when temperatures fluctuate during winter. Sometimes only a portion of the plant is affected. If your rose of Sharon will be misshapen by pruning just the damaged section, you may want to prune it back severely to within a few inches of the ground. That way it will resprout from the base with many new vigorous shoots. Because it already has a well-established root system, it could put on 5 or 6 feet of growth this first year.

Forcing Blooms

Q What does forcing a pussy willow mean?

A Forcing refers to clipping a few branches in late winter or early spring and spurring them into bloom indoors. Collect a handful of 20-inch-long twigs from plants such as pussy willow, forsythia, flowering quince, peach, or redbud. Soak the twigs in room-temperature water in a bathtub or large bucket, then stand the twigs in a vase of water located in a cool, bright spot. The buds will swell and the flowers will open slowly.

Q How long will it take for the forsythia branches that I cut from my yard to begin blooming indoors?

A If the cuttings are taken close to their natural flowering time, the twigs will begin blooming in a few days. If the cuttings are taken in midwinter, it might take several weeks for flowering to occur. Change the water frequently to prevent bacterial growth.

Winter Hardiness

Q I have a hydrangea bush that is planted in full sun and is watered once a week. It has not bloomed in four years. Why?

A Bigleaf hydrangea (*Hydrangea macrophylla*) forms next year's buds late in the season of the current year, so harsh winter weather or late-spring frost damage can wipe out the flowerbuds. The vegetative (leaf) buds are hardier than the flowerbuds, so the bush may grow normally otherwise. Also make sure you're not doing any pruning from late summer through spring. Prune only right after the blooms fade.

Q This spring my forsythia bloomed only on a couple of branches near the ground. Why didn't it have flowers on the entire shrub?

A Forsythia flowerbuds often can be damaged during midwinter if a prolonged warm spell is followed by a sudden drop in temperature. The branches near the base of the shrub may have been protected by snow, insulating them from fluctuating temperatures.

For more tips on forcing branches, go to *bhg.com /shrub-forcing.*

Flowering Shrubs

Q **What are some good flowering shrubs to add color to the landscape?**

A You have many excellent choices of flowering shrubs from which to choose. Here are some to consider: 1. Beautybush (*Kolkwitzia*), 2. Bluebeard (*Caryopteris*), 3. Butterfly bush (*Buddleja*), 4. Lilac (*Syringa*), 5. Forsythia, 6. Hydrangea, 7. Oleander (*Nerium*), 8. Rhododendron, 9. Spirea (*Spiraea*), and 10. Viburnum.

Shrubs for Shade

Q We have a rather shady yard. What shrubs could we grow?

A Here are 10 great ones. 1. Yew (*Taxus*), 2. Hydrangea, 3. Abelia, 4. Japanese aucuba (*Aucuba*), 5. Pittosporum, 6. Fothergilla, 7. Summersweet (*Clethra*), 8. Bay laurel (*Laurus*), 9. Fringe tree (*Chionanthus*), and 10. Buddhist pine (*Podocarpus*).

1

2

3

4

5

6

7

8

9

10

Shrub Renewal

Q I moved into an old house this past winter. It has an overgrown row of shrubs. My first thought was to yank them out, but that seems like a lot of work. What do you suggest?

A Before you go to the cost and effort of replacing your shrubs, see whether they can be revitalized. Renovation involves using good pruning techniques to cut the oldest and thickest stems down to ground level and remove them. In your case, it sounds as though most of the stems are likely to be pruning candidates, so you'll need a little patience. The basic rule is to cut out no more than one-third of the bush at a time. If done gradually over several years, this process completely renews old shrubs.

Q On which shrubs can you cut out the old stems without harming the bush?

A Renovation pruning works best on multistem shrubs with shoots of differing ages and sizes. These shrubs respond well to renovation pruning: barberry, beautyberry, bottlebrush buckeye, deutzia, flowering almond, flowering quince, forsythia, kerria, lilac, mock orange, privet, rose of Sharon, spirea, staghorn sumac, and weigela

Q When is the best time to renovate my overgrown shrubs?

A Thin the shrub when it's dormant by removing the oldest and thickest stems. Use long-handle loppers to cut stems up to 1 inch in diameter. A pruning saw is a better tool to use for large stems.

Q I have some overgrown junipers. Will they grow back if I cut them to the ground?

A Such severe pruning will likely kill the plant. If you want to reduce the size of an overgrown juniper, cut it back gradually over a three-year period. Junipers can be cut back to green tissue, but avoid cutting into older wood that has no green foliage. If the plants are bare at their base, you may be better off removing the overgrown shrubs and replacing them with new ones. Start pruning the new shrubs during their first few years of growth to shape them and maintain their desired size. Minimize the amount of pruning you'll need to do by choosing varieties that won't overgrow the space you have for them.

Shrub Renewal

Q I just moved into a house that is surrounded by an overgrown landscape. Is it possible to chop some of the shrubs down and hope they regrow?

A Many gardeners inherit shrubs that have been neglected for years. Overgrown shrubs can be reclaimed using one of two pruning methods. The appropriate method is determined by the growth habit of the shrub. Some plants, such as barberry, can handle renewal pruning (clipping off all the branches 4 to 6 inches above ground level) and will spring forth with healthy new growth. Other plants, such as rhododendron, may die if cut back severely. But these sensitive types can be shaped with rejuvenation pruning.

Q When is the best time to cut shrubs all the way back to the ground?

A Perform renewal pruning in late winter or early spring, before the shrub begins to grow. Clip off all the stems 4 to 6 inches above ground level. The plant will send up new shoots during the growing season. The following winter, selectively remove about one-third of the stems, keeping those that create an attractive framework. After that, prune the shrub annually to maintain the desired form.

Q Which shrubs can be cut back to the ground with no ill effects?

A The following shrubs will withstand renewal pruning: barberry, bluebeard, bush cinquefoil, crape myrtle, flowering quince, forsythia, glossy abelia, heavenly bamboo, mock orange, ninebark, privet, redtwig dogwood, flowering almond, shrub rose, spirea, and weigela.

Q If I cut all the branches off my overgrown forsythia and lilac, how long will it be until they bloom again?

A Both of these shrubs bloom on old wood. Newly planted shrubs often take several years to reach blooming size. Overgrown shrubs that are cut back severely also could take several years to return to their blooming state. Your shrubs almost certainly won't bloom again next year, but if growing conditions are good, they might produce some blooms the following year.

For more ideas on what to prune when, go to *bhg.com/pruning.*

Deer-Resistant Shrubs

Q **We have a terrible deer problem. Are there any shrubs that they won't eat?**

A Here are some shrubs that deer generally avoid: 1. Barberry (*Berberis*), 2. Boxwood (*Buxus*), 3. Butterfly bush (*Buddleja*), 4. Forsythia, 5. Gardenia, 6. Juniper (*Juniperus*), 7. Oleander (*Nerium*), 8. Scotch broom (*Cytisus*), 9. Deutzia, and 10. Smoke bush (*Cotinus*).

Arborvitae

Q **Back in October I bought some 'Emerald Green' arborvitae and planted them in my backyard. They were brown on about half of the shrub. Now that spring is here, should I cut off all the brown branches?**

A When you can tell that deciduous shrubs in your area are greening up, go ahead and snip out the dead parts on your shrubs. Make sure the shrubs get about 1 inch of water per week this growing season. Baby them this year so that new growth is encouraged and sustained. Mulch your shrubs well after the ground freezes.

Q **How do you care for a 'Danica' arborvitae? The needles are turning brown.**

A 'Danica' arborvitae is a small shrub that doesn't grow more than 2×2 feet. It needs regular watering and should be kept out of windy areas. Protect it from wind and water as needed to prevent browning. You can shear it to keep the rounded shape that it develops in the landscape, but avoid cutting back farther than the existing green needles. If cut back severely it may not resprout.

Q **I have several arborvitae growing in the backyard. This year four of them turned brown and are dying. Last year I had to replace two different ones for the same reason. Could it be because of too much water back there, as my neighbor suggests?**

A Arborvitae is indeed not very tolerant of wet soils. If the damage is occurring over winter, it may be because the soil drains poorly and the roots suffocate. If the drainage on the site can't be improved, you might try installing a berm and growing the trees at the top of the berm to raise their roots out of the wettest soil. Or you could grow another type of plant that better tolerates wet soils. Unfortunately, few evergreens tolerate wet soil conditions.

Q **I am thinking about planting several arborvitae along my fence. If I purchase 2-foot-tall plants, how long will it take for them to reach 4 to 6 feet in height?**

A The speed at which any plant grows depends on the growing conditions, weather, and the particular variety. Often it takes a year or two for a plant to recover from transplanting; in the process, growth is limited. However, container-grown arborvitae may suffer little transplant shock. With good growing conditions, most arborvitae will add 3 to 12 inches of new growth per year, depending on variety. If your plants are moderate growers, it should take about four to five years for them to reach 4 to 6 feet in height.

Azalea

Q **I take good care of my azaleas, but they continue to die. I know they should come back and grow even bigger the following year, but they don't even survive one growing season. Help!**

A Several things may be at the root of your azaleas' problem. First, azaleas prefer acidic soil. If your soil is alkaline, your plants will surely suffer. Amend the soil to be more acidic if necessary. Most azaleas prefer moist but well-drained soil, so make sure that the azaleas in your garden have adequate drainage. If the soil is poorly drained, add compost to loosen the soil or grow the azaleas in a raised bed with better drainage. Keep plants watered during times of drought. Make certain that the azaleas you're growing are adapted to your locale. Some stores may carry plants that are not fully hardy in your location.

Q **When is the best time to prune azaleas?**

A It's best to prune azaleas right after their flowers fade. Deadhead deciduous and evergreen azaleas by pinching off wilted blooms between your thumb and forefinger. To keep azaleas looking natural, eliminate dead wood, cutting back the oldest stems at the base.

Q **If I cut the wilted flowers from my azaleas, will they bloom again this year? I've heard that deadheading promotes rebloom.**

A Most azaleas bloom only once a season. An exception are the Encore azaleas, which bloom again in summer and/or fall. Although taking off dead flowers won't make other types of azaleas bloom again, it will make them look better. When the flowers are spent, snap them off where they join the center of the leaf clusters.

Q **I received a potted azalea. I've kept it outside, and it's doing well. I'd like to transplant it into my yard. I know it likes acidic soil, but I don't know how much sun/shade it needs.**

A Azaleas sold by florists and other retailers as gift plants require well-drained, acidic soil (around pH 5.5–6.0) and partial shade. Although well-drained soil is a must, they appreciate good moisture—keep them from drying out, especially in times of drought. Most florist azaleas are hardy in Zones 7–10. Gardeners who live outside that range will need to treat the plants as annuals or short-lived gift plants.

Boxwood

Q **Can boxwoods be pruned or cut back at any time?**

A Whether you are sculpting boxwood (*Buxus*) into a perfect orb or simply shaping it a little, prune it in late winter and again in mid- to late June. For a graceful, natural appearance, trim boxwood by hand. Over time, boxwood often develops a leafy outer shell and a twiggy interior. Maintain a dense, leafy interior by increasing light penetration. To do this, annually thin the plant by snapping out 6- to 8-inch-long twigs by hand at major branches.

Q **I want to plant a small hedge of boxwood around my herb garden. What varieties do you recommend?**

A Boxwood is an excellent choice for edging beds or paths and can be grown in sun or moderate shade. Littleleaf boxwood (*Buxus microphylla*) and common boxwood (*B. sempervirens*) are widely available. Littleleaf boxwood has small medium-green leaves, which often turn a yellowish green in winter. Common boxwood has larger darker-green leaves but is reliably hardy only into Zone 6. Korean boxwood (*B. microphylla* × *koreana*) is an extremely hardy form of littleleaf boxwood. It can be grown in protected sites in Zone 4 and throughout Zone 5.

Q **When starting a topiary from scratch, is it best to start with a small plant or a larger plant? I plan on using boxwood to make a swan.**

A Because you plan to use boxwood, I'd start with a large specimen since the plant has a slow growth rate. And because boxwood responds well to shearing, you can cut it back severely to shape it into the general form that you want. Continue to shape the topiary as the shrub grows.

Q **The tips of my boxwoods are yellow. My neighbor says they got frozen over the winter and are dead. Is there anything I can do?**

A It's not uncommon for boxwoods to suffer some winter burn in areas with cold winters. The best thing to do is to trim off the yellow/brown foliage. The boxwood will readily resprout from below the cut, filling in to make a fuller shrub.

Broom

Q I bought a shrub called sweet broom (*Cytisus × spachianus*). No one seems to know anything about it. It's a beautiful shrub with tiny yellow flowers and unusual foliage. I just want to find out more about it.

A Your plant is a vigorous evergreen shrub with fragrant, golden-yellow flowers in late winter and early spring. It can grow 10 feet tall and wide, and it does best in full sun and well-drained soil. In fact, it's very drought-tolerant. It's also sometimes sold by the names Scotch broom, *Cytisus canariensis*, or *Genista fragrans*.

Butterfly Bush

Q I am new to gardening and need lots of help. Can you trim a butterfly bush to keep it the size you want?

A You can control the size of butterfly bush (right) to some degree by cutting it back to within a few inches of the ground in late winter. It's best not to prune during the growing season. Pruning at that time will remove the blooms. If you need a small butterfly bush, choose a dwarf type. Lo & Behold ('Blue Chip'), for instance, stays under 3 feet tall.

Q I cut back my butterfly bush almost to the ground right at the beginning of spring. I have yet to see any growth. Did I cut it back too far?

A Butterfly bush can be cut back completely to the ground with no ill effects. If it fails to resprout, it's not the pruning job that killed it; instead weather conditions over winter are to blame. Butterfly bush tends to be short-lived. It's not unusual for the shrub to die out over winter after several years, especially if drainage is poor in the area where it is growing.

Q I purchased a butterfly bush last year. Should I prune off last year's branches? If so, when?

A In Zones 4 and 5, treat butterfly bush as a perennial (not a shrub), and prune it to ground level in late winter. Most winters, the plant will be killed back to the ground in these areas, but it will send up new shoots from its root system in spring. Butterfly bush waits until the soil is warm before emerging in spring, so allow plenty of time for your plant to send up new shoots. In warm areas, gardeners can cut back their butterfly bush or leave it standing. If the bush is not cut back, however, the shoots become scraggly. For more compact form and a tidier appearance, cut back all old stems to about 4 to 6 inches above the ground in late winter or early spring. Because butterfly bush blooms on new growth, no blooms will be sacrificed.

Camellia

Q **My camellias get many buds, but only one or two open. The rest turn brown and hard. In spring and summer the shrubs get morning sun and afternoon shade. I also have difficulty keeping azaleas alive in the same bed. What's up?**

A Because your azaleas won't grow either, my guess is that your soil isn't acidic enough. Both species need acidic soil. Test your soil to determine its pH. Once you know the soil pH, make the necessary adjustments. (Sulfur is typically used to lower soil pH.) Also, feed your camellias in early spring with a fertilizer designed especially for acid-loving plants.

Q **Two years ago I planted two camellias, one on each side of my front porch steps. The leaves have started curling and are pale. Why is this happening?**

A If the plants are near your porch and under an overhang, they may not be getting enough water. It's easy to overlook an overhang when planning the landscape—until the plants dry out. Young plants recently transplanted are particularly sensitive to drying because their roots are limited to a small root ball. Water your camellias regularly or move them farther away from the overhang. Are the steps concrete? If so, the lime that naturally leaches from the concrete may be harming the camellias. To thrive, camellias need acidic soil.

Q **Can a camellia be moved? If so, when do I do it? I am moving and would love to take this beauty with me.**

A Yes, a camellia can be moved. You'll have the best success moving a young plant in late winter or early spring, before new growth begins. Because this plant is evergreen, dig as large a root ball as possible and transplant it immediately. If your shrub is large, chances are it will not transplant well. You may be happier purchasing a young plant to start at your new location. With proper siting and care, it will soon catch up to where the older plant would be.

Chokeberry

Q **I would like a Zone 3 shrub for shade and sandy soil. It should be 3 to 6 feet tall and wide. Any suggestions?**

A What about *Aronia melanocarpa*, black chokeberry? It has small white flowers in spring followed by blackish fruits that hang on through winter and attract birds. The cultivars 'Elata' and 'Autumn Magic' are good bets. Fall color is usually deep red.

Cotoneaster

Q **About a month ago I planted nine cotoneasters. I have had to trim several brown branches off these bushes. The ground seems to be watered enough. It's on drip irrigation supplemented with handwatering to make sure the plants are getting enough water to start. What else should I be doing?**

A Cotoneasters are in the rose family and are susceptible to a bacterial disease called fireblight, which could be causing the brown stems that you're observing. Usually you can keep the problem under control by pruning out the affected branches, cutting well beyond the observed dieback. Sterilize your pruning shears between each cut to avoid spreading the disease.

Dogwood

Q **Our front yard is very shady, and the soil in that bed is always moist. I planted some azaleas and hydrangeas that have survived there. Are there other shrubs that we could plant for variety?**

A Shrubby dogwoods (above right) would also be a good shrub choice for a moist, shady site. Redtwig dogwood (*Cornus alba* 'Sibirica') develops colorful red stems; yellow twig dogwood (*C. sericea* 'Flaviramea') has bright yellow stems; and kelsey dogwood (*C. sericea* 'Kelseyi') is a dwarf red-stem form that reaches only 2 feet tall.

Q **When and how should I prune my redtwig dogwood?**

A Prune your plant in late winter or early spring. Remove about one-third of the oldest, thickest canes to encourage new, vigorous canes to develop.

These new canes will decorate your landscape with splashes of red this fall and winter because one-year-old twigs have the intense fiery red color that gives redtwig dogwood its name. If you continue to remove one-third of the oldest stems each year, your dogwood will always have brightly colored, vigorous shoots. Overgrown redtwig dogwoods can also be cut back completely to 6 inches above ground level. They will quickly send up new shoots.

Q **When we bought our first home, we inherited some overgrown shrubs. I need your help with the redtwig dogwoods. Should I prune these shrubs before or after they bloom?**

A Redtwig dogwood and red osier dogwood (*C. stolonifera*) bear small white flowers, but unlike their treelike cousin, flowering dogwood, they are primarily prized for their colorful red stems. Prune them in late winter or early spring while they are still dormant. You could prune them to the ground annually so they put on all new growth and stay more compact.

Euonymus

Q **I have three burning bushes that are nine years old. For the past two years these bushes have turned color early and by the end of August have dropped their leaves. Any ideas why this is happening?**

A Trees and shrubs that turn color early are usually under stress. Look for things such as mechanical damage to stems, construction damage to roots, drought, or pests. Make sure your shrubs have adequate water and good soil (a shot of slow-release fertilizer in late spring is good). Mulch with shredded leaves or wood chips to protect the soil surface from drying and cracking.

Q **The leaves on my burning bushes are drying up. The plants line my home's foundation and get plenty of water.**

A Burning bush (*Euonymus alatus*) can be susceptible to leaf scorch, a problem caused by hot temperatures. It's usually more severe on younger branches. Although you say your plants are getting a lot of water, I wonder whether it's enough. Growing along a foundation exposes them to high temperatures and perhaps soil that dries out quickly. If your roof has an overhang, the soil next to the foundation may be extremely dry. I'd be sure to keep the plants well mulched and use a drip system for watering near their roots.

Q **I have several burning bushes. I've heard that they are not good for the environment. Should I replace them?**

A In some regions burning bush has become an invasive plant. If that is the case in your area, consider replacing them with native plants such as red chokeberry (*Aronia arbutifolia*) or Virginia sweetspire (*Itea virginica*). You could also replace them with the native euonymus, Eastern wahoo (*Euonymus*

atropurpureus), also called spindle tree. It doesn't produce the spectacular fall color, but does bear attractive berries.

Q **Can you give me some information on Greenlane euonymus? It appears on a landscape blueprint of my yard. I assume it is a groundcover.**

A Wintercreeper, or *Euonymus fortunei* 'Greenlane', is an evergreen shrub that often grows as a groundcover. It grows well in partial shade, but tolerates full shade. Although the young plants may be small, they mature to 3 to 4 feet tall and spread to 6 feet. Wintercreeper is hardy in Zones 5–9. These plants aren't for every garden though. They're considered invasive in some areas because they might escape from gardens and naturalize in the wild. Check with your county extension service to see whether it's all right to grow it in your yard.

Firethorn

Q **What kind of fast-growing bush or hedge should I buy that has thorns on it?**

A It sounds like you want to put up a barrier. Scarlet firethorn (*Pyracantha coccinea*) is hardy in Zones 5 or 6 to 9, and it grows 6 to 18 feet high and wide. It readily forms an impenetrable barrier to keep unwanted traffic out of your yard.

Forsythia

Q **When do I prune forsythia bushes? How severely can they be pruned?**

A Prune forsythias after they bloom. How far back to cut them is up to you; you can take the entire shrub clear to the ground if you want or remove just the oldest stems. Some people nip them back to a tidy rounded shape 2 to 4 feet high and that's OK, too, as long as it's done right after the blossoms drop off. If you prune later in the season, you'll be removing next year's flowerbuds.

Q **Why didn't my forsythia bloom this spring? It bloomed fine last year.**

A There are a couple of common reasons for forsythias not blooming. In very cold winters, forsythia flowerbuds can be killed, eliminating bloom the following spring. Sometimes all flowerbuds above the snow line are killed, whereas buds near ground level are unaffected because those stems were insulated by the snow. Two forsythias with greater flowerbud hardiness are 'Meadowlark' and 'Northern Sun'. These cultivars will bloom even if the temperature dips below -30 to -35°F. Improper pruning is another common cause of lack of bloom. Forsythia flowers form on the previous season's growth, so prune immediately after the flowers fade. Pruning later in summer or fall removes the next year's flowerbuds.

Fuchsia

Q **I've heard that fuchsias attract hummingbirds. Is that true?**

A Hummingbirds love red tubular flowers. Fuchsia is a great plant to provide them if you can grow them. Fuchsias prefer partial shade and protection from summer heat. Hardy fuchsia (*F. magellanica*) will grow in Zones 6–10.

Gardenia

Q I love the fragrance of gardenias. Do you have recommendations for the best ones to grow?

A Gardenia varieties vary in size, cold hardiness, light preferences, and when and how often they bloom, so it's best to choose the variety that best suits your climate and site. In the Coastal South, everblooming 'Veitchii' is popular. In the Mid-South and Pacific Northwest, look for 'Kleim's Hardy' or 'Daisy'. Both are hardy to about 10°F. In California, 'Mystery' is a favorite variety.

Q My gardenias are developing yellow leaves. What could be causing this?

A Cool soil temperatures (below 70°F) during the growing season or a pH above 6.5 can cause gardenia leaves to turn yellow. Gardenias grown outdoors often shed a few yellow leaves in winter, which is normal. The best remedy for yellow leaves is to feed plants with a good azalea fertilizer, which contains the three major plant nutrients (nitrogen, phosphorus, and potassium) as well as sulfur, which helps acidify the soil. Yellow leaves may also be a symptom of overwatering or an infestation of root-knot nematodes.

Q I'm frustrated trying to get my gardenias to bloom. They form buds, but the buds drop off before they open up. How can I stop this problem?

A The causes of blossom drop could be too little light, over- or underwatering, high temperatures, or low humidity. Bloom problems on outdoor gardenias are most often due to improper pruning. Gardenias should be pruned only to control their size or to shape the plants. Plan before you plant so you don't have to constantly prune a plant to keep it inbounds. Most well-sited gardenias need little if any pruning. If you prune your plant, do so in early summer, after spring's flowers have come and gone. Buds that open in spring form in late summer or autumn.

Q What insect pests should I be watching for on my gardenias?

A Prevent problems with aphids, spider mites, scale, and other small insects on your gardenia by spraying plants every 4 to 6 weeks with insecticidal soap. If you grow gardenias in pots outdoors in summer, always inspect plants and spray them with insecticidal soap before you bring them indoors in autumn to keep pests from moving in too.

Hibiscus

Q I have several hardy hibiscuses in my flowerbed. How do I divide them and when? I trim them back in spring, and they grow really big with stalks so heavy that I have to stake them.

A Hardy hibiscus (*H. moscheutos*) can grow quite large in the garden, and division is challenging. Division of their crowns requires a hacksaw and a lot of work and agony. You can relocate them when they get too big for their space in the garden. Another option is to cut the new growth back in early summer to 10 to 12 inches from the ground. This cutback will delay bloom by several weeks, but can help keep them from becoming as tall and top-heavy.

Q I purchased three hibiscus plants. They were blooming when I bought them, and I kept them in the container. Can I bring them indoors?

A Hibiscus fall into two major categories. The tropical types have flowers with petals that curve back and have large central stamens. The hardy types can have even larger flowers, but they are flatter, more like dinner plates. If you have tropical hibiscus, you can overwinter them indoors in a sunny window (or outdoors in Zones 9–11). If you have hardy hibiscus, get them in the ground as soon as possible and cover them with a bit of mulch after they go dormant in the fall. They will not survive indoors.

Q I just moved to Florida and planted a hibiscus tree in the front yard. It is growing, but it has fewer and smaller leaves now than when I bought it. Some are yellow and fall off easily. Other hibiscus plants I see have large, green leaves and look full and more healthy. It is still flowering. I don't know if it needs to be pruned, and if so, how?

A Your hibiscus is stressed and needs every bit of leafy canopy it has right now, so don't prune it. First, check the planting depth and make sure you didn't set it any deeper than the plant was when in the pot. If it is deeper, the plant would benefit from being lifted and replanted. Next, apply a 2- to 3-inch layer of mulch on top of the soil. Extend the mulch as far as the branches of the hibiscus reach. Mulch will help keep soil temperatures cooler in the hot summer sun and aid the root system in establishing itself. Make certain that the soil in the old root ball remains moist. Hibiscus requires quite a bit of moisture to thrive. The yellowing could be caused by lack of water in the root zone.

Q I planted two hibiscus plants last year, and they have not sprouted this spring. Will they come back?

A Are these hardy or tropical hibiscus plants? If they are tropical hibiscus (*H. rosa-sinensis*) and you live in an area with freezing temperatures, the plants likely died over winter and will not come back. If they are hardy hibiscus (*H. moscheutos*), it's normal for the plants to die back to the ground over winter but resprout from the crown when temperatures have warmed consistently. In this case, cut the old stems to the ground and be patient. Hardy hibiscus are slow to sprout in spring.

Honeysuckle

Q **My honeysuckle is covered with weird, deformed shoots. They are twisted and bunched up. What is wrong with it? Should I prune it?**

A The problem you're describing sounds like damage from honeysuckle witches' broom aphid. As aphids feed on the stem tips of Tatarian honeysuckle (*Lonicera tatarica*), below, they inject a toxin into the plant stems that causes the misshapen shoots to form. If left unchecked, the problem can eventually kill the plant. Pruning out and destroying the witches' brooms may help. Another option to consider is complete removal of the honeysuckle. This problem will recur year after year. Two honeysuckles that resist these aphids are the white-flowering 'Freedom' and red-blooming 'Honey Rose'.

Hydrangea

Q **I have a hydrangea that was planted about 10 years ago. It grows beautifully every year but has never bloomed. What can I do?**

A There are several reasons why hydrangeas don't bloom. 1. Plants can grow but won't bloom in dense shade. 2. It's planted where winter temperatures kill the flowerbuds. Mophead and lacecap hydrangeas are less cold-hardy than other types. 3. If you prune in late summer, fall, or winter you're probably pruning away the flowerbuds. Prune bigleaf hydrangea (*Hydrangea macrophylla*) right after blooming; prune smooth (*H. arborescens*) and panicle hydrangeas (*H. paniculata*) in early spring.

Q **A blue hydrangea that I bought at the flower shop is sitting in a pot in my kitchen window. Can I plant it in the backyard?**

A If you live in Zone 6 or warmer, your blue hydrangea should survive the winter when planted outdoors. In colder zones, the plant will probably die back to the ground over the winter and not bloom in the landscape. In addition to preferring a site in partial shade, this shrub thrives in moist, well-drained soil rich in organic material. Grow the plant in acidic soil (pH 5–5.8) to keep the flower color blue. To acidify the soil around your hydrangea, work iron sulfate into the soil when preparing the planting hole.

Q **Should I prune twiggy branches from hydrangeas in spring?**

A For bigger flowers and a tidier look, give your hydrangeas an occasional trim. Pruning times depend upon the types of hydrangeas you grow. Prune bigleaf hydrangea only after it blooms in summer. Retain thick new stems and some old canes. Prune out weak shoots and canes with no green growth. Smooth hydrangea blooms on new wood and therefore can be cut 6–12 inches from the ground in early spring. Trim panicle hydrangea in early spring to control its loose growth and encourage it to produce larger flowers.

Q I planted a snowball hydrangea last year. It survived the winter, but it didn't flower this summer. Any suggestions?

A Snowball, or smooth hydrangea (*H. arborescens*) prefers rich, well-drained soil that stays consistently moist. It does best with morning sun and afternoon shade, or dappled shade all day. Your new plant might still be adapting to its new location and putting more energy into root growth than flower production. Excessive nitrogen fertilizer or improper pruning can also cause a lack of flowers. Pruning in late spring or early summer will remove potential flowers.

Q What do I do with the dried flowers from last year that are still on my hydrangea? Should I prune them off?

A To avoid cutting off this year's flowerbuds, cut the stems of the dried flowers just above where you see the top set of leaf buds on the stem. If they're in decent shape, use them for crafts or dried flower arrangements.

Q How much sun do hydrangeas need? Mine, next to my house, wilt in full sun.

A Most hydrangeas like part shade, but they don't care for heat or a location where they dry out readily. If your hydrangeas are under a roof overhang, the sun may be less of a problem than the dryness. An overhang will prevent the plants under it from getting much moisture. Keeping your plants well-watered and mulched can help counteract the droughty conditions there.

Q My oakleaf hydrangeas have never bloomed for me in four years. The plants are about 5 feet tall and wide. I prune them back considerably in the spring. They are located in partial shade. What's up?

A This is an easy one: Stop pruning in the spring. By pruning your oakleaf hydrangea (*Hydrangea quercifolia*) in spring, you're removing the flowerbuds before they get a chance to bloom. Prune oakleaf hydrangea only in summer right after the flowers fade. Although oakleaf hydrangea prefers a partially shaded spot, too much shade keeps it from blooming.

Q I love the way dried hydrangeas look in arrangements. What is the best way to dry the flowers for indoor use?

A Hydrangeas are easy to air-dry. Cut hydrangea flowers at any stage from green to brown. Remove all foliage from the cut stems. Hang the stems upside-down individually in a warm, dry, airy spot until they are completely dry. Wrap the flower heads in tissue paper for protection before drying if you prefer. If this technique seems like too much bother, simply allow the flowers to dry on the plant, then pick them when you are ready to make your arrangement.

Ixora

Q My ixoras are getting leggy. How and when do I prune them to keep them looking full?

A Ixora (*Ixora coccinea*) benefits from rejuvenation pruning. This three-year process involves removing old, leggy branches. In early spring of year one, cut one-third of the oldest, thickest branches to ground level; in year two, remove half of the remaining large stems; in year three, remove the last of the old, woody shoots. Beginning in year one, the plant will send up dense new growth from its base that will create an attractive, rounded shrub. Keep the new growth in check by pruning back new shoots by one-third their length in early spring.

Juniper

Q Can you suggest a type of juniper that would make a good groundcover for a sunny western slope?

A Many junipers (*Juniperus*) make excellent groundcovers in sites with full sun and well-drained soil. Creeping juniper (*J. horizontalis*) is one of the lowest growing at only 6 to 8 inches tall. 'Bar Harbor', 'Blue Rug', and 'Blue Chip' are cultivars with blue-green foliage. Shore juniper (*J. conferta*), which grows 1 to 2 feet tall, makes a great groundcover, especially in coastal areas or locations subject to salt spray. Japanese garden juniper (*J. procumbens*), makes a good 2-foot-tall groundcover, but it is susceptible to juniper blight, a fungal disease.

Lower-growing forms of savin juniper (*J. sabina*) are also excellent groundcovers. 'Arcadia' and Broadmoor' have bright green foliage; 'Skandia' has blue-green needles.

Q I planted four junipers, and one looks like it is dying. I have been watering them every day, and I don't know what is wrong. Please help.

A Junipers like well-drained soil. If you are watering every day, the roots may be dying from overwatering. While the plants may need watering frequently right after planting, within a few weeks of planting you should be able to water only once per week (or perhaps twice per week if the soil is quite sandy.) It's much better to water deeply and less frequently than to apply a little bit of water every day.

Lilac

Q I inherited a row of lilac bushes 12 to 15 feet tall when I bought my house. They rarely give me flowers. I trim them after they bloom, but the flowers are small and don't last long. Any tips would be great.

A If your plants are very old, they may be types that naturally lack large or long-lasting flowers. Here are some ideas for reinvigorating your lilacs and increasing their blooms in the future. Feed your lilacs with some 10-10-10 fertilizer if they've been growing in the same spot for a long time. Make certain your lilacs are getting plenty of sunshine. They bloom best in full sun. If the plants are tall, old, and scraggly, prune back one-third of the oldest, thickest stems to the ground. Follow this routine for two more years until you have renewed the entire shrub.

Q Four summers ago I planted an old-fashioned lilac, which still hasn't bloomed. Before I dig it up, can you advise me on ways to make it bloom?

A Here are several reasons why a common lilac may not bloom:

1. It was pruned between midsummer and winter, removing its flowerbuds for the next season. Prune only in late spring, right after normal bloom time.

2. It's an old variety of lilac that takes six years or more to bloom. You may simply need to be patient.

3. It needs full sun. If the plant receives fewer than six hours of direct sunlight daily, it will never bloom well.

4. Your winters are too mild to allow it to set buds. Common lilac grows best in cold-winter areas (Zones 3–7). If lack of cold is the case, a Meyer lilac (*Syringa meyeri*) may be a better match for your garden. Meyer lilac flowers better in the South than most other lilacs.

Q My purple lilac has poor color this year. How can I ensure better color next year?

A Flower color is influenced by several conditions, including the weather. For example, warm temperatures often encourage pale blooms; cool temperatures often encourage more intense blooms. Soil moisture plays a part too: If your plant is dry, the flowers will be pale. It's unlikely that the flower color will permanently be pale. Be patient and hope for better weather next year.

Q I need advice on pruning a large, overgrown lilac. I love the flowers, but the shrub looks ugly.

A Common lilac (*S. vulgaris*) has an unattractive way of growing tall and developing bare stems. You

can revive these forlorn lilacs through renewal pruning. This entails cutting all the branches back to within 6 inches of the ground in early spring. The shrub will send up new shoots during the growing season. In late winter of the following year, select and retain several strong, healthy shoots to form the shrub's framework; remove all others at ground level. Lilac wood requires three or more years before flowering, so you'll sacrifice flowers for a few years.

Q I have a lilac that I would like to propagate. How long does propagation take? How long before it roots and shows new growth?

A Layering is a simple way to propagate your lilac. Just follow these steps:

1. In spring, choose a flexible outer stem and carefully bend it until the tip touches the ground.

2. With a sharp blade, carefully make a diagonal slit in the stem 12 inches from the tip, where the branch will touch the ground. Dip the cut in rooting hormone.

3. On either side of the slit, peg the branch to the ground with landscape staples or rocks. Pile some soil on the slit and pat it down. Mulch with leaf litter and keep the branch watered throughout the summer.

4. The next spring, after roots have grown from the wounded stem, sever the connection between your new lilac and its parent. Wait a few weeks before moving the new plant to a site where it has space to mature.

Magnolia

Q Three years ago I purchased a magnolia shrub. Although it produces leaves and a few buds in the spring, it has not grown. Is there something I should be doing?

A It often takes shrubs several years before they begin to grow and bloom well. If this is just the third year since planting, I wouldn't worry about slow growth unless the plant is also showing other signs of distress such as browning or yellowing foliage. Make sure your plant has good growing conditions (full sun and well-drained soil) and a site that's not too exposed. If your plant gets too little sun, is in heavy clay soil, or was planted too deeply, it may take longer to become established.

Oleander

Q I have an 8-foot-tall oleander in front of my home. I would like to trim it back to 2 to 3 feet tall. What can I do?

A Maintaining a 2- to 3-foot-tall plant is unrealistic unless your oleander is a dwarf cultivar. If you trim the plant back to 2 to 3 feet tall, it will send out new branches just below the cut, leaving the base of the plant bare. That said, leggy stems indicate that your plant needs corrective pruning. Begin by completely removing one-third of the large, woody stems. Cut the remaining stems back by one-fourth of their height. Late next winter, remove several more of the large, woody stems if necessary, and tip prune the branches. Oleander grows vigorously and requires annual late-winter pruning.

Q I have several oleanders in my yard, and I am having trouble with the leaves turning yellow. The plants are in a sunny, well-drained area. How can I treat this problem?

A Yellowing of oleander leaves is a common symptom that the plants are too dry. Get out your hose and flood the root zone of the plants with water, then wait an hour or two and do it again. In California, yellowing of oleander leaves that begins at the tip and spreads inward is a sign of a bacterial disease called oleander leaf scorch.

Q My oleanders aren't thriving. They're growing in part sun. I water them when they're dry. Do I need to fertilize them too?

A Oleanders do best in full sun; if yours are in partial sun, they may fail to thrive because they're getting too little light. Transplanting them to a sunnier spot may solve the problem. In most average soils, oleanders do well without fertilizing. If your yard has especially poor soil, the plants might benefit from fertilizer in spring.

Potentilla

Q **Why are my potentillas dying? The leaves turn brown and die. The plants were blooming and looking great until about a month ago.**

A Sudden browning of potentilla (*P. fruticosa*) foliage may indicate a root problem. I suspect that poor drainage or overly wet soils may have contributed to your potentilla's problems. Potentilla is also susceptible to spider mites in hot, dry weather. Foliage first develops a speckled yellow coloration, and webbing may be evident. If the problem continues untreated, leaves may turn brown and die. If you see early signs of spider mites, wash them off the plants with a forceful water spray or use an insecticidal soap to kill them.

Rhododendron

Q **My rhododendron didn't bloom this year. Do I have a male plant instead of a female?**

A Rhododendron produces flowers that have both male and female parts in the same bloom—so two different plants are unnecessary. Severe winter cold could have killed the flowerbuds but left the vegetative buds unharmed. Because flowerbuds form on rhododendron the previous growing season, stressful weather conditions such as drought may have limited flowerbud formation. Also, if you pruned your rhododendron late in summer or in fall last year, you may have removed the flowerbuds for this spring.

Q **How often do I need to separate my newly planted rhododendron?**

A Rhododendrons should never need division. They also rarely need pruning. If you need to shape or limit the size of a rhododendron, make pruning cuts in late spring after the plant blooms. Also, remove dead, diseased, and weak wood annually in late spring.

Q **What is causing my rhododendrons to wilt? The leaves are rolling up. I can't see anything wrong with the plant.**

A Rhododendrons naturally roll their leaves during severe cold in winter. There may be nothing wrong with your plant that a little warm weather won't cure. If the wilt is happening during warm weather, I suspect your plant may have rhododendron wilt. This disease is caused by a soilborne fungus (*Phytophthora*), which is most likely to develop in poorly drained, wet soils. Disease symptoms include stunted growth, leaf yellowing, and drooping leaves that roll inward. Usually only one or two branches on a plant are affected at first. To remedy the problem, improve soil drainage and aeration as soon as possible. If plants are young, dig up the plants and replant them in a raised bed, adding organic matter to the soil to improve drainage.

Rose of Sharon

Q **How and when do I prune my rose of Sharon shrubs so they fill out and become thicker? Mine are getting tall and skinny.**

A Prune rose of Sharon (*Hibiscus syriacus*) in late winter or early spring. If you want fewer but larger flowers, prune the plants back hard. For more but smaller flowers, prune lightly. These plants naturally have an upright growth habit—typically growing about 10 feet tall and 6 feet wide. How close together are your shrubs? If they're crowded, they may be stretching for light. If the plants are close enough to be touching, transplant some of them.

Q **I'd like to transplant a rose of Sharon to the north side of my garage and plant another one with it as a privacy border. How far apart should they be? When should I transplant them?**

A Rose of Sharon is not likely to do well on the north side of your garage. The shrub needs full sun (at least 6 to 8 hours of direct sun a day). Instead of rose of Sharon, consider shade-tolerant shrubs, such as summersweet (*Clethra*), or a trellis with a shade-tolerant vine. Perhaps you can find a sunnier spot in your yard for rose of Sharon. Spring and autumn are the best time to move it.

Q **This spring, many branches died on my rose of Sharon. I cut out the dead branches, but it still needs pruning. How and when do I do this? This plant is 22 years old; I don't want to lose it.**

A I'm sorry to say it, but your shrub may be coming to the end of its lifespan. Rose of Sharon is not a long-lived shrub. Try cutting it back severely to stimulate new growth, then fertilize in spring with a slow-release fertilizer. Your rose of Sharon may fail to bloom next summer because of the vigorous pruning.

Q **How do I know where to prune a rose of Sharon to grow as a tree? I don't know where to start.**

A If you want to grow rose of Sharon as a single-trunk tree, look for the strongest, straightest stem. Cut out all others that arise from the ground. As the plant grows, remove any branches that form on the lower half of the trunk. Eventually, your plant will reach its mature height (typically 10 to 12 feet). Keep the trunk clear of new branches, and thin excessive growth in the canopy when it gets out of hand. The best time to prune your rose of Sharon is in late winter or early spring.

Spirea

Q I have two Goldmound spireas. When is the best time to prune them?

A The best time to prune spireas (right) is immediately after they flower. If you don't care about flowers, you can prune them during the winter when the plants are dormant.

Q I transplanted a nice spirea when I moved three years ago. It is green but has not had a single flower in three summers. It gets late morning sun until about 3 p.m. Any suggestions to encourage blooms?

A Is this a white or pink blooming spirea? The white types typically bloom only in early spring. If they are pruned in summer or fall, you'll remove flowerbuds for the following year. You indicate that the shrub is growing well vegetatively, so perhaps it is getting too much nitrogen fertilizer, which promotes leafy growth, but suppresses flowering.

Sumac

Q How and when do I prune a Tiger Eyes cutleaf sumac?

A The best time to prune most deciduous shrubs is when they are dormant. A cautionary note: Removing the stem tips of sumac can cause the plant to produce suckers (shoots arising from underground) 10 feet or more away from the main stem. If you don't want your sumac to spread rapidly, avoid pruning it.

Check out our online story on the best summer-blooming shrubs at *bhg.com/summer-shrubs*.

Summersweet

Q I planted a summersweet last year. Brown capsules appeared last fall. Should I prune off these capsules or leave them alone?

A You can prune off the capsules this spring to spruce up summersweet (*Clethra alnifolia*) a bit, but there is no need to do so. The capsules will not interfere with flower production this season and eventually will drop off on their own.

Viburnum

Q Do I need two Blue Muffin viburnums for cross pollination? I have one but it didn't flower or get berries on it this year. I planted it last year.

A You do not need two plants for fruiting on this shrub. The plant, however, must be mature to flower and fruit. It may take several years to reach flowering and fruiting size, but after that, your Blue Muffin viburnum should bloom and fruit reliably.

Q I have a beautiful doublefile viburnum that bears cascades of white layered flowers each spring. Parts of the bark are dying and peeling off. Other branches have already sprouted leaves, and the clusters are starting to form. Should we wrap the branches?

A If the bark is peeling on the branches, the damage is already done, and wrapping them will not help. In fact, it might promote decay by trapping moisture under the dead bark. The peeling bark could be an indication of an insect infestation. Wood borers or periodical cicadas are possibilities. Did you by chance have an outbreak of periodical cicadas in your area last year? The egg laying of the adults sometimes can girdle stems and cause twig dieback. You can check for borers by pulling back the loose bark to see if you can find borer trails or exit holes (like shot holes). If borers are present you may want to treat the viburnums with a systemic insecticide.

Q Will Brandywine viburnum thrive in a poorly drained site?

A Most viburnums, including Brandywine (*V. nudum* 'Bulk') generally like well-drained soil; however, arrow-wood viburnum (*V. dentatum*) will take soggy conditions. Some other shrubs that take wet soil include

winterberry (*Ilex verticillata*), summersweet (*Clethra alnifolia*), black chokeberry (*Aronia melanocarpa*), redtwig dogwood (*Cornus alba*), hardy hibiscus (*Hibiscus moscheutos*), and purple osier willow (*Salix purpurea*).

Q My husband bought a snowball viburnum. I know nothing about how to care for this plant. How much sun does it need?

A A couple different viburnums are commonly called snowball viburnum by gardeners, but the most common is *Viburnum plicatum*. It's popular because of its clusters of attractive white blooms in late spring. Unlike most viburnums, it doesn't produce colorful fruits. This shrub generally grows about 10 feet tall and 12 feet wide and is hardy in Zones 6–8. It likes a spot in full sun to partial shade and moist, well-drained soil. Another shrub commonly called snowball viburnum is *V. opulus*, also known as European snowball. It is less desirable because it is susceptible to aphid damage.

Weigela

Q **I'd like to start some more weigelas. Can I divide them?**

A The best way to propagate your weigelas (*Weigela florida*) is from stem cuttings. Take cuttings from the tips of weigela stems just as they begin to firm up (softwood) or when they are firm and slightly woody (semihardwood). Cuttings should be about 4 inches long and have at least three sets of leaves. Remove all flowerbuds and any lower leaves that would be buried in the rooting medium. Dip the cuttings in rooting hormone, then place them in a pot filled with loose potting medium and water the medium well. Cover the entire pot with a plastic bag and place the pot in indirect sunlight or under artificial lights indoors. Once the cuttings form roots and begin to grow, transplant them into individual containers.

Q **When is the proper time to prune weigela?**

A Weigela blooms most heavily in spring and sometimes will rebloom later in summer. Prune the shrub right after the first flush of blooms. If you cut it before the flush of spring blooms, you will forfeit the flowers that are developing.

Yew

Q **I have a beautiful yew that I received from a friend who moved away. I have read that they are highly poisonous. Is it as deadly as I have read? I have a child who is 16 months old.**

A All parts of the yew (*Taxus* spp.) are poisonous if ingested. At the same time, several cancer treatment drugs are based on parts of the yew plant. People vary in their reactions—some may be highly susceptible to the toxins, others may have a mild reaction. The best approach with children is to teach them not to eat anything in the landscape because so many plants can be harmful to small ones if ingested.

Q **My landscaper planted a Japanese yew two years ago in front of my house. Most of the needles on the bottom half are yellow and falling off. What can I do?**

A If the soil stays too wet or soggy, the roots of yew may suffocate. Yews in poorly drained soils are also susceptible to phytophthora root rot, a fungal disease which can kill the plant. Make certain that downspouts direct excess moisture away from the root zone of the yew. If the soil is poorly drained, it may help to amend the soil with compost or plant it in a raised bed.

Vines for Specific Sites

Q I need a hardy flowering vine to climb the picket fence around our air-conditioner. Can any vine withstand full sun in the afternoon in addition to the heat from the air-conditioner unit?

A One of the toughest perennial vines for a situation such as this is trumpet vine. It's vigorous, fast-growing, and spreads by suckers and seeds, so you don't want to plant it close to your house's foundation. Passionflower and climbing rose are a couple more sun-loving vines that will produce an abundance of blooms. Several annual vines can do well in these conditions too. Some of my favorites are black-eyed Susan vine (below) and purple hyacinth bean.

Q I have a shady spot where I'd like to grow a flowering vine. What would you suggest?

A Most flowering vines bloom more prolifically in sun. However, some vines bloom and grow well in shade. Here are several to consider: Fiveleaf akebia (above right),

climbing hydrangea, Dutchman's pipe, false climbing hydrangea, hardy kiwi, and trumpet honeysuckle.

Q I would like to cover a chain-link fence with a flowering vine. Which plant would you recommend for this fence?

A You're in luck—a lot of vines will work for your situation. Your hardest chore might be choosing just one!
Annual vines: Black-eyed Susan vine, cup and saucer vine, cypress vine, moonflower, and morning glory.
Perennial vines: Fiveleaf akebia, clematis, passionflower, and trumpet vine.

Learn about the best perennial vines for your garden at *bhg.com/vines*.

Fragrant Vines

Q **Could you suggest a blooming vine that also has a nice fragrance?**

A You have quite a few vines from which to select for fragrance and bloom. Here are some great vines for fragrance: 1. Armand clematis (*Clematis armandii*), 2. Confederate jasmine (*Trachelospermum jasminoides*), 3. Madagascar jasmine (*Stephanotis floribunda*), 4. Moonflower (*Ipomoea alba*), 5. Pink Chinese jasmine (*Jasminum polyanthum*), 6. Rose (*Rosa*), 7. Sweet autumn clematis (*Clematis terniflora*), 8. Sweet pea (*Lathyrus odoratus*), and 9. Wisteria (*Wisteria*).

Bittersweet

Q **I have a serious problem with bittersweet taking over my lilacs. I've pulled and cut as much as I see, but I can't seem to get rid of it. How can I get rid of it once and for all?**

A Oriental bittersweet (*Celastrus orbiculatus*) is a formidable foe because birds eat the seeds and spread them about, and the plants spread by developing shoots that sprout from roots. Simply cutting back the plant often stimulates the growth of new stems and root suckers. To kill a mature plant, cut back all top growth, then treat the stumps with a brush-killer herbicide.

Q **My bittersweet is seven years old. Two years ago it had a wonderful crop of fruits, but last year it didn't produce. Can I do anything this year to ensure berries?**

A American bittersweet (*C. scandens*) depends on pollination for good berry production, so you need more than one vine. Yours produced fruits, so it's a female vine. Male flowers are borne on a different bittersweet plant. If a nearby male plant died or was removed, you'll need to plant another in order for your female plant to be pollinated.

Q **I have bittersweet growing on my back fence. How do I harvest it for the berries?**

A Harvest bittersweet when the first yellowish capsules of the fruit split open and you see the orange-red fruit inside. Cut stems to the length you desire, tie them together into small bundles, and hang them upside down in a warm, dry location out of direct sun. As the fruits dry, more capsules will split to reveal the fruits inside.

Q **Must I plant more than one bittersweet vine to get the berries?**

A Bittersweet produces separate male and female plants, so you'll need at least one male plant nearby to pollinate female plants for the berries. Unfortunately there's no way to determine the sex of an immature plant, so plant several vines to ensure that you have at least one male among your plants.

Bougainvillea

Q How do I prune my bougainvillea? It is massive, and I would like to reduce its size.

A Bougainvillea tolerates heavy pruning. You can safely prune off about three-fourths of the plant in late fall or early spring. Avoid the need for repeated severe pruning by lightly pruning the plant every year in late fall or early spring. Use a sharp pair of pruners to cleanly remove spent blossoms, several inches of new growth, and dead or diseased twigs.

Q I've had spotty luck with bougainvilleas. This year I bought a new one, which was beautiful, but now all the blooms are gone. How do I make sure it does well?

A Bougainvillea needs rather harsh conditions to bloom well. In addition to a site that gets at least a half day of sun, bougainvillea should rarely receive water beyond the month after it is transplanted. Fertilize your plants twice a year, using a high-potassium, low-nitrogen fertilizer. When bougainvillea fails to bloom, it is usually due to too little sun, too much water, or too much nitrogen fertilizer.

Q How do I propagate bougainvillea? I'd like to start some new ones from my vine.

A The easiest way to propagate bougainvillea is to layer the plant. In late summer or autumn, remove the leaves along a 12-inch section of growing stem. Make a diagonal cut along the underside of the shoot, creating a small flap. Lightly dust the flap with rooting hormone. Lay the stem along the ground and secure it with a U-shape wire pin. Cover the stem with about 3 inches of soil. Cut the new plant from its parent after the new one develops a strong root system (about a year after the process begins). Dig it up and plant it in its permanent new home.

Q I planted a dozen bougainvillea on a slope behind my house four months ago. They started off and bloomed in a vibrant, deep color. In the past few weeks, the flowers have faded and then started falling off. What am I doing wrong?

A Individual blooms on bougainvillea are not permanent. It may be that the fading that you're observing is simply the natural aging of the flowers (technically bracts surrounding the small white flowers). The plants may not be producing a lot of new blooms while they get established in their new location. As long as the foliage looks healthy, the plants are likely getting just the care that they need.

Clematis

Q How do I plant bare-root clematis? Believe it or not, I can't tell the root end from the vine end. Can you help?

A You're not alone in puzzling about which end is up on a bare-root plant. The root should have fine hairlike growths on it and be much more flexible than the stem part. When planting bare-root clematis, set it deep in the hole so the crown is 3 to 4 inches underground. Backfill the hole with compost. Bank more compost in a circle around the newly planted clematis and water well.

Q Should I prune sweet autumn clematis? Is spring the time to do it?

A The best time to prune your sweet autumn clematis (*Clematis terniflora*) is in early spring, long before it blooms. It doesn't require pruning—it's only something to do if you want to control the plant's size. To prune, cut back the stems to the lowest pair of buds or to the height where you'd like growth to start during the current season.

Q Sometimes, for no reason, one of my clematis vines dries up and turns crispy brown. A friend told me that a wilt disease causes this and not to plant another clematis in the same spot, since it will also get sick and die. Is this true?

A When clematis wilt strikes, it takes just days for the foliage to shrivel and die. Wind spreads clematis wilt, a fungal disease. *Clematis* 'Jackmannii' and some of its big-flower hybrid relatives are more prone to wilt than species clematis, which have better resistance. Although infected plants look dead, the disease typically affects the stems; the roots survive. New shoots may emerge from the ground. When wilt strikes, cut back the sick parts to healthy stems, even if you have to cut them below the soil. Apply a fungicide containing copper on any new growth that appears. Also, make sure you give clematis enough water to keep it from wilting from thirst.

Q How do I transplant clematis? I have moved some with luck and others with no luck. Are some varieties tougher than others?

A As you've already discovered, clematis plants don't like to be moved once established. If you must move them, the earlier in spring you can do it, the better, before they start new growth. Some clematis varieties are definitely more robust than others. Sweet autumn clematis (*C. terniflora*) and pink anemone clematis (*C. montana* var. *rubens*) are among the sturdiest.

Fig

Q **I live in Alabama and would like to plant vines along a section of a wood fence. I planned to use climbing fig but read that it can trap moisture and rot the wood. Is there another vine that would not cause moisture problems?**

A The small-leaf climbing fig (*Ficus pumila*) will attach itself to whatever it is growing on with small sticky pads, making a dense cover. This can accelerate wood rot. But any vine clambering on the fence would have a similar effect.

English Ivy

Q **We just purchased a house where English ivy is growing all over the trees and the house. The ivy stems are at least 3 inches thick, and it grows up about 100 feet. I'm afraid it will hurt the trees. What should I do?**

A You can prune English ivy (*Hedera helix*), above right, as severely as you need to, or remove it entirely. Ivy can grow up the trunks of trees with little danger of harming them, but it shouldn't be allowed to grow into the branches, where it can wrap around and girdle the stems, or stretch to branch tips, shading out the trees' foliage. You'll probably need to have a professional remove it from the trees if it has climbed too high and grown too thick.

Q **I was going to plant English ivy in my yard, but someone told me that I shouldn't plant it because it's invasive. Is that true?**

A English ivy can be invasive in some regions, such as the Pacific Northwest. In many areas, however, it remains well-behaved. Check with your local cooperative extension service or department of natural resources to find out whether English ivy is a problem vine in your locale.

Q **My English ivy is climbing up the brick wall of my house. Will it damage the house? Should I remove it?**

A Ivy climbing on a brick wall can be a beautiful sight, but it is potentially harmful to the wall. If you look closely at the stems of your ivy, you'll see rootlets. Holdfasts on the rootlets penetrate into the mortar between the bricks. English ivy growing on the wall accelerates the deterioration of the mortar. If you leave the ivy growing on the wall, you'll have to repoint your house sooner than if you remove the ivy. That said, keep in mind that ivy-covered brick walls are a centuries-old tradition. The brick wall of your house can support growth of ivy and be structurally sound for many years to come if you're prepared to keep up with the extra maintenance.

Honeysuckle

Q **I have a honeysuckle vine growing over my deck rail and onto an arbor. I am going to replace the deck rail and would like to know if the vine can survive a severe pruning.**

A Honeysuckle vine (*Lonicera* spp.), below, can be pruned back quite severely and still come back. Avoid severe pruning in late summer or early fall, however. Pruning at that time can force new growth that won't harden off before winter hits. Wait until winter or early spring to do the pruning.

Q **I have two honeysuckle vines. The leaves are covered with a whitish gray coating, and they aren't producing flowers. Is this some type of disease?**

A It sounds as though your honeysuckles have been infected with powdery mildew, a very common disease. Powdery mildew likes moist, humid weather and shows up as a gray, white, or silver powdery-looking substance on the leaves. It seldom is serious enough to require treatment.

Hydrangea Vine

Q **I had a flowering climbing hydrangea planted in a fairly shady spot for four years, then moved it to a sunnier spot. Neither place has produced a single flower. What might be wrong with this?**

A Climbing hydrangea (*H. petiolaris*) is a notoriously slow bloomer. I've had one for 10 years and it's had only one or two flowers so far. Moving your plant probably set it back a little since these vines don't like to be moved. Avoid fertilizer of any type. If it gets excess fertilizer it will develop leaves but few flowers.

Q **I planted a climbing hydrangea about five years ago, and it refuses to bloom. It receives morning sun. Last year I tried pruning it back in an effort to force it to bloom. Any help would be most appreciated!**

A Climbing hydrangeas are notorious for taking their time in getting established. The good news is that once a climbing hydrangea is established, it makes up for it. The vines put on wonderful growth and bloom beautifully once they get settled in your garden. If you prune it, wait to do so in late June or early July. The plants develop their flowers on last year's branches; if you prune in fall, winter, or spring, you could cut off the buds before they have a chance to open.

Jasmine

Q **What is the best way to care for a star jasmine and keep it blooming?**

A Star jasmine (*Trachelospermum jasminoides*), also known as Confederate jasmine, is hardy in Zones 8–10, with some varieties hardy in Zone 7. It prefers full sun to partial shade and well-drained soil high in organic matter. You can grow it in a container with some support to climb on or as a groundcover. It needs average water, although once established it will tolerate drought.

Q **I have two pink jasmine vines. They have finished blooming for this year and have grown very rapidly. Do I prune these vines?**

A You can prune your pink jasmine (*Jasminum polyanthum*) after it finishes its bloom cycle to keep it from becoming a tangled mess. Take out any crossing branches. If it is too long, you can prune it back harder to shorten the length of the vining branches.

Q **I have a jasmine and I was wondering how I can make a new plant from my existing one. Can I take cuttings and root them in water?**

A Jasmine roots easily from cuttings. Take 5- to 6-inch-long cuttings and remove leaves from the bottom third of the cutting. Dip them in rooting hormone and place the cutting into a pot with a high-quality potting mix. Place the cuttings in a shady spot and water regularly. If the air is dry, they'll benefit from the high humidity under the drape of a plastic film cover.

Q **I have successfully grown my Confederate jasmine in a container for several years. This summer some of the leaves started turning reddish and there are red spots on some of the green foliage. Is this some kind of disease?**

A Red spots on the leaves of your Confederate jasmine likely are from a fungal leaf spot, which usually develops during wet weather. If the weather has recently changed from wet to dry, further infection may not develop. If conditions remain wet and humid, it may be helpful to spray the plant with a fungicide to prevent additional infection.

Q **I live in Zone 7a. Last summer I purchased two star jasmines. This winter they have lost all of their leaves. Are they dead?**

A Star jasmine is a tender evergreen vine. Its response to cold is to drop its leaves to cut down on water loss. I expect that it will start to leaf out shortly in response to the spring weather, and you will have plenty of flowers later on. Don't expect it to hold its leaves all winter in Zone 7a, unless you can protect it from winter cold in some fashion.

Mandevilla

Q **Where is the best place to plant mandevilla? Does it require shade or sun?**

A Mandevilla vines (below) are tropical plants that need a fence or trellis to scramble over. They also require full sun—at least six to eight hours of sunlight a day—in order to bloom well.

Q **What do I need to do to take care of my mandevilla? I love its pink flowers.**

A Several species of mandevilla have become popular container plants in the North and landscape plants in the South. 'Alice du Pont' is a well-known variety. Plants are not hardy but may be overwintered in a greenhouse or bright sunroom where temperatures remain above 50°F. Outdoors, mandevilla requires full sun to part shade. Keep the soil moderately moist, and fertilize regularly

through the summer. In late summer, cease fertilizing and reduce watering. Prune it back in late winter. Take the plant back outside when all danger of frost is past.

Morning Glory

Q **I would like to plant morning glories along a wood fence. Where's the best place to put them? What care do they need?**

A Morning glories (*Ipomoea*) need a spot in full sun. If there's too much shade, they won't bloom. Water them throughout the summer to encourage lots of flowers. Fertilize them sparingly unless your garden has very poor soil; too much fertilizer encourages leafy growth at the expense of blooms. In areas that experience short summers, start your morning glory seeds indoors a month or two early.

Q **Our morning glories are overrunning the roses and apple trees as well as the birdfeeder. How do I get rid of them without killing other plants?**

A Wherever morning glory is allowed to shed seeds, it quickly becomes a persistent summer weed. Fortunately, these vining annuals are easy to pull or hoe when they're young. To kill morning glories that have entwined themselves in other plants, use scissors or sharp-tipped pruning shears to clip the main stem close to the ground. Then simply allow the vines to shrivel. Many excellent large-flower varieties reseed only modestly.

Learn about the best annual vines for your garden online at *bhg.com/annual-vines*.

Passionflower

Q **I would like to grow a passionflower, but I don't know anything about how to care for one. Where should I plant it?**

A Passionflower (*Passiflora incarnata*) thrives where it gets at least a half day of sun. The exotic purple flowers appear from early summer to autumn, but each blossom lasts only a day. If pollinated, the flowers develop into egg-shape fruits, which pop loudly when tread upon—hence the common name of maypop vine. After the vines die back in late autumn, trim away the current season's growth. New stems will sprout from roots in spring.

Trumpet Vine

Q **I bought a trumpet vine two years ago and it hasn't bloomed. What can I do to get it to bloom?**

A Trumpet vine (*Campsis radicans*) is notorious for taking its time to bloom. It's common for plants to take several years to start flowering. Trumpet vine needs full sun and well-drained soil to thrive. If yours doesn't have these growing conditions, flowering could be delayed.

Q **Last year I severely pruned an overgrown trumpet vine. In the past few weeks it has sent up new plants all across my lawn. How can I kill these new plants?**

A Trumpet vine activates dormant root buds when the parent plant is threatened. You may continue to see sprouts popping up for another year or two. Repeated mowing will kill them, or you can use a sharp knife to cut them off just below the soil line. It takes

persistence to kill off the shoots. Avoid letting the shoots grow for long without removing them. By constantly mowing or pruning them off, you'll eventually starve the roots of energy.

Q **I have a trumpet vine next to my garage. The hummingbirds love the orange blossoms, but the vine causes damage to the siding. How can we get rid of it?**

A Trumpet vine (above) can be very difficult to eliminate. Dig out as much of the root system as you can. Then watch for sprouts that come up. Use a paintbrush to apply a brush-killer herbicide to the sprouts. It may take repeated applications over the course of a year to knock out the remaining root system.

Wisteria

Q Why doesn't my wisteria bloom?

A It can take wisteria more than seven years after it's planted to bloom. If your wisteria was planted in heavy soil, shade, or other situations it doesn't like, the vine may fail to bloom. Too much nitrogen causes a plant to put on leafy growth at the expense of flowers. If your wisteria is growing near a lawn area, the roots may be absorbing the nitrogen-rich lawn fertilizer. In Zone 5, plants may not bloom after severe winters because the cold freezes out the buds. Pruning the roots with a shovel sometimes helps wisteria to bloom sooner, but this technique stresses the vine. Instead, focus on growing the plant in the right spot and pruning it properly for good blooming.

Q My wisteria has been growing great foliage for many years, but it never blooms in my Zone 5 garden. Are some kinds hardier than others?

A Gardeners in Zone 5 should grow varieties such as 'Clara Mack', which have increased hardiness. In Zone 4 try Kentucky wisteria (*Wisteria macrostachya*) cultivars 'Aunt Dee' or 'Blue Moon'.

Q Are there different kinds of wisteria? Which are the best ones to grow?

A There are more than 50 wisteria varieties available to gardeners. If you have a small garden or lack a sturdy structure on which to grow wisteria, substitute a smaller type, such as Kentucky wisteria or American wisteria (*W. frutescens*). Chinese wisteria (*W. sinensis*) and Japanese wisteria (*W. floribunda*) are considered invasive in many areas. The American forms are smaller and don't grow as quickly, making them better suited to small gardens.

Q I bought a 5-foot-tall Chinese wisteria. I love this plant but am afraid to plant it in the ground because friends tell me it's aggressive. Can I put it in a large pot and keep it pruned to 8 feet tall?

A Chinese wisteria is aggressive, but you can trim it severely without hurting it. Prune it after flowering and again once or twice during the summer by trimming back long shoots to the principal stems. If necessary, prune in winter, retaining a main trunk and dense branching structure. Avoid removing the spurs (compact, woody stems with short internodes). These spurs are where most blooms develop.

Q I want to start a wisteria from seed. How should I germinate the seed?

A Wisteria is easy to grow from seed, but seed-grown plants may not bloom for 10 to 15 years. Plants grown from cuttings or layered from a flowering plant usually begin flowering much earlier than seedlings. If you'd still like to start one from seed, collect the mature (brown) seedpods and remove the seeds. Allow the seeds to dry, then store them in the refrigerator until spring. Sow seeds in spring after soaking them in water for 24 hours.

Q I'd like to get a wisteria vine for my yard. Can you tell me the best place to plant it and what care it needs?

A Wisterias aren't easy vines to grow. The plant requires full sun (at least six hours a day) and well-drained soil. Especially important is a sturdy support, such as a pergola, because wisterias grow large and fast. Planting it too deeply may delay or prevent blooming. Prune your wisteria twice a year to keep it from growing out of bounds and to keep it flowering well.

Q How should I prune my wisteria?

A Wisteria normally needs pruning twice per year. Prune in summer, just after the spring flush of growth. Cut off the tips of all the side shoots. Remove any new shoots as well. Prune again in winter. Cut back the main stems by about half. Shorten the side shoots that were pruned in spring. Cut them back to a couple inches from the flowering spurs (which look like little pegs). This encourages the production of more flowering spurs, which means more flowers next spring.

Q My wisteria refuses to bloom. It gets a lot of sun and I do not fertilize it at all. My parents have a wisteria that blooms without fail. We live close to each other so the soil is not any different. What does this vine need?

A Wisteria can be very stubborn if it's not completely happy. Sometimes they won't bloom if they are not getting enough sun or if they are being overfed. It also depends on how they started life. Wisteria that's been grown from seed is very slow to bloom, usually taking 10 to 15 years to reach maturity. It's best to grow wisteria as a cutting from a parent that's already blooming. Your reluctant bloomer may have been started from seed rather than a cutting.

Pruning Wounds

Q Should I paint the large cuts I make when pruning trees?

A A tree generally seals itself effectively, and an untreated wound seals better than a painted one. Research shows that pruning paint can seal in moisture and promote decay. In most cases, you're better off avoiding the use of tree paint or wound dressings, but there are exceptions. Trees that are troubled by diseases or pests may benefit from wound dressing to keep out the pest. For example, an oak pruned during the dormant season seals itself effectively with no extra care. However, an oak that needs to be pruned in spring or summer (from storm damage, for instance) should be sealed with wound dressing to prevent sap beetles, which carry oak wilt fungus, from being attracted to the open wound.

Q We have some broken cordyline leaves. What should we do?

A When a plant has broken stems, it's best to make a clean pruning cut so that the stem can begin to seal. Damaged stems and torn foliage are good entry points for disease. In the case of your cordyline, trim the damaged leaves at the main stem.

Q My Japanese maple has a spot on the trunk where the bark has lifted from the trunk, exposing bare wood. The tree is about 5 inches in diameter. How should I treat this?

A This sounds like a sunscald injury. It happens when bark on a thin-bark species, such as maple, warms up on sunny winter days then becomes damaged when it freezes after sundown. Score the bark with a sharp knife, removing any pieces that could harbor insects or moisture. Don't remove any more of the bark than you absolutely have to. If the wound extends one-fourth of the way or less around the tree, it likely will recover.

Next fall, wrap the bark with tree wrap to protect it from further damage. Be sure to remove the wrap in spring.

Q I recently pruned my maple tree, and now sap is flowing out of the cut. Will this hurt the tree? Should I put anything on the wound?

A The best time to prune maples and other trees with heavy late-winter sap flow is after they have fully leafed out in early summer. Unless you don't mind stained trunks, avoid pruning your maple tree in late winter when the majority of other trees are pruned. Maple, walnut birch, American hophornbeam, and American hornbeam have free-flowing sap that seeps from open wounds in late winter and early spring. The sap flow doesn't harm the tree, but it can create unattractive wet streaks on the bark. There is no need to seal the cuts with wound dressing. Allow nature to take its course in sealing off the cuts naturally.

Deadheading

Q What does "deadheading" mean?

A Deadheading means removing a plant's flowers as they fade. On some plants this encourages more blooms. The best time to deadhead is right after flowers fade. This practice not only improves the plant's appearance, but it also removes developing seeds. Because the plant is no longer putting energy into seed development, it can put more energy into vegetative growth and developing more flowers.

Q How far back should I cut my perennials when I deadhead them?

A The best technique to use for deadheading depends on the type of flower. Remove the entire bloom stalk of delphinium, hosta, and other plants that flower from a single stem. Similarly, deadhead individual flowers of plants that produce single blooms on long stems, such as Shasta daisy and coneflower. Cut back plants that produce plumes, such as Russian sage and astilbe, just below the bulk of the flowers. Shear plants, such as threadleaf coreopsis, that produce flowers at the same level as the foliage.

Q Is it OK to cut back the foliage of shrubs and perennials in late summer when they don't look good anymore?

A You can cut back herbaceous perennials (those in which the stems die back to the ground over winter) if their foliage is tattered and unattractive. However, it's best to leave shrubs alone in late summer. Pruning them in late summer can stimulate new growth on their woody stems that won't have time to harden off before winter weather arrives.

Q Should shrubs be deadheaded similar to perennial flowers?

A Few shrubs require deadheading, but some look more attractive if their spent flowers are removed. For example, many people like to remove the seedpods of lilac because they can detract from the foliage. Avoid removing spent flowers of shrubs, such as viburnums, which develop attractive fleshy fruits.

Pruning Roses

Q How much should I prune my roses back before winter?

A Unless the rose canes are quite long, and likely to whip in the winter wind, it's best to leave them unpruned going into winter. However, depending on the method of winter protection you use for your roses, you may need to prune some stems to contain the rose under the soil or mulch used to protect it.

Q How do I know how far back to cut my roses after winter? When is the best time to do it?

A Take a cue from the rose itself for timing and place to make the cutbacks. Wait until the plant begins to send out new growth in the spring. Make your cuts just above a healthy developing shoot as the leaves are unfolding. Check the color of the stem. Healthy stems will be bright green; damaged ones will be blackened.

Q After a harsh winter, my roses look terrible. Can I cut them all the way back to the ground?

A Severe pruning is one way to invigorate an old rose. If the rose is grafted (look for a swollen knob near the base of the plant), be certain to make the pruning cuts above the graft union. Remove any shoots that develop below the graft; they won't be the same variety as the top. The best time to do this drastic pruning on your rose bush is in late winter, just as the rose is coming out of winter dormancy.

Q I don't see any graft union on my rose bush. How do I know how far back to prune it?

A Some roses are grown on their own rootstocks. If your rose is a miniature or one of the landscape roses, it's likely that it is growing on its own roots. With these roses, it makes little difference where on the main stem you make a pruning cut because all shoots that develop will be of the same variety.

Q I have no idea where to begin in pruning my hybrid tea rose bush. Can you help?

A A good place to start is to remove any dead or damaged wood. Next, cut off any suckers growing up from the root. Also remove any spindly or very old growth and canes that are rubbing against each other. Finally, trim the remaining canes. You can trim the canes that you want to keep anywhere from several inches above the graft union to several feet tall. The more severe cutback will result in a shorter bush, but it will take longer to return to bloom.

Q Do I need to apply a protective coating on the cut canes where I pruned my roses?

A There is no need to apply fingernail polish or other sealants to rose-pruning wounds. Make pruning cuts at a 45-degree angle, so that water sheds from the cut. The rose should heal fine on its own.

Q How do I prune a climbing rose?

A The method to use in pruning climbing roses depends on the type of climber. If yours blooms just once per year, prune it severely right after it blooms. It will bloom next year on the shoots that develop this season. Reblooming types may be pruned in late winter to remove excess growth. This will remove some flowering wood, but because they bloom on new wood as well as old wood, they'll still produce blossoms this year.

Q When I cut rose flowers, where should I make the cut?

A When cutting hybrid tea roses and other reblooming long-stem types, make the cut just above a 5-leaflet leaf. For roses that bloom in clusters, snip off the rose just below the individual bloom.

Pruning Shrubs

Q Should I prune the dead blooms from my butterfly bushes?

A Deadheading butterfly bush by removing the spent blossoms promotes continued bloom on the bush and makes it more attractive. Prune the dead blooms back to the next blossom or set of leaves.

Q Should I deadhead my hydrangeas?

A Most hydrangeas need no deadheading. The spent flowerheads dry naturally on the plant and can be an attractive addition to the fall and winter landscape. The exceptions to the hydrangea deadheading rule are the reblooming types. Endless Summer and Forever & Ever Series hydrangeas bloom on new wood, so they can rebloom if you cut off the spent blossoms. If you'd like to encourage another bloom cycle on these hydrangeas, remove the flower clusters as they begin to fade. Cut them off at the first set of leaves below the bloom.

Q I recently purchased six Knock Out roses. Do I need to deadhead them?

A Knock Out roses have taken the market by storm for good reason. They are almost carefree, blooming throughout the summer into fall with little maintenance. Their habit of self-cleaning means no deadheading, a boon to gardeners strapped for time, and indeed they do bloom over and over again. Pruning can be done in early spring. First remove any dead, damaged, or dying stems. Then trim to shape.

Q My friend told me that I must deadhead all the old blossoms from my rhododendron bush. She said I won't get any blossoms next year unless I do this. I think she must be mistaken because I've seen beautiful rhododendrons in parks that have never been deadheaded.

A You are correct. You don't need to deadhead rhododendrons. Removing the spent flowers does make them look better and can help them bloom a little better next year. But leaving the spent flowers on will not prevent them from flowering next year.

For information on which pruning tools to use in which situations, check out our online story about pruning tools at *bhg.com/pruning-tools*.

Q A big section of my bridalwreath spirea died last season. This spring, another section died. Is there any way to salvage this plant? Can I cut it to the ground and start over?

A Spirea does respond well to severe pruning. The best time to do so is while it is dormant in late winter. Spring or early summer is the second-best time. You can cut it back to within 4 to 6 inches of the ground. It will likely take several years for your bridalwreath spirea to bloom again. The pink-flower types of spireas can be cut back in late winter and will still bloom this year.

Q Could you tell me how to prune a redtwig dogwood? Does pruning out one-third of the old canes mean taking all canes down one-third of the plant's height? Or does it mean taking one-third of the old canes out to the ground? If pruned to the ground how much regrowth can be expected in one season?

A Pruning out one-third of the oldest canes means removing one-third of the canes all the way to the ground. If your shrub had 12 stems, you would remove the four oldest, woodiest stems as close to the ground as you can. The newest, youngest branches have the best red color. As they age they lose their color until they're a dull gray. Dogwood shrubs sucker from the base and form a clump of stems. Removing old stems results in new red shoots from the ground. The new shoots grow fast. You should see several feet of growth on the new suckers during their first year.

Q I have some boxwoods that are turning yellow. Early in the spring I pruned off the winter-killed leaves, and the shrubs looked pretty good. Now they are showing small areas that are green, but most of the plant is yellow. Is this fatal, or can this be treated?

A The timing of the yellowing suggests that this is also winter injury. Often internal stem tissues that conduct water and nutrients may be damaged over winter, but the damage doesn't show up on the leaves until the temperature warms, and the plant is no longer able to get enough moisture and nutrients through the damaged conducting tissues. Go ahead and cut them back to the healthy green sections. They can grow out from even a small healthy green section.

Q I have six gardenia bushes approximately 4 feet tall. They bloom every spring and fall, but they are becoming leggy. How and when do I prune these?

A Immediately after the fall bloom period is done, prune them into the tidy shape that you want in your garden. Remove no more than one-third of the plant. You'll find that your gardenias only need pruning once every two or three years to keep them from becoming leggy again.

Pruning Shrubs

Q **Should I cut off all of last year's dead blooms on my lilac?**

A Cutting off a lilac's dead, faded blooms will help the plant bloom better next year because it won't put energy into making seeds. That said, many gardeners find their lilacs bloom fine without deadheading. So it's not something you must do.

Q **My hydrangea and lilac bushes had only a few blooms but lots of foliage this spring. Can I prune them now in September?**

A The best time to prune hydrangea or lilac is in early summer, right after they finish blooming. By late summer the plants have already made next year's flowerbuds. If you prune them from late summer through spring you'll be cutting off the flowerbuds and preventing your plants from blooming. Both types of shrubs will bloom better if they grow with adequate sunlight. Perhaps the site is too shady for them.

Q **How and when do I prune dwarf lilac bushes? Two of mine were poor bloomers this year.**

A Prune lilac bushes shortly after they finish blooming. They may need some thinning—removing some of the oldest stems all the way to the ground—if they have a lot of stems emerging from the base. Otherwise simple pruning to shape the shrub is all that is needed. Avoid pruning late in the growing season because that will remove next year's flower buds.

Q I have dead shoots on my hydrangea. Can I cut them out now?

A You can cut dead branches on hydrangea or any other shrub whenever they appear. It's a good idea to cut them out because dead stems can serve as an entry point for insect and disease problems.

Q How and when should I prune my hydrangea?

A The amount and type of pruning to do on a hydrangea depends on the type of hydrangea. A good starting point, though, is to prune out any dead or damaged branches that you see at the end of winter, regardless of the type of hydrangea. Most lacecap (*H. macrophylla*) and mophead hydrangeas bloom on old wood, so they should receive minimal pruning until after they bloom. Otherwise, you're cutting off their blooms for this year. When pruning after bloom, cut back to just above a side branch or a node (where the leaf emerges from the stem.) Reblooming hydrangeas such as Endless Summer or the Forever & Ever Series can be treated like the lacecaps and mopheads. The only difference is that they also bloom on new wood, so if you want to cut them back in late winter, you can and will still get blooms this year. Panicled hydrangeas of the 'Annabelle' type can be pruned back to the ground in late winter. They bloom on new wood, so a severe cutback doesn't affect their bloom. Instead it cleans up the old brush and allows the new growth to come in strong.

Q I have two huge oakleaf hydrangeas. The blooms are beautiful but weigh the branches down to the ground. I need to prune them but don't want to harm them. Can they be kept pruned to a smaller size? When is the right time to prune?

A You can prune oakleaf hydrangeas, but they will grow back to this same size within a couple years. Pruning severely will remove the flower buds. It's best to prune oakleaf hydrangeas as little as possible, although you can shape them a bit in late winter or early in the growing season by cutting out errant branches or cutting back to a side growing shoot or branch. If the plant is too large for its space, it would be better to move it or replace it with a plant better suited to the site.

Q I have two male holly bushes that have become unsightly due to bare spots and pruning that has left it misshapen. When can I prune them? Can I remove half of the height to start new growth?

A Holly bushes can be pruned quite severely with no ill effect to the plant. Late winter or early spring is the best time to prune. While it's good to prune as little as necessary to shape the plant, you can prune back into old wood and expect the plant to resprout.

Pruning Evergreens

Q I have a 'Bracken's Brown Beauty' magnolia growing in my Zone 5b yard. I would like to prune a few bottom branches. It's now 3 years old and about 6 feet tall. When should I prune, and what is the best method?

A The ideal time to prune 'Bracken's Brown Beauty' southern magnolia is in late winter, from February until growth begins in the spring. As you prune, keep in mind that even for small trees, approximately two-thirds of the total height of the tree should be branches and only one-third of the height should be trunk. For your 6-foot-tall tree, that means only the bottom 2 feet should be trunk, and the upper 4 feet should have branches. This ratio is necessary for the tree to have enough leaf structure to support good growth. Wait until the tree grows taller to remove many of the lower branches. When removing lower branches, cut back to just outside the branch collar (swollen area next to the main stem or trunk). If cutting back branch tips, cut to just above a side branch or leaf node (the point where the leaf attaches to the stem).

Q Is it OK to trim arborvitae in spring?

A You can trim arborvitae in spring, but be sure not to trim too far back. If you remove all of the outer green needles on a stem it may not regrow. Instead, prune off only a portion of the green fans on a shoot.

Q My rosemary plant that I've had for about three years started dying this year. Should I be dividing or pruning? And if so, how and when?

A Rosemary usually doesn't send up multiple shoots from belowground, so it's not easily divided. However, it can be pruned quite severely to remove dead portions of the plant or to keep it trained to a certain shape. You can also propagate new rosemary plants by taking cuttings of the healthy growth or layering a stem to the ground.

Q How do I prune my pine tree?

A Pines are particular about their pruning method. If you need to completely remove a branch, you can cut it off at the main stem almost anytime. But pruning to shape the tree should be done only when the tree is in the candle stage. This occurs in late spring when the new shoots are elongating, and before the new needles have fully developed. You can cut back these new shoots by one-half to one-third, but avoid pruning into older wood. Pines can form new buds only at this stage.

Q There is a dense hedge of hollies planted along the foundation on both sides of my front door. They overpower the tiny front yard. Can I trim them 12 to 18 inches shorter? Is it best to do it all at once or gradually?

A Hollies (*Ilex* spp.) can be pruned any time of year; many people prune in November or December so they can use the cuttings for holiday decorations. Unlike many evergreens that won't send new growth from older branches, hollies can produce new buds anywhere along the stem after they've been cut back. That means you can remove as much as 12 to 18 inches of stem. However, there will be a period during which they'll look like they've gotten an ugly buzz cut. One way to avoid that is to prune selectively. Work through the shrub and cut one-third of the branches back, leaving the others at their full length. After new green shoots emerge on the cut branches, cut back half of the remaining branches. When those branches sprout, cut back the final third.

Q Why do cedar trees lose their lower growth?

A Lower branches of red cedars (*Juniperus virginiana*) usually die because they are being shaded by the upper branches. At low light intensities, growth is reduced, and eventually the shaded branches die. You can prune upper branches to thin or shape them so that they're always shorter than the lower branches. Doing so will help you keep branches all the way to the base of the tree.

Q I have beautiful nandinas that are more than 10 years old. Some are quite tall and leggy. When should I prune them and how?

A The best time to prune nandina is in winter, when it is dormant. Cut about one-fourth of the stems down to the ground. Then cut one-third of the total stem height off one out of every four remaining stems. Next, prune about one-fourth of the stems two-thirds of the height of the plant. Leave the final fourth of the stems uncut. This will create a layered effect and should result in a fuller canopy of foliage.

Q I would like to know when and how much to prune upright yews.

A Yews respond well to most kinds of pruning. Many cultivars are compact and maintain a tidy shape without any pruning at all. If you would like to shear or shape your yew, trim the stem tips in early to mid-summer. If the plant requires more severe pruning, a good rule is to remove no more than one-third of the plant in a single year. Although yews can resprout from a severe cutback, it's quite a shock to them if more than one-third of the shoots are removed at one time.

Pruning Deciduous Trees

Q **I have two weeping cherry trees. The branches have grown down to the ground and across my flowerbed. Can I trim the branches about 1 foot from the ground?**

A You can trim back weeping branches that drape too low to the ground. If you're doing major pruning it's best to wait until late winter while the plant is still dormant. If just a few branches need trimming, you can do that at any time.

Q **When is the best time to top my trees?**

A The short answer is: Never. Topping trees is never a good idea. The regrowth from a topping cut will be weakly attached and susceptible to wind damage. Instead, reduce the height of the tree by crown reduction. In this type of pruning, you cut the tallest shoots back to a more lateral growing branch, thereby reducing the height of the tree. It's best to have an arborist or tree pruning professional do this work for you. The best time to prune most deciduous trees (those that lose their leaves) is in late winter.

Q **My maple tree has a large limb that needs to be removed. How can I do that without damaging the tree?**

A Whenever you must remove a large limb from a tree, follow this three-step process:
1. Make an undercut on the branch 12 to 18 inches from the main trunk.
2. Make a second cut on top of the branch a couple inches farther out on the stem. Continue cutting from the top until the weight of the branch causes it to break off at the undercut.
3. Remove the branch stub remaining on the trunk by cutting just outside the branch bark ridge (swollen area where the branch attaches to the main stem).

Q **I love my crabapple tree, but its branches are very long and lanky. If I prune them back a bit, will it encourage it to become denser?**

A Heading back pruning (cutting stem tips back to a bud on the stem) is one way to encourage thicker branches and more branching on the stem. The ideal time to prune is while the tree is dormant in winter, but it can also be done early in spring.

Q My two-year-old Japanese maple has lots of small shoots growing at its base. Should I prune off the new young shoots, and if so when is the best time to do so?

A It's OK to prune the shoots arising from the base of the tree at any time. These shoots are called suckers. They are robbing the tree of vigor, and if you let them go, they will adversely affect the shape of the tree. Also, if they arise from the roots rather than the stem, the shoots could look quite different from the rest of the plant.

Q When is the best time to prune a maple tree? After a severe windstorm last fall, it split in two. The remaining half looks pretty good, but one limb is close to our roof. We would like to take it off, but we are unsure when to do it or if we should.

A I strongly suggest that you have a local certified arborist come out and give you an opinion on this tree. You can remove any limbs endangering your home at any time. Get the advice on the safety of the tree from the arborist who can tell you if it's worth saving or if any trimming will make it more likely to split.

Q My shade trees have crusty green splotches on their bark. Should I remove these spots? Are they harming the trees?

A The pale green substance on your tree's bark is lichen. It's fairly common, and is harmless to the tree. Attempting to remove it would damage the bark and make the tree susceptible to diseases.

Q What's the best way to thin out the branches of a tree that's casting too much shade?

A If the tree isn't too large, you may be able to remove enough low-hanging branches with a pole pruner.

Make any cuts at the main stem or branch juncture. If you can't reach the branches that need removal with a pole pruner, it may be best (and certainly safest) to hire the job done professionally.

Q I would like to know the best way to prune my willow tree. I usually trim it from the bottom to keep it from covering my house.

A Willow can be a rampant grower. Fortunately, it withstands rather severe pruning. In Europe they are often pollarded—cut all the way back to the main trunk each winter or at least every couple years. You need not prune that severely, but rest assured that you can prune the tree almost as much as you'd like to keep it in shape. Avoid pruning during rainy periods, which can promote disease development or late in the growing season, which can result in growth of shoots that won't be winter-hardy.

Pruning Vines

Q I have a trumpet vine that I purchased about 10 years ago. Now this vine is spreading and overpowering my deck. I have cut it back, but it comes back and has spread to areas where I don't want it.

A Trumpet vine is such a rampant grower that it's what many gardeners would call invasive. It can send long runners underground and spring up 8 or 10 feet away from the original vine. You should be able to keep it tamed in the turf with regular mowing, but watch for it in distant landscape beds and tear it out whenever you find it. If the supporting structure for it is not strong enough to bear the vine's rampant growth, you may be best off completely removing it.

Q I have a wisteria vine that has never bloomed. Am I pruning it wrong? Should I prune it in spring or wait until later in summer?

A It's not timing as much as how you cut it back. In summer, after bloom occurs (or would occur, in your case), cut new shoots back to 6-inch stubs. In winter, do the same. The blooms usually occur on the first few buds formed on the previous year's shoots. So don't strip all the new growth away each time you prune, or you will be pruning off the flower buds. Lack of bloom may simply be because your wisteria is not old enough to bloom. Make sure the vine is getting at least six to eight hours of sunlight per day, and give it another couple years to mature. You could replace with 'Blue Moon' wisteria, which usually flowers within a year or two of planting.

Q I've had a clematis vine for three years now and it has never bloomed. How do I get it to bloom?

A Are you pruning the clematis? If you cut the vine back to the ground every winter you may be removing all the flowers. Clematis falls into three pruning groups. Those that bloom once in spring or early summer should be pruned right after they flower. Pruning them in winter removes their blooms for the year. Those that bloom on new wood (usually late-season bloomers) can be cut back to 1 to 2 feet above the ground in late winter. Reblooming types bloom on old and new wood. Prune this type of clematis in late winter as for those that bloom on new wood. But also pinch the new growth occasionally to encourage branching and stimulate more blooms.

Q I have kudzu vine overtaking my yard. How do I prune out this awful weed?

A Kudzu is a tough plant to eradicate. Your best bet is to cut it off at the base of the vine and paint the freshly cut stump with a brush killer. Pull the rest of the vine down after it's been severed from its roots.

Edible Gardening

Easy-to-Grow Vegetables

Q I'd like to start a vegetable garden, but have never grown anything before. Do you have any suggestions for which crops would be the easiest to grow?

A Start with some of the easier ones, and you'll build your confidence and graduate to growing a broad variety of produce. These crops offer relatively trouble-free growing, are quick to harvest, and require a minimum of work: 1. Bush beans, 2. Cabbage, 3. Cucumbers, 4. Onions (from sets), 5. Peas, 6. Potatoes, 7. Radishes, 8. Summer squash, and 9. Tomatoes.

Crop Rotation

Q My husband and I would like to grow a few more vegetables than usual. I've heard that in a large garden it's best to rotate where the vegetables are planted each year. How do I do this?

A The basic rule of rotation is to avoid planting any closely related vegetables in the same spot for at least three years. Some common plant families include the following:
1. Tomato: Tomatoes, peppers, potatoes, and eggplant
2. Squash: Cucumbers, melons, pumpkins, winter squash, summer squash, zucchini, and gourds
3. Beans: Green beans, wax beans, lima beans, soybeans, snow peas, snap peas, and garden peas
4. Cabbage: Cabbage, broccoli, cauliflower, Brussels sprouts, kohlrabi, kale, and collards.

Q What are the advantages of crop rotation in the vegetable garden?

A By rotating crops, you help prevent disease and you ensure that your plants get proper soil nutrients. For example, verticillium wilt can survive several years in the soil and affect tomatoes and potatoes. To keep from spreading the disease season to season, plant susceptible vegetables in different garden spots from year to year so the disease will be less likely to carry over. Rather than follow your tomato crop with tomatoes or potatoes, instead plant corn, carrots, or members of the squash family. Use crop rotation for better plant nutrient management too. Corn, for instance, uses more nitrogen than peas or beans do. In fact, members of the bean family actually add nitrogen to the soil through nitrogen fixation. By planting corn where beans or peas grew last year, you can keep your soil's nutrients better balanced and reduce the amount of fertilizer needed.

Gardening in Shade

Q My garden is almost totally shaded on one side. What vegetables can I plant in the shade?

A Few vegetables will grow in shade. If the shady side of your garden gets some sun during the day, I'd try leafy greens there—especially ones that tend to bolt in hot weather, such as lettuce and spinach. They somtimes even do better in partial shade than in full sun. If your garden gets at least four to five hours of sun, beans, broccoli, potatoes, peas, and rhubarb should produce for you as well.

Ashes in the Garden

Q My dad wants to use the ashes from our charcoal grill on the garden. Will this have any effect?

A Ashes from charcoal grills should not be added to gardens because of chemicals used in processing charcoal. Wood ashes, on the other hand, are safer for garden use. They have fertilizer value—generally less than 10 percent potash, 1 percent phosphate, and trace amounts of micronutrients—but their main effect is to raise the pH. If you live in an area with alkaline soils, adding wood ashes to the garden soil could cause nutrient deficiencies.

Seed Starting

Q How early can I plant peas and lettuce? It takes so long to warm up where I live, but I know that peas and lettuce can tolerate cool soil. Which varieties of lettuce and peas should I use?

A Peas and lettuce can be planted as early as six weeks before the last frost, as long as the soil is moist but not muddy. It's important to get peas in as early as possible. Yields drop dramatically on later plantings because peas tolerate heat poorly. Plant lettuce at two-week intervals through early summer so you can extend the harvest into midsummer.

Q I have some vegetable seeds left over from last year. Will they still be good to plant this year?

A Some vegetable seeds store well from one year to the next and others don't. To be certain, do a germination test on them. Moisten a paper towel and line up 10 seeds along one edge; fold the edge over

the seeds. Roll up the paper towel. Place the paper towel in a covered tray or plastic bag in a warm (room temperature) location and keep it moist but not soggy. In a few days, unroll the towel to see how many seeds have germinated. If germination is poor, it's best to discard the seeds.

Q Does it matter how early I plant my vegetable garden? There's a lot of rain here in the spring, and it doesn't seem like a good idea to plant while the soil is wet.

A Tilling soil when it is wet turns it into a sticky mess. It's perfectly OK to delay planting of tomatoes, peppers, beans, and other plants that like warm weather. However, if you wait until days become long and warm to plant cool-season crops such as lettuce, spinach, or peas, their flavor suffers and they quickly go to seed. Prepare the soil in raised beds in fall and cover them with polyethylene film through the winter to make sure you get an early start on the spring planting season. The film will keep excess moisture off the soil as well as warm the bed earlier in spring.

Q I live in Zone 5. When should I start my veggie seeds indoors?

A Starting seeds usually is a matter of counting backward from the last frost date in your area. Other gardeners in your neighborhood or the county extension service can help you in determining that. Then read the back of your seed packets. It will tell you how many weeks before the last frost date to start your seeds. For example, for peppers start seeds 8 to 10 weeks before setting them out.

Transplanting

Q **I just planted three tomato plants. They are now turning almost white and look like they are dying. The same problem is showing up on my cucumber plants. Could the weather be affecting them or is this a disease?**

A The response that you're observing on your tomato and cucumber transplants is typical of sunscald and windburn on new transplants. After growing in a protected greenhouse or other spot indoors, transplants benefit from a gradual hardening off before transplanting outdoors. It's best to place them in a protected spot out of the wind and out of direct sun for a week or so before actually transplanting them to the garden. Your plants may recover fully. Make sure they have adequate, but not too much, moisture. And it may still help to protect them from winds by erecting a shield on the windward side of the plants.

Q **All of my seedling pepper plants are turning yellow. What is the cause and what can I do?**

A Yellow leaves on seedlings may indicate a lack of nutrients or moisture stress. This is common in seedlings that have outgrown their starter pots or cell packs. Transplant them into the garden or into larger containers with fresh soil. Feed the peppers with a balanced fertilizer for vegetables.

Q **My garden hasn't had rain in over a month. I water daily, but my tomatoes aren't growing much. What can I do to get them to start growing?**

A It's hard to imagine that fast-growing annuals like tomatoes might be suffering from transplant shock, but it's possible. They're devoting their energy to establishing their root systems before sending up a lot

of new top growth. Be sure you're watering deeply when you water so that the roots are encouraged to go deep. I like to set the sprinkler on mine and run it for an hour. With deeper watering, you can get away with watering just once or twice a week. You might also consider using a starter fertilizer so that nutrients are readily available when the plants need them.

Q **Our family enjoys the flavor of homegrown lettuce, but I have trouble starting it in the ground. The seeds either don't germinate, or they come up so thick that thinning out the seedlings becomes a tedious job. What's the trick?**

A Try jump-starting your plants indoors from seed. It's easier and faster to transplant seedlings exactly where you want them than to thin out the leafy crowd in the ground. And because you'll be planting seedlings instead of seeds outside, you'll also have a head start on the growing season—a plus in areas with short summers.

Raised Beds

Q We want to plant a vegetable garden, but the ground is hard clay. We plan to build a raised bed and bring in fill dirt. What type of wood should we use?

A Raised beds of any type should be constructed out of rot-resistant materials. Pressure-treated lumber is usually the least expensive, but some have concerns about the treated products leaching into the soil. You could line the wall of the bed with heavy plastic if this is a concern for you. Other rot-resistant woods to consider are cedar and redwood. Costs vary from region to region, so you may want to check prices of what is available in your area. Other materials to consider are composite lumbers made from a combination of vinyl and wood fibers. These usually are more expensive, but will last longer than wood. In the Better Homes and Gardens® Test Garden, the cedar raised beds are rotting away after 10 years, but the ones built of composite materials show no signs of rot or decay.

Q We're building a raised-bed vegetable garden on top of clay soil. Should we dig up the clay base first?

A If you make the raised beds deep enough, it isn't necessary to till up the underlying clay. However, mixing in some of the new soil with the existing clay can help prevent the formation of a soil texture barrier through which roots and water won't easily penetrate. The rooting depth for most vegetables should be at least 1 foot.

Q I grew vegetables in a raised bed last summer. I haven't done anything to the soil since I planted last year. What should I do to get the soil ready for this year?

A I like to add a fresh layer of organic matter to the bed's surface and work that into the soil. Compost, rotted manure, leaf mold, or peat moss will help. At planting time, add a timed-release vegetable fertilizer, and dig it into the soil as you till, in preparation for planting. Keep the bed weed-free between growing seasons. By removing weeds before they set seed, you'll cut down on the need to weed while crops are growing.

Q Is it OK to eat fruits and vegetables planted near a railroad tie retaining wall?

A Creosote oozing from railroad ties can be toxic to plants. But most railroad ties used in landscaping no longer have fresh creosote that oozes into the soil. If in doubt, you can place a plastic liner behind the retaining wall so that nothing can ooze into the soil, and roots will not come into contact with the creosote.

Learn how to build raised beds online at *bhg.com /raised-beds.*

Season Extenders

Q We get frosts late in the spring in our garden. Is there anything we can do to get our vegetables started earlier outdoors?

A Floating row covers work well for protecting whole beds of crops such as salad greens from several degrees of frost. At season's end, the insulation from a row cover can extend the harvest of larger plants such as zucchini and tomatoes. Old sheets supported by metal hoops also make good covers. Many synthetic row covers are light enough to drape directly over the crop. Synthetic-fabric row covers may also be left on all season to give insect protection to such pest magnets as eggplant and cabbage.

Q What is a cloche? I think this has something to do with frost protection.

A Cloches, in essence, are miniature greenhouses that protect plants from the elements. Glass cloches aren't vented; move them daily to keep plants from sizzling in the midday sun. Eliminate this daily chore by employing cloches with vents, such as milk jugs or any vented hot cap that allows heated air to escape. To use a milk jug, cut off the bottom, remove the lid, and place the top of the container over your plant. Use cloches until after the last spring frost and again when frost threatens in fall.

Q Is there a way to warm up the soil in spring to get veggies started sooner?

A Soil's insulating properties can make for slow gardening in spring. Plant in raised beds, where the soil warms faster because the beds are above the main soil surface, even if only by a few inches. For gardens that aren't raised, warm the soil before you plant by covering the area with sheets of clear or black plastic or dark landscape fabric.

Q I would like to plant a winter vegetable garden. I live in Zone 8. What would be the best veggies to plant and when?

A Cool-season vegetables are the best ones to plant for a winter vegetable garden. These include cabbage family (*cabbage, broccoli, cauliflower, Chinese cabbage, Oriental greens, kohlrabi, etc.*), radishes, green onions, peas, spinach, and mesclun. Timing depends on the average first frost date and the days to maturity for the vegetables you plan to plant. Because days are shorter in fall than at spring planting time, it's often a good idea to add a couple weeks to the stated days to maturity on the seed packet. Plant early enough in late summer so that the crops will mature before a hard freeze. You can also extend the season by using floating row covers or other frost protection devices.

Asparagus

Q I purchased asparagus roots. What is the correct way to plant them?

A Asparagus requires well-drained soil with a near neutral pH. Many references suggest digging a trench, then making mounds on which to plant the asparagus, but this isn't necessary. Dig a trench only deep enough to cover the roots with 4 inches of soil. To tell which side is up on a dormant asparagus plant, look for knobby lumps, which are most numerous on the top. Spread out the roots as you plant them, like spokes of an umbrella.

Q How much asparagus can I harvest? I've heard that if I pick too much, I could hurt my plants.

A The first year after planting, pick only large spears (pencil-size diameter or greater) that emerge early in the growing season. In the second year, gather all the spears you want for a month, beginning with the emergence of the first spear. In subsequent seasons, limit your picking to a six-week period. If you overharvest asparagus, the plants will produce fewer spears, because they will have less time to store energy and develop the next year's crop.

Q Do I need to keep all asparagus shoots picked so none of them develop into fern?

A During the harvest season, pick the asparagus patch clean. If you leave some shoots to develop into fern, asparagus beetles are likely to lay their eggs on the ferny growth. As the eggs hatch, the larvae feed on and distort developing shoots. Even with thorough harvest, the beetles may become a problem and require treatment with an insecticide.

Q My grandma said that I could sprinkle salt on my asparagus beds to control the weeds. Is that true?

A Asparagus is more salt-tolerant than a lot of plants, so it may not be damaged by an application of table salt to the soil. However, I don't recommend it. Salt destroys soil structure and may wash into other parts of the garden, injuring other crops. Keep your asparagus bed mulched with weed-free straw or other organic mulch to prevent weeds from germinating. Hand-pull or hoe out weeds that grow through the mulch.

Beans

Q **I want to grow pinto and red kidney beans for use as dried beans. When is the best time to plant and harvest them?**

A Wait until all danger of frost has passed to plant shell beans. They produce best when grown in double rows (two parallel rows about 6 inches apart). Begin harvesting beans for cooking fresh as soon as the pods become leathery. To dry beans, allow them to mature until the pods turn tan. If a prolonged spell of rainy weather strikes while your beans are drying, harvest them and finish drying them indoors.

Q **I noticed holes in the leaves of my bean plants. After close inspection I found green and yellow bugs about the size of ladybugs on the leaves. I have been picking them off and killing them because I don't want to use pesticides. Any suggestions?**

A It sounds as though your beans are being attacked by Mexican bean beetles, which are closely related to ladybugs. The good news is that bean plants are quite resilient and can tolerate a lot of feeding injury from the beetles with no loss in yield. So if the infestation is not heavy it may be unnecessary to control them. If control is needed, you might consider using spinosad (Captain Jack's Deadbug Brew), a natural product made from bacteria. You could also try using floating row covers as a barrier to keep the beetles off the beans.

Q **I got a late start on my vegetable garden. Can I still plant green beans in late June?**

A Throughout most of the country you can plant green beans from approximately the last frost date in spring through mid- to late July. In fact, making new plantings of beans every couple weeks ensures a steady harvest of this vegetable.

Q **Some animal is eating my string beans. How can I stop them?**

A It sounds like you have hungry rabbits or deer in your garden. Tender young plants in spring are irresistible to them. You might try a physical barrier like a fence or cages over your plants. Your vegetables are most vulnerable in early spring; if you can make it through the first several weeks, more food sources sprout up elsewhere and your problem may lessen. You could also spray the plants with a repellent labelled for use on vegetables, such as Liquid Fence.

Broccoli

Q How do you harvest broccoli? Do you just snap it off, and more shoots will grow from the side?

A Use a sharp knife to cut off the head before it starts to flower and turn yellow. If you leave the plant in place, it will develop more smaller heads in the remaining leaf stalks.

Q When can I safely plant broccoli seedlings that I bought from the garden center?

A Broccoli likes cool temperatures and tolerates frost, but exposure to too much cold can make the plant develop a head prematurely, and the plant may be permanently stunted. In spring, the prime planting time is one to three weeks before your last expected frost date. If you love broccoli, plant it again in midsummer for an autumn harvest.

Q I live in central Oklahoma. My broccoli is not heading out, but it has beautiful foliage. It has been hot and rainy. Please tell me what I need to do to get it to head out.

A Broccoli is sensitive to hot weather and can experience heat delay. Excessive heat can also cause misshapen heads on broccoli. You may need to wait for the weather to cool down in order to get heads on your broccoli. Also, how long have your broccoli plants been growing in the garden? Some varieties take longer to develop than others, but eventually your plants should develop heads.

Brussels Sprouts

Q My Brussels sprouts develop a fungus and melt from the top down. The fungus also appears on collards. Any ideas?

A It sounds like your Brussels sprouts and collards suffer from a bacterial infection similar to black rot, which attacks cabbage. You may be able to prevent (or at least reduce) its spread to your crop this year by removing all plant debris in your garden from last year. If you water, a trickle system or weeping hose is better at preventing the spread of disease than a splashy overhead system.

Cabbage

Q How can I prevent my cabbage heads from splitting open?

A To prevent split heads on cabbage, harvest them when they are fully developed and solid. If you can't harvest immediately, dig around one side of the plant to disrupt the roots so that they will take up less water.

Q There are green worms chewing holes in my cabbage. What can I do?

A Three species of cabbage worms chew on leaves of cabbage-family crops (cabbage, broccoli, cauliflower, Brussels sprouts, kohlrabi, and kale). Imported cabbage worm, cabbage looper, and diamondback moth larvae chew holes through the leaves. Use floating row covers to prevent adults from laying eggs on plants. Or handpick worms from the plants. The biological insecticide Bt is effective against all three species of cabbage worms.

Cauliflower

Q I tied up the heads of my cauliflower when they were about the size of a doorknob. Some grew beautifully into nice heads, but some didn't. They were loosely formed, with very little of the white top. What happened?

A Cauliflower can be temperamental to grow. It sounds as though you did the right thing in tying up the leaves to blanch the heads to keep them white. Those that failed to develop fully may have been stressed previously. This can lead to button heads, small heads that fail to expand. If the heads were loose and ricey in appearance, you may have blanched them too long. Overmature cauliflower develops this grainy appearance. Normal blanching time is four to eight days.

Chinese Cabbage

Q I would like to know how to grow bok choy. Do you have to tie the leaves up around the plant as it grows?

A Bok choy Chinese cabbage is relatively easy to grow during cool conditions. (It often flowers and goes to seed prematurely if the temperature is too high.) Treat it as you would regular cabbage or broccoli. They are closely related. It requires no special care such as tying up the leaves. It naturally forms a loose cluster of upright stalks as it matures.

Corn

Q **How do I know when it is time to pick my sweet corn?**

A Corn is ripe when silks are brown and dry on top but still yellow just under the husk. Watch for the silks to change color from greenish yellow to brown as the ear of corn matures. Many gardeners check how filled-out the cobs feel before harvesting, but if you grow different varieties, those that have thin cobs may seem as though they are still filling out. Some gardeners peel back the husks to look at the developing kernels. Avoid peeling back any more husks than you must, because the act invites corn earworms, raccoons, and some birds to feed on your corn.

Q **What does it take to grow good sweet corn? The ears never fill out well when I grow it.**

A Sweet corn needs warm temperatures for best growth. It needs full sun and prefers a soil pH between 5.8 and 6.5. Plant two or more rows of the same variety side by side to ensure good pollination. Because corn is wind-pollinated, pollen from one row must fall or blow onto the silks of an adjoining row to pollinate the kernels. Plant corn in a block of shorter rows to ensure better pollination.

Q **In the seed catalogs I see some letters by the names of some sweet corn varieties. What do they mean?**

A High-sugar sweet corn may be either supersweet or sugary enhanced. The supersweet varieties have the "shrunken 2" gene, abbreviated "sh2." Sugary-enhanced varieties are designated "se." Regular sweet corn is sometimes labelled "sugary" or "su". Look for these designations in seed catalogs or on seed packets. The reason they are sweeter than regular sweet corn is

that sugars in these types of sweet corn are slower to convert to starch.

Q **I like the flavor of supersweet sweet corn. Does it require any special care?**

A One consideration in growing supersweet sweet corn cultivars is that they are slow to germinate and have reduced seedling vigor. Wait to plant until the soil has warmed to at least 60°F, and sow seeds shallowly. These sweeter corns should be isolated from other types of corn. Cross-pollination with regular sweet corn results in a starchy kernel. Plant at least 250 feet away from other types of corn. Another option is to stagger planting dates, or select cultivars that mature at different times so the tasseling periods don't overlap. Plant at least two weeks apart, or use varieties with at least 14 days' difference in maturity.

Cucumber

Q **How far apart should I plant cucumbers from squash to prevent them from cross-pollinating and ruining one another?**

A Cucumber and squash are not related closely enough to cross-pollinate, so they may be planted next to each other with no danger of cross-pollination.

Q **Every year, my cucumbers are hollow in the center. What could be causing this?**

A Hollow fruits are a common problem. They usually result from a combination of nutrient deficiency and irregular watering. Keeping the soil consistently moist, but not wet, will help. Too much nitrogen in the soil may make the fruits grow too fast. Reducing the amount of fertilizer would help if this is the case. The hollow centers have little effect on the quality of the fruit, although affected ones are sometimes bitter as a result of the moisture stress.

Q **I am growing a 'Bush Whopper' cucumber plant. Instead of growing long and straight, the fruits grow in a C shape and are skinny at one end. What causes this?**

A A couple things can cause what you describe. Misshapen cucumbers often are caused by hot, dry conditions during fruit set, soil that's not fertile enough to support the plants, or poor pollination. The problem happens more frequently in late summer because of high temperatures. The best prevention is to keep your plants mulched to maintain more uniform soil moisture, and improve your soil with lots of organic matter to aid water-holding capacity. If you have good soil, poor pollination is a likely culprit. Avoid using insecticides in your garden that can kill bees that act as pollinators.

Q **All of my cucumbers are bitter and just plain nasty-tasting. What is the problem?**

A Bitterness in cucumbers is caused by a natural compound produced by the cucumber. This compound tends to be produced in highest amounts when the plant is under stress from lack of water, excessive heat, or poor fertility. Keeping plants watered well and mulched should help prevent the problem. It also helps to grow varieties with less natural bitterness. 'Sweet Success', 'Sweet Slice', 'County Fair', 'Carmen', and 'Diva' are a few to try. Look for "bitter-free" in the description of the cucumber variety.

Lettuce

Q **My lettuce comes up really nice, and then after a couple weeks it turns brown and rusty and dies. What causes this problem?**

A This sounds like a fungal disease problem. Both botrytis mold and Rhizoctonia can attack lettuce. Both are more severe when conditions are wet. Make sure the area has good air circulation to dry the foliage quickly. And if the soil remains too wet, consider growing your lettuce in a raised bed. Although lettuce will tolerate partial shade, it grows best in full sun.

Q **My lettuce is turning bitter. Is there anything that I can do to prevent that from happening?**

A Lettuce is a cool-season vegetable. When day length is long and temperatures are hot, it bolts (goes to seed) and becomes bitter readily. You can't do much to control the weather, but you can make successive plantings of lettuce at two-week intervals so that you always have immature plants that are less likely to develop the bitter flavor associated with bolting.

Mesclun

Q **What is mesclun?**

A Mesclun is simply a mix of salad greens that are grown together in the same bed or row. Many seed companies develop their own blends of lettuces and specialty greens such as arugula, mustard, and endive, with varying degrees of spiciness. Try several to determine which combinations you like best.

Melon

Q **Last year I had some beautiful cantaloupes and watermelons, only to find one morning that snails had devoured them. I have animals around, so I don't want to use snail bait. Do you have any suggestions?**

A Some gardeners have suggested protecting melons with old nylon stockings. I've yet to try it, but it seems like it would work. You can sprinkle crushed seashells, diatomacous earth, or sharp sand around plants to dissuade slugs and snails. You could also train your melons on a trellis, using the nylon stockings as a sling to support the weight of the developing melons. Keeping the fruits off the ground makes them less attractive to the snails.

Q **This is the first time I have grown canteloupe, and I'm not sure when to pick them. Do they ripen any after you pick them?**

A It can be difficult to tell when cantaloupes are ripe simply by looking at them. The surest method is to test the stem. If the stem slips loose with a gentle tug,

the cantaloupe is vine-ripe and ready to eat. If the stem is still firmly attached, it's too early to harvest. Fruits will ripen some after harvest, but they develop best flavor if allowed to ripen on the vine.

Q **My muskmelon plants' leaves turn yellow, then brown, and the vines wilt. I water daily, fertilize as instructed on the package, and sprinkle with a granular insecticide to keep off the bugs. What is the problem?**

A The problem sounds like bacterial wilt, a disease spread from plant to plant by striped and spotted cucumber beetles. To diagnose the disease, cut off a wilted stem near the base of the plant, then gently squeeze out the sap. Touch a knife to the sap and withdraw it slowly. If your plant is infected with bacterial wilt, you'll see white ooze that strings out in a fine thread as you withdraw the knife. There are no good chemical controls for bacterial wilt. Remove and discard all infected plants as soon as you notice the infection. Handpick the beetles off the plant, or use floating row covers until after the blooms have begun to appear. Spinosad is a natural product that can keep beetles under control.

Q **If my cantaloupe plants have not started to show melons by the end of July, should I cut back the tips to encourage melons to start?**

A Most melons require about three months from seeding to fruit development, so if you started yours late, they will fruit late. Male flowers develop first on the vine. Male flowers have slender stems, while the females have a small bump at the base of the flower. Only the female blooms result in fruits if they are pollinated. Pinch the main shoot now, and as soon as you see any melons developing, pinch back the shoots beyond them to encourage the first-set fruits to develop fully.

Onion

Q How do I grow yellow and red onions? How do I store them?

A Buy seeds or transplants from a reliable seed company or garden center. You can also grow onions from sets, but the onions that develop from sets will develop seedheads and will not store as well as those grown from seeds or transplants. Plant the onions where they'll get full sun and grow in well-drained soil. 'Southport Red Globe' is an old standby red type that stores well. 'Stuttgarter' is a yellow type for storage.

Q What's the best way to store onions?

A By late summer, when the onion bulbs have developed to full size, stop watering the plants. Doing this lets the green tops dry and encourages the bulbs to go dormant. Avoid the temptation to break over or remove the foliage before it dies down naturally. When the onions are dry, store them in mesh bags and hang them in a cool, dry, dark place. They'll store longest at temperatures just above freezing. Prevent them from freezing, however, because frozen onions will turn to mush. Inspect them regularly for signs of sprouts. Use sprouting bulbs as soon as possible.

Q My onions didn't develop very large bulbs. What's the trick to getting nice big bulbs like I see in the store?

A Be sure you have the right variety for your climate. Onions are day-length dependent for bulb formation. Types for southern climates may not form large bulbs in the North, just as northern types won't grow very large in southern areas. A few varieties, such as 'Candy Hybrid' and 'Superstar Hybrid', are intermediate in day-length requirements and can be grown almost anywhere.

Garlic

Q How do I harvest my garlic? What is the best way to store it?

A Harvest garlic when the tops begin to dry and discolor naturally. This usually happens in late summer or early autumn. Dig rather than pull bulbs to avoid stem injury. Place the bulbs in a well-ventilated area to dry for several weeks. After the bulbs are dry, cut off the tops and roots to within 1 inch of the bulbs. Garlic stores best at 32°F, but a refrigerator works well too.

Pepper

Q **My green peppers do not get very big. Any ideas why?**

A The problem could be that there are too many peppers on the plant. Plants have only so much energy—too many fruits can demand more energy from the plant than it can provide. Thinning the extra fruits soon after they set can help. The size of your pepper plant's fruits may be related to the variety that you're growing. Some peppers remain small at maturity, while others form the big, bell-shape fruits common in the supermarket.

Q **What's the difference between sweet red peppers and green peppers?**

A The short answer is "About two weeks." Red peppers are simply fruits that remain on the plant until they ripen. Some varieties ripen to yellow, orange, or chocolate brown instead. Ripe peppers are sweeter and have more nutrients than green ones.

Q **I am having a hard time with my habanero peppers. The blossoms never form fruit. They yellow and fall off. My Thai peppers are fine and are growing and producing right next to the habaneros. Can you help?**

A Pepper blossom drop (often more severe in some varieties than others) is caused by temperature fluctuations during pollination. Normal pollination and fruit set fail to occur when nighttime temperatures fall below 58°F or daytime temperatures rise above 85°F. Below or above this range, the blossoms may fall off. If partial pollination occurs and fruit begins to set, the fruit often becomes misshapen or rough. Irrigating to cool the plants is one way to minimize this problem.

Q **My bell peppers have small dark spots on them. What is this and how can I get rid of it?**

A It sounds as though your peppers may have bacterial spot. This disease affects leaves and fruit and develops in moist weather. On the pepper fruits, bacterial spot appears first as small, water-soaked areas. Eventually the spots become dark, raised, and scablike. This disease usually comes from infected transplants. Make certain that you purchase plants from a reputable supplier. Avoid wetting the plants' foliage when watering, and wait until the plants dry to work in the garden. Destroy affected plants at season's end, and plant peppers in a different location next season to prevent the disease from carrying over.

Potato

Q **Is it true that you can grow a potato plant from a regular potato? How is this done?**

A It's best to grow potatoes from specially grown seed potatoes that are certified disease-free. The potatoes you purchase in the grocery store may have been treated with a sprout inhibitor to prevent them from sprouting in your pantry. However, if you have some potatoes that are beginning to sprout, simply plant a piece of the sprouting potato in the ground. After three months or so new spuds will develop below ground. Potatoes are ready to harvest when the plants begin to turn yellow and die back.

Q **Some of my potatoes are poking above ground and turning green. I've heard that they are poisonous. Should I throw them away?**

A Potatoes exposed to sunlight will turn green. The green tissue does contain a bitter alkaloid that is mildly poisonous. However, removing the green portion of the potato before eating it is sufficient; you need not destroy the tuber. To prevent the problem, hill soil or mulch around the potato plant to protect the developing tubers from exposure to sunlight.

Q **Something is eating holes in the leaves of my potato plants. I saw some large yellow-and-black beetles. Are they the culprits?**

A It sounds as though your potatoes have Colorado potato beetles. Plant potatoes as early as possible in spring. By the time the beetles attack, the crop will be mature enough to escape significant damage. Another option is to wait to plant until early summer. By the time the potatoes emerge, most beetles will be gone. Late-planted potatoes will mature in fall. If you have a small planting, handpicking beetles is an effective control. Place floating row covers over plants to prevent adult beetles from getting to the plants. Bacteria called Bt (*Bacillus thuringiensis san diego* or *Bt tenebrionis*) control Colorado potato beetle larvae.

Q **Why do my potatoes have a scaly substance on the peel?**

A It sounds as though your potatoes are infected with potato scab, a fungal disease that persists in the soil over long periods. Potato scab is most severe in warm, dry soil that's slightly alkaline. If your soil pH is above 5.5, lower the pH with powdered sulfur. Rotate your potato patch so each place is used for potatoes only once every 3 to 4 years. And plant resistant varieties; several have high scab resistance.

Pumpkin

Q I had great success growing big orange pumpkins for Halloween my first year, but for the last two years there has been a problem. The plants start out great, then begin to slowly die. I still get a few pumpkins, but I have to harvest early. What's happening?

A When pumpkins or summer squash slowly wilt to death, the culprits are usually squash vine borers. There are three ways to prevent serious borer damage:
1. Cover plants with floating row covers until they begin to blossom.
2. Inject beneficial nematodes into the base of the plants' hollow stems every 4 to 6 inches; nematodes quickly kill the vine borers.
3. Inject the stems with Bt (*Bacillus thuringiensis*). You may also be able to save the plant by slitting the stem lengthwise near the base, digging out the borer, and covering it with moist soil.

Q I planted pumpkin seeds, and only one plant grew. It bloomed through much of the summer but didn't produce one pumpkin. What did I do wrong?

A Did you notice any insects, such as bees, around the flowers? If they were absent, that may be the reason. Male flowers have a slender stalk attaching them to the vine. Female flowers have a swollen base that looks like a miniature pumpkin. If both are present on your vine, you can compensate for lack of insect pollinators by hand-pollinating the female blossoms. Take an artist's brush to gather pollen from the male blossom early in the morning. Transfer the pollen to a freshly opened female blossom. Within a few days you should see the swollen base beginning to enlarge into a pumpkin.

Rhubarb

Q A good friend gave me a rhubarb plant. I have been growing it now for more than a year, and the plant is very leafy. Do I trim it back? How do I harvest it?

A Rhubarb leaves are not edible, but the leaf stalks (*petioles*) make a good pie. Wait until the plant is at least 1 year old, then harvest the stalks in spring and early summer. The stalks at the outer edge of the plant can be pulled off at the soil line when the leaves are fully open and developed. Just take hold of the stalk close to the soil line, and give a slight twist as you pull. Never take more than about a third of the stalks at one time. Stop harvesting rhubarb before midsummer, and let the plant continue to grow.

Q Should I cut the seed stalks out of my rhubarb plant?

A Flowering does not affect the flavor or edibility of the rhubarb plant. However, most gardeners cut down the stalks before the flowers bloom so more of the plant's energy remains in the roots to help produce more leaves and edible stalks.

Squash

Q **My summer squash plants have been blooming for a couple weeks, but they haven't produced any squash yet. What's wrong with them?**

A Most squash plants produce many male flowers before female flowers appear. Because only the female flowers can develop into fruits, it's common for the plant to bloom for a while without setting any squashes. Male flowers have a slender stalk, and females have a swollen base that looks like a miniature squash. Squash depends on honeybees and other insects for pollination. If your garden has few bees, fruit may fail to set due to lack of pollination. You could try hand pollination. Use a small brush or cotton swab to transfer pollen from the male flower to the female flower.

Q **I can grow other squashes and gourds with success, but I have no luck with zucchini. I get nice-looking plants and a bunch of little fruits, then they rot. What's wrong?**

A Your zucchini rot might be gummy stem rot. Stressed plants are more likely to contract diseases. Grow zucchini plants where they've not been grown before, avoid high-nitrogen fertilizers, and mulch the plants so the fruits do not sit directly on the soil's surface. Mulch also prevents dramatic fluctuations in soil moisture, which cause plant stress and blossom-end rot, another common disease of cucurbits.

Q **My squash vines were growing beautifully, but all of a sudden they wilted and died. What would cause them to do this?**

A Sudden wilt is likely caused by the squash vine borer. Borers come from the eggs of adult moths. After plants begin to bloom, closely inspect the base of the vines and stems for tiny reddish brown eggs and wipe them off. If a borer does manage to hatch, you can tell by the appearance of a mass of crumbly borer excrement on the vine. Use a small, sharp knife to slit open the vine lengthwise at that point and remove the white larva. Mound soil up around the stem to encourage new rooting. The plant often survives if you catch the borer early enough.

Q **My squash vines are overrun by gray bugs. What can I do to kill them?**

A These pests are squash bugs. They can do much damage by sucking juices from the leaves, which then wilt, darken, and die. Watch for a cluster of shiny brown eggs on the top or undersides of leaves, groups of green or powdery gray nymphs with black legs, and $5/8$-inch-long dark brown adults with a shield-shape body. Remove each of these and drown or crush them. Soap sprays and chemical controls work on nymphs but not adults. Be sure to clean up plant debris before winter. Plant varieties of squash that are resistant to squash bugs. 'Butternut' is one of the best resistant cultivars.

Sunflower

Q Can I save and dry sunflowers to get my own seeds?

A Yes, you can. After the flowers have bloomed and the petals around the edge of the flower have wilted, watch for the back of the flowerhead to turn yellow. At that point, cut the head, leaving some stalk attached, and hang it in a warm, dry area until it is brown and dry. If you leave it on the stalk to dry outside, it may rot, or birds may eat the seeds before it's time to harvest them. When the head is dry, rub the seeds out of the head, holding it over a bag. Then shell the seeds and roast them or eat them raw.

Sweet Potato

Q How do I grow sweet potatoes?

A Grow sweet potatoes from young plants called "slips." Plant them 12 to 18 inches apart in rows 3 to 4 feet apart after the soil warms up in spring. Plant in raised beds or ridges; these soil ridges warm up earlier in spring and drain better than a level planting area. Harvest sweet potatoes just before the first fall frost. Carefully dig under the roots to lift them. To cure the roots for storage, place them in a warm (85°F), humid location for 10 to 14 days. Then store them at 55°F for up to four months.

Q Are yams the same thing as sweet potatoes?

A Technically, they are not the same thing. True yams are starchy tubers grown in tropical climates. They are not grown in the United States. However, sweet potatoes are often called yams, and the terms are commonly used interchangeably. The U.S. Department of Agriculture requires that the term "yam" always be accompanied by the term "sweet potato."

Q When I dug my sweet potatoes, they were covered with a dark, scabby coating. What is this? Are they safe to eat?

A Your sweet potatoes are infected with scurf, a fungal disease. The fungus grows only on the skin, so the interior of the sweet potato is unaffected. However, infected roots won't store well, so use them first. Avoid planting sweet potatoes in the same area for at least three years after an infection occurs. Make sure that you plant disease-free sets. And avoid overwatering. The problem is worse in wet soils.

 Check out our online vegetable garden plans at *bhg.com/veggie-gardens.*

Tomato

Q I had never heard of pruning tomatoes until a friend suggested that I do so. What difference will it make?

A Indeterminate tomato plants grow and put on flowers and fruit until the end of the season. Selective pinching and pruning can keep the plants in check and open the canopy to better air circulation and sunlight. Where summers are hot, you may want to keep more leaves to shield the fruit from the strong sun. In cool climates, pinching out some of the suckers (secondary stems that are produced out of a leaf axis on the main stem) can create better air circulation and reduce disease problems.

Q My tomato seedlings are getting tall and spindly. Should I cut them back to make the stalks bigger? Do I need to transplant them into bigger pots?

A Tomato seedlings grow best at temperatures between 65 to 72°F. Bright light helps them become stocky, not spindly. If the plants are big enough that their root systems are filling the pots they're currently in, transplant them into larger pots. If the root systems aren't filling the pots yet, transplanting them is unnecessary. Brush your tomatoes daily. Gently brush your hand across the top of the plants. Research shows that doing so makes sturdier transplants.

Q What's the best way to transplant my tomato seedlings into the garden?

A Tomatoes are sensitive to cold temperatures, so wait until all danger of frost has passed to set out your plants. Dig a trench deep enough to completely cover the root ball. Lay the tomato on its side in the trench, gently bending up the top of the stem as you rake soil around it. Because a tomato can grow roots from its stem, bury most of it for a stronger, more stable plant. Soak with a gentle sprinkle, not a blast from a hose. Mulch with dried grass clippings, straw, newspapers, or plastic garden film.

Q I planted my tomatoes in mid-May, but they may have been slightly hurt by some cold weather. The leaves are a little yellow, and I'm wondering if there is anything I can do to save the plants, or will I have to start over?

A If the tips of the plants' leaves are still green, they will probably recover when the temperatures climb again. If the leaves are completely yellow, you should pull the plants and start over. To prevent this from happening again, wait to plant until the nights stay above 50°F, or provide some protection for your young plants.

Q How can I protect my tomato transplants from a late frost? I have already planted them in the garden.

A You can use a milk jug with the bottom cut away as a temporary greenhouse for a week or two, until the plant is too big for the jug and the nights are warmer. You can leave the cap on the milk jug, but be sure to uncap the jug during the day when temperatures are above 50°F. Other devices have been developed in the last few years, such as water-filled tubes to place around the plants to insulate them against cold air. These can protect plants from subfreezing temperatures.

Q Some of my tomatoes need staking, while others seem to stand up on their own. What's the best way to treat tomatoes regarding support?

A Determinate tomatoes can usually stand on their own without additional support. The plants are small enough to stay upright when they start producing fruit. That said, keep an eye on your determinate plants; you may have to give the prolific producers some support. Something as simple as tying the plant to a wooden stake or poles can do the job. Indeterminate tomatoes have a tendency to become lanky and rangy, especially the cherry types, so plan on providing support.

Q What's the difference between tomatoes that are "determinate" and those that are "indeterminate"?

A Determinate varieties of tomatoes, also called "bush" tomatoes, are bred to grow to a compact height, usually 4 feet or less. The plants stop growing when fruit sets on the terminal, or top, bud. All the crop ripens at or near the same time. Avoid pruning or sucker removal because it severely reduces the crop.

Indeterminate tomatoes also are sometimes called vining tomatoes. They grow and produce fruit until killed by frost and can reach heights up to 10 feet. These plants require substantial caging and/or staking for support.

Q I was thinking of growing a tomato like 'Beefsteak' rather than a smaller, patio variety. What size pot should I use?

A Most tomatoes do just fine in a 14-inch pot or larger. The keys to healthy potted tomatoes are consistently moist soil and regular feedings. Consistent soil moisture helps eliminate plant stress and prevent disease. Plants in pots tend to use all the available nutrients in the pot, and tomatoes can be heavy feeders. Containerized plants should have full sun.

Tomato

Q **My tomatoes are not ripening. I have plenty of them on the plants, but they are not turning red. The ones that have ripened have been tough and not flavorful. I water about every other day, daily when it's very hot.**

A Tomatoes that are late to ripen usually are overfed and overwatered. Once the vines reach the size you want, cut back on the fertilizer. Reducing water, even to the point where a little stress (slight wilting) shows before you water again, can push the plant to ripen its fruit. If your season is long, you may wish to water enough to keep more tomatoes setting on the plant, but doing so will slow the others' ripening.

Q **My tomato plants are full and lush, but I don't have many blossoms or tomatoes. What might be wrong?**

A Tomatoes will fail to set fruit when daytime temperatures are above 90°F and/or nighttime temperatures below 55°F. Too much nitrogen in the soil could produce lush leaves but prevent fruit formation. And too little moisture could prevent fruit development. Water and mulch your tomatoes to keep the soil moist.

Q **How do I ripen green tomatoes indoors? I have lots of them I picked just before frost.**

A You'll have the best luck with "mature green" tomatoes. These are the ones with a whitish coloration. Best ripening occurs when temperatures are kept at 70 to 75°F. To speed ripening, you can place ripe bananas or apples with the tomatoes. These fruits give off ethylene gas, which promotes ripening. If you have lots of tomatoes, store them in a ventilated box one layer deep. To prolong storage, keep them in a cool, dark, humid room. Protect from direct sun.

Q **My tomatoes aren't ripening correctly. The top of the fruit never colors up well. I've tried leaving them on the plant longer, but they remain yellowish green. What can I do?**

A It sounds as though your tomatoes have a physiological condition called yellow shoulder. No one knows for certain what causes it, but it seems to be related to many factors, including high temperature, high soil pH, a low magnesium-to-calcium ratio, lack of potassium, variety, and possibly a virus. You might try other varieties of tomatoes that would be less susceptible to this disorder.

Q My tomatoes are all gnarled and distorted. What would make the fruits misshapen?

A Tomato fruits distorted at the blossom end are called catface tomatoes. This scarring is a physiological problem related to initial fruit development during bloom. Cool weather during fruit set or injury from 2,4-D herbicide drift can cause catfacing. Fruits that set in warm temperatures are usually unaffected. By the time you see the problem, the conditions are probably in the past. Wait for the plant to outgrow the problem. Some heirloom varieties of tomato normally produce fruits with deep lobes rather than the smooth fruits you may be familiar with from the grocer.

Q My tomatoes are cracking and splitting open. What am I doing wrong?

A Tomatoes are affected by two types of cracking. Radial cracks run from the stem end toward the blossom end; concentric cracks form circular patterns around the stem. Cracking is usually caused by changes in the growth rate of the fruit. Rapidly growing tomatoes are more susceptible. Wide fluctuations in temperature and rain promote cracking too. Maintain uniform soil moisture to help prevent cracking. Some varieties are more crack-resistant than others.

Q My tomatoes have corky greenish spots on the fruits. What causes this?

A The damage you're describing fits that of stink bug feeding. The stink bugs pierce the fruits and inject a substance that prevents normal ripening near the injection point. Insecticidal soap can provide some level of control.

Q This summer we're having tomato problems. They're rotting on the bottom, and some of the green ones are turning black. What can we do?

A When a tomato turns black or brown on the bottom, it has blossom-end rot. This problem is caused by calcium deficiency in the tissue. The best way to prevent blossom-end rot is to plant tomatoes in well-drained soil. Mulch your plants to maintain even soil moisture, water during periods of drought, avoid cultivating near the shallow roots, and use moderate amounts of nitrogen fertilizer. Some varieties are more susceptible to the condition than others. You might try growing a different type of tomato.

Tomato

Q **My tomato plants have huge green worms that are completely stripping the plants. What are they?**

A It sounds like your plants have been attacked by tomato hornworms. They are large (up to 4 inches long) green caterpillars with white stripes on each side of the body. The worms often escape detection until much of the foliage is gone because they blend in so well with the green leaves. If you see hornworms on a plant, simply pick them off by hand (use gloves if you're squeamish), and crush them underfoot. If the hornworm has small white cocoons attached to its body, leave the hornworm alone. The cocoons contain the larvae of a parasitic wasp that is a natural parasite of the hornworm.

Q **The leaves on my tomato plant are curled and rolled up. I don't see any bugs or leaf spots. What's causing this?**

A Some varieties of tomato develop physiological leaf roll. 'Beefsteak', 'Big Boy', and 'Floramerica' are three susceptible varieties. The margins of leaves roll inward toward the central vein, and leaflets become leathery. Fluctuating soil moisture, and excessive heat or pruning are the usual causes. The problem is mostly cosmetic. Tomato yields are unaffected.

Q **My tomatoes suddenly wilted and died this summer. My neighbor said it was because of my walnut tree in the backyard. Will walnuts kill tomato plants?**

A Many plants can be affected by a toxin produced by walnut trees. Tomatoes are particularly sensitive to the substance known as juglone. Because tree roots can extend three to four times the distance of the spread of branches, plants 50 to 60 feet from the tree's trunk may be affected. Tomato plants that come into contact with walnut roots can wilt about the time the fruit is setting. Juglone eventually kills the plant. To prevent this problem from happening again, plant tomatoes beyond the tree's root zone or grow them in large tubs.

Q **What plants are beneficial to tomato plants when planted next to one another?**

A Tomatoes are heavy nitrogen feeders, so legumes that fix nitrogen, such as beans, peas, and peanuts may be good partners for tomatoes. Marigolds may repel nematodes. Avoid planting other plants in the same family as tomatoes—pepper, potato, and eggplant—because these get some of the same pest problems as tomatoes.

Q My tomatoes were beautiful and healthy until about midsummer. The leaves turned yellow, then brown, and now they are dead. I planted tomatoes in this same spot and had bumper crops the last two years.

A Your tomatoes may have been hit by early blight or septoria leaf spot, fungal diseases that are most active during humid weather. If you see disease symptoms appearing on your tomato plants, such as yellow lesions that turn brown and crispy, spray the plants with a disease-control product for vegetables. Do this once a week for three to four weeks. Spraying won't get rid of spots that have already begun to develop, but it will protect new growth from becoming infected.

Q Why does the foliage on some of my tomatoes die? Not all of the plants are like this.

A Several diseases affect tomatoes, including early and late blights, septoria leaf spot, verticillium wilt, and fusarium wilt. Varieties differ in their susceptibility to these diseases. Mulch well to prevent the spread of disease spores that live on the soil. Plant in a different place every year to prevent the spread of diseases. Provide good airflow around the tomato plants. Choose disease-resistant varieties. Look for any combination of the letters V, F, N, and/or T on the plant tag. Consider spraying your plants with a protective fungicide spray.

Q How should I replenish my soil after planting tomatoes?

A Change the location where you plant your tomatoes each year. This helps prevent soil pests and diseases from building up in any given spot. If moving the tomato patch is not feasible, try building a raised bed at the site. Adding fresh compost can keep soil life active enough to reduce the likelihood of disease or pests building up. If you are strapped for space, lay a bag of compost on its side, slit it open, poke holes in the underside, and plant directly in the compost-filled bag. Provide good air circulation around plants and avoid wetting the foliage. If foliar problems persist, you may need to spray with a protective fungicide.

Q My tomatoes blighted this year. What can I do to make sure that it doesn't happen again next year?

A It's important to remove and discard all spent foliage and fruit from the garden in fall to prevent diseases from overwintering in the garden. Clean tomato cages and trellises with a disinfectant such as a 10-percent chlorine bleach solution to kill lingering spores. Rinse metal cages with water afterward to prevent corrosion. Unfortunately there are no early-blight-resistant varieties of tomatoes, so you'll have to watch for disease development again next year.

Planting Fruit

Q **When is the best time to plant fruit trees and berries?**

A In most areas, early spring, when the plants begin to emerge from dormancy, is the ideal time to set out any deciduous plant, including fruits. If you wait until later in spring, look for plants grown in containers; they transplant more easily than bare-root plants after they have emerged from dormancy. In mild-winter regions, late fall is a good time to plant fruit trees and berries. Cool temperatures through the winter allow the plants to become established before the stressful heat of summer sets in.

Q **How long will it take after planting fruits to harvest a crop?**

A Most dwarf fruit trees begin bearing 2 to 5 years after planting, but standard-size ones may take 7 to 10 years or more to produce their first crop. Small fruits such as grapes, raspberries, blackberries, and strawberries usually begin to bear the year after planting. Everbearing types can produce a crop later in the first season of growth.

Q **I'd like to grow some fruit trees in the yard. What should I consider before I decide what to grow?**

A Most fruit trees require full sun and well-drained soil. If your yard is shady, it may be best to let someone else grow the fruit for you at an orchard. Some fruits require cross-pollination for fruit set. Apples, pears, plums, and some sweet cherries fall into this category. Two trees of different varieties should be planted within about 100 feet of each other for cross-pollination. Fruits can be attacked by many disease and insect pests. To minimize the amount of spraying you'll need to do, choose varieties that are resistant to disease problems whenever possible.

Q **I'd like to grow some berries in my backyard. Which would be the best kinds for a beginning gardener to grow?**

A Generally, strawberries, blackberries, and raspberries are the easiest small fruits to grow. Grapes (which need a lot of pruning to maintain their productivity) and blueberries (which need moist, acidic soil) are moderately difficult to grow.

Pollination

Q **I just bought four different kinds of fruit trees. On the tags it says that they need cross-pollination. What will happen if I have only one of each tree?**

A Some fruit trees are "self-fruitful," meaning they don't require pollination from a different tree to bear fruit. Even for trees that are self-fruitful, yields are often increased if another variety is planted nearby for cross-pollination. If another variety of fruit tree of the same species is within 500 feet or so of yours, and you have bees and other insects in the neighborhood, they will likely take care of the pollination for you. It won't work to just plant another tree of the same variety. For example, pollen from a 'Fuji' apple won't pollinate another 'Fuji' apple, but it would pollinate a 'Gala' apple. And it's impossible for an apple tree to pollinate a pear, cherry, peach, or plum.

Q **Do I need to plant two kinds of raspberries and blueberries to get fruit from them?**

A Most small fruits, such as raspberry and blueberry, will bear fruit without cross-pollination, so you can get a crop with just one variety of each. However, their flowers must be pollinated in order to develop into fruits. If you spray insecticide during bloom time, you could kill the pollinators and prevent good fruit set. Although blueberries are self-fruitful, they often produce better if cross-pollinated.

Q **My apple and peach trees produced a bumper crop last year but almost nothing this year. Do I need to place some bees in my yard for better pollination?**

A Many fruit trees have a tendency for alternate bearing, that is, they produce a heavy crop one year and very little the next. This is because the trees

are unable to support a heavy fruit load and at the same develop lots of flower buds for next year's crop. To even out the crop from year to year, thin excess fruits if the tree sets a heavy crop.

Preventing Fruit Set

Q **Is there any way to keep fruit trees from producing fruit? I like the trees, but the fruits end up being messy every year.**

A Other than removing the tree, there is no permanent solution to this problem. Commercial growers use a spray to thin fruit. These sprays reduce the crop by applying plant hormones that cause fruit drop. When they're applied during or right after bloom, the mess is negligible. A commercially available fruit preventer is Florel. The spray must be applied during bloom and must thoroughly cover the entire tree. Ironically, when you remove the crop, the tree puts more energy into the next year's fruit buds, ensuring a big crop if you let it go.

Apple & Pear

Q **I want to grow apples but don't want to have to spray all the time. Are there any varieties that don't need to be sprayed?**

A Many apples are susceptible to diseases such as apple scab, cedar apple rust, and fire blight. Backyard orchardists should consider growing varieties that are resistant to these diseases to avoid pesticide sprays. Scab-resistant cultivars include the early-season varieties 'Redfree', 'Prima', 'Jonafree', and 'Sir Prize'. For midseason production try 'Novamac', 'Liberty', or 'Freedom'. 'Enterprise' and 'Goldrush' are resistant late-season varieties. Depending on your region, you'll also have to contend with insect pests such as codling moth and apple maggot.

Q **The leaves on my apple tree get black spots, turn yellow, and fall off. Many of the fruits also develop corky black spots on them. Is this some kind of disease?**

A The symptoms you describe are those of a fungal disease called apple scab. You can spray protective fungicides to prevent the disease, but you'll have to spray repeatedly. If you don't want to spray your tree regularly, consider growing a scab-resistant variety (see answer at left) instead.

Q **Each year the apples on my tree get brown spots and worm trails through the fruit. How can I prevent this from happening so I can harvest more apples?**

A The usual, chemical way to achieve blemish-free fruit is with a regular fruit-tree spray program. Your county extension service or a local garden center can give you a complete program for spraying your trees. However, some good nontoxic methods have recently become popular. Hang sticky red spheres in the trees to trap the insects when they come to lay their eggs. When used properly, the spheres offer as much or more protection as spray. Use scent lures to make the traps much more effective.

Q **I saved seeds from some apples. Will they come up if I plant them? How should I plant them?**

A Most apples are grown from grafted trees and will not come true from seed. The seeds might germinate, and they could develop into productive trees, but the fruit will not be the same kind as the apple from which the seeds came. Trees you purchase will fruit in a much shorter time. A seed-started tree could take 8 to 10 years to fruit. Also, apple trees started from seed will have no dwarfing characteristics. Unless you have a large yard, they may be too big for your site.

Q How do I know when to pick my apples? I've never grown them before.

A The most certain way to know when to pick apples is to pick one and taste it! The fruit should have developed a good color for the variety. Mature fruits will have dark brown seeds. Cut through the core to check this. Apples will also ripen off the tree, but not if picked too green. If you plan to store the fruit for a long time, pick the fruit slightly on the green side because it will continue to ripen a bit after harvest. However, for best flavor allow the fruit to ripen on the tree.

Q We just moved into a house that has several badly neglected old apple trees on the property. I don't want to lose them. What do I need to do to rejuvenate them so we can harvest fruit in the fall?

A Apple trees generally can be completely renovated with five to six years of knowledgeable pruning. It may be unrealistic to expect a good crop for several years, until you get the trees back into shape. A good place to start is by removing any dead or damaged branches in late winter while the tree is still dormant. Next take out crossing branches and those growing inward, downward, or strongly upright. Thin out branches growing directly on top of one another. However, you should remove no more than about one-fourth of the branches each year.

Q Last year was the first time my pear tree bore fruit, but by the time the fruit ripened, it was rotten. What can I do differently so I can harvest a good crop?

A Unlike virtually every other fruit, pears must be picked when they are still quite hard. They ripen from the core outward. If pears are allowed to remain on

the tree until you can feel or see ripeness, the fruit becomes mushy and brown. If you cut open a pear and find that the seed coat has darkened from white to brown or black, the pear is ready to be picked. Once harvested, most varieties ripen in a week or two. Speed up the process by sealing the pears in a bag with a ripe apple or banana.

Q I have a 'Bartlett' pear that doesn't produce. How do I get it to bear?

A If it blooms each spring, your tree may not be bearing fruit because it needs a second variety nearby to pollinate it. If you don't have room for a second tree, have a second variety grafted onto your tree so you'll have a branch of pollinating blossoms within the canopy of your 'Bartlett'. If your tree has not bloomed yet, it may be a maturity issue. Standard-size pear trees may take five years or more to reach bearing size. If your tree gets fewer than six hours of direct sunlight per day, excess shade could be causing lack of production. Pears bear on spurs on two-year-old or older wood. Excessive pruning can keep the tree from bearing fruit by removing the fruiting spurs.

Blueberry

Q I'd like to grow blueberries. What do I need to know to be successful?

A If your soil isn't acidic enough, the plants won't do well. If you live in an area with high-pH soil, amend the soil with an acidifying agent such as sulfur or iron sulfate. Next, find the right type of blueberries for your area. If you live in the South, a rabbit-eye type, such as 'Powderblue' or 'Tifblue', is best. To get fruit, grow two cultivars together. If you live in the North, plant a northern highbush type, such as 'Legacy' or 'Earliblue'. Most northern highbush types don't require a second cultivar to help them produce good fruit crops. In the far North (Zone 4 or colder), half-high types 'Chippewa', 'Northsky', 'Northblue', and 'St. Cloud' are your best bets.

Q I purchased a house that has blueberry bushes. They're planted in a bed covered with river rock in full sun. Should I remove the rock and replace it with mulch?

A The rock may cause overheating of the soil and injury to the shallow roots of blueberry. If you want to replace it with shredded bark, pine needles, or another organic mulch, simply pick up the rocks, pull out any weeds, and spread the new mulch over the surface. Because blueberry roots are shallow and are easily damaged if you cultivate the soil's surface, avoid the temptation to dig anything into the soil. If you want to enrich the soil, spread a shallow layer of compost or composted manure over the soil, then add your new mulch.

Q I want to grow blueberries near a spruce. I've heard that the 'Top Hat' variety tolerates part shade. Will the spruce needles that drop off the tree kill the blueberries?

A If the area you plan to plant is shady enough that lawn won't grow, it's not likely to be sunny enough for blueberries, which need six to eight hours of sunlight a day. If grown in too much shade, blueberries produce spindly new growth and poor-quality fruits. Lack of moisture is a concern when growing blueberries near a spruce tree. The tree roots soak up most of the available water. Spruce needles will not hurt blueberries if the plants get enough sun.

Q We planted three blueberry bushes last year. The plants have very yellow leaves. What should I do?

A Check the soil pH to make sure it's acidic enough. Blueberries prefer a low pH (5.0-5.5). When the pH is too high, iron chlorosis sets in. The leaves turn yellow, but often the veins remain green. You can apply iron chelate to the foliage to quickly green up the plants, but the long-term solution is to add sulfur or sulfate to the soil to lower the pH.

Brambles

Q What can I add to my soil to make blackberries sweeter?

A Do you know what type of blackberry you're growing? Some varieties are naturally quite tart. You can improve the general quality and flavor of the fruit by keeping the soil around the plants well-covered with organic mulch. In the end, you can't overcome the heritage of a naturally tart variety, but you can get it to produce its best possible fruit. If you don't like the fruit you have even after trying the above recommendation, replace it with a sweeter-tasting variety.

Q I have blackberry bushes all over my yard. I want to keep a few around to have blackberries for pies but would like to get rid of the rest. What is the best way to kill them?

A You can get rid of the plants you don't want by spraying them with a woody brush-killer herbicide. Be sure to cover nearby cultivated plants—including the lawn—to prevent damage by the herbicide. Some blackberry root buds may survive and send up shoots the next season, but you can eliminate them by chopping them down with a sharp hoe. If you prefer not to use an herbicide, you could cut off the blackberry vines at ground level. Mow or chop off any shoots that resprout.

Q Why have I never gotten fruit from my 10-year-old raspberry bushes?

A The problem may be the variety of raspberry you're growing. For example, a spring-bearing variety planted in your climate might be suffering from frozen fruit buds. Although raspberries are hardy in Zones 4–9, they deacclimate very quickly during warm winter weather. A cold snap later in winter can cause dieback or damage to fruit buds. Build a raised bed in full sun with lots of organic matter in the soil and plant a new raspberry variety that's suitable for your climate.

Consider growing an everbearing raspberry such as 'Heritage'. That way, even if the summer crop is frozen off, you'll get a crop in fall.

Q I planted new raspberry bushes last spring that grew rather tall and spindly but produced no fruit. Do I cut those back this spring so they grow fuller, or should I just leave them alone?

A In general, it takes two years for a raspberry cane to produce fruit. It grows vegetatively the first year, fruits the second year, then dies. Meanwhile, new canes come up from the base of the plant during the second year. These will become the fruiting canes the year after the first batch dies. If the one-year-old canes are cut off during winter, your raspberries will not produce fruit because you have no two-year old canes left in the patch. A twist on this system is that of everbearing raspberries. They grow vegetatively through the summer of their first year, but in late summer, the tips of the first year canes produce fruit. Those tips die the first winter, but the rest of the cane fruits the following summer, then dies completely.

Citrus

Q **How do I start an orange tree from seed? We picked up oranges at the store that have wonderful flavor, and we'd like to grow our own.**

A Although you can easily grow seeds collected from store-bought citrus, the plants they become may produce less than high-quality fruit. However, seed-grown citrus can make for attractive foliage plants indoors. If you'd like to grow citrus for fruits, purchase a grafted named variety from a reputable nursery. To grow citrus from seed, remove the seeds from the fruit and plant them immediately. Use a seed-starting mix or potting soil, placing seeds about 1 inch deep in the medium. Moisten the mix and move it to a warm location until germination occurs.

Q **Where can I grow citrus trees? How should I prune them?**

A Grow citrus trees where they'll get plenty of sun and in acidic, well-drained soil that's enriched with organic matter. Most types of citrus do not tolerate temperatures below 30°F. Maintain an open growth habit by removing overlapping or excess shoots. Remove older, bearing wood to continually stimulate new growth, because most old wood becomes unfruitful after a while. Cut off shoots or limbs at the point where they join another limb. Cutting back the ends of shoots instead of removing old branches can cause lots of small, brushy growth that blocks sun from the interior and encourages disease development.

Q **I'm growing oranges, lemons, and grapefruit for the first time. What pests will I have to spray for?**

A Several common pests attack citrus, including whiteflies, scale insects, mealybugs, and sooty mold. Combat pests by using horticultural oil or insecticidal soap applied directly to the foliage.

Q **Last year my Meyer lemon tree was covered with flowers and had a dozen lemons. I moved it outside in late May. This winter it only had two flowers. I usually give it liquid fertilizer once or twice a week. How can I get it to produce more flowers?**

A It's fine to move your lemon tree outside for the summer and keep it inside in the place where it's happy for the winter. Stop feeding it during the winter, and water less frequently. The soil should be allowed to dry slightly between waterings during the winter. Overfeeding will reduce flower and fruit production and cause weak roots. Feed in spring and summer only once a month. Use an acid fertilizer specifically formulated for citrus. Remove the tree from the pot every few years and repot the plant with new soil.

Grapes

Q I recently moved to a house that has grapevines. They are in need of care, and I have no idea where to start.

A Grapes are vigorous growers that generally need some pruning every year. Winter is the best time to prune them. You can cut back grapes severely if necessary. There are several options when it comes to pruning styles. Do you want to grow the grapes to maximize fruit production, or do you simply want to keep them inbounds? Best fruiting comes from two-year-old wood. Are the grapes growing on a trellis or sprawling over a pergola? How vigorous are the varieties of grapes that you have? All these questions need to be answered to provide detailed pruning instructions.

Q How do you trim or prune grapevines on an arbor?

A Do you want to grow the grapes for harvesting quality fruit? If so, when your vines are dormant, prune them to canes with spurs, removing 90 to 95 percent of the previous year's growth. Leaving the vines unpruned can result in a tangled mess that invites disease, looks untidy, and reduces the fruit quality. If your vine fails to cover the arbor the way you'd like with this type of pruning, prune the plants less.

Q My grapes were looking good earlier this summer, but now they're shriveling up before ripening. What's wrong with them?

A It sounds as though your grapes have been attacked by black rot, a fungal disease of grapes that shows up in warm, humid weather. Infection starts as leaf spots followed by small light-brown spots on half-grown grape berries. The spots enlarge, and the berry shrivels, turns black, hardens, and mummifies. These mummies remain attached to the cluster. Take steps early next season to prevent the disease from returning. Remove

mummies and diseased tendrils from the vines. Make sure the plants are growing in a sunny area with good air movement. Apply a protective fungicide early in the season, beginning at bud break, all the way through bloom for good control of black rot.

Kiwi

Q Can you tell me how to grow hardy kiwi? I have a couple vines that are several years old, but they have never produced fruit.

A Because they bloom early in the season, kiwi flowerbuds are susceptible to spring frosts. Even if plants grow well, a late spring frost may wipe out the entire fruit crop for the season. Most kiwis have separate male and female plants. If you don't have at least one male and one female, your plants may not produce fruit. You could plant several more vines to increase the likelihood that you'll have at least one of each. Or you could grow a variety such as 'Issai' that produces fruit on a single vine.

Peach, Plum & Cherry

Q **I've had a peach tree for six years that I purchased from a local garden center. Though the tree is beautiful, the fruits taste awful! They're not sweet, and the texture isn't good. Can you help me?**

A If the tree is otherwise healthy, your tree may be an accident. Most peach trees are grafted onto a rootstock, meaning that the top part of the tree is a different variety from the roots. Sometimes the graft fails and the entire tree grows from the rootstock. Rootstock types often don't have good fruit. Unfortunately, you won't know this until the tree bears its low-quality fruit. Take the fruit to the nursery to show the error and ask for a replacement tree. Or you could have someone graft a desirable variety onto your tree.

Q **Although our peach tree develops loads of little green fruit each year, none of the peaches ever grows large enough to harvest. The tree gets plenty of sunshine. What's wrong?**

A Too much fruit can spoil the harvest. Small fruits will mature and ripen, but their diminutive size makes for poor-quality fruit. What your peach tree probably needs is a thorough thinning. As soon as the green peaches reach about 1 inch in diameter, selectively thin by pinching some of them from the branches. Leave the largest, healthiest-looking fruits to ripen, spaced about 6 inches apart.

Q **Leaves on my peach trees are puckered and turning red. Is it something I should be worried about?**

A It sounds as though your tree has peach leaf curl, a fungal disease that is most prevalent in a cool, wet spring following a mild winter. New leaves are distorted and puckered and have a reddish cast. Leaves turn yellow

or brown and drop. It's easy to control peach leaf curl with a dormant spray just as buds are beginning to grow. By the time you see the puckered red foliage, it's too late to do anything for the crop. Rake up and destroy fallen leaves to help cut down on the amount of fungal spores overwintering under the tree, and apply a fungicide in late winter next year to prevent a recurrence of the disease.

Q **My peach trees grow well and have always produced good-tasting fruit. However, every year I battle brown rot, which shows up just before harvest time. I don't like to use pesticides. Can you help me?**

A Brown rot is a serious problem on most stone fruits, including peaches, plums, cherries, and apricots. Sanitation is one way to limit the problem. Remove mummified fruits over winter, and prune out infected twigs. Thin shoots for better air circulation. Some varieties have more resistance to this fungal disease than others. Grow resistant types when possible. However, for good control, you may need to spray a protective fungicide. Check with your local cooperative extension office for the latest recommendations.

Q I planted two dwarf plum trees, and one is turning brown. The trunk of the tree is oozing a clear sticky liquid. Do you have any idea what's wrong with the plum tree?

A The oozing sticky liquid on the trunk is a symptom of a borer, a type of insect that tunnels under the bark and can kill the tree. It may be too late to save this tree that has turned brown, but you may need to apply protective insecticides on the other one to prevent it from getting borers also.

Q Our plum tree is dropping fruit before it is ripe. I have been watering once a month but do not think this is enough.

A There are several reasons that could cause plums to drop fruit early. As you suggest, excessive drought is one of them. Weekly watering is best for plums. A heavy fruit set—too heavy for the tree to sustain—could also lead to premature fruit drop. Thin fruits so that they are about 3 inches apart. Early in the season, an insect called the plum curculio can feed on developing fruit, leaving a C-shape scar. The damaged fruits often fall off. If that is the case, next year spray an insecticide to control the curculios.

Q How do I get rid of cherry worms?

A I assume that you're referring to the worms that get into the fruits of cherries. The adults are flies that lay their eggs on the fruits. Once the fruits are infested, there is little you can do. However, to prevent them you can hang yellow sticky traps in the tree to determine when the adult flies are present. Spray the tree with an insecticide labeled for use on food crops when adults first appear. Repeat the spray two more times at 7- to 10-day intervals. To reduce the population for next year, place black plastic or a tarp under the tree to catch fallen fruit and prevent the worms from burrowing into the ground where they pupate.

Q It never fails. Just when I'm about ready to pick my cherries, the birds get them. How can I save my cherries?

A The most effective way to protect your cherries from marauding birds is to place a bird net over the tree before the cherries ripen. You could also try one of the bird-scare devices available from garden centers. These include inflatable owls, plastic snakes perched in the tree, reflective ribbons, and aluminum pie pans. Birds get accustomed to these scare devices quickly, so it's important to wait until just before the cherries are ripe to place them in the tree.

Strawberries

Q **What's the difference between June-bearing and day-neutral strawberries? Which should I grow?**

A For a harvest that comes on all at once, choose June-bearing strawberries. As the name implies, they bear a single crop in June in Zones 5 and north, earlier in warmer zones. With good care, you can harvest a crop from these plants for four to five years. Look for varieties such as 'Earliglow', 'Honeoye', and 'Totem'. Day-neutral strawberries bear fruit throughout the growing season. The plants are smaller than their June-bearing cousins because more energy goes into fruiting. Look for varieties such as 'Tristar' and 'Tribute'.

Q **What do I need to do to protect my strawberry patch for the winter?**

A In cold-winter regions, strawberries need winter protection. The traditional mulch is straw (*hence the name strawberry*). Shredded cornstalks or marsh hay may be more readily available. Use whatever you can easily find. Apply the mulch 2 to 6 inches deep after the plants have experienced several freezes in the mid-20s. It's important to wait until cold weather settles in so the plants are dormant.

Q **When should I remove the winter mulch from my strawberries?**

A Pull the mulch off the crowns of the plants in spring when growth begins. This usually happens after high temperatures hit the low 70s for several days in a row. Be on the alert to rake the mulch back over the plants if frosty nights are predicted during bloom.

Q **I've heard of bare-root trees, but I see that strawberries are sold that way too. Is it better to plant bare-root strawberries or to buy them in pots?**

A Choose bare-root or potted. Bare-root strawberries are available in late winter and early spring. They're usually sold in bundles of 10 or 25 and are often less expensive than potted plants. Plant the roots as soon as the ground is workable in spring, taking care not to bury the crown, the area where the top of the plant meets the roots.

Learn how to grow strawberries in a strawberry jar at *bhg.com/strawberry-jar*.

Q Can you really grow strawberries in a pot? I've always planted them in the garden, but I saw a pretty strawberry pot at the local nursery and I'm wondering if that works.

A With a strawberry jar you can grow these delicious berries on a balcony or patio. Start by filling the pot with good-quality potting soil. As the soil level reaches one of the pot's pockets, put in a strawberry plant. Continue until you reach within 1 inch of the top of the pot. Then plant a couple plants at the top. Place the pot in a sunny location and keep it well-watered. Because these strawberries are not set in the ground, you'll have to water them more often than the ones you have in your garden.

Q I planted a few strawberries, and now they are crowded. There are runners everywhere! Can I dig them up and put them farther apart? Can I cut off the runners?

A If you're overrun by runners, train them into the space between the rows in your strawberry patch to create new rows of young plants. Then remove the old rows so their spaces become the new aisles. Discard the old plants, because they're less productive than the new daughter plants. The best time to get rid of the parent plants is right after the patch has finished bearing in early summer. That way the daughter plants have most of the growing season to get established and set fruit buds for next year's crop.

Q My strawberry plants are two years old and produce only small, weirdly shaped berries. What's wrong with them?

A From your description, I suspect that your strawberries are being attacked by tarnished plant bugs. This insect feeds on developing blossoms. The toxin they inject while feeding causes misshapen fruits, sometimes called nubbins, to develop; the tip end of the berry becomes hard and seedy. Spray with an insecticide just before the blossoms open. Avoid using insecticide during bloom to prevent injury to pollinating insects.

Q When and what kind of fertilizer should I apply to my strawberries?

A The best time to fertilize strawberries is right after they finish bearing their main crop. If you fertilize first thing in spring, they will grow excess foliage that can hide the developing berries. Unless you have soil test results that indicate otherwise, apply a complete fertilizer, such as 10-10-10.

Growing Herbs

Q I'm growing basil, chives, cilantro, dill, parsley, and thyme. When do I harvest these herbs?

A Harvest basil by pinching the stems before flower stalks develop. Cut one-third to one-half of chives leaves to about 1 inch above the ground, or harvest individual leaves as you need them. Snip off the fresh leaves from the base of the plant for use as cilantro; allow seeds of this annual to ripen for coriander. Cut the fernlike leaves of dill, or wait for the plant to flower and go to seed before harvesting. Harvest the leaves of parsley. Use scissors to harvest thyme, leaving at least half of the plant in the garden.

Q Herbs do not do well for me, though I can grow parsley and basil. It may just be too hot and humid for most of the year where I live. Do you have any suggestions?

A Because parsley and basil grow well for you, try your luck with dill, cilantro, and chives. Grow mint in an area that is protected from hot afternoon sun. You might also try growing some of the tropical herbs. Cuban oregano (*Plectranthus amboinicus*) combines the flavors of oregano, thyme, and savory. Ginger (*Zingiber officinale*) survives in Zone 9, as does lemongrass (*Cymbopogon citratus*). These three tropical herbs can be grown in containers in colder areas. Curry leaf (*Murraya koenigii*) is a small tree whose leaves are used in curry dishes. It is also hardy to Zone 9.

Q I'm growing rosemary, lemon thyme, and chives together in a clay pot. How can I keep them through the winter? They're getting crowded. Should I separate them?

A You can repot them individually in late summer so they have some time outdoors to get used to their new containers. Then before frost hits, bring them indoors and place them on a sunny windowsill (a south-facing window is essential) or under grow-lights. You can also plant the chives and thyme directly in the garden and let them spend the winter outdoors. Rosemary is hardy only to Zone 7, so it needs an indoor home during the winter in cold regions.

Q I want to grow herbs that smell wonderful. What are the top fragrant herbs to grow?

A Fragrance is subjective, so experiment to find the ones that you like best. Here are some to consider:
1. Basil (*Ocimum basilicum*)
2. Rosemary (*Rosmarinus officinalis*)
3. Lemon verbena (*Aloysia triphylla*)
4. Scented geraniums (*Pelargonium* spp.)
5. English lavender (*Lavandula angustifolia*).

Culinary Herbs

Q **I'd like to grow some herbs to use in cooking. Which ones would be the best for that purpose?**

A Grow herbs that produce the flavors that you like. Some of the more common ones to consider are: 1. Basil, 2. Chives, 3. Dill, 4. French tarragon, 5. Oregano, 6. Parsley, 7. Rosemary, 8. Sage, and 9. Thyme.

Shade-Tolerant Herbs

Q My yard has a lot of shade. Are there some perennial herbs that I could grow there?

A Most herbs need full sun for best growth. However, here are a few you can try in partial shade: 1. Sweet flag (*Acorus gramineus*), 2. Angelica (*Angelica archangelica*), 3. Sweet woodruff (*Galium odoratum*), 4. Goldenseal (*Hydrastis canadensis*), 5. Sweet Cicely (*Myrrhis odorata*), 6. Lady's mantle (*Alchemilla mollis*), 7. Lungwort (*Pulmonaria*), 8. Mint (*Mentha*), and 9. Bee balm (*Monarda didyma*).

Basil

Q I'd like to try growing some basil. What do I need to know about growing it and using it?

A Basil is a fast-growing annual herb. It loves warm weather, so wait until late spring to plant it outdoors. To keep plants producing plenty of new leaves, pinch off flower spikes as soon as they appear. Enjoy basil fresh—the leaves don't retain their flavor well when dried. Sprinkle fresh chopped basil on sun-ripened tomatoes, add it to pasta salads, or puree it into pesto.

Q I love growing herbs, but I'm having a hard time choosing which basil to plant. There are so many to choose from. Are some better than others for cooking?

A Greek bush basils grow shorter and more compact than others. The delicate flavor of these basils makes them perfect for using raw or adding at the end of cooking. Look for 'Spicy Globe', 'Piccolo Verde', and 'Fine Green'. Purple basils add color to your herb garden. The plants won't grow as fast or as full as their green counterparts. Use this basil in cooking as you would the green types; just add it later in the cooking process to allow it to keep as much of its purple color as possible. Sweet basil's large, thick leaves and pleasing flavor make it the standard basil used in cooking.

Q I read something about different-flavored basils like lemon and licorice. Do these really taste different from regular basil?

A Lemon basil has a distinctive lemony aroma. Cinnamon and licorice basils, sometimes called Thai basil, have aromas reminiscent of their namesake flavors, and are frequently used in ethnic cuisines. All have distinct, spicy flavors different from regular basil.

Q Can you freeze fresh basil? We love fresh basil, but can't eat it all now.

A You can freeze basil, but its texture suffers. A better solution is to make pesto out of the basil and freeze the pesto. Grind the basil with olive oil, pine nuts, and Parmesan cheese, and freeze it in ice cube trays. After the cubes are frozen solid, pop them out of the tray and store them in airtight freezer bags.

Bay

Q How do I dry bay leaves for cooking?

A Sweet bay (*Laurus nobilis*), below, can be grown as a houseplant if you provide it with medium to bright light and cool to moderate temperatures. Harvest full-size leaves and place them on an absorbent paper towel in a well-ventilated dark area until they are dry. In about a week or so, the leaves should be dry.

Q With the addition of a new deck, I have decided to grow sweet bay in a container on the deck. I am wary of using fertilizers because these will be consumed. Can you suggest what type of fertilizer to use? Is there a harmless organic one?

A Herbs will be more aromatic and more flavorful if they are grown with very little fertilizer. You probably won't need to supply any fertilizer at all. If you must, you can mix dried cow manure into the soil or use a fish emulsion fertilizer according to directions.

Cilantro & Dill

Q I live in central Florida and have planted dill and cilantro in pots. They get full sun all day. They keep going to seed. I keep clipping them back, but the new growth just keeps flowering. What am I doing wrong?

A Dill and cilantro are annual herbs that do not care for hot weather. In response to high temperatures they attempt to complete their life cycle by going to seed. You can try planting successive crops of them. Make new seedings about every two weeks to have a steady supply of young plants that haven't bolted and gone to seed. Place them in a partly shaded location where the soil remains damp and cool with plenty of organic mulch. You will get much better crops during the cooler times of the year.

Ginger

Q Recently I planted a piece of sprouting ginger root, which I have been keeping moist. Once it breaks the soil's surface, what is the best way to care for it?

A Edible ginger root (*Zingiber officinale*) grows best in a humid place where it is shaded from hot summer sun. It also needs excellent drainage. Allow the plant to dry out in autumn. When the leafy tops die back, you can harvest some of the roots and leave the others to regrow next spring. Ginger is hardy only to Zone 9, so you may need to transfer the root to a container and keep it indoors in a dry place through the winter.

Check out our online story on easy-to-grow herbs at *bhg.com/easy-herbs*.

Lavender

Q How often should lavender be trimmed? How close to the woody part can I cut?

A Cut lavender back hard in spring to perhaps half its height. Spring pruning promotes bushiness and removes dead tips, which are common after winter exposure. Most of the buds that lavender sets each fall for the next year's bloom are on its youngest woody stems, so avoid cutting these all the way back to the ground. As soon as the plant finishes its main summer bloom, shear it—that is, give it a haircut to remove the spent flowers. Shearing may promote a second, albeit smaller, flush of bloom.

Q I planted lavender five months ago, and it is dying. Parts of the plant turn light green, then brown, and seem to wilt away one branch at a time. I water it daily and fertilize once a week. What am I doing wrong?

A Lavender is extremely drought-tolerant, and does not like wet soil. If you're watering every day it may be developing root rot. It should not need watering more than once or twice per week at the most. Also, lavender grows best with low fertility. Avoid fertilizing it.

Q Can you grow lavender indoors?

A Lavender is not a very happy indoor plant. If you can provide bright light such as in a sunroom or conservatory, you might have some luck, but lavender usually declines rapidly indoors.

Q What's the difference between English lavender, French lavender, and Spanish lavender?

A The most commonly grown type of lavender is English lavender (*Lavandula angustifolia*). It is hardy to Zone 5, and most varieties grow 1 to 2 feet tall. French lavender (*L. dentata*) bears purple flower spikes on plants 3 to 4 feet tall and is hardy in Zones 8–10. Spanish lavender (*L. stoechas*) has tender flower stalks with winglike petals. It grows 2 to 3 feet tall and is slightly less hardy than English lavender.

Mint

Q No one told me that mint is so invasive! Is there anything I can do to control it?

A Mint seems to grow anywhere and quickly spreads by rhizomes (underground stems). To keep mint from growing where you don't want it, plant it in a deep container. Set the container above ground, or sink it into a garden bed. Leave 1 or 2 inches of the pot's rim above the soil line so the stems won't creep over the edge. Another option is to grow the mint in a contained bed. For example, limiting it to a small space bordered by the foundation of your house and a sidewalk would prevent the rhizomes from taking over the rest of your yard.

Q I have mint that has spread into my lawn. Is there any way that I can get rid of it without killing the grass?

A If the lawn is completely overrun by the mint, consider total renovation. This involves killing the entire lawn area with a nonselective herbicide such as glyphosate (Roundup). Late summer is the best time to do this. After the grass and mint are dead, reseed or resod the affected area. If the mint is confined to a small area, you may be able to control it with repeated applications of a broadleaf herbicide designed to kill perennial weeds such as clover and dandelions.

Q I recently got a plant from a local nursery that was called pineapple mint. The leaves smell just like fresh pineapple. Do you know what I can use it for?

A The most commonly sold form is variegated pineapple mint (*Mentha suaveolens* 'Variegata'). The green leaves edged in white are an attractive addition to the garden. But be forewarned: Like all mints, it is invasive. You can use it as you would any other mint, in drinks or as a garnish. Use it in dishes where you want a refreshing, fruity touch.

Q Will mint survive winter outdoors in Chicago, or do I have to bring it indoors?

A Mint will overwinter in your garden with no problem if it's planted in the ground. In fact, mint can take over your garden so be sure to plant it along a walk or someplace it can't spread. You may want to plant it in a container and bury the container close to the rim just to keep it from spreading too much.

Parsley

Q Last year our parsley was bitter. Is there something we can add to the soil to prevent this?

A In general, bitterness is caused by lack of water or other stress to the plant. Parsley can be attacked by aster yellows, a disease spread by leafhoppers. Infected plants usually develop yellowing foliage, and flavor could be affected. Protect plants from leafhoppers with a floating row cover. Remove and destroy infected plants. If parsley overwinters, it will have more bitterness the second year. Start new plants each year to maintain mild-flavor foliage.

Q I planted six parsley plants and they are doing great. My question is how and when do I start picking it?

A You can start to harvest parsley as soon as the plants are well-established and growing well. Particularly if you plan to use only a few leaves at a time, it's easiest just to snip off a few of the oldest leaves, keeping the new growth intact. Later, as the plant is nearing full size, you can shear off the entire top, and new growth will emerge from the center.

Rosemary

Q Will my rosemary plant make it through the winter outside?

A Rosemary (*Rosmarinus officinalis*) above right, is hardy in Zones 7–10 and protected areas of Zone 6. In colder areas, grow it outside in containers to avoid having to dig it up in fall before bringing it inside for the winter. Overwintered rosemary performs best if kept at 40 to 50°F with good air circulation. Because it is evergreen, it needs bright light. I keep mine in a cool

greenhouse. Don't expect much growth on the plant through the winter; the idea is simply to keep it alive. Keep the soil moderately dry. Rosemary can develop root rot if kept too wet.

Q How can I make new starts off my rosemary plant?

A The best way to create new rosemary plants is by taking softwood cuttings. Do this in late spring, using 3- to 4-inch-long pieces from the strongest branches. Remove the lower two-thirds of the foliage. Dip the stripped stem into rooting hormone, shake off the excess, and insert the cutting into seed starting mix. Water the cuttings frequently to keep the rooting medium moist but not soggy. Cuttings should root within several weeks or months.

Stevia

Q **I'd like to grow the herb stevia as a natural sweetener. What care does it need? How do you harvest it?**

A Stevia (*Stevia rebaudiana*) grows best in full sun with good drainage. Start with transplants from a reliable nursery; plants grown from seed vary in their level of sweetness. Harvest stems for drying in fall. The cooler temperatures and shorter days of fall intensify the sweetness in the leaves. Cut stems from the plant; strip the leaves and dry them on a screen in a sunny spot with good ventilation.

Thyme

Q **Is there any special trick to growing thyme? Mine is not doing well.**

A Thyme (*Thymus vulgaris*), right, likes hot, dry, sunny sites similar to its native Mediterranean climate. Water when necessary to maintain soil moisture, but avoid overwatering. Shear off the flowers when the plant finishes blooming to keep energy concentrated in leaf production rather than in setting seed. Pest and disease problems are few. Occasionally spider mites may attack the plants. A forceful water spray will remove them. Root rot from overwatering or poorly drained soil is the most severe problem. Avoid overwatering, and grow the plant in a raised bed if drainage is poor in your garden.

Q **How do I harvest and dry thyme?**

A Harvest the entire plant by cutting it back to 2 inches above the ground in midsummer. Tie the stems in a bundle and hang them upside-down in a cool, dry place to dry. When the leaves are dry, crumble them off the stems and store in an airtight glass jar for up to two years. You can expect one more harvest before the season ends.

Q **What do I need to do to protect my thyme over the winter?**

A Thyme is perennial in Zones 5–9. It overwinters well as long as it is planted in a sunny, well-drained site. Thyme remains semievergreen through the winter. If you would like to provide a little extra protection, mulch the plants with straw or evergreen branches after the soil freezes. Next spring, after growth begins, remove any dead foliage.

Pests

Ants

Q I have trouble with ants. Do you have any solutions for killing them all over my yard?

A Ants rarely harm the garden; they are more of a nuisance than anything else. The petite crawlers are probably dining on honeydew left behind by problem-causing aphids on your trees. A strong spray with the hose might dislodge aphids, and thus eliminate the ants' food source. Raised anthills are prevalent in areas with a large number of ants. Destroy hills by dousing them with several gallons of boiling water.

Q How do I get rid of leaf-cutting ants? They are eating all the leaves off my trees and plants.

A Leaf-cutting ants are difficult landscape pests to control, because they devour many landscape plants. Control of cutting ants needs to be a neighborhood effort. Get your neighbors together and devise an action plan. Begin by identifying the location of colonies, then choose a cutting-ant insecticide. Follow application directions carefully, and be sure to repeat the application as suggested. It's important for your neighborhood to join you in this control effort, or the ants will simply relocate temporarily, then return to your garden as soon as the coast is clear.

Q I have carpenter ants invading a tree in my landscape. How can I get rid of them?

A Carpenter ants normally invade only wet or decaying wood. If they're attacking one of your trees, it's likely that the tree has internal rot, which may make the tree a structural hazard. Get a certified arborist to assess the tree's overall health. If the tree is a hazard, have it cut down. If the tree is still structurally sound, have an exterminator treat it for carpenter ants.

Q What's the best way to get rid of fire ants?

A If you want to eliminate all ants in an area, start with broadcast bait. Several days later, apply a contact insecticide, and repeat every four to eight weeks. This program is the most expensive and uses the greatest amount of pesticide. Individual mound treatment gets rid of the ants temporarily, but they may reappear elsewhere in the yard. To prevent fire ants from entering your home, treat outdoor colonies near the home, and apply an outside barrier of insecticide such as chlorpyrifos or a pyrethroid around the foundation. If you see fire ants indoors, use bait labeled for indoor use.

Aphids

Q My garden is infested with aphids. What is the best remedy to eliminate these pests without using chemicals?

A Remove aphids from plants with a strong spray of water from the garden hose. Spray every other day if necessary. Fragile plants, as well as sturdy plants that are heavily infested, may need a pest-control product such as Safer's insecticidal soap, a nonchemical, soap-based mixture that's formulated for soft-bodied insects such as aphids. Apply the product, which is available at garden centers, weekly for two to three weeks.

Q The leaves on my snowball viburnum are all curled and twisted. What is causing this?

A Your snowball viburnum (*Viburnum opulus*) has snowball viburnum aphid. This aphid feeds in clusters at the tips of the branches, causing leaf curl and twisted, distorted stems. Snowball viburnum is usually the only species affected; other viburnums are immune. The aphids are protected inside the curled leaves, but you may be able to dislodge them with a high-pressure spray from the garden hose. Damage from viburnum aphids is mostly cosmetic. Although they disfigure plants, the overall health of the plant is unaffected.

Q I would like to know how to get rid of the ants and aphids on my trumpet vine. The ants are on the flowers, and it looks like they may be harming the flowers.

A The ants won't cause direct harm to your trumpet vine, but they may be "farming" aphids. Ants often tend or encourage the aphids or other sucking insects because these insects secrete a sticky honeydew, which the ants feed on. Check the vine closely for the presence of these other insects. If necessary, you can control the aphids, and that will make the ants go away.

Q My corkscrew willow is dripping sticky sap. I found some small black bugs on the tree. Is it normal for a willow to drip sap, or is it from the bugs?

A I'm betting that your willow tree has aphids. These soft-bodied insects can be black, green, or yellow, and produce a sticky sap called honeydew. They are easy to eradicate with insecticidal soap, or you may be able to dislodge them with a forceful spray of water. They usually don't cause serious harm to trees.

Bees & Wasps

Q **I have just installed a patio and want to landscape it. What plants will provide fragrance and flowers near the patio but not attract bees?**

A The blooms that most plants produce are as attractive to bees as they are to you. You can create an equally lovely look without blooms, however. Start with ornamental grasses. Add in other plants grown for their foliage interest. Examples include coleus, caladium, sweet potato vine, rex begonia, hosta, and ferns. For fragrance, consider herbs that have scented foliage such as pineapple sage, mint, rosemary, and lemon verbena.

Q **Can you tell me how to prevent bees on my hummingbird feeders? The hummingbirds will not use them when the bees are on them.**

A Bees are especially attracted to leaky hummingbird feeders, so make sure your feeder is working properly. They also favor fermented sugar water, so change the solution in your feeder frequently. Bees prefer hummingbird feeders that hang in direct sunlight; try locating your feeder in a shady location. If this doesn't work, try the decoy method: Mix a concentrated sugar-water solution (2 parts water to 1 part sugar), pour it into a shallow plate, and place it near your hummingbird feeder. Each day, move the plate a little further away from your hummingbird feeder. Remove it entirely after several days.

Q **It appears that we have a nest of aggressive bees in a ground nest in a bed of ivy. The bees are black and yellow. What is the best method to get rid of them?**

A These are likely ground-nesting wasps that can be easily upset if their nest is disturbed. The best way to combat them is with a wasp spray. If you know where their nest is, just spray it from a safe distance to kill them. Early morning is the best time to spray.

Q **We have yellow jackets nesting in our lawn. What can I do to get rid of these unwanted insects?**

A Yellow jackets are a type of wasp whose populations build up in late summer. Throughout most of the summer they are beneficial insects, feeding on caterpillars and flies. But in late summer they switch to a high-carb diet, which is why they're attracted to sugary soda pop. If the nest is in an out-of-the-way location, your best bet may be simply to avoid the nest. All but the queen will die out over the winter, and she'll take up residence in a different spot next year. If you must destroy the nest, use carbaryl (Sevin) dust. Wait until dusk when all the yellow jackets are back in the nest. Sprinkle some carbaryl into the opening of the nest, and move slowly away.

Beetles

Q My eggplant leaves have small holes throughout them, as if someone stuck pins through the foliage. What happened, and how do I stop it from happening again?

A It sounds as though your eggplant was attacked by flea beetles (right), small black insects that have strong back legs, allowing them to jump like fleas. To deter the beetles, use floating row covers in spring, right after you plant. Remove the row covers after you see that most flea beetle damage on adjacent plants has stopped and before temperatures get too high in summer. Simply planting your eggplant outdoors a little later than usual in spring can help too. Luckily, feeding of flea beetles has little effect on fruiting.

Q I am struggling to protect my pine trees from pine beetles, which got into my neighbor's trees. Two of mine look dead, and two more appear infested. How do I prevent the beetles from spreading?

A Pine beetles normally feed on weakened or stressed trees, but when populations explode they attack healthy trees too. Pine beetles are best managed on a community-wide basis, which usually requires the prompt removal of infested trees. Avoid cleaning up trees by trimming them. The scent of pine pitch in the air sometimes attracts more pine beetles. Check with your city forester or state department of forestry about efforts they may have underway to manage pine beetles.

Q I have hard-shelled red bugs on a lot of my lilies. What are they, and how do I get rid of them?

A It sounds as though your garden has lily leaf beetles. Adult beetles are ¼ to ⅜ inch long. Larvae resemble slugs, with a swollen orange, brown, yellowish, or greenish body and a black head, and cause more damage than adults. Adult beetles overwinter in the soil or plant debris. If you have only a few lilies in your garden, handpick adults, larvae, and eggs to reduce populations. The natural insecticide neem kills larvae and repels adults. Several chemical insecticides, including carbaryl (Sevin), malathion, and imidacloprid, are effective on adults and larvae.

Q Ladybugs are invading my house this fall. What should I do about ridding my house of them?

A Multicolor Asian ladybugs are a type of beetle that invades homes in fall in search of a site for overwintering. Like their American cousins, the Asian ladybugs are (generally) beneficial insects. They feed on harmful aphids and other insects. However, their sheer numbers can be a nuisance, and they can inflict a mildly painful bite. Vacuum them up and destroy those you find inside. Caulk cracks around doors, windows, vents, and electrical outlets to keep them out of the house.

Japanese Beetles

Q Japanese beetles are a serious problem in my area. Are there any plants that I should avoid planting because they attract the beetles?

A Japanese beetles attack many different kinds of plants, but these are some of their favorites: 1. Canna, 2. Astilbe, 3. Azalea, 4. Crape myrtle, 5. Grape, 6. Hollyhock, 7. Linden, 8. Raspberry, 9. Rose, and 10. Viburnum.

Japanese Beetles

Q I have had problems with grubs and Japanese beetles for the last few years. Most of our neighborhood has used the little bag traps, but this isn't solving the problem. Would milky spore help?

A Japanese beetle traps are usually ineffective for controlling the beetles. The pheromone scent in the trap actually attracts more beetles into the area. For long-term control, milky spore will be helpful, but you may not see results until the following season because the spores work at killing the grubs that turn into beetles rather than the beetles themselves. If your garden has only a few Japanese beetles, kill them with soapy water. Go out early in the morning with a bucket of soapy water. Hold the bucket under a flower or branch where Japanese beetle adults are resting. Tap the branch; the beetles will drop off into the soapy water where they'll be killed.

Q Last year we planted 15 rose bushes surrounding our deck. They have been plagued by Japanese beetles. What will work to kill the beetles?

A The only quick method of getting rid of Japanese beetles is with a spray of malathion or carbaryl (Sevin). You could also consider your roses a trap crop for the Japanese beetles. Because roses are one of their favorites, the beetles congregate there. See the response to the previous question for the technique of killing Japanese beetles in soapy water.

Q Can you suggest some plants that Japanese beetles won't attack?

A Several plants that seem to be immune to Japanese beetle feeding:
1. Dogwood
2. Forsythia
3. Ginkgo
4. Lilac.

Other plants that Japanese beetles tend to avoid include American holly, arborvitae, boxwood, fir, hemlock, juniper, magnolia, oak, pine, redbud, red maple, and tamarisk.

For more information on Japanese beetles, check our online story at *bhg.com/Japanese-beetle*.

Beneficial Insects

Q **I know that ladybugs are good for the garden, but are there other insects that I should be encouraging to come to my yard?**

A Beneficial insects are those that feed on other insects. Assassin bugs, dragonflies, lacewings, pirate bugs, praying mantises, and soldier beetles are good bugs that you should encourage in your yard.

Q **How do I keep the ladybugs from eating away at the basil in my garden this summer?**

A Ladybugs are the good guys. They eat aphids and other small insects in your garden. If you're seeing orange ladybugs on the basil, they are having lunch.

They will stay around as long as there are tender insects on the menu. When the live food gets scarce, they will move on to another location. If you want them to leave sooner, spray them off the plant with your hose. This will dislodge the ladybugs and their prey.

Q **How do I attract praying mantids to my garden? Where can I purchase them?**

A The way to attract praying mantids to your garden is to create a good habitat for them. Avoid use of chemical sprays, and leave undisturbed, natural areas for them. You can purchase praying mantids from several companies including Planet Natural, Peaceful Valley Farm Supply, and Buglogical.

Biological Control

Q I don't like to use pesticides of any kind in my garden. What kind of natural products could I use to keep bugs at bay?

A In addition to the beneficial insects mentioned on page 312, many spiders and mites eat other insects and mites. Parasitoids are somewhat like predators. They attack by laying eggs on or inside the pest insect. The unsuspecting pest then becomes food for the developing parasitoid. The good insect hatches out from the shell of the pest, and the cycle continues. Look for the parasitic wasps *Encarsia formosa* to control whiteflies, and *Trichogramma ostriniae* to control European corn borers. Beneficial nematodes can be effective in controlling insects that live in the soil, such as grubs.

Q Are there other natural insecticides that I could use in my garden in addition to Bt?

A The most common pathogen you'll find on the shelves is Bt, also known by its full name, *Bacillus thuringiensis*. This bacteria is harmless to pets and humans. Spinosad is another bacterial-base insecticide. You'll also find pathogens that are insect-specific viruses and fungi.

Physical Controls

Q I sometimes use floating row covers for frost protection in spring and fall, but I've heard they can also be used to protect my plants from bugs. How does that work?

A Thin row covers make the best pest barriers because they retain little heat. Drape the row cover over the plants you want to protect, allowing plenty of growing room, then secure the edges with pins, boards, or soil. Let the row cover float over the tops of plants, or keep it aloft with hoops. Better yet, stud the bed or

row with a few upright plants, such as dwarf sunflowers or corn that do a good job of raising a row cover up over the tops of squash, pumpkins, or young flowers that might be devoured by bugs.

Q My neighbors and I are having problems with cutworms destroying the seedlings in our gardens. How do we get rid of them?

A When you find the tops of young plants lying next to the stubs, cutworms are the most likely cause. Protect transplants from cutworms with collars made from paper towel rolls, or wrap the base of each seedling with aluminum foil. Extend the collars ½ inch into the soil. Beneficial nematodes, sold as Grub-Away, will kill cutworms in the soil within a few days.

Borers

Q I've heard there's a new borer affecting ash trees in some parts of the country. Is it true that all the ash trees in those areas are being removed? Should I avoid planting any ash trees?

A Emerald ash borer has the potential to be devastating to ash trees in the landscape and in native forests throughout North America. For now, containment is the primary control strategy. When an infestation is discovered, all ash trees nearby are destroyed in an attempt to prevent the borers from spreading from tree to tree. There is no need to apply insecticide to your ash trees if you don't live near an infection zone. If you're thinking of planting a new shade tree and live in the Great Lakes region, consider planting something other than an ash.

Q I have several varieties of iris. The leaves are healthy, but the plants don't bloom, even though they're growing in full sun. I noticed that one rhizome has holes in it and is spongy. What could the problem be?

A The spongy rhizome may be a sign of iris borer. The borers hatch in midspring and chew their way down to the rhizome. Once in the rhizome, they continue to feed, hollowing out the insides. Foliage may yellow from injury to the rhizomes. Larvae crawl out of the rhizome in late summer to pupate. Moths hatch in early autumn and lay eggs on iris foliage and nearby garden debris. To control iris borer, clean up and destroy garden debris around irises in late fall or early spring before eggs hatch. If you find borers in rhizomes, dig up the plants, remove the borers, destroy badly damaged sections, and replant healthy ones.

Q Squash vine borers kill my zucchini plants every year. How can I keep my zucchini plants productive?

A The squash vine borer larva (below left) is a grublike caterpillar that gets into plant stems. It feeds inside the stem, causing wilting and death of the plant. If you have only a couple vines, you may be able to keep the borer at bay by handpicking adults and eggs. Adults look like black wasps with orange-red markings. They lay dull red eggs on the main stem near the ground. You may be able to prevent egg laying by wrapping stems with aluminum foil or old nylon stockings. Or try using floating row covers to exclude the borer adults from plants. If all else fails, apply an insecticide every 7 to 10 days, starting when the vines begin to run.

Q My apricot tree has sap on the trunk. The majority of leaves are turning brown and starting to drop. What is causing the problem?

A If there are large droplets of exudate on the main trunk or branches, your apricot tree may have borers, a type of insect that tunnels under the bark. You may be able to kill the borers by inserting a wire into the hole where the sap comes out of the trunk. In late spring or early summer spray the main trunk and branches with carbaryl to kill the moths that lay the eggs that hatch into the borers.

Butterfly Plants

Q I'd like to attract butterflies to my yard. What plants should I grow to attract them?

A A good start to attracting butterflies is to grow the plants that their larvae eat. Here are some to consider: 1. Elm, 2. Flowering crabapple, 3. Citrus, 4. Passion flower, 5. Pink turtlehead, 6. Rose, 7. Tulip tree, 8. Violet, 9. Willow, and 10. Yarrow.

1

2

3

4

5

6

7

8

9

10

Butterfly Plants

Q **Which flowers are good for attracting butterflies?**

A Flowers that produce a lot of nectar and have a "landing pad" will attract butterflies. Here are some good ones: 1. Aster, 2. Butterfly bush, 3. Butterfly weed, 4. Pentas, 5. Garden phlox, 6. Lantana, 7. Citrus, 8. Purple coneflower, 9. Liatris, and 10. Joe-pye weed.

1

2

3

4

5

6

8

9

10

Caterpillars

Q My sedums are under attack by a little green worm. When it is not curled up on the sedum leaves, it is eating them! What can I do? Is there an organic solution?

A If there are just a few caterpillars, pick them off plants by hand and drop them into a bucket of soapy water. If you don't want to touch the insects, combat caterpillars organically with Bt (*Bacillus thuringiensis*) or spinosad.

Q My juniper has little brown bags hanging in it. It looks like something is eating the juniper, but I don't see any bugs.

A The little brown bags you're seeing in your juniper are the protective cases of bagworms. The worm inside each bag eats the buds and foliage of the juniper. Bagworms have a single generation per year. Eggs hatch in late spring, and new larvae begin to feed immediately. If your trees and shrubs have few bagworms, handpicking is an option. Pick them off the plant and squash them. If you notice that your plant has immature bagworms, you can spray it with Bt (*Bacillus thuringiensis*) in late spring or early summer after all the eggs have hatched. Many chemical insecticides are also labeled for control of bagworm.

Q Every year when I plant geraniums, I see little green worms. They start eating the flower and leaves. What are they, and how do I get rid of them?

A This sounds like the geranium budworm caterpillar. It usually appears in June and July. The budworms themselves can be hard to control, but you can knock them out by using a biological control such as Bt (often sold as Dipel at garden centers). It will naturally prevent caterpillars from doing damage to your plants without harming other creatures. The geranium budworm also attacks other flowers such as petunia.

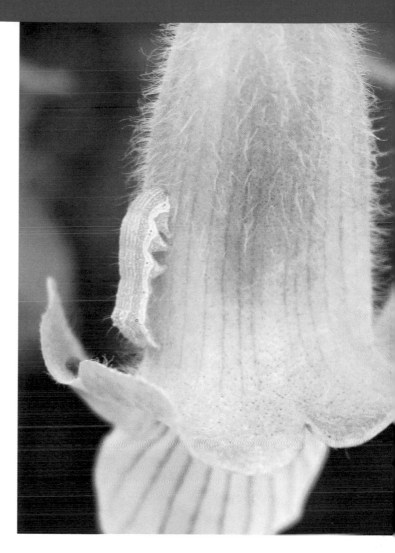

Q My broccoli is full of green worms! How do I control them?

A Several green caterpillars feed on broccoli and other cabbage-family crops. The cabbage looper, imported cabbage worm, and diamond-back moth are serious pests of these crops. You can keep your broccoli worm-free by covering plants with a floating row cover so the adult butterflies and moths can't lay their eggs on the plants. If your broccoli already has some worms blissfully chomping away, use the bacterial insecticide Bt. Insecticidal soap or chemical insecticides may also be used to control them.

Cicadas

Q **I just moved into a home in which old shrubs need to be replaced, but I don't want to plant new ones if cicadas are going to eat them up. Will my plants be safe?**

A Periodical cicadas have a 13- or 17-year life cycle. They get the press because of their enormous numbers in years that they emerge. Adults lay eggs in branch tips. In response to egg laying, twigs split and dry up. Established trees and shrubs can handle the loss of a few branch tips, but young plants can be severely disfigured. If periodical cicadas are expected to emerge in a given year, it may be best to postpone new landscape plantings until late summer or fall, after the adult cicadas have died. Recently planted trees and shrubs can be protected from egg-laying adults by covering the plants with fine-mesh nylon netting or cheesecloth.

Earwigs

Q **One of my potted plants has become a haven for earwigs. I sprayed it, but they are still there. I have two cats and have to be careful with insecticides, but I can't stand the bugs. What should I do?**

A Earwigs love dark, damp places such as flowerpots, and they can become numerous in moist, mulched beds. Trapping earwigs is usually more effective than spraying. The least messy trap is a section of damp newspaper rolled into a tube, baited with a moistened crust of bread, and secured with a rubber band. Place a few of these around your plants overnight. Earwigs will crawl inside at night. In the morning, gather up the traps and throw them away.

Grasshoppers

Q **Every few years I lose my garden to grasshoppers. What can I do to save my garden?**

A Grasshoppers are easiest to control with an insecticide such as acephate (Orthene) or carbaryl (Sevin) when they are young. Mature grasshoppers are nearly impossible to kill with an insecticide. You might also consider a small flock of chickens to help control the population in late summer. A few birdbaths combined with shrubs and small trees provide water and shelter for grasshopper-chomping birds. At the end of the growing season, till your garden to expose grasshopper eggs to killing temperatures during the winter.

Q **Is there a natural way to control grasshoppers in the garden? I hate to use chemical sprays.**

A The biological control *Nosema locustae* is a protozoan disease of grasshoppers. It can be an effective long-term control, but it is not quick-acting. You may see some reduction in grasshopper numbers a few days or weeks after application, but in general it takes about a year after applying for it to affect grasshopper populations. *N. locustae* is sold under brand names such as Nolo Bait, Semaspore, and Grasshopper Spore.

Gypsy Moths

Q **Which trees are most susceptible to gypsy-moth feeding?**

A The favorite food of gypsy moth larvae is oak trees (1). Other trees that they like to eat include: 2. Arborvitae, 3. Apple (and crabapple), 4. Cottonwood, 5. Canadian hemlock, 6. Hawthorn, 7. Linden, 8. Maple, 9. Pine, and 10. Spruce.

Gypsy Moths

Q After seeing the damage done by gypsy moths, I'd like to make sure that the new tree I plant won't be stripped by them. Which trees are resistant to their feeding?

A These are some good species to plant to avoid gypsy-moth feeding injury: 1. American sycamore, 2. Balsam fir, 3. Black locust, 4. Black walnut, 5. Catalpa, 6. Eastern red cedar, 7. Flowering dogwood, 8. Golden larch, 9. Ash, and 10. Holly.

Mosquitoes

Q I can't work in the yard without mosquitoes attacking me. I'm worried about West Nile virus. How can I protect myself from these pesky biters?

A Follow these tips for minimizing mosquito troubles.
1. Wear light-color clothing. Long sleeves and pants add more protection.
2. Mow and trim regularly. Overgrown brush and tall weeds are the optimal mosquito habitat.
3. Avoid dawn and dusk. Mosquitoes are most active as the sun comes up and just before it goes down.
4. Use a mosquito repellent. Many experts recommend a formula that contains DEET.
5. Eliminate standing water. Stagnant water is a mosquito breeding ground.

Plant Bugs

Q Something is attacking my black-eyed Susans, veronicas, and asters. Whatever it is makes spots all over the leaves. Can you tell what it is and how to control it?

A Your flowers are being attacked by plant bugs. No, really. Although many gardeners call anything with six legs that crawls around in their garden a bug, there is a specific group officially known as plant bugs. The immature and mature bugs feed on succulent leaf tissue, producing small tan or bleached spots on leaves. Your plants can tolerate a few damaged leaves. (Pick off spotted leaves to improve the plant's appearance.) If the problem continues, spray plants with an insecticide.

Q My flowers have something that looks like bubbles on the stem. What is this?

A You described the telltale signs of spittlebug (above). In spring they feed on plants by sucking fluids from plants, but they seldom cause severe damage. If you see only a few of them in your garden, don't worry about controlling them. If you dislike the looks of the frothy foam, blast it off the stem with a forceful spray of water.

Q How can I get rid of squash bugs? They killed my zucchini, and now I'm afraid they'll kill my pumpkins.

A Protect your plants with a row cover. Install the cover at planting time, and leave it on until the plants begin to bloom. Once flowers appear, remove the cover so bees and other pollinators can get to the flowers. Squash bugs will move in, but by then your plants will be robust enough that they should produce well despite the insects. Reduce squash bug numbers by handpicking them off your plants and dropping them into a container of soapy water for easy disposal. Examine plants for squash bug eggs (brick red clusters on leaves), and destroy them before they hatch into nymphs.

Sawflies

Q Something is eating the needles off my mugo and Scotch pines this spring. I see something that looks like caterpillars on the needles. What are they?

A European pine sawflies attack mugo (*Pinus mugo*), Scots (*P. sylvestris*), red (*P. resinosa*), and Austrian pine (*P. nigra*) in early spring. The adults look like flies, but the larvae resemble caterpillars. Larvae feed on needles and can strip one-year-old needles right down to the branch. The grayish green larvae feed in a group, and freeze into position when disturbed. Because these are not true caterpillars, Bt (*Bacillus thuringiensis*) will not control them. However, you can handpick them off plants and drop them in soapy water to kill them. Or spray with insecticidal soap, horticultural oil, or an insecticide labeled for use on trees.

Scale

Q My euonymus has white bumps on the leaves and stems. What are they, and how do I get rid of them?

A It sounds as though your euonymus has scale insects. Heavy infestations cause leaf drop and may kill the plant. The females lay eggs under their waxy white coating when temperatures rise in spring. Eggs soon hatch, and crawlers spread over the plant and begin feeding. You can spray the plants with dormant oil spray during the winter to kill the overwintering females. If the infestation is severe, cut the plants back near ground level in spring and spray the new growth with an insecticide to kill the crawlers.

Q I have been battling scale insects, and I am losing. What can I do to save my plants from this pest?

A Scale insects look like small raised bumps on plant stems and leaves. Insecticides are effective only when the young larvae (crawlers) are moving about the plants. To monitor crawlers, place pieces of double-sided tape on your plants; check them weekly for the presence of tiny beige dots, or tap infested twigs over a piece of white paper and look for moving specks. When the crawlers are active, spray the plants weekly with an all-purpose insecticide. On seriously infested plants, spray monthly with light horticultural oil. In spring and autumn when temperatures are mild, occasionally use insecticidal soap instead of the oil.

Q My mugo pine has small white flecks on its needles. I can scrape them off with my fingernail. What is this?

A If your mugo pine looks as though it has been spattered with white paint, it likely has pine needle scale. Adults are difficult to control, but the crawler stage is easy to control with insecticidal soap or horticultural oil. Eggs hatch in midspring, about the time that white bridalwreath spirea blooms. Watch for the crawlers, and spray to thoroughly cover needles and stems.

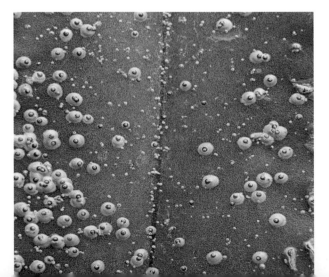

Slugs

Q **What can I do about slugs? They munch on just about everything in my garden.**

A To control slugs, grab a flashlight and handpick the creatures from plants at night or just before dawn. Or make a slug trap from a plastic yogurt carton. Bury the carton in soil (without the lid) so its top is level with the soil's surface, and fill it with beer. Place several of these traps around your garden; empty them every few days, and restock them with fresh beer. The slugs are drawn to the beer and fall into the cartons, where they drown. Watering in the morning, rather than at night, also helps to discourage slugs.

Q **We have a lot of hostas, and slugs that just love them. We've tried trapping them with beer in a container, but that hasn't worked for us. Can you suggest anything else?**

A If beer bait doesn't work for you, spread crushed eggshells around your hostas. Slugs don't like crawling over the sharp edges of the eggshells. Iron-phosphate-based baits such as Sluggo, Escar-Go!, and Worry Free are harmless to birds and mammals but take care of slugs right away.

Q **I've heard that copper can repel slugs. Does it really work? How do you install it?**

A Copper can be an effective repellent for slugs. When the slugs crawl across the copper, the moisture in their slime trails sets off an electrical current through the copper. Because slugs don't like to get shocked any more than you or I, they avoid crossing the copper. Of course, if you set up a copper band, and some slugs are already inside it, they won't want to leave either! And a copper band can be expensive for circling an entire garden.

Snails

Q **I'm growing lupine for the first time this year. It started coming up, but something is already chewing on its leaves. I have a lot of snails in my yard; could it be that?**

A Yes, snails could be devouring your lupine seedlings. Try sprinkling the soil around the seedlings with diatomaceous earth. For tender-bodied pests like snails and slugs, crawling across the diatomaceous earth is like crawling across shards of glass. Diatomaceous earth is fairly safe to handle, but be careful not to inhale any of the powder.

Check out our garden insect pest slide show online at *bhg.com/garden-pests*.

Spider Mites

Q **I always get spider mites on my indoor plants at this time of year. Is there an effective way to keep these pests away from my houseplants?**

A Spider mites (right) don't like high humidity but thrive when the air is warm and dry. To prevent them, provide a moist atmosphere for your plants. This might mean giving the plants a shower once or twice a week. To combat the pests, use insecticidal soap or a houseplant insecticide that specifically says it will kill spider mites. Spray the upper and lower surfaces of the leaves, and repeat the spray according to label directions.

Q **How can I tell if my spruce has spider mites?**

A Place a sheet of white paper beneath a branch or stem. Give the branch a sharp tap. If mites are present, you'll see tiny flecks that begin to crawl around on the paper. You may also notice fine webbing on the foliage. By the time webbing has formed, mite populations are high and should be controlled. Spruce mites are different from most mites in that they do most of their damage in the cool weather of spring and fall. Other mites are most prevalent during hot, dry weather.

Q **What's the best way to control spider mites?**

A Keep mite populations low by dousing plants with a forceful water spray. You can also spray with insecticidal soap or horticultural oil. These products work by coating the mites, so thorough coverage is essential. Several commercial miticides are available at garden centers as well.

Termites

Q **Are termites attracted to wood chip mulch? We don't want to use it if it might bring in termites.**

A Any wood in contact with soil can be attractive to termites. It's unusual for them to infest mulch, but it can happen. Instead, termites are more likely to attack decaying stumps or fallen limbs that contain large pieces of dead wood. As long as you keep the wood-based mulch a foot or so away from the house's foundation, you should be able to see any mud tunnels that termites make as they cross the barren zone. Also, bark mulch contains few wood fibers, so it is even less attractive to termites than wood chips.

Thrips

Q My gladioluses came up just fine but never really bloomed. The flowers that opened were brown and dry. I checked for pests but didn't see anything. Any ideas?

A Gladiolus is commonly attacked by thrips that feed on the shoots and flowers, leaving behind silver-streaked foliage, stunted plants, and flowers that fail to open. The thrips most likely nested in your gladiolus corms and will appear again next year if you don't take action. Dig the gladiolus corms in autumn and store them in an unheated garage or shed where the temperature remains at 35 to 40°F; thrips will be eliminated in these near-freezing temperatures. Control thrips during the growing season with insecticidal soap.

Vine Weevils

Q Something is eating half-moon notches on the edges of my rhododendron's leaves. What sort of insect would be doing this?

A It sounds as though your rhododendron is being munched by black vine weevils. It feeds at night on more than 100 different kinds of garden plants. Larvae feed on plant roots and occasionally on stems. If stems are girdled, the plant may be killed. This insect is difficult to control because adults are active at night, and larvae develop underground, protected from insecticides. No insecticides are labeled for controlling larvae, but adults may be managed by spraying plants with an insecticide in late spring. You may also be able to reduce larval populations by cutting back on irrigation to keep the soil dry.

Whiteflies

Q How do I get rid of whiteflies?

A Ladybugs and several types of tiny wasps attack whiteflies. Or you can spray horticultural oil or insecticidal soap without worrying about harming the good bugs. Alternate the sprays by applying the oil one week and the soap the following week. Meanwhile, nab some whiteflies by installing yellow or blue sticky traps near severely infested plants. (You can make traps by coating pieces of yellow or blue plastic with honey, or you can purchase traps from your local garden center.)

Q I've had difficulty dealing with whiteflies in the past. Please recommend whitefly-resistant varieties of plants.

A Whiteflies have hundreds of hosts, so naming resistant plant types is difficult. Here are some tips to help you keep the tiny pests at bay.
1. Select plants that have hairy leaf surfaces.
2. Carefully inspect all plants before bringing them home.
3. Remove plants that seem especially attractive to whiteflies.
4. Use insecticidal soap and yellow or blue sticky traps to help suppress whiteflies.

Anthracnose

Q I recently noticed red and brown spots on my young dogwood's foliage. I've been told that it is most likely infected with anthracnose. What is this disease, and how can I control it?

A Anthracnose is a serious fungal disease that plagues dogwoods. Weakened trees and those suffering from drought, nutrient deficiency, or other diseases are most susceptible. Dogwood grows best in partial shade; morning sun with afternoon shade is ideal. If yours is growing in a shady site, the foliage may remain wet for long periods after rain or dew, providing conditions favorable for development of the disease. Consider pruning out some surrounding growth to increase airflow and promote drying. The best control measure for your infected tree is to prune out the diseased twigs. Sterilize the pruners in alcohol or dilute bleach between cuts to prevent spreading the disease. Fungicide sprays are most effective when applied early in the season, just before buds open.

Q My hydrangea is getting black spots on its foliage. Is this the same thing as black spot on roses and how do I treat it?

A There are two fungal diseases that may be causing the black spots on your hydrangea. Cercospora leaf

spot starts on the lower leaves and works its way up. The spots are usually no larger than ¼ inch in diameter. Anthracnose spots are larger—as much as 1 inch in diameter—and can appear anywhere on the plant without necessarily starting from the bottom up. The treatment for both of these diseases is similar. Remove all fallen leaf debris where the pathogen will overwinter. Fungicides won't clear up the spots this year but may be used as a preventative next year. Watch for signs of the disease and begin spraying as soon as they appear.

Q I recently planted a red maple, and it now has light brown spots on the leaves. What could be causing this?

A The light brown spots on the foliage may either be anthracnose or a symptom of transplant shock. In either case, you likely need not do anything other than make certain that the tree is adequately watered this year to get its roots established. Anthracnose is a fungal disease that sometimes attacks maples in wet spring weather, but as soon as temperatures warm up and conditions are drier, goes away.

Q Every spring my sycamore tree drops a lot of its leaves. Why does it do that, and how can I stop it from happening?

A Your sycamore tree is suffering from anthracnose. By the time you see leaf drop and twig dieback, the infection period is usually over. Trees typically develop new leaves by early to midsummer. Reinfection is unlikely as warm, dry weather conditions arrive. Repeat infections over the years can result in distorted growth from cankers and dieback, but fungicide sprays are seldom necessary. Cut down on the amount of fungus in the area by raking up and destroying fallen leaves. If your tree is small, you could prune out cankered twigs, but that is impractical on a large, established tree.

Aster Yellows

Q Some of my marigolds stay green and never fully develop. What could be causing this? Will it affect other plants?

A Your marigolds have become infected with aster yellows. Remove infected plants to decrease plant-to-plant spread. These types of plants are most likely to be infected by aster yellows: 1. Aster, 2. Blanket flower, 3. Broccoli, 4. Celosia, 5. Gladiolus, 6. Lettuce, 7. Marigold, 8. Petunia, 9. Purple coneflower (infected plant shown), and 10. Tomato.

Botrytis

Q **A lot of my strawberries get a fluffy gray mold on them just as they turn ripe. How can I control this fungus?**

A Your strawberries have gray mold, also called botrytis blight (below). The disease is most common during cool, humid weather. Blossoms and berries become infected when a healthy bloom or berry touches an infected one, the ground, or a dead leaf. Pick and destroy infected fruit to get the source of new infections out of the patch. Mulch plantings with clean straw, pine needles, or other mulch to keep fruits off the ground. Keep proper spacing between plants to promote air movement and drying. If necessary, spray with a protective fungicide that's safe for edibles.

Q **Some of the flowers in each cluster of blooms on my geraniums always turn brown. The leaves also have brown spots. What should I do to prevent this problem?**

A Your geraniums are infected with botrytis blight. The problem is usually temporary. When the weather warms up and dries out, the problem goes away on its own. You can help prevent the spread of the disease by clipping off and destroying affected flowers

and leaves. Give plants wider spacing so they'll have better airflow around them and dry out more quickly. Use drip irrigation to avoid wetting foliage and flowers when watering. If the problem persists, spray with a protective fungicide.

Q **My peonies have blackened leaves. Should I cut them down now and throw the leaves in the trash? How do I prevent this from happening next year?**

A The fungal diseases botrytis and phytophthora attack peonies when conditions are cool and wet. Remove and dispose of the affected plant parts immediately. In fall, after frost kills the rest of the plant, remove all aboveground plant parts. If the soil in your garden is poorly drained, dig the plants, amend the soil with compost, and replant. It's possible that the diseases won't show up again next year if the weather is drier. If necessary, spray the plants next year with a fungicide.

Q **I have roses, clematis, and bearded iris that had some flowers that opened normally, while others just shriveled up and got slimy. I don't see any bugs or disease on them. What could this be?**

A The flower buds that wilt and turn gooey before opening are being affected by disease. It may be botrytis blight, a type of fungus that is widespread during cool, cloudy, wet conditions. As weather conditions improve, it usually goes away on its own. It's also possible that bacterial disease can cause the symptoms you describe, although bacteria usually also create a foul-smelling odor. If you don't notice any bad smell with the gooey buds, it's most likely botrytis. You may help prevent the spread of these diseases by removing and destroying the affected buds.

Canker

Q I've been told that my blue spruce tree has cytospora canker. The arborist said there is no cure for this disease. Isn't there something I can do to help the tree?

A Your arborist is correct; there is no fungicide labeled for the control or prevention of cytospora. Your best bet is to keep the tree in good health. Fertilize the tree if growth is poor. Water during dry periods. Control insect pests that may infest the tree. And avoid injury to the trunk and branches. If the disease gains a foothold, prune out dead and dying branches several inches beyond the cankered area. Disinfect pruning shears between cuts with 70 percent rubbing alcohol or a 10 percent chlorine bleach solution.

Q I have a chokecherry tree that started developing growths on the trunk and branches. What can I do about these growths?

A Chokecherries are susceptible to a fungal disease called black knot canker. The source of infection is often wild chokecherry trees growing nearby. To control the disease, remove the galls (swellings on the stems) over winter, pruning at least 4 inches beyond outward signs of swelling. Cut out knots on trunks down into healthy wood, and at least ½ inch outward from visible swellings. In the spring, spray the tree with a fungicide containing thiophanate methyl or captan just before the buds open then two more times at 7- to 10-day intervals.

Q I've been hearing a lot lately about sudden oak death. My oak tree has dead spot on its trunk. Do you think that this could be caused by sudden oak death?

A Sudden oak death affects many species. Some hosts develop bark cankers; others develop foliar symptoms. Those that develop bark cankers (mostly

oaks) usually die. If disease symptoms develop only on leaves and twigs, death is unlikely. In susceptible oaks and tanbark oaks, the first symptom of the disease is usually a bleeding canker in which thick sap oozes to the bark's surface. Symptoms on foliar hosts include leaf spots and twig cankers. Some shoot dieback may also be seen. For more information on sudden oak death, visit the California Oak Mortality Task Force's website at *suddenoakdeath.org*.

Q I have a maple tree that has a big gash at the base of the trunk. It looks like the tree is dying. How can I save it?

A It sounds as though your maple may have lawn mower blight (above). Bumping into the trunk with a lawn mower can damage the bark, opening a wound in which canker fungi can gain a foothold. Prevent the problem by mulching around the tree so that you need not trim so closely to it. If the canker extends halfway around the trunk, the tree is not likely to survive. If less than one-fourth of the circumference is affected, the tree may be able to outgrow the damage.

Crown Gall

Q I just noticed several corky swellings on the stems of my euonymus bush. Is this a disease or insect?

A Your euonymus has crown gall, a plant disease caused by a soil-inhabiting bacterium. Many species of plants are susceptible to the bacteria, which can remain in the soil for several years. The bacteria produce a substance that stimulates rapid cell growth in the plant, causing gall formation on the roots, crown, and sometimes branches. Galls are most often found at the soil line (crown) of the plant.

Q One of the shoots on my rose bush died this spring. When I looked closer, I noticed a gnarled woody growth surrounding the base of the dead stem. Will this kill my rose bush?

A You can't eliminate crown gall from your rose (below), but the plant may survive for many years. Prune out and destroy affected stems below the galls. Disinfect pruning shears after each cut. If you want to replace it, replant with a resistant species. Among those resistant to crown gall are abelia, andromeda (*Pieris*), barberry (*Berberis*), deutzia, holly (*Ilex*), leucothoe, Oregon grapeholly (*Mahonia*), serviceberry (*Amelanchier*), and sumac (*Rhus*).

Damping-Off

Q I am starting seeds and have read about damping-off disease. How can I keep my seedlings safe?

A There's no effective treatment for damping-off once it occurs—your best bet is to prevent it. Use sterile planting containers (use new ones, or scrub recycled containers with a solution of 1 part chlorine bleach to 9 parts water.) Fill the containers with sterile potting mix, and maintain good air circulation by installing a small fan near seedlings to keep air moving. Avoid excess water. If your plants are already infected, you may be able to save some seedlings if you allow the soil to dry out between waterings.

Q I've tried starting flower and herb seeds indoors in our kitchen window, but it's always been a big disaster. The seedlings sprout, but they soon grow spindly and fall over. What's the problem?

A Seedlings that remain wet in a warm, humid environment will fall prey to diseases such as damping-off fungus. If your seedlings are collapsing at the base, that could be what's happening to them. Water only when the soil surface feels dry to the touch. Your spindly seedlings may need more consistent light. Fluorescent shoplights provide an inexpensive source of steady light. Place one 1 inch above the plants as they first emerge. Keep the light turned on for 16 hours each day. Gradually raise the light source as the seedlings grow taller, keeping the bulb 1 or 2 inches above the uppermost leaves.

Fire Blight

Q I have a pear tree that has several branches that suddenly turned brown and died back. What would cause this?

A Your pear tree has fire blight, a bacterial disease. Symptoms include brown or black leaves that cling on the tree. In severe cases, the entire tree may be killed. Avoid pruning susceptible trees and shrubs during the growing season. However, if the disease gets started, pruning out affected branches can stop its spread. Prune 8 to 12 inches below the blackened area. Sterilize your pruning tool between each cut by dipping it in a solution of 1 part chlorine bleach to 9 parts water. Avoid fertilizing your pear tree. Succulent growth from high-nitrogen fertilizer is more susceptible to fire-blight attack.

Q I know that apples and pears can get fire blight. Are any other plants susceptible to it?

A Pear and quince are the most susceptible plants to fire blight. Apple, crabapple, and firethorn are also frequently infected by the bacterial disease. Other rose family relatives, including rose, spirea, mountain ash, contoneaster, serviceberry, and loquat, occasionally may develop an infection.

Q My pear tree just started getting red spots on its leaves, then the leaves turned dark brown and dry. It seems to be spreading fast. How should I treat this problem?

A I would guess that the problem is fire blight. The rapid color change to brown or black is very typical of the disease. Pruning out the affected areas is one way to keep it under control. Sterilize your pruners between each cut. Because it is caused by a bacteria, most fungicides won't control the disease; however streptomycin or copper-containing fungicides can be effective.

Leaf Spots

Q **My impatiens bloomed beautifully, but the leaves are spotted and turning yellow. What can I do about this?**

A There are several possible causes for the spotting and yellowing of leaves on your impatiens. Tomato spotted wilt virus has become a serious problem on many ornamentals, including impatiens. Once the plant is infected with this virus, there is no cure, so remove the plant to prevent further spread. Your impatiens may also be showing symptoms of fungal leaf spot. Drought, lack of nutrients, and harsh growing conditions all stress a plant, making it less resistant to fungal diseases. Promote healthy impatiens by planting them in an area that receives afternoon shade and by watering and fertilizing the plants regularly.

Q **Our crabapple gets yellow leaves with black spots and drops them early in the summer. Is this something I should be spraying for?**

A The conditions you describe sound like apple scab. This fungal disease is present every year, but some years it is more severe than others. Its development is accelerated by wet weather. Defoliation can be severe on susceptible varieties. You can spray with a fungicide to prevent the disease. It will take at least two or three sprays at weekly intervals beginning with bud break in spring. Rather than setting yourself up for yearly spraying, however, consider replacing your susceptible crabapple with a resistant variety.

Q **My roses have yellowed leaves with fuzzy black spots on them. Is this a disease? Do I need to spray something to get rid of it?**

A Black spot (above right) is a common fungal disease on roses. The disease usually starts as irregular black spots on leaves. Leaves turn yellow and drop. If you grow susceptible rose varieties in areas where black spot is a problem, you'll almost certainly have to spray fungicides to keep the problem under control. However, you can avoid the need to spray by choosing disease-resistant roses and growing them in a favorable location. Plant roses in a sunny area with good air circulation. Avoid wetting the foliage when watering, and remove spotted or yellowing leaves from the plants. In fall, clean up all diseased leaves and remove diseased canes.

Q **I have a rhododendron that is about four years old. There are some small brown spots on the leaves. Any suggestions as to what could be wrong?**

A Rhododendrons are susceptible to several fungus diseases, including cercospora leaf spot, anthracnose, and gray blight. Cercospora causes odd-shaped spots with yellow margins. Heavily diseased leaves will drop off. Anthracnose causes round brown spots that extend all the way through the leaf. Gray blight starts with spots, then spreads to large areas, causing a gray discoloration and eventual leaf drop. Usually leaf spots are nuisance diseases, not really harming an otherwise healthy plant. Continue to fertilize gently, water during dry spells, and mulch to keep the soil moist. Remove fallen leaves and other litter to minimize the source of fungus spores.

Powdery Mildew

Q Powdery mildew is making my phlox and asters suffer. What can I do?

A Full sun and good air circulation are key to avoiding powdery mildew. Thin plants, beginning in late spring. Avoid getting the plants' foliage wet—especially later in the day. When selecting plants that are especially susceptible to powdery mildew, such as phlox, zinnias, and roses, look for varieties that are resistant to the disease. For example, 'David' garden phlox has excellent resistance to powdery mildew.

Q My garden is mildew heaven. The bee balm, phlox, lilac, pulmonaria, and black-eyed Susan all have it. There must be one plant that's really susceptible and giving it to the rest. Can you tell me which one I should take out?

A Each plant species is prey to its own fungus species. You simply see the same symptom on different plants. When mildew is prevalent among species, watering problems and poor air circulation may be the real culprits. Zinnias and phlox are more prone to mildew if their leaves stay moist for long periods. Bee balm and pulmonaria are more susceptible when grown too dry. Where air doesn't circulate well, mildew spores have more time to grow and take hold on a leaf. Pruning to thin overgrowth can help. You might replace some varieties that you already have with disease-resistant types.

Q Can powdery mildew infect lawns? The shady section of my lawn has a whitish powder on it. What can I do to get rid of it?

A Powdery mildew infects many species of plants, including lawn grasses. The disease is more unsightly than damaging. It slows the growth of the grass plant, weakening it and making it more susceptible to other problems. Excessively fertilized lawns are more susceptible to powdery mildew. Fertilize and irrigate only moderately in shaded areas to help prevent the disease. Reduce shade and improve air circulation by pruning surrounding trees and shrubs. If the problem persists, consider overseeding with grasses more resistant to mildew. An alternative is to replace the grass with a shade-tolerant groundcover.

Q My garden is behind my garage. It gets lots of sun, so I am puzzled as to why the plants in one corner never do well. They turn whitish and die off sooner than the rest of the garden. What's going on?

A From what you describe, it sounds as if you have a powdery mildew problem in your garden. I suspect that poor air circulation may be the culprit. In places such as corners of yards where fences meet buildings or in spots where plants are close together, the air circulates poorly, leaving the surfaces moist. When the plants stay damp, there's more of a chance for disease organisms to stake their claim. You might try planting disease-resistant varieties in that corner.

Rust

Q **My lawn has an orange cast to it. When I mow, my shoes turn orange! Is this a kind of rust? How do I get rid of it?**

A It sounds as though your lawn has rust, a type of fungal disease. The disease usually shows up in mid- to late summer when cool-season turfgrasses are growing under stressful conditions. Symptoms on leaf blades include orange pustules full of powdery orange spores. You shouldn't need to spray your lawn to control rust. Instead, fertilize and water the lawn to provide better growing conditions. Late summer and fall are the best times to fertilize your lawn. Water as needed through the summer to prevent moisture stress. If the rust persists, you can overseed with rust-resistant varieties.

Q **I've heard about the new daylily rust disease. Will I need to spray my daylilies to control it?**

A Similar to other rust diseases, daylily rust produces bright yellow or orange spots with raised pustules. Eventually leaves turn yellow and dry up. If you suspect that your daylily plants are infected with rust, remove all infected foliage and bury the trimmings. Sterilize tools

with 70 percent rubbing alcohol or a 10 percent bleach solution to prevent spread. Wash your hands, gardening gloves, and clothes afterward to prevent spread to the rest of the garden. Some daylilies show good resistance to rust. The All-American Daylily Selection Council (*daylilyresearch.org*) tests for rust resistance on the top varieties it recommends.

Q **My juniper trees have slimy orange balls on them. What are they?**

A It sounds as though your juniper trees have cedar-apple rust. The orange balls you see are the fruiting body of the fungus. The first year of infection, the fungus forms a brownish green swelling 1 to 2 inches in diameter on the juniper branch. The following spring, during warm, rainy weather, the ball sends out jellylike orange projections that produce spores that spread the disease to apple trees. Cedar-apple rust is not a serious problem on junipers, although infected twigs may die. On apples, the disease shows up as orange spots on leaves and fruit. Again, the tree is not permanently damaged, but the fruit can be seriously disfigured.

Q **I have a hollyhock that has little round rust-color spots on the underside of the leaves. Any thought on how to get rid of it?**

A Hollyhock rust is difficult to control. You can minimize the damage by removing all leaves with rust spots on them, and by cleaning up infected leaves on the ground. Don't put the infected plant parts in the compost pile—burn or bury them. If you begin spraying with fungicides early in the season, and continue treatment over the summer every 7 to 10 days, you may keep the problem under control. One solution is to keep the plants cleaned up as best as possible, and plant something in front of them to cover the naked hollyhock stems as the defoliation progresses through the summer.

Sooty Mold

Q **My camellia has black soot covering on its leaves. What is this? Will it hurt the plant?**

A Sooty molds (below) are caused by fungi that grow in the sticky honeydew left on the foliage by feeding from sap-sucking insects such as aphids, mealybugs, and scales. The black coating cuts out some light to the leaf so photosynthesis is reduced. More serious is the insect infestation that caused the honeydew. Aphids may be easily controlled with insecticidal soap or dislodged with a forceful water spray. Mealybugs and scales can be more difficult to manage. Use an insecticide labeled for treatment of these pests to control them. Remove sooty mold from plants by wiping leaves with a wet rag or washing it off with a forceful spray of water.

Virus

Q **The leaves of my roses have unusual zigzag yellow streaks on them. Someone said this is a virus. Is this true?**

A It sounds like your problem is rose mosaic virus. Plant pathologists haven't found evidence showing that rose mosaic is spread by insects or pruning shears, but the problem could spread if the roses are growing close together and their roots are intertwined. There is no treatment for rose mosaic so removing the infected plants is the best method to prevent further infections in the garden.

Q **The leaves of my tomato plant are deformed and mottled yellow and green. The fruits that develop are also mottled and misshapen and don't taste very good. Is this something in the soil?**

A The symptoms you describe are those of mosaic virus—either tobacco mosaic virus or cucumber mosaic virus. Smokers may carry tobacco mosaic virus on their hands. There is no cure for mosaic viruses. Keep aphid populations under control by spraying with insecticidal soap. If you are a smoker, wash your hands thoroughly before working in the garden. If you notice infected plants, remove and destroy them to prevent spread.

Q **How can I get rid of tomato mosaic virus? I smoke but never touch the plants unless I've washed my hands.**

A When you do spot the disease in your garden, remove and destroy every bit of the infected plant. Wash your hands frequently and disinfect your tools by scrubbing them with scalding hot soapy water for at least 5 minutes. Look for tomato varieties with a "T" on the label, indicating resistance to the tobacco mosaic virus. Resistant varieties include 'Celebrity', 'Hawaiian', 'Sweet Chelsea', 'Park's Whopper', and 'Tropic'.

Wilt Diseases

Q **I miss the elm shade trees that used to line the streets years ago. Is Dutch elm disease always going to be with us, or are there some elms that can survive the disease?**

A Dutch elm disease is caused by a fungus that invades and plugs the water-conducting tissues of elm trees. Plant breeders are working on resistant elm hybrids, so one day you may again see the graceful forms of elms arching over streets. A few resistant cultivars include Accolade, 'Dynasty', 'Frontier', 'Homestead', 'Patriot', 'Pioneer', 'Sapporo Autumn Gold', and 'Urban'. However, it's unlikely that city foresters will again return to the practice of planting entire sections of the city with the same species. Diversity in plant types helps prevent epidemics such as Dutch elm disease.

Q **I've been told my maple is dying of verticillium wilt. I thought verticillium was a problem on tomatoes. What can you tell me about this disease?**

A Verticillium wilt affects many ornamentals as well as fruits and vegetables such as tomatoes. Maple is one of the susceptible species. The disease is caused by a soilborne fungus that enters the tree roots and spreads up into the branches through the water-conducting vessels. Some maples may recover from infection, so avoid rushing to remove wilted branches. They may leaf out again next year. If the branch dies, however, cut it out. No chemical control is available for the disease, but you may be able to help your tree overcome the disease by stimulating new growth with fertilizer and adequate water during dry periods.

Q **My tomato plants' leaves turned brown then yellow, and there are dark streaks on some of the stems. Should I trim off the sick leaves and stems?**

A Symptoms of the wilt diseases and the fungal leafspot diseases on tomato (above) can look similar. However, usually the leafspot diseases develop distinct spotting of the leaves before turning yellow then brown. You can spray a fungicide to protect the foliage from getting leafspot, but sprays are ineffective on vascular wilts. Instead, look for resistant varieties, designated by "F" or "V" after their name. These letters stand for resistance to fusarium and verticillium wilts, respectively.

Q **My cucumbers start out fine, but they wilt and die suddenly. Why?**

A Your cucumber plants are infected with bacterial wilt. Striped or spotted cucumber beetles may spread the disease. They transmit the disease to the plant through feeding wounds. The only control for bacterial wilt is to control the beetles. A floating row cover can exclude the beetles, but you'll need to remove the cover for a few hours each day or hand-pollinate flowers to get fruit set. Plant wilt-resistant varieties if possible. You can also spray vines with an insecticide to control beetles.

Q My beautiful red oak tree has some dying branches on it, and I'm afraid it might be oak wilt. What does oak wilt look like? If it is oak wilt, what can I do to save the tree?

A You should suspect oak wilt if your tree has wilting, bronzing leaves that fall prematurely. Oak wilt is caused by a fungus that spreads through water-conducting tissues. Red oak branches may die quickly. Dieback in white oaks happens at a much slower pace. Prune out dead or damaged branches, taking care to avoid injury to healthy trees. Open wounds during the growing season attract sap beetles that spread the disease. Unless you are pruning out dead or storm-damaged branches, avoid pruning oaks except during the dormant season. Keep trees growing vigorously by watering during periods of drought and by fertilizing periodically.

Q The leaves on my rhododendron are rolling up and wilting. What could be causing this?

A If you see drooping and rolling of foliage during the growing season, it's likely that your rhododendron has a wilt disease caused by the soilborne fungus phytophthora. Phytophthora is most often a problem in poorly drained, wet soils (such as by a downspout). Fungicide treatment is ineffective. A better solution is to change the growing conditions. Improve soil drainage and aeration if you want to continue growing the plant in the same location. Incorporate compost or other organic matter to loosen heavy soils. Consider installing a raised bed to improve drainage, and transplant your rhododendron into the amended raised bed.

Yellowing Leaves

Q The leaves on my maple tree are turning yellow, but the veins remain green. Is this some kind of virus?

A The symptoms you describe are typical of iron chlorosis (below). It is often caused by high soil pH that makes iron unavailable to the plant. If can also be caused by other stress factors, such as compacted soil. Iron chelate applied to the foliage can quickly green up the leaves. But for a long-term solution, work at lowering the soil pH by amending it with sulfur.

Q The leaves on my shrubs are turning yellow. What's wrong with them?

A Several conditions can cause yellow leaves on plants. Nutrient deficiencies can show up as yellowing foliage. Over- or underwatering can lead to leaf yellowing and loss. Root rots also may cause leaf yellowing. Various fungal diseases and insect feeding may also cause leaf yellowing. To properly diagnose the cause of the yellowing, look more closely for additional signs or symptoms. Have there been any recent changes in the care of the shrubs, such as unusually dry or wet conditions? Has any work been done recently in the root zone of the plants?

Birds

Q **Our condo has a small pond in the center of the complex. Canada geese have invaded the pond and taken over our lawns. Is there a way to keep them from making a mess of everything?**

A There is no easy solution to managing geese. However, there are steps that you can take to reduce run-ins with geese. Keep all vegetation mowed down around ponds to eliminate nesting cover. Keep the neighbors from feeding the geese. Once geese associate your condo complex with food, they'll keep coming back for more. Commercially available bird-scare devices include reflective tape and balloons. You can make your own scarecrow, or tie aluminum pie pans to a string. Change the scare devices every couple days to keep the geese from getting used to them.

Q **Woodpeckers are attacking several trees in my yard. What can I do to protect the trees from the birds?**

A Woodpeckers often drill into trees that are infested with insects. In these cases, the insects are probably causing more damage than the birds. Identify the insect pest (frequently a borer) and treat the tree accordingly. Sometimes, though, woodpeckers attack trees for no apparent reason. You can deter them by hanging objects in the tree, such as strips of brightly colored plastic, Mylar, or aluminum foil; pie tins or compact discs displayed like mobiles; or inflatable rubber snakes or globes with eye designs painted on them.

Q **Something is drilling holes in a gridlike pattern on the trunks of my trees. Are these borers? Will they kill my tree?**

A It sounds as though your trees have been found by a yellow-bellied sapsucker (yes, there really is a bird by that name!). The sapsucker is a type of woodpecker that drills holes in precise rows to drink the sap that flows from the wounds. The bird also feeds on insects that are attracted to the sap. If the injury is substantial, an individual branch or even the entire tree can be killed. Wrap the affected trunk or branches with burlap. Or use sticky repellent such as Tanglefoot or Stik'em Special from a garden center. Apply the repellent to the trunk. When the bird lands on the sticky goo, it finds the perch unpleasant and moves on.

Q **How can I keep birds out of strawberries and raspberries? I always have a good crop, but the birds generally get to them before I do.**

A You can buy lightweight netting to drape over the plants. Make sure that it is suspended with stakes so that it doesn't sit on the plants—if that happens, birds just peck through the holes. Also make certain that the netting is securely fastened to the ground so that birds won't fly in under the netting.

Cats

Q I have four cats that use my gardens as a litter box. I've tried commercial repellents, but none seem to work. Are there any herbs or flowers that may assist in deterring them?

A Because commercial repellents haven't worked for you, consider physical barriers, such as mats of flexible plastic spikes or buried plastic forks (tines sticking up). In a corner of your garden, plant catnip (*Nepeta cataria*) or catmint (*N. × faassenii*) and install a sandbox for the kitties. The cats will find the plants irresistible, and they'll prefer to dig in the sandbox rather than the heavier soil in your garden. These distractions may occupy the cats' attention enough to keep them from exploring the rest of the garden.

Q Our new home is on a street that's home to outdoor pet cats. The cats use our mulch as a litter box. Is there anything we can do to keep cats out of our yard?

A Most municipalities now have regulations about cats at large. Your local animal control officer may help you with this. Otherwise, you could try several cat-scaring methods. Motion-sensor-triggered contraptions that spray water at animal intruders can keep cats at bay. Repellents work well in many situations. Try a liquid formula that you apply with a sprayer.

Q Do you have any suggestions on how to keep cats from using my flowerbeds and garden as a litter box? I tried cayenne pepper, but it didn't last long.

A There are a number of cat repellent sprays that you can try, including Cat Stopper, made by Messina Wildlife. If sprays don't work well for you, you might try laying chicken wire over the soil in the areas the cats prefer to use. The chicken wire will prevent them from scratching the soil and often forces them to go elsewhere.

Q How can I keep cats from using my flowerbeds as a litter box?

A The most effective way is to use a spray repellent on selected areas of your garden. Liquid Fence makes a dog and cat repellent that is reported to work very well on cats and it won't hurt them. You can buy Liquid Fence at most garden centers and home centers.

Chipmunks

Q The chipmunks have eaten every single green tomato that developed on my tomato vines. How can I keep them away?

A Chipmunks are hard to deter. You could try covering your plants with grow netting. You can buy this at most garden centers or online from Gardener's Supply. There are also spray repellents designed to repel these rodents, but if you have a high population of chipmunks, you may still observe some damage.

Q How in the world do I get rid of chipmunks in my flowerbeds? They destroy my bulbs and leave holes behind.

A The first step is to limit their food supply. Chipmunks feed on spilled birdseed beneath feeders, and they steal food from pet food bowls. Although chipmunks love tulips and many other bulbs, they avoid eating daffodils. Plant plenty of those, as well as crocus, which they also leave alone. Watch for them early in the morning and late in the afternoon, and see if you can locate their homes. If you discover that they're nesting beneath a woodpile or another source of cover, you may be able to move the cover—and the chipmunks—a good distance away from your garden.

Crayfish

Q My backyard borders a creek. The lawn near the creek is developing small mounds of soil with a hole in the middle of each mound. I can't find anything in the holes. What could be causing this? How can I get rid of them?

A It sounds as though your yard may have crayfish (or crawdads, as they are sometimes known). Crayfish invade lawns that are constantly wet, whether from a high water table near a body of water, as in your case, or from poor drainage or overwatering. There's no pesticide labeled for control of crayfish, so changing the environment to discourage them is your best bet. Rather than trying to grow a lawn next to the creek, perhaps you could install a naturalized wetland or bog. Then even if the crayfish make their mounds, mowing won't be an issue.

Deer

Q **The deer around here eat everything! Are there some plants that they won't eat?**

A If deer are hungry enough, they'll eat just about anything. But these plants are ones that they generally avoid: 1. Astilbe, 2. Bald cypress, 3. Flowering dogwood, 4. Forsythia, 5. Foxglove, 6. Ginkgo, 7. Juniper, 8. Pulmonaria, 9. Russian sage, and 10. Oleander.

Deer

Q Over the winter, deer ate some of our arborvitae shrubs. Should I prune now or wait to see if they come back this spring?

A Wait and see how the shrubs look when the new growth emerges. The plants may look rather unsightly during the first growing season, but if you can tolerate the view, it's worth the wait to see how the natural growth compensates for the damage.

Q Deer have eaten the leaves off my hostas, leaving just the stems. Should I cut the plants back to the ground? Will new growth appear this summer?

A Leave the hostas alone. They should recover with some new foliage before fall unless the deer come back. Don't cut back the damaged foliage because even though it's unsightly, any green tissue remaining continues to photosynthesize and build up energy in the plant.

Q How do I repel deer?

A There are a handful of deer deterrents to try, but deer adapt quickly so be prepared to change tactics frequently. Try these techniques:
1. Fill nylon stockings with human hair or bars of deodorant soap, and hang them around the garden.
2. Make a smelly spray by mixing 3 eggs, 1 cup of skim milk, and 1 quart of water in the blender. Spray on plants, reapplying after rain.
3. Make a hot pepper spray by mixing 2 tablespoons of Tabasco sauce into 1 gallon of water. Spray it on garden plants, reapplying after rain.
4. Coyote urine repels deer. Put it into an empty plastic bottle with a piece of cotton rope running as a wick through a hole in the bottle. Coyote urine is available at some hardware stores, well-stocked garden centers, and from several online suppliers.

Q This year several very large hostas were eaten by deer. Other than spraying with coyote urine what can I do to ward off their destructive behavior?

A The only sure way to keep deer out of your yard is to put up an 8-foot-tall fence (left). Some gardeners have found success with repellent sprays such as Deer-Stopper, Deer-Off, Deer-Away, and Plantskydd, but not every spray works for every gardener, so it may take some trial and error. Otherwise, you can grow plants that they typically don't eat.

Check out our lists of deer-resistant plants by region at *bhg.com/deer-plants*.

Dogs

Q **I sodded my yard, but my puppy is burning holes in the lawn when she urinates. I was going to give her a food additive that is supposed to stop the burning effects on the lawn, but I was told the additive can cause bladder infections. I was advised to sprinkle lime on the spots. What's your opinion?**

A Sadly, there's not much you can do except flush the area thoroughly with water after every urination. You could create a small, fenced-in corner of the yard where you can place the puppy every time it needs to go. That and walking the dog instead of letting it run in the backyard would help. Adding lime won't. The spots happen because the urine is full of salts—and that's why flushing with water helps; the water dilutes the salts to levels that will not harm your lawn.

Q **I want a nice garden in my backyard, but it's also home to my two dogs. Are there trees and plants I can use that withstand dog traffic?**

A It's going to be hard to have a perfect-looking landscape with two dogs using the space. In general, with dogs, it's best to use shrubs instead of perennials, mulches instead of grass or groundcovers, and raised beds or planters for colorful annual flowers. Those three practices can give your garden a leg up while your dogs enjoy the yard.

Q **How do I clean up weeds in my yard without poisoning my pups?**

A If you don't mind a few stray dandelions or a patch of clover here or there, you may not need to spray at all for weeds. You may be able to keep weeds to a tolerable level by pulling them out of the lawn and mulching planting beds to prevent weeds from growing

around trees, shrubs, and perennials. A dousing with boiling water kills most weeds. (Use caution; the boiling water kills desirable grass and flowers too.)

Q **My dogs use my flowerbeds as a place to sleep. How can I prevent them from lying on the flowers?**

A The surest way to protect plantings is to separate them from your pets with a physical barrier, such as a fence. Or you could try using dog-repellent chemicals to deter your dogs. Another option is to keep your dogs in a kennel or in the house when you aren't around to supervise them. Another option is a buried electric fence that works with a collar that your dog wears. A beeping sound or a small electric shock can train your dogs to keep out of areas delineated by the buried wire.

Moles

Q We have moles in our garden. We were told that one way to get rid of them is to pour gasoline into their holes and seal them. Is this true?

A Pouring gasoline into their tunnels would pollute the groundwater and could be dangerous to you. Home remedies purported to control moles abound; none are terribly effective. You'll undoubtedly find someone who tried a remedy that "worked." In all likelihood, the moles simply moved on to better feeding grounds, and there was no connection between the supposed treatment and their disappearance.

Q Is there some kind of poison I can use to get rid of the moles in my yard?

A Moles dine on grubs and earthworms that live in the soil. Poison baits are ineffective because the moles are not attracted to the grain-based baits. Reduction of grub populations by applying a natural pest control, such as Grub-Away nematodes, may force the moles to move elsewhere. But it may also cause them to dig with renewed energy to find grubs to feed on. A proven mole repellent is castor-bean oil, in liquid or dry form. Liquid Fence makes a mole repellent in the shape of a worm that you can place in the mole tunnels.

Q I have moles in my lawn. If I control the grubs in my lawn, will the moles leave?

A It's a common misconception that controlling grub populations will get rid of moles. Moles do eat grubs, but the No. 1 food source of moles is earthworms. Moles will eat almost any insect larva they come across while digging through the soil. Rather than assuming that grubs are to blame because you see moles digging in the lawn, check to see how many grubs are present. Unless your lawn has more than 10 grubs per square foot, chemical treatment for grubs is likely unnecessary.

Q Do traps really work to get rid of moles?

A Trapping is the most effective means of ridding your yard of moles. It can be a tricky process because the traps must be set in an active runway. If the mole fails to trip the trap within a couple days of your setting it, move it to a different runway. You can determine which runways are active by stepping down on the raised ridges created by the moles. They'll tunnel through active runways and raise the ridge again.

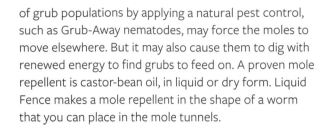

Q Something is digging in my garden and destroying my bulbs. I think that it might be a mole. How can I tell?

A Moles are dark gray with blue-black or brown tones, although you're unlikely to see them because they spend virtually all of their time belowground. They're built for digging with a long, pointy snout; narrow, slitlike eyes; large padded feet with cupped claws; and a short, virtually hairless tail. Moles are insect eaters, feasting on grubs or worms. Although they're often accused of gobbling bulbs, they aren't the guilty party—it's voles that gorge on bulbs and perennials, eating them from belowground. Chipmunks and squirrels also eat bulbs, but they dig them up before devouring them.

Q I have mole tunnels just about everywhere in our lawn and flowerbeds. Is there a natural way to get rid of the moles? I don't want to use chemicals because I have a dog and a creek in our backyard.

A Products containing castor-bean oil are proven repellents to moles. They don't kill the moles, but drive them away. Most last for about 90 days. Some are applied as a spray. Liquid Fence company also makes a bait in the shape of earthworms that are made to be stuck down in the mole tunnels.

Q How can I rid my garden and yard from pesky moles?

A Patience is often the best solution for moles. These carnivores are in your garden to dine on earthworms. As the weather warms and the soil dries, the worms go deeper into the earth. The moles follow them to the lower depths, and surface damage will be less likely. If you can't wait it out, mole traps or repellents containing castor-bean oil are effective.

Q Moles are invading my gardens. They have eaten my iris rhizomes and the bark off some of the shrubs. Last year they tunneled under and ate my carrots. Any suggestions?

A It's doubtful that moles are causing these problems in your garden. Moles are carnivores that dine almost exclusively on earthworms and grubs. They do not damage plants or eat them. It's likely you might have voles, which are a form of field mice that often use mole tunnels to get around safely. To eradicate voles, you can use mousetraps or any product designed to kill or eliminate mice. For moles, you can use a repellent product containing castor-bean oil.

Rabbits

Q Rabbits gnawed on my shrubs this winter. Will my plants be all right?

A If the shrubs are the type that send up new shoots from the root system, I wouldn't worry because new stems will come up regardless of rabbit damage to them. Remove the damaged stems at ground level, and let the new shoots take over. If, however, your shrubs are the type that don't send up new stems, and the rabbits ate off the bark all around the stems, the girdled shoots will die. Cut back the girdled stems to just below the injury. Most deciduous shrubs will send out new growth below the cut.

Q Rabbits are eating my perennials as soon as the plants come up. How can I keep these pests away?

A The best defense against rabbits is a 3-foot-tall chicken-wire fence (1-inch mesh or smaller) with another 6 inches buried in the soil. Or you can try odor repellents such as blood meal or fox urine. These usually need to be reapplied frequently. Spray-on taste repellents such as hot pepper spray are also available. It must be put directly on the plants, so rabbits get a good taste of it when they settle in for their snack. It also needs to be reapplied periodically.

Q Can I use mothballs to keep rabbits out of my garden?

A Many gardeners seem to think that mothballs must be a safe rabbit repellent to use in the garden because they can use the product in their home. These products are not natural; they are toxic pesticides labeled for use only indoors. Their specific purpose is to repel moths, not to deter rabbits.

Q I have a sunny yard and am looking for drought resistant perennials that are also rabbit resistant. I already have lots of daylillies and lavender, as well as salvia. What else would you suggest?

A If they're hungry enough, rabbits will eat anything, but here are some additional perennials to try: bear's breeches, yarrow, artemesia, campanula, Jupiter's beard, snow-in-summer, foxglove, purple coneflower, tansy, iris, beebalm, beardtongue, santolina, scabiosa, and lamb's-ears.

Rabbits

Q Are there any plants that bunnies won't eat? They ate every perennial and shrub I planted last year.

A Rabbits usually avoid plants with hairy leaves or ones that are poisonous. Here is a short list to get you started: 1. American holly, 2. Butterfly bush, 3. Forsythia, 4. Juniper, 5. Chives, 6. Pine, 7. Deadnettle, 8. Spruce, 9. Thyme, and 10. Wintercreeper euonymus.

Squirrels

Q Help! I have 30 or 40 tulips planted in my yard. Every time they produce buds, squirrels bite them off. How can I stop them?

A To defeat squirrels, your options are repellents or traps. To protect your tulip buds, use a taste repellent such as hot-pepper wax spray. You may still lose a few tulip buds, because the squirrels don't smell the hot pepper; they have to taste it for it to be effective. Look for squirrel repellents at local garden centers and pet stores or from mail-order companies. In some areas you may be able to live-trap the squirrels and move them to a local park or greenbelt area. Check with your state conservation department about the legality of live-trapping.

Q The squirrels in my yard chew on everything, from gnawing off maple twigs to chewing up my deck and birdfeeders. What can I do?

A Squirrels are rodents. When there is a shortage of acorns, other nuts, or tree bark to chew on, squirrels may revert to gnawing on other hard objects such as the siding on your house or your deck or birdfeeder. You may be able to keep them at bay by covering their favored chewing sites with metal flashing or hardware cloth. Squirrels gnawing on branch tips in spring is usually a temporary phenomenon. They feed on the expanding buds and lap up the nutrient-rich sap from the wounds they make. Once the tree is fully leafed out, they move on to a different food source.

Q Squirrels are eating my ginger. They attack before the plants get aboveground. Spraying around the roots seems useless. What should I try next?

A Because you know that squirrels like your ginger, your best bet is to keep it out of their reach. To do this, build a chicken-wire or hardware-cloth cage (with ½-inch mesh or smaller) around the plants. Squirrels won't think twice about climbing inside to dig for what they want, so cut a piece of mesh to fit over the top of the cage as well.

Q How can I keep squirrels out of my flowerbeds? They are digging in my planters and eating my hostas.

A First, make sure that there are no birdfeeders around where they can get food. For planting beds, cover the surface of the soil with chicken-wire mesh so that growth comes through the holes. Sometimes putting a layer of gravel over bulbs deters digging. You can also spray squirrel repellents around your plants, although these must be reapplied after rain.

Voles

Q **Last year voles burrowed under my perennials, feasted on the roots, and ate the new growth above the soil. I caught some with mousetraps placed throughout my garden, but it seemed like a futile attempt. Do you have any suggestions for getting rid of them?**

A The best way to control voles is to use traps. Peanut butter alone or mixed with oatmeal lures these chewing rodents effectively. Dry or liquid castor oil treatments will repel voles. Snakes and owls prey upon voles. Depending on where you garden, you might consider hanging an owl nest box or adding a snake to your garden.

Q **I saw something that looked like a mouse in my garden, but someone said it probably was a vole. How can I tell the difference?**

A Voles are about the color and size of mice but have a shorter tail. The rodent you saw in your garden is most likely a vole rather than a mouse. They speed along the earth through established runways in grass, mulch, or groundcovers, as well as burrow belowground. Accurate identification may not be important. You can control either pest with mousetraps.

Q **After the snow melted this spring, I saw trails all over the lawn. What caused this?**

A Voles create runways (above right) at the soil surface under the cover of snow. They also gnaw on the bark of trees and shrubs, often girdling them at the soil line. You can protect individual plants or beds by putting up a fence of ¼-inch-mesh hardware cloth buried 1 foot into the ground (to prevent them from tunneling underneath) and extending 1 foot above the ground. Keep your garden free of grassy areas and hay or leaf mulch, which provide hiding and breeding places for the voles. Tunnels in the lawn usually fill in quickly when the grass begins growth in the spring.

Woodchucks

Q **How do I stop woodchucks from eating my flowers and plants?**

A Your best bet for deterring woodchucks, also known as groundhogs, is to make them find a better place to live than your yard. There are several odor repellents formulated for woodchucks. You could fence your garden with chicken wire, which must be buried 12 inches below the ground and extend at least 3 feet above the ground. Leave the top part of the fence unattached to posts so it will bend outward if woodchucks try to climb it. Another solution is to get a dog that likes to chase woodchucks.

plant, the entire plant (including the roots) will be affected. Common systemic herbicides include 2,4-D and glyphosate (Roundup). "Preemergent" means that the herbicide must be in place before the weed begins to grow to be effective. Most crabgrass preventers are pre-emergent herbicides.

Q Is there a good, safe weed killer that I can use to kill an overgrown bed of weeds?

A Safe is a relative term. Glyphosate (Roundup) herbicide will control most weeds and not harm your soil. It's a systemic herbicide that goes through the plants' foliage into the roots and kills the plant without leaving residue in the soil. (It has no soil activity.) On really tall, tough plants like thistles you may have to spray several times. Use caution around any plants that you'd like to save. Glyphosate is nonselective, meaning it will kill any green plant that it contacts.

Herbicides

Q What kinds of precautions do I need to follow when spraying weed killer around the plants in my garden?

A Protect nearby plants. Always wait for warm, still weather with no rain forecast in the next day to spray. Spot treat in tight places. For best results, mix a small amount of herbicide. Add a few drops of dishwashing liquid to help the mixture adhere to the leaves. Use a small paintbrush or sponge to dab it directly onto the plants you want to kill.

Q I'm confused by some of the terms I hear related to week killers. What do systemic and preemergent mean?

A Systemic means that the herbicide moves through the plant, so if you spray it on one part of the

Weed Control

Q **Can I use tar paper and old roofing shingles to keep weeds and grass from growing in my garden?**

A Although both products you mention are effective in blocking out light and holding down weed growth, I advise against using these materials because they can contain chemicals that leach into the ground and adversely affect your plants. Instead, use sheets of newspaper covered with mulch, or landscape fabric. Even old carpet strips are a safer alternative.

Q **I seem to be fighting a losing battle against the weeds in my garden. What can I do to keep the weeds out?**

A Mulch covers open spaces and discourages weeds. But even with mulch, every garden has weeds. Here are some tips to win the war against them:
1. Weed early and often, and avoid letting weeds become mature enough to bear seeds.
2. Pull weeds when the soil is moist. When the soil is dry, use a sharp hoe to slice them off.
3. Keep weed seeds from sprouting by applying preemergence herbicides.
4. Till soil as little as possible because working the soil pulls weed seeds to the surface.

Q **Each spring I discover that my flowerbeds have sprouted a bed of weeds. What can I do to prevent this?**

A Keep your bed of flowers from becoming a bed of weeds by topping the garden with a layer of mulch and by weeding it often. Finely shredded organic matter is one of the best mulches for flowerbeds. Other good choices include shredded pine bark, wood chips, pine straw, and cocoa-bean hulls. Spread a 1- to 3-inch-deep layer of mulch over the bed. Keep it a few inches away from plant stems.

Q **I start the garden year with good intentions, but by midsummer the weeds have taken over. How can I keep them from getting the upper hand?**

A Handweeding sounds worse than it really is. Dedicate yourself to 10 minutes of weeding two or three times a week. You'll be amazed at the large area you can cover in such a short time. Don't allow the weeds to get ahead of you. Take frequent strolls through the garden to enjoy the flowers. At the same time pull a few weeds and be alert for developing pest problems. If you control weeds early in the season, you'll have little trouble by midsummer.

Broadleaf Weeds

Q When we moved here, a vine with leaves shaped like arrowheads was growing on our chain-link fence. Each year it becomes more invasive, wrapping itself around my perennials and spreading through the ground. Could you help us stop this monster?

A To get rid of bindweed, allow the plants to grow about 6 inches high, then cut them down. Repeat throughout the entire growing season. This procedure forces the plants to exhaust the food reserves they hold in their roots. Late in summer, treat surviving bindweed with a herbicide. Bindweed also grows from seeds, which can remain viable for 50 years. Consistent weeding and the generous use of mulches are the only ways to achieve good long-term control.

Q How can I kill lawn ivy?

A Lawn ivy, also known as creeping Charlie, is difficult to control. Broadleaf weed killer will knock it back, but it usually requires two applications. Another option is a home remedy using 20 Mule Team borax treatment. Dissolve 10 ounces of Twenty Mule Team Borax into 4 ounces of warm water, then dilute it in 2½ gallons of water. Spray the solution evenly over 1,000 square feet of lawn. Treat your lawn with borax no more than once every two years. Even a slight overdose can make your soil toxic to plants. If you find small amounts invading an area, pull it before it gets out of control.

Check out our online weed identification guide at bhg.com/weeds.

Q How do I get rid of broadleaf weeds in my yard?

A Treat broadleaf weeds, such as dandelion, with broadleaf weed spray. Most garden centers carry broadleaf weed sprays with names such as Weed-B-Gon or Dandelion Killer. Apply the broadleaf weed spray in spring or fall when temperatures are moderate and weeds and grass are actively growing. Weed preventers often include broadleaf weeds on their labels, and they will prevent new seeds from germinating, but the weed preventers will not have an effect on established plants.

Q How do I get rid of wild violets in the flower garden? I have dug them up by the roots and they still come back more prolific than before.

A Violets can be tenacious, especially in damp shade where the soil is compacted and acid. The best solution is to dig as many violets as you can and remove them, roots and all, in the spring. If any sprout afterwards, dig those out as well. Do this conscientiously for several years and you will gradually win the battle.

Q Can you advise me what to use to get rid of the white clover in my lawn?

A You'll get the best control from a liquid broadleaf weed killer with the ingredient Trimec. But consider whether you really need to control the clover. In years past, white clover was a common ingredient in grass seed mixes. You don't have to eradicate it to have a beautiful, lush green lawn. In fact, the clover fixes nitrogen in the soil, so you can reduce the amount of fertilizer you apply to the lawn. And the clover in the lawn may prevent rabbits from harming your flowers; clover is one of their favorite foods.

Q For the past two years, my garden has had an orange vinelike weed that starts in midsummer in my coreopsis and then spreads. I have tried to see where the vine grows from but have not found a stem that goes into the ground. Please help.

A The weed that you describe is dodder, an annual parasitic plant that derives its nourishment from other plants. Once the dodder has attached itself to the host plant you cannot remove it. You can cut it out by removing it and the host plant, but because seeds can lie dormant in the soil for several years, the problem likely will return in the future. A preemergent herbicide containing DCPA (Dacthal) or trifluraline (Treflan) is fairly effective in preventing germination. (Make certain that the perennials you use the herbicide near are on the label.) Watch for signs of the vining stems and remove them before they have a chance to flower and set seed.

Q I moved to a new home, and my yard is covered with thistles. I regularly mow them, but they seem to be spreading rapidly. What can I do?

A Some people dig up thistles. This rarely works because any small piece of the root that is left in the ground will send up a new shoot. Regular mowing is easier and more effective than the backbreaking work of digging up the taprooted growers. Alternatively, cut the thistle at ground level with a sharp knife. If you do this consistently (every few weeks), the thistle roots will be exhausted and cease to sprout new shoots. If you have a lot of thistles, you may need to apply repeat applications of a broadleaf weed killer.

Q What can I do about crown vetch, which is a real problem in my yard?

A Crown vetch is often used as a groundcover on steep roadside banks. Although it may serve a good purpose along a roadside, in a backyard it can become invasive. Spray it with glyphosate (Roundup) if possible. It may take repeat applications to kill the extensive taproot of this legume. Otherwise, keep pulling it. I planted one plant 10 years ago and am still finding stragglers trying to survive in my garden.

Grassy Weeds

Q **Crabgrass has invaded my flowerbeds. It looks terrible. Should I start from scratch by removing the existing plants, or can I get rid of the crabgrass with a weed killer?**

A The first step you should take is to confirm that the grass growing in your flower beds is crabgrass. Grasses can be tricky to identify, so consult an expert at a garden center, nursery, or cooperative extension office if you aren't certain. It's important to know whether the grass in your flowerbeds is a perennial or an annual. If it is crabgrass, the plants growing now will die when freezing temperatures arrive. However, it's still a good idea to remove the plants because they'll set seed and come back even stronger as new plants next year. Crabgrass sprouts best in bare soil. By covering the soil with mulch, you'll prevent many seeds from germinating.

Q **I have some crabgrass in my yard. I tried some weed killers, but they only turn the grass brown. Can you help?**

A Crabgrass (below left) is a warm-season annual grass that isn't evident in the lawn until mid- to late summer. If you see a rough-looking grass in the lawn in spring, it must be some type of perennial grass. While you can apply crabgrass preventer in early to midspring to prevent its growth later in the year, there are no selective controls for weedy perennial grasses. Products labeled for spraying on existing crabgrass are much less effective than preemergence controls. As you note, they may simply cause browning of the weed rather than killing it.

Q **Last year I dug and dug many onion grass bulbs out of my flowerbeds. This year they have returned with a vengeance. Is there any way to get rid of these?**

A Wild onion is difficult to control, especially in a groundcover bed where no selective herbicide is labelled for use. The seeds and bulblets of wild onion can lie dormant for several years, so even if you get rid of all that are present, they likely will resprout. In a lawn you can use a combination herbicide that contains 2,4-D, MCPP, and dicamba, but this product should not be used around trees and shrubs. If you decide to start over in the infested area, spray the entire area with Roundup, wait several weeks for new bulbs to sprout, and spray again.

Q **Is it possible to get rid of nutgrass growing in my lawn?**

A Nutgrass, also known as nutsedge, has grassy foliage but is not a true grass. If you're persistent, pulling out all new shoots you see every couple weeks, you may be able to get rid of a small patch of nutsedge in your lawn by hand-pulling. For herbicide options, look for products with "nutgrass killer" in their name. Often, nutgrass becomes a problem because of poor drainage. If this is the case, you may be able to discourage it by improving the drainage and drying out the site.

Q **Our beautiful bluegrass-sodded lawn is being taken over by a trailing grass, perhaps zoysiagrass. Is there any way to eliminate it without destroying the good turf?**

A If you have a weedy, creeping grass in your bluegrass lawn, you have no good options. It really doesn't matter whether the weedy grass is zoysiagrass, Bermudagrass, creeping bentgrass, or some similar rogue grass. The only way to truly get rid of the undesirable grass is to kill the entire infested patch with glyphosate (Roundup), then reseed or resod the affected area. Treat only the undesirable grass; glyphosate kills bluegrass too. But it leaves no residue in the soil, so you can replant quickly after the weedy grass dies.

Q **I have quackgrass in my yard that invades my flowerbeds. How do I eradicate it?**

A Any digging or disturbance of the area in which quackgrass grows only breaks up the runners into smaller pieces, each of which can start a new quackgrass plant! In my experience, a nonselective herbicide such as glyphosate (Roundup) is the best solution for removing quackgrass. It often takes a couple applications. The first one kills back the top growth and most of the roots, but usually additional shoots of quackgrass appear several weeks later. Once the new shoots are 6 to 8 inches tall, hit them with glyphosate again. This type of persistence will usually get rid of the quackgrass.

Q **Is there any way to get rid of wiregrass? We seem to have an abundance of it in our flowerbeds, and no matter how many times I weed, it continues to come back.**

A Wiregrass is another name for Bermudagrass. It can spread rapidly by underground rhizomes. If digging is ineffective, you could apply Roundup with a paintbrush so you touch only the grass and not your flowers. (Roundup will kill your flowers, too, if it comes into contact with them.) A second or third application often is needed to kill wiregrass.

Q **Is there a way to rid my yard of crabgrass organically?**

A Corn gluten is a preemergent herbicide that suppresses many weeds by killing germinating seedlings. It won't have any effect on weeds that are already present. If you have weeds already growing that you're trying to get rid of, you'll likely need to spot treat with a nonselective herbicide. Concentrated acetic acid (a more potent form of vinegar) will burn back weeds, but it also kills grasses that it comes into contact with. Of course, pulling weeds by hand is also an organic control.

Poison Ivy

Q **Poison ivy is growing on my trees and in my shrub border. What's the best way to get rid of it?**

A You can get rid of poison ivy by handpulling (wear gloves, a long-sleeve shirt, and pants to prevent skin contact) or digging out the roots. Make certain you get the entire root, or it will resprout. If you're particularly sensitive to poison ivy, avoid this method because the chemical that causes skin irritation is present in all parts of the plant. Vines growing on trees can be difficult to pull out. Cut the vine at its base and carefully remove it from the tree. Apply glyphosate (Roundup) or triclopyr to new shoots that emerge from the base of the old plant. Repeat applications of herbicide are usually necessary for complete control.

Q **I got a rash after working out in the yard. How can I tell if it was poison ivy?**

A Poison ivy can be identified by its compound leaf consisting of three leaflets. The leaflets are 2 to 4 inches long with pointed tips. The plant grows as a shrub or as a woody vine. In late summer, the plant may produce waxy grayish-white berries. In fall, leaves turn red or orange. If you come in contact with poison ivy, wash with soap and cool water immediately. Avoid burning the poison ivy vines you remove. Breathing the smoke or coming in contact with tainted clothing can cause a rash. Many nonprescription poison ivy relief products are available at drugstores, but you don't want to have to use them if you can avoid it.

Brush Control

Q **How do I get rid of the briars and brush that keep popping up all over my property?**

A Get quick results by using a brush-killer herbicide. Follow label directions carefully. If there are relatively few plants to remove, cut off the brush at ground level, then apply the herbicide to the stumps, particularly the open wounds.

Q **I'm having a problem with invasive ivy. It grows through the neighbor's chain-link fence, onto our lawn, and up the back wall of our brick garage. The space between our garage and the fence is very narrow and difficult to access. How do I kill the ivy on my garage?**

A If you slice through the stems with a sharp spade at the fence line, you can use a brush killer on the stems that encroach on your garage without killing everything on your neighbor's property. Follow application directions for the brush killer carefully, and avoid applying it to the soil. If the space between the fence and the garage is quite narrow, you may want to consider putting down gravel or pavers so that the ivy can't root in on your side of the fence. Then, when it does send out shoots onto your property, it will be easier to trim them off before they attach to the garage.

Poisonous Plants

Q I have small children and two dogs. I don't want any poisonous plants in my yard. Which ones should I avoid?

A This list is only a start, but here are some common poisonous landscape plants that you may wish to avoid planting:
1. Rhododendron, 2. Wisteria, 3. Castor bean, 4. Cherry, 5. Foxglove, 6. Datura, 7. Lantana, 8. Larkspur, 9. Oleander, and 10. Yew.

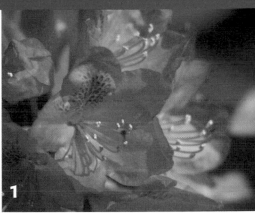

1

2

3

4

5

6

7

8

9

10

Invasive Plants

Q I don't want to plant anything in my yard that will become invasive. How can I find out if a plant I want to grow might become invasive?

A Whenever a plant seems to like your yard a little too well, begin to control it early, before its high spirits become a headache. Better yet, check a plant's invasive reputation before adding it to your landscape. One of the best websites for this information is *invasive.org*, where you can search for invasive plants by their name or the state where they are a problem. Some plants that are well-behaved in certain regions may be problematic in others.

Q I have garlic mustard everywhere on my property. How can I control it?

A Garlic mustard is an invasive weed throughout much of the Midwest and Northeast. Cut off flowering stalks before they go to seed to prevent the plant from spreading seed and to break its biennial life cycle. Remove the cut stems from the site because cut stalks sometimes mature their developing seeds. After several years of cutting, you should have your patch of garlic mustard under control. Of course, you'll need the cooperation of neighbors, too, if garlic mustard is growing on their properties.

Q I have a tall plant that's come up in my garden. It's now blooming with purple flowers. I fear that it may be purple loosestrife. What should I do about this plant?

A If you identify your plant as purple loosestrife (below), dig it out and destroy it. In addition to a stout taproot, expect to find a network of shallow roots spreading from the primary plant. If the plant in your garden is holding seeds, place a paper or plastic bag completely over the seed-bearing spikes and clip them off before you begin digging, to prevent accidentally spreading seeds.

Q I have a problem with invasive porcelain berry, blackberry, raspberry, and mint. How do I regain control?

A Blackberry and raspberry spread by canes, so you can usually keep them under control by digging and/or pruning out the unwanted shoots. Mint spreads by runners, so it needs to be kept confined in a container. Porcelain berry spreads not only by vining, but also by seedling berries. So until the main vine is removed, you'll have a constant source of new plants. It may be best to kill them all off with a nonselective herbicide.

Gardening Basics

Compost

Q **I've had a large compost bin for two years. The pile is composting, but slowly. How can I speed up the process?**

A Add thin layers of topsoil or finished compost to your pile to introduce microorganisms that create compost. Water enough to keep it moist but not soggy. Turn your compost regularly to keep it aerated. If that doesn't produce compost as quickly as you desire, turn the pile more often, add more nitrogen-rich (green) materials, and shred or chop the carbon-rich (brown) materials before adding them to the pile.

Q **I've been advised to locate my compost pile in a shady area. I always assumed a compost pile should be located in a sunny area. What do you recommend?**

A Compost piles usually work best if they are located in sunny spots. (They warm up faster and stay warmer than shaded ones.) However, if you live in a dry climate or are unlikely to water your pile during dry periods, it's a good idea to locate your pile in at least partial shade to keep it from drying out too quickly or too much.

Q **I'd like to compost my garden waste but don't know much about it. How do I get started?**

A Compost is a mix of high-carbon and high-nitrogen materials combined proportionately with soil, air, and moisture. Carbon-rich materials include straw, hay, leaves, sawdust, shredded newspaper, and pine needles. Nitrogen-rich materials are generally succulent green plant parts, such as grass clippings, weeds, perennial flower prunings, and vegetables. Kitchen scraps, such as eggshells (rinse them first), vegetables and fruits, and coffee grounds, can also be added. Avoid adding meat scraps, bones, or grease.

Q **Will composting kill diseases that have infected plants in my garden?**

A There is a debate about adding diseased plants, or weeds with seedheads, to compost. Some experts think that the heat of a properly working compost pile will kill the diseases and seeds. Others doubt it's worth the risk. To be safe, avoid using such materials in your compost pile.

Q **When should I add compost to my perennial garden?**

A The best time to add compost to a perennial garden is before you plant anything in the garden. This allows you to work the compost into the soil where it does some good. You can also add compost when you divide or transplant your perennials. Work some into each planting hole. You can spread a thin layer of compost over the entire garden in late fall.

Q I am interested in different styles of compost bins that are easy to construct. I want to make one and need some designs to choose from. What would you suggest?

A You can make a compost bin from just about anything. One consideration, though, is how important it is for your compost bin to look attractive. If it's in full view of the deck, you may want to spend a little more cash to build a state-of-the-art bin. Here are some suggestions:

1. Wrap snow fencing around a square of metal stakes.
2. Stack concrete blocks in a square several feet high.
3. Stand four pallets on end and wire them together.
4. Make a ring of woven wire fencing.

Q Can I speed up the decomposition of the autumn leaves from my yard so the compost will be ready in spring?

A Fallen tree leaves need to be mixed with high-nitrogen materials to break down quickly. You can add a nitrogen fertilizer or manure if you don't have enough "greens" on hand. Compost needs warmth to break down yard waste. As temperatures cool off in fall, the heat will have to be generated from within the compost pile. That means active management of the pile on your part. Turn the pile weekly to mix the browns and the greens, and to move the colder outer layers to the warmer interior of the pile. The leaves will compost if left alone. It just takes longer.

Q Composting seems like a lot of work. Is there an easy way to do it?

A As some gardeners say, "Compost happens." If you don't want to go to the trouble of layering browns and greens or mixing and watering, you can simply pile your yard waste in an inconspicuous spot and let nature take its course. The organic matter will eventually break down into compost. It may take a several years rather than several months. But if you're patient, you can get wonderful finished compost with this laissez-faire method.

Mulch

Q The builder landscaped our new home, sodding the front lawn and planting various perennials and shrubs. The plants are surrounded by mulch. About a week ago, I saw two foamy yellow piles on the mulch. What is it and how do I get rid of it?

A It sounds as though you have a slime mold (below) growing on your wood mulch. Slime mold generally develops when moisture is plentiful. There's not much you need to do except cut back on the moisture a bit. Luckily, the fungus won't harm anything, and it will disappear on its own when the weather warms up and dries out.

Q What type of mulch—cypress, pine, or hardwood—is best to use on our perennial beds? The mulch will be against our foundation.

A Any organic mulch will work well in your perennial beds, including shredded bark or leaves, cocoa bean

hulls, and pine needles. Keep the mulch a few inches from your foundation to deprive small rodents of a place to call home. Whatever mulch you use, be sure to put down a layer 2 to 4 inches thick. If you use less than that, weeds may still grow through it; if you use too much mulch, you may restrict the amount of oxygen getting to the plants' roots. Replenish mulch every year or two as it decomposes.

Q One landscaper touts mulch as a panacea for garden problems. Another says that although it helps in some areas, it can be as bad as it is good. Who should I listen to?

A Mulch discourages weeds, adds nutrients to the soil, and protects tender plants during cold winter months. Mulch creates a perfect haven for earthworms, which love to slither through the stuff, aerating the area and leaving behind soil-enriching castings. But the mulch also may harbor slugs and snails, which love to eat the luscious plants that grow up through the mulch. You may have to put out slug traps to contain the additional pests that can come with the use of mulch.

Q How do I know how much mulch to use? Is there a formula?

A Spread most mulches 2 to 4 inches deep. Bulk mulch is sold in cubic yards. To determine the number of cubic yards you'll need, divide the number of cubic feet you need by 27. As an example, if you have a 20×25-foot garden you want to cover with mulch to 4 inches deep, multiply 20 feet by 25 feet by 0.33 feet (4 inches is one-third of a foot). This gives you 165 cubic feet; divide that by 27 to get about 6 cubic yards. Another way to think of it is that a 2-cubic-foot bag will cover 8 square feet about 3 inches deep.

Q I've heard conflicting information regarding grass clippings. I used clippings as mulch. Some people say it may give the plants a disease. Is this correct?

A You can use grass clippings as mulch (right), but be aware of a few things. If you put down fresh grass clippings in a layer more than 2 inches deep, the clippings can form a mat that discourages air from penetrating the soil. This mat will eventually rot and smell. Make certain that the grass from which the clippings were cut has not been treated with any herbicides that might be harmful to plants.

Q I want to add a mulched cutting garden to my yard. I've read mixed reviews on the use of fabric weed barrier. I have a large birch that I do not want to lose. Will the weed barrier be a problem for the tree?

A I've had bad experiences with fabric weed barriers because weeds can grow in the mulch on top of them. These weeds are difficult to pull because their roots grow through the fabric. The product can be difficult to remove, especially once soil accumulates on top of it. Keep in mind that if you grow annuals that need replanting each year or perennial flowers that need to be divided occasionally, the fabric weed barrier will be an obstruction to digging in the bed. A more appropriate use of the weed barrier fabric is around trees and shrubs that remain in place once planted.

Q I have a garden that was covered in leaves to protect my plants through the winter. When I cleaned the bed, I noticed that my plants had started to grow even though they weren't getting light. They have yellow-white stems and leaves. Are they going to grow right?

A Although your plants may look damaged now, they're not really in serious condition—so there's little reason to worry. After a few days in the sun, your perennials should be just fine. They will color up quickly and grow normally. In the future, check for growth of perennials under the mulch a bit earlier. If left in place too long, winter mulch can smother the emerging perennials. It can also hold in excess moisture, causing them to rot.

Q When should I remove the mulch that I use to cover and protect my plants in winter?

A Remove winter mulch in late winter or early spring when you observe new growth under the mulch. Also, if you see mold developing on the plants, it's time to pull back the mulch. Keep in mind that winter mulch protects plants from sudden temperature changes, so acclimate your plants by pulling off the mulch gradually as the plants show signs of new growth. Do keep some of the mulch handy, just in case frost is predicted and you need to protect the tender new growth.

Mulch

Q **I've just planted a new tree beside the front entrance to my house. Is there any benefit to mulching around the trunk, or should I let the grass grow back?**

A A layer of mulch 2 to 4 inches deep around your newly planted tree will save water, decrease stress on the tree, and ensure that grass doesn't compete with the tree for nutrients. The ring of mulch also will keep you and your lawn mower away from the trunk and reduce nicks in the bark, which open up paths for insects and disease to get in. Keep the mulch about 3 to 4 inches from the trunk to keep rodents from hiding there and gnawing the tree bark.

Q **I added a flowerbed next to my home and mulched it with wood chips from trees. Is there a danger of termites getting under my house from the mulch?**

A Termites generally attack solid wood and leave bark mulch alone because it doesn't provide a suitable place to live or hide. Be certain to keep the mulch from directly touching siding or wood walls where termites like to dine. Keep the mulch 6 to 12 inches away from any wood structures on the home. If termites cross the wood-free zone, you'll be able to see the protective soil tubes they build. That will allow you to treat them before they become established in your home.

Q **We put down some wood-chip mulch around our foundation plantings last spring. Soon afterward I started noticing tiny black specks on the house siding. They're virtually impossible to remove. Did the mulch cause the specks? How do I get rid of them?**

A It sounds as though your mulch has developed artillery or shotgun fungus. The black specks are spore masses of the fungus. Artillery fungus has the ability to "shoot" its spores at objects such as light-colored house siding, fences, or cars. The spores stick to most surfaces and are almost impossible to remove. This fungus develops in wood-based mulches under cool, moist conditions. Cypress, cedar, redwood, and pine bark mulch seem to be resistant to the fungus.

Q **How do I decide how much mulch to buy? Where do I go to find the kinds of materials that make good mulch?**

A Here are a few guidelines to get you started: Wood mulches are sold in bags or in bulk. A 2-cubic-foot bag will cover 8 square feet about 3 inches deep. The amount of gravel needed to cover an area will vary with the size of the pebbles. Generally, a ton of rock covers 100 square feet. When buying in bulk, estimate that 1 cubic yard of material will cover 100 square feet about 3 inches deep.

Rock Garden Plants

Q **I'd like to start a rock garden. What are some good plants to try?**

A Rock garden plants require excellent drainage. Here are 10 perennials to get you started on your project: 1. Basket-of-gold, 2. Bellfower, 3. Bloody cranesbill, 4. Creeping phlox, 5. Evergreen candytuft, 6. Hen and chicks, 7. Lavender, 8. Sea thrift, 9. Sedum, and 10. Snow-in-summer.

Plants for a Sunny, Dry Yard

Q **My yard is sunny and dry. What plants would you suggest for me to grow?**

A You have many choices, particularly if you water the plants until they become established. Try these: 1. Bearded iris, 2. Blanket flower, 3. Butterfly weed, 4. Crape myrtle, 5. Japanese kerria, 6. Mugo pine, 7. Purple beautyberry, 8. Rugosa rose, 9. Sedum, and 10. Star magnolia

Q I applied cocoa-hull mulch around the birch tree on my front lawn so I wouldn't have to weed around it. Is that the best mulch? What do I do if it gets moldy?

A Cocoa bean hulls (right) are a popular, if slightly expensive, mulch that will do just fine around your birch. They tend to mat and get moldy during hot, wet weather, but that won't harm your tree, and the mold usually washes off with rain or watering. If you decide that the smell of chocolate is too enticing for your inner chocoholic, other good mulches for your birch include shredded bark, wood chips, and pine needles.

Q I've seen mulch that is made out of recycled tires. It looks like organic mulch and seems to make sense environmentally. Are there any faults to using it?

A Rubber mulches are often used in playground areas at schools, athletic fields, and parks. The sponginess of the rubber adds cushioning for falls. Drawbacks of rubber mulch include the odor and, more importantly, the fact that rubber mulch does not break down over time as organic mulches do. Because the rubber does not decompose, it would be hard to remove from the garden. That could be a problem if you need to replace any plants that die or redo the plantings.

Q Can mulch go bad? We bought some bagged mulch that had an unpleasant odor, but we used it anyway. The plants are dying back where we applied it.

A Yes, mulch may be unfit to use. If organic mulch such as wood chips decomposes without enough oxygen, anaerobic decomposition sets in. When this happens, the mulch produces alcohol and organic acids that can be toxic to plants. In addition, the pH of such

mulch can be extremely low. Anaerobic conditions usually develop in large, wet mulch piles, or in bagged mulch with water in the bag. Good mulch has a pleasant, humusy smell; anaerobic mulch has a sour smell. Fortunately, you don't need to throw out the sour mulch. Simply spread it out in a thin layer for a few days on a hard surface such as your driveway or patio. Once the smell subsides, the mulch should be safe to use.

Q My perennial bed doesn't have any earthworms. How can I encourage them?

A Start mulching with shredded leaves, and the earthworms will come. I have a corner in my garden with heavy clay that is almost like subsoil. I started a compost pile there and within a year I found hundreds of worms beneath the pile. Mulching with shredded leaves will accomplish the same thing. Also, after a good rainfall, feel free to pick up earthworms from your sidewalks and introduce them to the site.

Soil Amendments

Q How do I figure out how much lime to add to my soil?

A To determine whether your soil needs lime and how much, you need to answer these basic questions: What is the current pH of your soil? What do you want the pH to be (based on the plants you want to grow)? What is your soil type? To get this information, you'll need to have your soil tested. Contact your county extension service or a commercial soil-testing laboratory to order a soil test kit. The results will indicate whether your soil needs lime and how much to add.

Q My new garden has heavy clay soil that's difficult to dig into, and it's lumpy and clumpy. How can I improve the soil so I can plant some things to dress up my new home?

A The best and only practical way to improve clay soil is by incorporating organic matter. Compost, rotted manure, and leaf mold will eventually turn clay soil into usable soil. If you're starting a new garden, spread 2 to 3 inches of organic matter over the soil and work it into the top 6 to 8 inches. If you have existing planting beds, you may be able to dig compost into pockets around the plantings. It's a lot of work up front, but it will be worth the effort in the end.

Q I'd like to loosen up my clay soil by adding some sand to it. How much sand should I add?

A Adding sand alone to a clay soil is not a good idea. When sand and clay are mixed, the smaller clay particles stick to the larger sand particles, creating a dense layer of soil that's something like concrete. If you get the right combination of sand and clay, you'll end up with adobe bricks. It's a much better idea to add organic matter—such as peat moss or compost—to a clay soil. As organic matter breaks down, it helps create larger spaces between the clay particles and enriches the soil.

Q I've heard that drywall is good for amending clay soil. How does it work? What's the best way to add it to the soil?

A Drywall (sheetrock) won't necessarily help your soil. Its main ingredient is gypsum, and gypsum is used effectively to amend soils high in sodium. Gypsum needs to be ground to a fine powder to react with the soil. Unless your clay soil has a lot of salt in it, though, the gypsum will be of little use in improving the soil.

Plants for Sandy Soil

Q The soil in my area is sandy. I'd like ideas for plants in my sunny yard. Are there any plants that will thrive here?

A Here are some plants that grow well in sandy sites: 1. Butterfly bush, 2. Juniper, 3. Flowering quince, 4. Japanese barberry, 5. Japanese pittosporum, 6. Kerria, 7. Santolina, 8. Bayberry, 9. Pomegranate, and 10. Trailing lantana.

Raised Beds

Q I've been told it's good to garden in raised beds. Why are they better?

A Raised beds provide better drainage and earlier warming in spring. Better drainage means less likelihood of root rots developing. In the case of vegetables, more plants can be grown in a smaller area than with conventional row-cropping techniques because no space is needed between rows. Another good thing about raised beds is that no one walks on them, so the soil never becomes compacted and tilling the soil each season is easier to do. For gardeners with limited mobility, raised beds can be built to any height, so less bending and reaching are needed to work with the plants.

Q I'd like to try gardening in a raised bed. What's the best way to make one, and what do I use to make it?

A Wood is commonly used to make raised beds. It is easy to work with and attractive. If you plan to grow edible plants, and are concerned about the safety of treated wood, use a naturally rot-resistant wood, such as red cedar, black locust, or redwood. Under most

circumstances, rot-resistant woods will last 10 to 15 years. Four feet wide is convenient, because lumber is readily available in 4-foot lengths; with this width, the center of the bed is easily accessible from either side. If the bed will be accessible only from one side, limit the width to 3 feet. As for depth, most plants need at least a 6- to 12-inch root zone, but even deeper is better. Fill the raised bed with topsoil and compost, and garden away!

Q I'm preparing to landscape my backyard, which has rock-filled clay soil. Is there a good way to improve the soil? Do I need to sift it, remove all the rocks, then add topsoil? Is there anything I can add to the existing clay that will enable me to grow a wide variety of plants?

A Though it would be a big job, the best thing would be to dig out and replace some of the rocky clay soil with fresh topsoil. As another option, you could build raised beds or berms to plant in and simply cover the soil's surface with about 1 foot of fresh topsoil mixed with organic matter. If adding loads of soil isn't an option, you'll have to rake or pull the stones. Once you have removed enough of the stones to easily work the soil, amend it liberally with organic matter (such as compost) to loosen the clay.

Q What is double digging? Does it help plants to grow better?

A With double digging, you remove the top 12 inches of soil (or the depth of a garden spade), set it aside, then loosen the next layer of soil. If you like, add and mix in several inches of organic matter as you turn over each layer. Top off the lower layer with the amended upper layer. This is hard work; it helps if you have a strong back. You can get some of the same benefits with less digging by building raised beds.

Plants for Clay Soil

Q **My yard consists of heavy clay. What will grow well in this nasty stuff?**

A These plants will thrive in clay soil: 1. Bur oak, 2. Potentilla, 3. Callery pear, 4. Lilac, 5. Obedient plant, 6. Peony, 7. River birch, 8. Forsythia, 9. Viburnum, and 10. Red-osier dogwood.

Fertilizers

Q A soil test revealed that my garden soil is alkaline (pH 8.0) and low in nitrogen and phosphorus. What do I need to do to fix it?

A Most plants grow best in soil with a pH of about 6.5. To lower your soil's pH, use a soil acidifier, such as soil sulfur or ammonium sulfate. Follow the directions on the package. Adding organic matter to your soil will increase nitrogen levels. Another way to increase them is by adding ammonium sulfate or any granular fertilizer containing nitrogen in the form of nitrate or ammonium. Phosphorus is more stable in the soil. To increase the phosphorus level, add superphosphate, rock phosphate, or bonemeal.

Q I read that used coffee grounds are a good fertilizer for a flower garden. Is this true?

A Coffee grounds contain a small amount of nitrogen, so they contribute nutrients to the soil. They are also slightly acidic. This is good for some soils, but not for all. I recommend composting the coffee grounds instead of just dumping them on the garden. In the absence of a compost pile, work some grounds into the soil around your acid-loving plants, such as azaleas, blueberries, and hydrangeas.

Q What's the difference between blood meal and bonemeal? Can I use them together?

A Bonemeal and blood meal are amendments that add nutrients to soil, and they can be used together. Blood meal is dried and powdered animal blood; it increases soil nitrogen levels. Bonemeal is ground animal bones; it increases soil calcium and phosphorus levels. Blood meal and bonemeal take time to break down and make their nutrients available to plants. They are quite safe to apply around plants with little danger of burning from overapplication.

Q I'd like to add some well-rotted manure to my garden. Can you tell me how much I should use?

A Because manure varies in nutrient content, and fertility needs vary from soil to soil, there's no "best" ratio for adding manure or other forms of organic matter to your garden. But generally you can spread a layer of manure about 1 or 2 inches deep over the garden in winter so that by spring the rains and snows have helped leach excess salts and ammonia. Avoid applying fresh manure directly on a garden where plants are growing because it could burn the plants. The more aged the manure, the better.

Plants for Alkaline Soil

Q The pH in our landscape is quite high—nearly 8.0. Are there some plants that will grow at this high pH?

A These plants tolerate high pH, and should do well in your yard: 1. Chinese juniper, 2. Cornelian cherry, 3. Deutzia, 4. Forsythia, 5. Fragrant sumac, 6. Golden rain tree, 7. Persian lilac, 8. Queen-of-the-prairie, 9. Russian olive, and 10. Yellowwood.

Plants for Acidic Soil

Q I know that blueberries need acidic soil to grow well. Which other plants grow well in acidic conditions?

A Here are some additional woody plants that grow well in acidic conditions: 1. Azalea, 2. Camellia, 3. Canadian hemlock, 4. Holly, 5. Japanese pieris, 6. Lupine, 7. Mountain laurel, 8. Pin oak, 9. Scotch broom, and 10. Scotch heather.

Q What do the three numbers on a fertilizer bag mean?

A All fertilizers list their nitrogen (abbreviated as N), phosphorus (P), and potassium (K) content as percentages on the label. This is called the fertilizer analysis. A 24-8-16 fertilizer contains 24 percent nitrogen, 8 percent phosphate, and 16 percent potash. The remaining 52 percent may be other minor fertilizer elements (such as iron or sulfur) or filler (carrier) for the nutrients. The percentages on the label are always listed in the order N–P–K.

Q Does it make a difference what kind of fertilizer I use on my flowers and lawn?

A Lawns generally need more nitrogen than flowers. A commonly recommended formulation is 24-8-16. You can use any fertilizer with a similar ratio even though the analysis is different. A 25–5–10 (ratio is 5:1:2) fertilizer will work as a substitute because it is also high in nitrogen. For flowers, a 10–10–10 fertilizer would be a better choice. Flowers prefer lower levels of nitrogen. You could substitute 20-20-20 or 11–8–8 fertilizer for flowers, because these ratios are also close to 1:1:1.

Q Which fertilizers are considered organic? Are they safer to use than other fertilizers?

A Organic fertilizers may be derived from plant materials (compost, alfalfa meal), from animal sources (manure, bonemeal), or from naturally occurring minerals (greensand, rock phosphate). Most release their nutrients slowly, so there is little danger of burning plants by applying excess. However, most have a low nutrient content per pound of material, so large volumes of them must be used, and they generally cost more per pound than manufactured fertilizers.

Q I know that most fertilizers contain nitrogen, phosphorus, and potassium. What do each of these do for the plant?

A In simple terms, nitrogen promotes plant growth. It is associated with leafy, vegetative growth. Nitrogen is part of the chlorophyll molecule, which gives plants their green color and is involved in creating food for the plant through photosynthesis. Phosphorus is involved in transferring energy from one point to another in the plant. It's also critical in root development and flowering. Potassium helps regulate plant metabolism and affects water pressure regulation inside and outside of plant cells. It is important for good root development. For these reasons, potassium is critical to plant stress tolerance.

Watering the Lawn

Q I don't want to water my lawn all summer, but I do want it to survive during hot, dry periods. Can I water it just part of the time?

A If you don't care about keeping your lawn lush and green all summer, lightly irrigate with ½ inch of water every 3–4 weeks to keep the roots and crowns alive. This is not enough water to stimulate new growth, but it will keep the growing points moist enough to live. Avoid the temptation to give the lawn a soaking that could spur new growth, especially if you don't intend to continue watering. It's stressful to the grass to go in and out of dormancy.

Q Are there some types of lawns that don't need watering?

A Some lawn grasses are naturally more drought-tolerant than others. Warm-season grasses such as buffalograss, Bermudagrass, and zoysiagrass need less water to thrive and survive than cool-season grasses such as fescue, Kentucky bluegrass, or ryegrass. Turf-type tall fescue and fine fescue are fairly drought-tolerant and will remain green through most summers.

Q I'm going to be starting a new lawn. How much will it need to be watered?

A Keep a newly seeded lawn moist, but not soaked, while your grass seed sprouts. Too much water can inhibit germination. A light mulch over the seed will help keep the soil damp. As the new lawn grows, reduce the frequency of watering and increase the amount of water you apply each time. After four to six weeks, treat the new lawn as an established one. Completely soak a newly sodded lawn for about two weeks after placement, watering every day or two. This will help the root system to become firmly established.

Q When is it safe to run the irrigation system on my lawn? I've heard that I shouldn't water during the middle of the day because the sunlight will burn holes in the leaves.

A It's a myth that water droplets on plant leaves will focus the sun's rays and burn holes in the leaves. You can water any time of day without harm to the plant from the sun. However, watering during the middle of the day is more wasteful than watering in the morning because warm and windy conditions cause water to evaporate quickly. Water early enough in the day that the plant dries off before nightfall. If the foliage stays wet for a long time, diseases are more likely to develop.

Q We just bought our first home. Since I'm new at yard care, could you tell me what's the best way to water the lawn on a budget?

A Water heavily at infrequent intervals. On average, a lawn needs about 1 inch of water per week, from rainfall or irrigation. This will soak the soil to a depth of 4 to 6 inches. A thorough watering takes a while, however, so be prepared to leave the water running. Pause when the water puddles or runs off the yard, and let the water soak in before starting again. Most sprinklers and sprinkling systems apply water faster than the lawn can drink it up. Water soaks in at different rates in different soil types. If you have sandy soil, it could take as little as 15 minutes for ½ inch of water to soak in. With clay, it could take 10 times longer.

Q An area in my yard gets full sun, but the soil stays wet. The grass doesn't grow well there. Is there some way to cut down on the amount of water this area gets?

A You might consider installing a French drain. This is an underground perforated pipe, surrounded by landscape fabric and stones, to help direct excess groundwater away from a site. An easier solution is to grow plants that like wet soils. Sedges are grasslike plants that could make a good lawn substitute in this wet area.

Q Are inground sprinkler systems worth their extra expense to install?

A The answer depends on where you live and the size of your lawn. In arid western climates, inground irrigation systems are a must for almost any lawn that you expect to remain green. (If you have a tiny patch of turf, less than a few hundred square feet, portable sprinklers can suffice.) In wet climates, you'll have to weigh the convenience of flipping a switch to water versus dragging out the hose. Generally, the larger your lawn, the more practical an inground irrigation system will be.

Q Is it a good idea to water the lawn a little bit every day?

A The short answer is, "No." Frequent light waterings won't soak deeply into the soil. That causes the roots to develop only in the upper inch or so of soil. Less frequent but deeper soakings will encourage deep rooting and improve the stress tolerance of your grass.

Watering Landscape Plants

Q **Do evergreens need to be watered in the fall and winter?**

A If weather conditions are dry in fall, it's a good idea to water the evergreens in your landscape to prevent winter browning. They may need another boost of water in midwinter if conditions remain dry. Water when the ground is not frozen, so the water can soak into the root zone.

Q **Should I be watering my established trees during the drought we're having? Or will they survive on their own?**

A Well-established trees and shrubs can survive long periods of dry weather without supplemental watering. But if they suffer moisture stress, they may be more susceptible to attack by diseases, insects, or other environmental stresses. Younger trees and newer plantings should be higher on your watering priority list

than established ones. However, if the leaves on your established trees begin to wilt, if you notice a change in leaf color, or if the margins of the leaves turn brown, it's time to give these trees a good soaking.

Q **I'm building a small rock garden in sandy soil, so I added peat moss and topsoil into the top 8 to 12 inches. After a thorough watering, the water runs down the slope. What did I do wrong?**

A The runoff may be due to too much peat moss, which can form a crustlike surface on the soil. For a rock garden, I would suggest adding loam to your sand and leaving it at that, because rock-garden plants prefer soil that is on the sandier side. Once your plants become established, their root systems will help hold the soil in place. Until then, you may need to rig up some sort of retaining system using additional rocks to keep the water and soil from washing down the slope. Gravel mulch around the plants also will help keep the soil in place.

Q **All directions for new-plant care say that once a plant is established, you should water less frequently. How do you know when a plant is "established"?**

A As a general rule, it takes a full year in the ground before plants are established. Even so, you'll want to keep an eye on them during the second and third years if there is a prolonged dry spell. Most perennials can easily establish themselves within one year, but trees and shrubs, especially evergreens, can be more vulnerable going into winter if you have a dry fall, for example.

Check out our online tree and shrub care guide at *bhg.com/tree-guide.*

Q Because it's been so hot and dry this summer, I've been watering the trees I planted this spring every day, but they're still wilting. How can I save my trees?

A For starters, stop watering so often! It's much better to give your trees a thorough soaking less often than to water daily. If you're wetting only the surface (water may not be soaking in as fast as you're applying it), the soil in the lower part of the root ball may be completely dry, and your trees will suffer from lack of moisture. The opposite may also be true. If you're watering enough to soak the entire root zone of the trees daily, you may be drowning your trees.

Q I recently planted a new tree. How often should I water it?

A Water the soil deeply once every four to seven days. If it's warm and windy, water more frequently. Plants that were grown in pots require more frequent watering than those that were field-grown and balled and burlapped. Cover the root zone with mulch to help hold in moisture. Continue this watering regimen for at least the first year, or until the tree's roots expand out into the surrounding soil.

Q How do I know how much to water the new trees I just planted?

A A 2-inch-diameter tree needs about 15 gallons of water per week; a 4-inch-diameter tree, about 25 gallons. Use drip irrigation, or place a hose running at a slow trickle over the root zone. If in doubt about how much water you're applying, run the hose at a trickle into a bucket to measure the flow. If it takes 10 minutes to fill a 5-gallon bucket, you'll need to leave the hose at the root zone for 30 minutes for a 2-inch tree or 50 minutes for a 4-inch tree.

Q Our city parks department has placed something around their newly planted trees. They look like big green bags filled with water. What are they for?

A The large bags that you're seeing are a form of drip irrigation for trees. Commonly they hold about 20 gallons of water that slowly drips into the root zone of the tree. You may be able to find them at garden centers or home centers. Treegator is one widely available brand. You can also rig up your own homemade drip system for trees by poking several nail holes in the bottom of a 5-gallon bucket. Place the bucket near the trunk of a newly planted tree to allow the water to slowly soak into the root zone.

Watering Food Crops

Q **Is it better to use sprinkler or drip irrigation in my vegetable garden?**

A Drip irrigation (below) works well for vegetable beds for several reasons. It's relatively low cost and easy to install. It uses less water than sprinklers. And, perhaps most significantly, it cuts down on disease problems by watering only the soil, not the foliage of garden plants.

Q **I live in the south and we are having some extremely hot weather. I hear it's best to water early in the morning. Is this good advice?**

A A couple reasons exist for watering your garden early in the morning. Generally the wind speed is less in early morning, so less water is lost to evaporation. Also, by watering early in the morning, the plants will dry off during the day, and fewer disease problems should develop.

Q **How do I get rid of the gnats that live in the dirt? I've had hundreds of gnats this year around my vegetable seedlings indoors.**

A Fungus gnats lay their eggs in potting soil, which then hatch, grow and start flying around your house. Allow the soil to dry more between waterings. You could also use Bt (*Bacillus thuringiensis israelensis*) in a liquid form. It is an organic way to rid your potting soil of the juvenile gnats. Be forewarned: It smells awful. You can also use blue or yellow sticky cards to trap the adult gnats.

Q **My tomato seedlings have white mold growing on the surface of the soil. Will this hurt them?**

A White mold often appears on the soil surface if you've been overwatering. Be sure to use a sterile, soilless seed starting mix to grow in. Those two things will help you keep this problem at bay. Your seedlings should be fine, but reduce the amount of water you apply.

Plants for Wet Sites

Q A section of my backyard is always soggy. What plants could I grow there?

A Here are some plants that grow well in constantly moist soil: 1. Calla lily, 2. Cardinal flower, 3. Creeping Jenny, 4. Elephant's ear, 5. Japanese iris, 6. Japanese primrose, 7. Ligularia, 8. Ostrich fern, 9. Pink turtlehead, and 10. Spiderwort.

Plants for Standing Water

Q We have a pond with a shallow edge. What can we grow in the water besides cattails?

A These plants will grow in shallow, standing water: 1. Bald cypress, 2. Bowles' golden sedge, 3. Dwarf papyrus, 4. Giant reed, 5. Japanese sweet flag, 6. Marsh marigold, 7. Rush, 8. Taro, 9. Water lily, and 10. Yellow flag iris.

Q I'd like to catch rainwater in a rain barrel to use for watering my vegetable garden. Do I need to do anything other than direct the downspout from the roof into a barrel?

A Direct the flow of water into the barrel. It helps to use a screen over the downspout to prevent debris from washing into and collecting in the barrel. Place a tight-fitting lid on the barrel to keep out mosquitoes. Place a spigot in the lower portion of the barrel to drain the water for use in the garden. (Keep the spigot at least several inches above the bottom of the barrel to keep it from being clogged from sediment that may wash into the barrel.) An overflow pipe near the top of the barrel is a handy option. The overflow can be directed into a second barrel or simply aimed away from the house's foundation.

Q I have a big vegetable garden and have trouble keeping everything watered all the time. How often should I be watering?

A Many gardeners wait until they see their vegetables wilting before dragging out the hose. That can be a mistake. In order to remain productive, vegetables should suffer no moisture stress. That means supplying them with at least 1 inch of water per week from natural rainfall or through irrigation.

Q My potatoes were all knobby when I harvested them. Someone said it was because I didn't water enough. Is that true?

A Certain vegetables do have critical watering times at various stages of development. For potatoes, that is during tuber set and development. Lack of water at that time can, indeed, lead to knobby tubers. Other veggies and their critical stages are: Beans—pod enlargement; cucumbers—fruit enlargement; melons—flowering and fruit development; peppers—fruit set and enlargement; sweet corn—silking, tasseling, and ear development; tomatoes—flowering, fruit set, and fruit enlargement.

Water Recycling

Q Is it safe to use the water from our dehumidifier to water flowers in the garden? I'd like to conserve water if possible, but don't want to harm the plants.

A The water you collect from your dehumidifier is purer than the water from your tap. I wouldn't suggest drinking it, because bacteria could be growing in it, but it should be perfectly fine to use on your plants.

Q Can I use the rinse water from my washing machine to water plants in my landscape?

A Reusing water from the laundry, bathing, or sinks seems like an efficient way to recycle water. However, there are some drawbacks. All these sources of recycled water contain bacteria that may pose health problems. For this reason, most states regulate the use of these sources of water, called gray water. Check with local or state health authorities for the requirements in your area. You may need to install a filtration or settling system before you can use the gray water. Never apply it to edible crops; use it only on ornamentals. Using gray water can lead to significant water savings, but make certain that you do it right and follow the rules.

Water Quality

Q Is it OK to use softened water to water my plants?

A Softened water contains salts, which are not good for plants. Use unsoftened water for irrigating and watering plants. Usually water for outdoor hydrants bypasses the softening process. If you're using an indoor water source to fill watering cans, make sure that it also bypasses the softener.

Q Is it better to use rainwater or tap water for watering my container gardens?

A Rainwater is almost always better for plants than water from the tap. Even if your tap water is unsoftened (*see above*), it may contain chlorine, which can damage plants. Or it may have a high pH, which can lead to micronutrient deficiencies, especially in plants grown in containers with soilless mixes.

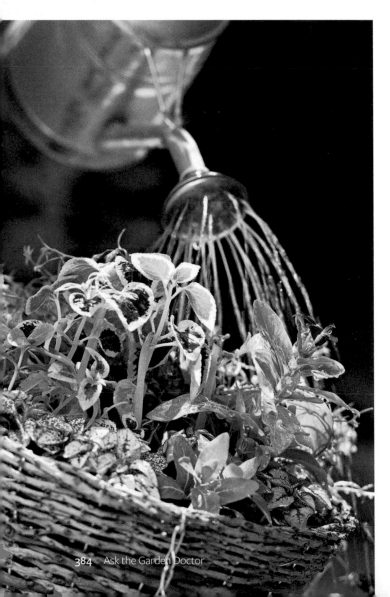

Rain Garden

Q I know that rain gardens are a good way to prevent runoff. What plants can be grown in a rain garden?

A Use plants adapted to periodic wet conditions. Here are some that work well: 1. Canna, 2. Obedient plant, 3. Calla lily, 4. Corkscrew rush, 5. Cardinal flower, 6. Prairie smoke, 7. False indigo, 8. Sedge, 9. New England aster, and 10. Switchgrass.

Sunscald & Sunburn

Q **My Japanese maple tree has a dead patch of bark on the trunk. Can I save the tree?**

A If the dead patch of bark is on the south or southwest side of the tree, it's likely that your Japanese maple was damaged by sunscald. Once the bark is injured, there is little you can do. Remove any loose bark, which may harbor insects or trap moisture underneath it. To prevent the problem from developing, wrap the trunk of newly planted trees over the winter with tree wrap, or paint the trunk with white latex paint to reflect the sun's rays. Remove the wrap during the spring and summer months.

Q **Can plants get sunburned?**

A Yes, although the process isn't quite the same as the sunburn you get on your first day at the beach each summer. Leaves (and stems) of plants adapt to the light level in which they are grown. On plants grown indoors, the leaf size, leaf thickness, and chlorophyll content will be much different from on the same type of plant grown in brighter light outdoors. If the plant is suddenly moved to brighter

light, leaves may become bleached or burned from excess sun. Prevent sunburn on your plants by gradually moving them to brighter light over a period of two weeks or so.

Light Requirements

Q **I would like to know what is considered "full sun." Is it just so many hours a day, or does it mean that the plants are in the sun during the hottest part of the day?**

A "Full sun" means that a plant needs direct, unfiltered sunlight for at least 6 hours a day. A plant that gets full sun all morning but is shaded in the afternoon has a much different growing environment from one shielded from the sun in the morning but exposed to full sun in the afternoon. Many plants that are classified as growing best in "partial shade" can take full morning sun, as long as they are protected from direct afternoon sun. Latitude and elevation play a role too. Gardens in the South receive more intense sun than those in the North. And gardens at high elevations are brighter than landscapes at sea level.

Q **I have a lilac growing under an ash tree. It's starting to grow crooked, as though it's reaching for more light. How can I keep it growing straight up?**

A Lilacs are best adapted to growth in full sun. When grown in the shade, they won't flower well and, as you have noticed, may grow in the direction of brighter light. Short of removing the ash tree to create full sun, you may not be able to keep your lilac growing straight upright. The only way to keep it growing straight is to provide it with uniform light all around. If you prefer to keep the ash tree, a solution may be to replace the lilac with a shade-tolerant shrub such as hydrangea, fothergilla, or viburnum.

Shrubs for Sun

Q My yard has absolutely no shade. What kinds of shrubs could I grow in this hot, sunny site?

A You have many choices of shrubs adapted to full sun and hot conditions. Here are 10 to get you started: 1. Spirea, 2. Caryopteris, 3. Potentilla, 4. Spreading juniper, 5. Lilac, 6. Crape myrtle, 7. Japanese barberry, 8. Beautyberry, 9. Firethorn, and 10. Weigela.

Perennials for Sun

Q I'd like to put in a perennial flowerbed on the south side of my home. It gets full sun, so it is usually hot and dry.

A These tough perennial flowers will withstand the intense sun and heat in your yard: 1. Bearded iris, 2. Blanket flower, 3. Butterfly weed, 4. Creeping phlox, 5. Daylily, 6. Coreopsis, 7. Purple coneflower, 8. Sedum, 9. Spike speedwell, and 10. Yarrow.

1

2

3

4

5

6

7

8

9

10

Lighting Systems

Q **Should I start my flower and vegetable seeds in the light or in the dark? Does it make any difference?**

A Most seeds germinate best in darkness. However, as soon as the seedling emerges, it needs bright light or it will stretch excessively. Seeds of a few plants actually require light for best germination. These are usually small seeds that should be sown shallowly or on the soil's surface where light can reach them. Among the plants that need light for germination are ageratum, California poppy, blanket flower, coleus, columbine, love-in-a-mist, snapdragon, Shasta daisy, strawflower, sweet alyssum, and lettuce.

Q **Can I use ordinary fluorescent shop lights to start all of my flower and vegetable seedlings in the house?**

A Fluorescent lights are the best lights to use for starting seeds indoors. Use one "warm" bulb and one "cool" bulb so you'll get the full—most natural—spectrum of light. Once seedlings sprout, give them 14 to 16 hours of light per day. Keep the lights about 4 to 6 inches above the seedlings. Avoid using incandescent bulbs to start your seedlings. These bulbs give off so much heat that your seedlings will suffer heat damage if you keep the seedlings close to the bulbs.

Q **I'd like to add landscape lights along the sidewalk to my front door. Will it be expensive to keep it lit all night?**

A Most landscape lighting systems use low-voltage (12V) lights. This low voltage makes the lights extremely safe; you're unlikely to get a shock even if you touch bare wires or hit a buried cable while digging in the garden. Low-voltage systems often use less energy than a single 75-watt bulb. To save even more energy, you could put the lights on a timer that would automatically shut them off at a predetermined time each night. Or consider a solar-powered system, which harnesses sunlight during the day to power the lights at night.

Q **It would be nice to add some lighting near our fire pit at the back of our lot. I'm not sure that I want to extend electric lines out there though. Are there other options?**

A Solar-powered landscape lights might work for you. Solar lights need at least 8 hours of direct sunlight per day to collect enough energy to provide sufficient nighttime illumination. This type of lighting works pretty well if you don't need to light up a large space and you won't need the light on all night.

Shade-Tolerant Perennials

Q My yard is quite shady. Which perennial flowers would be best for me to grow?

A Perennial flowers will grow best in partial shade rather than dense shade. Here are some to try: 1. Tiarella, 2. Astilbe, 3. Columbine, 4. Fringed bleeding heart, 5. Hosta, 6. Lady's mantle, 7. Lamium, 8. Monkshood, 9. Toad lily, and 10. Virginia bluebells.

Frost

Q I started plants in a small greenhouse. I know that my plants should be "hardened" before I plant them outside, but I don't know what this process involves.

A Hardening off (below right) means acclimating soft and tender growth—which has been protected from wind, cold, and strong sun—to outdoor conditions. Start the process of hardening off about two weeks before you intend to plant the seedlings outside. Water your seedlings well, then set them outdoors in a partially shaded spot. Leave the seedlings out for about 1 hour the first time. Repeat this process daily, gradually working up to a full day by the time they are scheduled to be transplanted into the garden.

Q I planted some pansies last fall. During a midwinter thaw, I noticed that some of them were pushing up out of the ground. I'm sure I planted them deeply enough. Why are they doing this?

A Your pansies are experiencing frost heave. As the ground freezes and thaws, the soil expands and contracts. In the process, the pansies' roots were pushed up and out of the ground. To prevent frost heave from happening again, cover the soil with a couple inches of organic mulch. The insulating effect of the mulch diminishes the effects of rapid temperature changes. Once the ground becomes frozen it will more likely stay frozen beneath the mulch until sustained warm temperatures arrive.

Q I have a 20-year-old shade tree that developed a split on its trunk last winter. It looks better this spring, but is there anything I should be doing to it?

A It sounds as though your tree has a frost crack. Frost cracks develop from the expansion and contraction of bark and wood during wide temperature fluctuations in winter. A weakened section of the bark splits open from the stress. The sudden break is often accompanied by a loud noise like a gunshot. Cracks usually close up during the growing season, but they may remain partially open. If a large split fails to close, consult an arborist to install a rod or bolt to hold it together.

Q My neighbor says that trees won't develop good fall color until we've had a frost. But I've noticed that some trees color up in late summer long before we've had a freeze. Do plants need to have frost for good fall color?

A There is a connection between cool temperatures and fall color, but frost isn't necessary. Most plants produce a variety of pigments all summer long, but for most of the year green chlorophyll is produced in such abundance that it masks any of the other colors. As the days grow shorter and nights get cooler, chlorophyll breaks down faster than it is produced by the plant. That allows other pigments to take over. The brightest colors develop when sunny days are combined with cool nights. A hard frost dulls fall color by turning the leaves brown more rapidly.

Spring Frost Dates

Q I know that I shouldn't plant my tender annual flowers until after the last spring frost. How do I find that date for my area?

A This map will give you a general idea when to expect the last spring frost in your area. To get a more precise date, check with your local cooperative extension office.

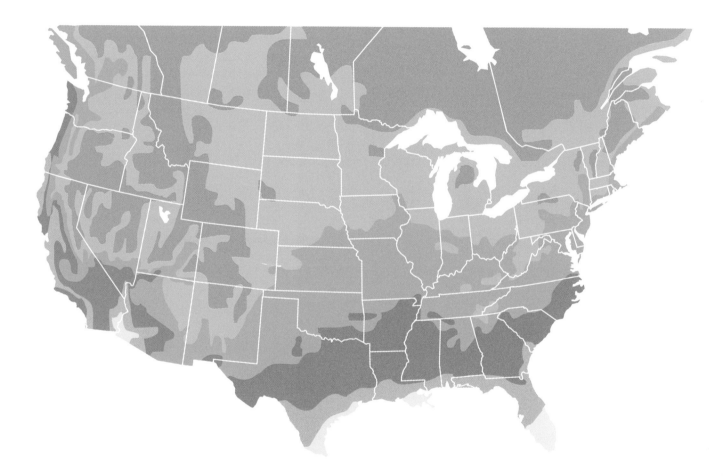

Average Dates of Last Spring Frost

- May 30 or after
- April 30 to May 30
- March 30 to April 30
- February 28 to March 30
- January 30 to February 28
- January 30 or before

Fall Frost Dates

Q I'm not sure that my tomatoes will ripen before frost hits this fall. When is the first fall frost likely to happen?

A Although the actual first fall frost date may vary widely from year to year, this map will give you some idea of when to expect a frost that might damage your tomatoes.

Average Dates of First Autumn Frost

- June 30 to July 30
- July 30 to August 30
- August 30 to September 30
- September 30 to October 30
- October 30 to November 30
- November 30 December 30

Hardiness Zones

Q When a plant is listed as hardy in Zones 4–9, what does that mean?

A The USDA Hardiness Zone map was developed by examining average minimum winter temperatures for various locations over many years. The USDA zones don't take into account the idiosyncrasies of your yard. You may have a protected spot where tender plants will thrive outside their usual zone.

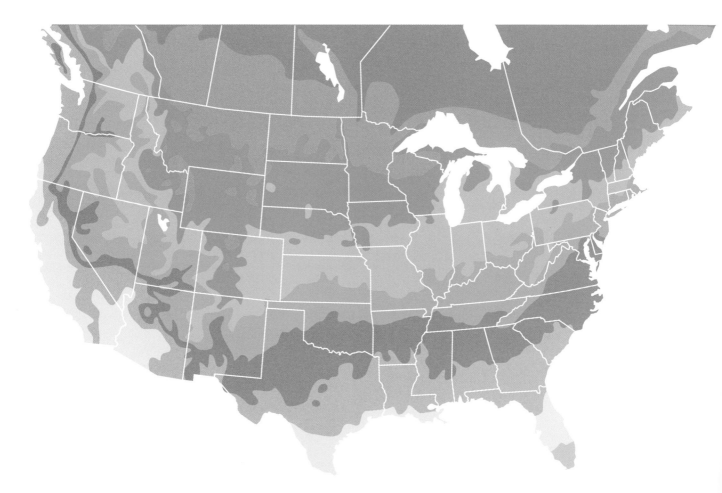

Range of Average Annual Minimum Temperatures for Each Zone

- Zone 2: -50 to -40° F (-45 to -40°C)
- Zone 3: -40 to -30° F (-40 to -35°C)
- Zone 4: -30 to -20° F (-34 to -29°C)
- Zone 5: -20 to -10° F (-29 to -23°C)
- Zone 6: -10 to 0° F (-23 to -18°C)
- Zone 7: 0 to 10° F (-18 to -12°C)
- Zone 8: 10 to 20° F (-12 to -7°C)
- Zone 9: 20 to 30° F (-7 to -1°C)
- Zone 10: 30 to 40° F (-1 to 4°C)

Microclimate

Q **I'd really like to grow rosemary in my Zone 6 garden, but have been told the plant is only hardy to Zone 7. Am I out of luck?**

A Most rosemary cultivars are fully hardy only to Zone 7, but several, including 'Madalene Hill', 'Arp', and 'Athens Blue Spires' are slightly hardier than most. If you find the right microclimate for them in your yard, you may succeed with them. A microclimate is a pocket in your yard that differs from the basic growing conditions in your area. Because rosemary thrives in full sun and well-drained soil in a protected location, those conditions are what you should try to duplicate.

Heat

Q **What does the term "growing degree days" have to do with gardening?**

A Growing degree days are a measure of accumulated heat during the growing season. They are calculated by taking the daily maximum and minimum temperatures, determining an average, and comparing that to a base temperature. Growing degree days directly relate to the growth and development of plants and insects. Below certain temperatures, no growth occurs (or it happens extremely slowly). At higher temperatures, development proceeds rapidly (unless it's so hot that stress sets in).

Q **I'm familiar with the USDA Hardiness Zones, but recently I heard about heat zones. Are they the same thing?**

A The American Horticulture Society (AHS) in conjunction with the USDA has expanded on the USDA Hardiness Zone designations to develop an AHS Plant Heat-Zone map. The USDA map tracks average winter cold. The AHS map measures the number of days that the high temperature reaches 86°F or higher at a given location. The reason this temperature is critical is that above 86°F, photosynthesis begins to shut down in most plants. That puts the plants under stress.

Q **It's been extremely hot here lately, and my tomatoes have stopped producing fruit. Is it because it's so hot?**

A Although tomatoes are a warm-season crop, it can get too warm for them. Generally, tomatoes grow bigger, better, and faster the warmer the weather. However, when daytime highs regularly top 95°F, the plant's pollen can be killed. With no live pollen to pollinate the flower, fruits fail to develop. Varieties such as 'Heatwave II' tolerate the heat better than do others. Other warm-season vegetables sensitive to excessive heat include pepper, eggplant, pumpkin, squash, and cucumber.

Temperature-Sensitive Plants

Q I love delphiniums and lupines, but find that they melt out quickly in the heat where I live. Are there other flowers that I should avoid?

A If you live in areas with hot summers, the following flowers are likely to be short-lived: 1. Calendula, 2. English daisy, 3. Globeflower, 4. Iceland poppy, 5. Lady's mantle, 6. Leopard's bane, 7. Monkshood, 8. Oriental poppy, 9. Pansy, and 10. Sweet pea.

Q Have you ever heard of buying bad seed? I have been using seeds bought at a local store, and I usually have to replant several times before germination.

A A lot of factors can affect the viability of packaged seed. For greatest longevity, they should be stored in cold, dry conditions. (I always keep my seeds refrigerated.) It's certainly possible that seeds held in conditions that are too warm or too damp may lose some viability. There are also considerable differences in seed vigor and viability from the outset. That is, some seeds may germinate but produce weak seedlings that may not emerge well. Vigor of the seed should be considered as well as viability. It's always a good idea to purchase seed from a reputable source, one who will stand behind the quality of the product.

Q Can I grow a strawberry plant from the fruit? Are the seeds from the fruit good to plant?

A Technically it is possible to start new strawberry plants from seed. You would plant the individual seeds from the surface of the fruit, not the entire fruit. However, it will take a long time for a plant from seed to grow to fruiting size. Also the plant that develops will be different from the parent plant, because strawberries are cross-pollinated, which means the seeds are genetically different from the mother plant. If you want more strawberry plants, it's much easier to root some of the runners, dig them up, and transplant them to a different location.

Q I have collected Johnny-jump-up, sweet pea, and marigold seeds over the summer. How long will these seeds last if dried out?

A Length of seed viability is dependent on several factors. Some species don't store well at all. The ones you mention are not particularly difficult to store, however. Store the seeds at low humidity and low temperature for longest viability. I put my seeds in airtight containers in an extra refrigerator and find that most types will last a couple years that way.

Q I am trying to start impatiens from seed. They just haven't done well. They're still only 1 inch or so tall. I've been putting them into our greenhouse during the day and bring them in at night. I keep them in shade as much as possible. What am I doing wrong?

A It sounds as though you got the seedlings to germinate just fine. Keep in mind that impatiens are heat-loving plants that need very warm soil. A heat mat often helps keep the plants going if your greenhouse is not warm enough. Also, although they are shade plants when grown outdoors, they will benefit from bright light indoors or in a greenhouse. A combination of low light and low temperature may be stalling the growth on your impatiens.

Seed Starting

Q Can I cut the seeds off the top of a basil plant and then plant them?

A Various basils often reseed themselves in the garden if the seeds are allowed to dry on the plant. You can collect the seeds for later sowing, but you must make certain that the seeds are mature first. The seedheads should be dry. You may want to place a small bag around the seedhead to collect the seeds in case the seeds mature before you catch them at the right stage. Keep in mind that if your basil is a hybrid, the resulting plants from the seeds that develop will be quite variable and may not resemble the parent plant.

Q Can I collect seeds from my existing garden zinnias to use for next year?

A Yes, zinnias will grow from seeds collected from your garden. The may not be exact carbon copies of the parent plants, but they should be similar. You'll have the best luck with heirloom or species types rather than hybrids.

Q I have some hollyhock seedlings with two leaves. I want to transplant them into the garden. How and when should I do that?

A The first set of leaves that develops on hollyhocks are called the seed leaves or cotyledons. Wait to transplant the seedlings until they develop another set of leaves. At that stage, they will be very tender and will require extra care if you transplant them directly into the garden. It would be preferable to transplant them into slightly larger containers first, let them develop new roots in the containers, then transplant them to the garden. But if you're careful and attentive to the seedlings you can transplant them directly from the seed-starting pot into the garden.

Q Can I reuse the seed-starting soil and peat pellets from last year that did not produce any plants after planting seeds?

A It's best not to reuse seed-starting mix or peat pellets because it's possible for them to harbor diseases that could kill the seedlings you're starting this year. You'd be best off adding last year's seed-starting mix to your compost pile and investing in new seed-starting mix.

Q My 'Foxy Mix' and 'Camelot' foxglove self-seeded in my garden. In places it is a mass of babies. Should I thin them or just let nature take its course?

A If the seedlings are as crowded as you indicate, thin them to several inches apart. If you want to transplant some to a different location, move them when they are just 1 or 2 inches tall. Be sure to water the transplants well.

Seed Starting

Q **Can I use those new energy-saving fluorescent bulbs that are supposed to provide natural light to start seedlings? Or must I use the expensive grow lights sold at garden stores?**

A You don't need to use the expensive grow lights. Fluorescent bulbs work fine for starting seeds. If you were keeping the same plants under lights year-round you'd probably want to invest in grow lights. The seedlings won't spend their entire lives under those lights, so the bulbs don't need to be full spectrum. Inexpensive fluorescent bulbs will work great.

Q **Can you get an apple tree to grow from the seeds of a 'McIntosh' apple?**

A The easiest way to grow the seeds of an apple is to plant the seeds in loamy soil in the garden in fall. Apple seeds need a stratification period (moist, cold treatment) in order to germinate. In spring, when the weather warms, they should germinate into seedling apple trees. Alternatively, you could plant the seeds in pots and hold them in a refrigerator over winter. One note: Because 'McIntosh' is a hybrid apple, the seeds will not grow into exactly the same kind of tree as their parent. So if getting 'McIntosh' apples is important to you, buy a 'McIntosh' tree rather than planting seeds.

Q **I was given paper impregnated with wildflower seeds as a gift. Unfortunately, there are no directions or even any species on the paper. What would be a good time to plant them on a sunny hillside?**

A Ideally, plant wildflower seeds when the plants growing in the wild would shed their seeds. With paper that is impregnated with wildflower seeds, start the seeds in a flat of moist seed-starting medium. Once the first pair of true leaves appear, you can transplant into small individual pots or peat pots. Plant them on your sunny hillside when the seedlings are growing vigorously. You'll have much better luck than if you sow them directly on the hillside.

Q **I want to find out what clay to use for making seedballs. Where could I find it?**

A Seedballs are a mix of clay and seeds to make sowing small seeds easier. If you can find heavy clay soil in your area, that will work. Or buy dry, powdered red clay at an art supply store, mix it with water and some compost, and use that as the basis for your seedballs.

Division

Q How do you propagate clivia?

A If you have an established clivia, you can dig it up and divide the clump. If it is a large clump, you can slice through the clump with a sharp spade to make several new plants. Or you can carefully tease apart the intertwined roots to start many new plants.

Q I have a 5-foot-tall ponytail palm that has four or five pups at the base. The pups are about 6 to 7 inches tall. When should I remove the pups?

A The pups of ponytail palm can be cut off the mother plant at any time as long as they have some roots attached. The best time, however, is when they're ready to go into a growth cycle, such as in early spring.

Q Can you split a bromeliad? I have one that has matured, and the top edges are starting to turn brown. I see three new sprouts coming from within the bottom of the leaves.

A Did the central mother plant flower? It's normal for the flowering plant to die after it blooms and for side shoots to take over. These offsets, or "pups," can be separated from the mother plant to start new plants. Slice through the main stem to remove pups. Dip the cut end in rooting hormone. Pot the offset in a lightweight soilless mix and keep it moist but not soggy. In a few weeks, new roots should form.

Q Do hybrid daylilies multiply by seeds, runners, or both? I saved some seeds. Would planting them be a waste of time?

A Thousands of hybrid daylilies are available. Unfortunately, none can be successfully propagated true-to-type from seed. Usually, the seeds collected from hybrid plants produce weaker or inferior plants (or plants that have traits of both parents, if two different plants were crossed to produce the seed). Because daylilies are so easy to propagate by division of their fibrous roots, I'd recommend using that method.

Read our online story about dividing perennials at *bhg.com/divide-perennials.*

Q My snake plant is growing in a large clump from one center point. Should I repot it or divide it?

A Snake plant is a tough indoor plant that can remain in the same container for many years. However, it does eventually become pot-bound, and can benefit from repotting or division. If yours has formed a solid ball of roots and stems, it may be time to divide your plant. Slice completely through the root ball with a sharp knife. (You could easily slice through twice to get four plants from your existing one.) Pot up each section into an individual pot, and you'll soon have enough plants to share with friends and neighbors.

Q When do you divided poppies?

A You can divide perennial poppies in mid to late summer, after they have finished blooming but before they begin growth in fall. Keep them well-watered after dividing.

Q When should I divide my coralbells?

A You can divide coralbells anytime from spring to fall. However, it's least stressful on the plant if you divide them during cool, moist weather in early spring or early fall. You want to divide and replant so that the new divisions have time to reestablish before the heat of summer or the rigors of winter set in.

Q When is the best time to divide my hostas?

A Hostas are extremely tough plants and can be divided and transplanted at almost any time that you can dig in the soil. However, it's best to divide the plants in early spring just as new shoots begin to poke up through the ground. It's easiest to dig up the entire clump to make the divisions. You can wash the soil off the roots and gently tease them apart. Or slice through the clump to get several large divisions.

Cuttings

Q I was told that you can cut pieces off a tomato plant, put them in water, and in seven days it should root. Is that true?

A Tomatoes root fairly easily. However, there are differences among varieties of tomato and woodiness of the stem cuttings as to how quickly they will root. Also, you will have better luck rooting them in moist potting soil rather than directly in water.

Q I have a childhood memory of my mother starting a potato vine by suspending a potato with toothpicks in a glass jar. I'd like to try this and wonder if you have any pointers.

A Your memories are right on target. Just buy a sweet potato that has obvious "eyes" and suspend the fat end in water by inserting toothpicks into the tuber and resting them on the lip of the glass or jar. Keep the tuber in a warm place with bright light. Sprouts should develop within several weeks.

Q I have an African violet with one stem but two shoots. I would like to divide it. What's the best way?

A It's relatively easy to propagate African violets. You can start a new plant from just one leaf by sticking the petiole (leaf stem) in moist potting soil. It will take several months, but eventually it will develop new roots and a new shoot. You could also slice off one of the crowns of your African violet, and stick it in moist potting soil to root it. This would speed the process since it just has to form new roots. Keep the soil moist but not soggy until new roots form. It would also speed the process to dip the cut end in rooting hormone before sticking it into the potting soil.

Q How do you propagate a pussy willow?

A Pussy willow is very easy to propagate. All you need to do is take branch cuttings in the spring when the pussy buds are visible but before the plant leafs out. Place the cut branches in water. Keep the water fresh by changing it every few days, and eventually the branches will form roots. When the roots are a few inches long, you can plant the branches in pots with potting soil or directly in the garden. Keep them moist until their roots become well-established.

Q How do I propagate a grapevine?

A Grapes can be propagated using hardwood cuttings, layering, or grafting, but for your purposes hardwood cuttings are probably the most practical. Cut pencil thick cuttings about 9 to 12 inches long from growth made the previous summer. Angle the top cut so that you can tell which end is up on the cutting. Bury the stems in a trench, and cover them with soil and straw for winter protection. In spring, dig up the cuttings and line them out, so that just the top bud is showing aboveground. With good care, about half of the cuttings should root and be ready for transplanting by the following spring.

Q I have a friend who has the most fragrant gardenia that her mother gave her many years ago. Neither of us knows how to get cuttings to root. I would love to get a plant started in my yard.

A Gardenias root rather easily from cuttings taken from new growth. Snip off a 4-inch-long section of stem and pot it up in sand, vermiculite, or perlite. Keep the cutting humid and it should root in 9 to 10 weeks. It may take a couple years for the cuttings to reach blooming size.

Q I have three large rhododendrons that I am going to lose because of foundation repairs. Is there a way to root a branch?

A You can propagate rhododendrons from cuttings, but the timing may not be right for your situation. Some types of rhododendrons propagate easier from cuttings than others. Here are the basics: Take stem cuttings several inches long from a semiwoody portion of the stem tip. Wound the base of the cuttings by scraping a bit of bark off two sides of the base. Dip the cutting in a rooting hormone solution and stick the hormone-treated base into rooting medium (2 parts sand to 1 part peat and 1 part perlite or vermiculite). Cover the container with the rooting medium and cuttings with plastic, and place under fluorescent lights. It normally will take at least two to four months for roots to develop.

Q I'd like help with making cuttings from a neighbor's hydrangea plant. What should I do?

A Many hydrangeas root easily from cuttings taken from late spring to midsummer. Cut a section of new growth about 4 inches long; it should root in three to four weeks.

Layering

Q Some of the branches of my hydrangea have rooted while laying on the ground. Can I divide and move that part of the shrub?

A The best time to move a layered stem is when the plant is still dormant. If you're careful to keep soil around the roots, get it replanted right away, and watered in well, you should have success by transplanting in early spring too. Cut through the stem that's attached to the mother plant. Dig a ball of soil containing the roots, and move the ball with soil intact to a new location. Place the root ball at the same level, water in, and mulch to preserve moisture.

Q What is the best way to get additional plants out of a wisteria that is more than 80 years old? The cuttings I have taken have not lasted.

A If you've not had good luck with cuttings, look for little runners around the base of the plant. You can dig these up and replant them to another sunny spot in the garden. If the vine has no shoots from the base, you could bend a section of vine down to the soil, make a notch in the stem, apply rooting powder, and cover with soil. Keep the area moist, and after several months, new roots should form on the buried stem.

Q I have a lilac that I would like to propagate. How long does propagation take?

A Layering is a simple way to propagate your lilac. In spring, choose a flexible outer stem and carefully bend it until the tip touches the ground. With a sharp blade, make a diagonal slit in the stem where the branch will touch the ground. Dip the cut in rooting hormone. Peg the branch to the ground with landscape staples or rocks. Pile some soil on the slit and pat it down. Keep the soil watered throughout the summer. Next spring after roots have formed, sever the connection between your new lilac and its parent. Wait a few weeks before moving the new plant to a site where it has space to mature.

Air Layering

Q My corn plant has just one stem, which is almost 8 feet tall. Can I cut off the stem and successfully reroot it? If I cut the trunk part, will new growth start on it?

A If you cut off the top of your corn plant (*Dracaena*), the cane that is left normally will resprout, although it may take several months to do so. You can use the stem tip that is cut off as a cutting, sticking it in a pot after dusting the cut end with rooting powder. If you're not sure about taking a cutting, you could also air-layer the plant. Rather than completely cutting off the top, simply make a notch in the stem about halfway around the stem. Prop it open with toothpicks. Dust with rooting powder. Wrap moist sphagnum moss around the stem and enclose the moss in clear plastic. Keep the moss moist until you see new roots developing. At that time, cut off the stem just below the roots, and pot up the new plant.

Grafting & Budding

Q **I have the roots of a rose. Is it possible to start a rose from the roots?**

A Many roses are grafted onto a rootstock that is different from the top, flowering part of the plant. So, for example, if the top part of the plant is a 'Peace' rose, it's likely that the root system is a wild, species-type rose that won't look anything like the 'Peace' rose. In recent years, some growers have taken to producing what are called own-root roses, meaning that cuttings are rooted and grown on their own root systems rather than on a grafted rootstock. In this case, a piece of the root would be the same as the top. However, the easiest way to propagate roses is from stem cuttings.

Q **I have a weeping Japanese maple. It has several shoots coming out of the base. Can I cut these shoots at the base and propagate them into new trees?**

A If these shoots are coming from the base of the plant, they probably aren't the same variety as the weeping top part of your Japanese maple. Most weeping varieties are grafted onto an upright growing trunk. Shoots sprouting from the base of the plant develop from the root variety. Your best option is to cut off these shoots at ground level and dispose of them. Although you could try rooting softwood cuttings, chances of success are slim unless you use rooting hormone and have a mist propagation system.

Q **The instructions for planting my rose bush say to plant the graft union several inches belowground. What is the graft union?**

A The graft union is the swollen, knobby part of the rose stem just above the roots. It's where a desirable rose was grafted onto the root system of a vigorous rose. In cold regions, you should plant the graft union several inches deep to protect it from winter cold.

Q **The garden catalogs I've been looking at advertise 3-in-1 apple trees. How do they get three varieties on one tree?**

A All named apple varieties are grafted onto a rootstock of some kind. In the case of 3-in-1 trees, three different varieties are grafted onto one rootstock. Instead of grafting near the soil line, these different varieties are grafted onto an upright trunk so that three major branches, each of a different variety, will develop on one tree.

Transplanting

Q I had to transplant my rhubarb plant. Even though it's only been a couple weeks since I replanted it, the plant is sending up a seed stalk and leaves on the rhubarb already. Should I cut off the seed stalk and leaf or just leave them?

A If the plant is sending up a seed stalk, go ahead and remove it so the plant puts no energy into producing seeds. However, keep all the leaves intact. They'll help the plant recover from the transplant.

Q We planted several Russian sage plants in our yard. Now we find that the Russian sages have taken up much more space than we intended. When can we transplant them?

A While it's possible to transplant Russian sage in midsummer, it would be much better to do so in late summer or early spring before growth begins. The stress and shock of transplanting in the heat and dry conditions of midsummer makes the success rate of transplanting much lower than when weather conditions are cooler.

Q When is the best time to transplant an established sedum?

A Sedums are tough plants that are best transplanted during the cooler temperatures of spring or fall, but you can also transplant them in summer. Succulent sedums also start readily from cuttings. I have often snipped off several inches of stem tips, stripped off the lower leaves, and simply stuck the cuttings in the garden where I wanted new sedum plants. Keep the planted cuttings moist, but not wet, and in a few weeks you'll have new sedum growing where you inserted the cuttings.

Index

A

Abelia, 208, 210

Acidic soils
plants for, 40, 135, 213, 216, 220, 222, 284, 288, 374
See also Soil pH

Adam's needle (*Yucca filamentosa*), 89

Aeration of soil, 126, 127, 183

African marigold (*Tagetes erecta*), 28

African violet (*Saintpaulia*), 7, 19, 402

Ageratum, 28

Air layering, 404

Ajuga (*Ajuga*), 41, 52, 91, 149, 198

Akebia, fiveleaf, 232

Alkali dropseed (*Sporobolus airoides*), 76

Alkaline soil, plants for, 373

Allergies, seasonal, 69, 71

Allium (*Allium*), 92
drumstick (*A. sphaerocephalon*), 92
See also Chive

Almond, flowering, 209, 210

Aloe, 11

Alternaria leaf spot, 39

Aluminum plant (*Pilea cadierei*), 7

Amaryllis, 20, 92

Anaerobic decomposition, of mulch, 367

Anemone (*Anemone*), 40

Angelica (*Angelica archangelica*), 298

Ammonium sulfate, to reduce soil pH, 372

Animal pests, 338–349
repellents for, 62, 265, 339, 342, 343, 346, 348, 349
See also specific animal pests

Annual plants, 24–39
cold-sensitive, 27
cool-season, 27, 35, 36, 38
as cost-saving strategy, 144
creeping, 28
deadheading, 31
easy, 27
frost dates and, 392
for hanging baskets, 25
hardening off, 27
heat-sensitive, 396
heat-tolerant, 24
low-growing, 28
medium-height, 28
pinching, 31
for pots, 24
rotating, 27
for sandy soil, 369
seeds
saving, 29
planting from, 26, 397
self-, 29, 38
storing, 29
shade-tolerant, 30, 32, 34
sun-tolerant, 32, 33, 38, 39
tall, 28
transplanting, 26, 27, 392
See also specific annual plants

Anthracnose diseases, 184, 198, 326, 332

Ants
aphids and, 306, 307
carpenter, 306
fire, 306
leaf-cutting, 306
on peony, 80, 81

Aphids
ants and, 306, 307
control methods, 307
honeydew, 306
ladybugs and, 309
and sooty mold, 335
on specific plants
daylily, 62
gardenia, 220
honeysuckle, 222
trumpet vine, 307
viburnum, 307
willow, 307
zinnia, 39

Apple
alternate bearing, 285
disease-resistant varieties, 286
diseases
apple scab, 286
cedar apple rust, 286, 334
fire blight, 286, 331
spraying for, 286
harvesting, 287
insect pests, 286
apple maggot, 286
codling moth, 286
gypsy moths, 319
nonchemical controls, 286
spraying, 286